DAPPER DAN FLOOD

Dapper
DAN★FLOOD

The Controversial Life of a Congressional Power Broker

WILLIAM C. KASHATUS

The Pennsylvania State University Press
University Park, Pennsylvania

A KEYSTONE BOOK®

A Keystone Book is so designated to distinguish it from the typical
scholarly monograph that a university press publishes. It is a book intended
to serve the citizens of Pennsylvania by educating them and others, in an
entertaining way, about aspects of the history, culture, society, and
environment of the state as part of the Middle Atlantic region.

Unless otherwise noted, all images appear courtesy of the Flood Estate.
Frontispiece: Daniel J. Flood, 1942 campaign photo.

Library of Congress Cataloging-in-Publication Data

Kashatus, William C., 1959–
Dapper Dan Flood : the controversial life of a congressional
power broker / William C. Kashatus.
p.   cm.
Includes bibliographical references and index.
Summary: "A biography of northeast Pennsylvania congressman
Daniel J. Flood, who served in the U.S. House of Representatives
from 1945 to 1980"—Provided by publisher.
ISBN 978-0-271-03618-2 (cloth : alk. paper)
1. Flood, Daniel J. 2. Legislators—United States—Biography.
3. United States. Congress. House—Biography. 4. United
States—Politics and government—1945-1989.
5. Pennsylvania—Politics and government—20th century. I. Title.
E748.F56K37 2010
328.092—dc22
[B]
2009027611

The Pennsylvania State University Press is a member of the
Association of American University Presses.
It is the policy of The Pennsylvania State University Press to use acid-free
paper. Publications on uncoated stock satisfy the minimum requirements of
American National Standard for Information Sciences—
Permanence of Paper for Printed Library Material, ANSI Z39.48–1992.

This book is printed on Natures Natural,
which contains 50% post-consumer waste.

For my parents,
*whose love and encouragement allowed
me to become a writer.*

CONTENTS

ILLUSTRATIONS

ACKNOWLEDGMENTS

Writing a book is an evolutionary process. Initially, it's a plaything, a pleasant diversion from the drudgery of the daily routine. Before long, however, a book becomes a mistress, making demands that take the author away from family, vacations, and other enjoyable pastimes. In the final stage, the book becomes a master that threatens to consume the author. If he's fortunate, the writer slays the master and the book becomes his own.

Writing about Dan Flood has, at various times over the last decade, been a plaything, a mistress, and a master. My wife, Jackie, and our sons, Tim, Peter, and Ben, have sacrificed the most. My decision to take a job at Luzerne County Community College—a three-hour drive from our home in southeastern Pennsylvania—limited my time with them to weekends. Jackie shouldered the responsibility of single parenthood without complaint, realizing how much this project meant to me and that I needed to be closer to the Flood Collection at King's College in Wilkes-Barre to complete it. Simple words cannot adequately express the love and respect I have for her. Perhaps our sons, whom I love as dearly, will one day realize the same passion I have for writing in whatever careers they choose.

The book is dedicated to my parents, who first suggested the idea of writing about Congressman Flood. More important, they gave me their unconditional support and financial assistance when I declared my intention to become a writer many years ago. For that, as well as for so many other things, my love for them is eternal. I am also very grateful to John "Dada" Kashatus, a great-uncle who was more of a surrogate grandfather to me. A onetime Democratic Party boss of Newport Township, Dada encouraged my early interest in politics and in his close friend Dan Flood. Both men were extremely colorful individuals with quick tempers and a penchant for the dramatic. But only those who knew them realized the singular importance they attached to public service and the welfare of the workingman. Not a day passes that I don't think about Dada, the lessons he taught me, and the love we had for each other.

Writing about Dan Flood has not been without reward either. Among the greatest benefits have been the people I've met over the years I've worked on the project. Michael O'Malley, the editor of *Pennsylvania Heritage*, first encouraged me to write about Flood for his magazine. Over the years he has offered me encouragement, the wisdom of his fine editorial skills, and his friendship. The late Robert Janosov, history professor at Luzerne County Community College and commissioner of the Pennsylvania Historical and Museum Commission, was a mentor who cultivated my interest in the Wyoming Valley's history. Sheldon Spear, emeritus professor of history at LCCC who was also working on his own biography of Flood, helped me to understand that not all of the congressman's activities were as disinterested as I had initially believed. Clark Switzer, a history teacher at Wyoming Seminary and an authority on local history, spent many evenings with me discussing Mr. Flood's congressional career and his important role in saving the anthracite industry. Janis Seeley, chair of the social sciences and history department at LCCC, gave me a flexible teaching schedule that allowed time not only for my research but also for extended weekends with my family. Dave Kozemchak, chair of the audiovisual department, offered helpful advice on whom to interview, and suffered my constant heckling. Nicole Saporito was another supportive colleague who provided an occasional home-cooked meal. Michael Hockenbury of the *Citizens' Voice* was helpful in restoring old newspaper photographs to their original clarity, including the magnificent image that adorns the cover of the book.

Special thanks are due to: William A. Breslin, executor of Dan and Catherine Flood's estate. Bill gave me unlimited access to the Floods' personal papers, photographs, and scrapbooks. He signed release forms for me to secure academic transcripts, agreed to several interviews, and provided invaluable advice on source material; Michael Clark, a longtime aide to Mr. Flood, who made important contacts for me with many of the congressman's former colleagues on Capitol Hill. He also agreed to several interviews and read early drafts of the manuscript; Robert Kulick, a special assistant to Mr. Flood, who provided access to important court records; Joseph Rish, professor of political science at King's College, who assisted me in navigating the holdings in the Flood Collection and read and commented on an earlier draft of the manuscript; Kenneth Wolensky, a historian with the Pennsylvania Historical and Museum Commission, who also reviewed the manuscript, offered many constructive suggestions, and recommended publication with Penn State Press; and attorney Peter Goldberger, who offered indispensable legal counsel. Without their guidance, this book would not have come to fruition.

Congressman Flood's family, friends, aides, former colleagues, and critics were also extremely helpful to me. They provided an invaluable pillar of my research, namely personal interviews. Some of these folks spent days with me, others gave me a few hours, and even those who answered a few questions over the telephone contributed to my understanding of Flood's unique personality and career: Bernard C. Brominski, J. Lawrence Brown, Frank Carlucci, Michael Cefalo, John Cosgrove, Joseph DeVizia, James Dyer, Joseph B. Farrell, Catherine Flood, Gerald R. Ford, Laura Kane Ganley, Paul Golias, William Hastie, John Kashatus, Sr., William C. Kashatus, Jr., James Kozemchak, Melvin R. Laird, James Lee, Robert Loftus, Thomas Makowski, Joseph McDade, Andrew McGowen, John McKeown, Tom Medico, Robert Michel, Francis J. Michelini, Ed Mitchell, Bernard J. Podcasy, Fred Rooney, Harold Rosenn, Ralph Rozelle, William W. Scranton, Sarah Sheerin, James Tedesco, and Jim Wright.

Another group of folks provided a second pillar of research by granting access to special collections, federal and state documents, photographs, and academic transcripts: Judith Tierney, director, Daniel J. Flood Collection, Kings College Library, Wilkes-Barre, Pennsylvania; Andrew Kuhl and David Meehan, Coughlin High School, Wilkes-Barre; Sheri Welch, registrar, Penn State University's Dickinson School of Law, Carlisle, Pennsylvania; Fawn Coleman, registrar, Harvard Law School, Cambridge, Massachusetts; Laurie Allen, research librarian, Van Pelt Library, University of Pennsylvania, Philadelphia; Gloria Ralph-McKissick and Audrey Davis, Federal Bureau of Investigation, Washington, D.C.; Mary O'Brien and Blain Delancy, Alumni Office, Syracuse University, Syracuse, New York; and Brenda Wright, Urban Archives, Temple University Libraries, Philadelphia.

Finally, Sanford Thatcher and his staff at Penn State Press were extremely helpful in the design and publication processes. Special thanks to Nicholas Taylor for his superb editing of the manuscript. Both parties also forgave me my constant criticism. Of course, any errors or shortcomings that remain are mine alone, as are the views presented herein.

*　　*　　*　　*　　*

During the early morning hours of Friday, June 23, 1972, U.S. Rep. Daniel J. Flood sat working in his Washington, D.C., apartment when news of the devastation in his northeastern Pennsylvania district reached him. Rains of Hurricane Agnes had caused the Susquehanna River to rise more than forty feet. Water was pouring over the dikes protecting the twenty-two communities clustered around Wilkes-Barre, and two hundred thousand people in the Wyoming Valley were homeless.

During the previous evening, residents scurried to the riverbanks to reinforce the dikes with sandbags. But by 12:15 A.M. their efforts had proven fruitless and Frank Townend, director of the Luzerne County Civil Defense, ordered them to evacuate the area. Shortly thereafter, Townend issued a similar directive evacuating patients from the town's hospitals and relocating important public records to higher ground. In a matter of hours Wilkes-Barre's entire downtown business district sat under nine to fifteen feet of water, much like the boroughs of Kingston, Forty Fort, Swoyersville, West Pittston, West Nanticoke, and Plymouth. In all, 20,000 homes, 150 factories, and 2,728 commercial properties were destroyed, resulting in damages of $1.038 billion.

Back in Washington, Flood called in the IOUs he had collected over the years as a senior member of the House Appropriations Committee. He began with secretary of defense Melvin Laird, a close friend who once served with him on the Defense Appropriations Subcommittee. Laird not only turned over his personal helicopter for Flood's use, but also issued general alerts to the Army Reserve, Navy Reserve, and the National Guard: "Congressman Flood would need help. Expect his call and take care of him."

By ten o'clock Friday morning, Flood was en route to Wilkes-Barre by helicopter. He established his headquarters at a recently constructed Naval Reserve Center, one of the many pork-barrel projects he financed during his nearly three decades in Congress. Like a general arriving to save his troops from a terrible defeat, Flood, with his typical flair for the dramatic, declared, "Stand by! This is going to be one flood against another!" During the next three days, Flood personally took charge of the rescue and relief mission, working around the clock to secure supplies, funding, and emergency legislation. House minority leader Gerald Ford, another longtime friend, agreed to give Agnes victim assistance top priority on the House floor. The army was ordered to send forty helicopters to hoist marooned residents from homes, treetops, and cars. When a fire broke out in Wilkes-Barre, Flood located a coast guard fireboat in New Jersey and arranged to have an air force C-130 fly it into the town. He fought both state and federal bureaucrats to obtain medical supplies and had 1,500 National Guard troops flown in to prevent civil unrest and looting. When Flood met with resistance from a member of the military brass, all that he had to do was to remind the general that he, "Dapper Dan" Flood, *was* the Defense Appropriations Subcommittee. He received what he had asked for.

In fact, Flood had exceeded his legal authority. Responsibility for such a disaster relief mission rested with the local and state governments. Unless those authorities requested federal assistance, Washington could not act. What's more, Townend, a retired general charged with the local civil defense, staunchly opposed federal intervention in state affairs. When Governor Milton Shapp phoned to ask if he should seek federal assistance, Townend rejected the notion, insisting that he had the situation "under control." Matters came to a head when Flood discovered that a local contingent of the Pennsylvania National Guard was heading out of the district for military exercises in Virginia. "What the hell are they going to Virginia for," he barked over the phone to Shapp. "We have a *real* war right here damn it! I want them to stay here!" Shapp mustered the courage to inform the congressman that such action could not occur until Civil Defense had requested a declaration of disaster. The order had to come from Pennsylvania's Civil Defense director, Lieutenant Governor Ernest Kline. Undeterred by Shapp's explanation, Flood placed a phone call to Kline.

"Is this Kline!?"

Flood by this point was so furious at having to navigate the state bureaucracy that he was screaming into the receiver.

"Yes, I assume this is Congressman Flood," replied the lieutenant governor, expecting the phone call.

"You're damn right it is!" The Pennsylvania legislator was on a roll. "Are you aware that appropriations for the National Guard are cleared by the House Defense Appropriations Subcommittee?"

Refusing to wait for the lieutenant governor's response, Flood continued, "Do you know that there has never been a better friend of the National Guard than Dan Flood? And I want those goddamned guardsmen to remain here!"

Kline tried to explain that the county Civil Defense director, General Townend, had "not made an emergency request for a declaration of disaster or military personnel," and that until he did the "Commonwealth's hands were tied." Flood didn't care. He spent most of Saturday morning circumventing Townend's authority by placing a series of phone calls to army generals, Lieutenant

Governor Kline, and his close friend, Secretary of Defense Laird. By noon, Flood achieved his goal. The local National Guard contingent did an aboutface en route to Virginia and returned to the Wyoming Valley.

At four o'clock Saturday afternoon, Flood huddled with his closest congressional colleague, Joseph McDade of neighboring Lackawanna County. Their primary concern was how to provide housing for the thousands of people left homeless by the natural disaster. The conversation would lead to the greatest federal disaster response to that date, the Agnes Recovery Act. Thousands of displaced homeowners would receive 1 percent Small Business Administration disaster loans, with the first five thousand dollars completely forgiven. The measure also provided for federally backed business loans in the millions at preferred rates, emergency grants for hospitals and medical centers, federal funds for local colleges, the rebuilding of bridges, a master plan for higher dikes, and the appointment of Office of Management and Budget director Frank Carlucci, a native of the Wyoming Valley, as coordinator of the recovery effort.

On Sunday afternoon, June 25, Flood, wearing army fatigues and standing on a hill with a sea of muddy waters in the background, appeared on television and announced, "Today I have ordered the Army Corps of Engineers not to allow the Susquehanna River to rise one more inch." It never did. Nobody argued with Dan Flood. Not Agnes, not the army, nor—at times, it seemed— the Almighty Himself.[1]

No wonder one of his constituents insisted that "Dan Flood is the next closest thing to God."[2] During his thirty-two-year congressional career Flood did more than any other single individual to rescue the dying economy of his congressional district, once home to a prosperous anthracite industry. His public career was one of unparalleled success in the accumulation of power at the national level and the use of that power to achieve practical results for his constituents at the local level. He understood the complexities of the old power politics and played the political game with sheer genius and a highly entertaining flair. Flood was a consummate "pork-barreler," a legislator who was successful in securing federal funds and projects for his own congressional district. He used his clout as a senior member of the House Appropriations Committee to channel billions of dollars into northeastern Pennsylvania. He worked his will by employing the common practices that greased the wheels of the political process in the post–World War II era: persuasion, manipulation, arm-twisting, and grandiloquent oratory rarely matched by his congressional colleagues.

"Method," however, was only part of Flood's effectiveness. Just as important was the colorful image he crafted. Known for his wardrobe of white linen suits, white ties, top hats, and dark, flowing capes, the former vaudevillian became a flamboyant sight on the floor of the House. He presented his addresses and arguments with the diction of an old-fashioned stage actor, and he reveled in the attention he attracted for each and every performance. The flamboyant image allowed him to reinforce his message at any given time by creating a subtle but profound memory for his audience, whether they were voters, congressional colleagues, or local Democratic Party leaders.

Essentially, Dan Flood's true genius was his ability to persuade others of his position. Like most successful legislators, Flood realized that winning reelection sometimes required him to exaggerate the facts, or to speak about topics that exceeded his knowledge, which was not an uncommon practice on Capitol Hill. Politicians, by definition, are not "moral" or "immoral," but "amoral." In other words, Flood never intended to mislead his audience about the truth. Instead, he simply made assertions that purported to describe "the way things were" and, in the process, exaggerated conditions to make his case more convincing.[3] What made Flood so beloved in northeastern Pennsylvania was that he defined the world—the "way things were"—through the eyes of his constituents. They were mostly blue-collar laborers and their families. Hard-working and intensely patriotic, they expected their congressman to act and deliver on their needs.

Predictably, the voters returned Flood to Congress for thirty-two years because of his remarkable persistence and an almost impeccable record of constituent service. While many legislators failed to see a project through to its completion, Flood never seemed to back down. The more difficult the challenge, the more relentless he became. An incurable workaholic, it seemed that Flood never missed a House roll call or a weekend in his district. He made sure to stay in touch personally with his constituents, holding Saturday morning "confessionals" at his Wilkes-Barre office and attending weddings, funerals, groundbreakings, and dinners for the balance of the weekend. No request was too big or too small for the pork-barrel congressman, who delivered time and again for his constituents.

Ironically, for all his flair, influence, and ego, Dan Flood was an enigma. Though he was a native of northeastern Pennsylvania's economically depressed anthracite region, he was hardly a product of it. Flood never worked a single day in the coal mines. Instead he enjoyed the luxuries of a comfortable middle-class lifestyle: parts of a childhood spent in St. Augustine, Florida; college at Syracuse University; law school at Harvard and later Dickinson; and a successful early career as an off-Broadway actor. When he abandoned his aspirations for the silver screen, he turned his attention to the law, local politics, and eventually the much larger stage of Capitol Hill.[4] Few, if any, of his constituents could boast of such a privileged background. Most of them were poorly educated mine workers and World War II veterans. To win their loyalty, Flood carefully crafted an image of physical prowess, military bearing, and devoted friendship to all. To that end, he lied about attending a military academy during his youth, exaggerated his scholastic and collegiate achievements, and pretended friendship to others when he was not a very warm or amiable person by nature. In fact, Flood had a nasty temper and could be imperious as well as extremely demanding on his staff. Nor was he shy about reminding others of the influence he wielded on Capitol Hill. Sometimes he would introduce himself by extending his right hand and saying, in a patronizing tone, "Flood . . . Defense." One member of the House press corps was so put off by the approach that he called him a "jackass" to his face.[5]

But Flood's own image making is only part of the challenge in understanding such an extremely complex personality. Previous accounts of his congressional career tend to be misleading in several respects.[6] First, the journalists suggest that his political career was one of unconditional success. In fact, Flood's reelection to Congress during the 1940s and early 1950s was not a forgone conclusion (as it was later on). He was an independent-minded Democratic candidate in a strongly Republican district controlled by a powerful—and corrupt—political machine. Flood's three electoral defeats in 1942, 1946, and 1952 can be attributed to low Democratic voter registration in Luzerne County and the negative campaigning, bribery, and voter fraud carried out by the corrupt Republican machine. But he managed to ingratiate himself with House Speaker Sam Rayburn as a first-term congressman in 1945. Rayburn not only assigned Flood to the House Appropriations Committee—a rare appointment for a freshman—but also mentored him. As a result, the young congressman established a powerful network on Capitol Hill that would allow him to successfully sponsor many important measures for his district, eventually earning the unconditional loyalty of his constituents.

Second, previous accounts focus on Flood's success at the art of pork-barrel politics, which often came at the expense of the national welfare. Flood, according to the argument, used his near veto power over the three-hundred-billion-dollar federal budget as a senior member of the Appropriations subcommittees for Defense, Labor, and Health, Education, and Welfare to channel billions of dollars into his own congressional district. To be sure, Flood was in the right place at the time, and he knew it. His shrewd manipulation of the legislative process was particularly useful in an era when the federal government was strongly committed to economic growth and development. Allying himself with such influential colleagues as Senators Lyndon B. Johnson, Robert F. Kennedy, and Paul Douglas and Representatives John Dent, Gerald Ford, Thomas "Tip" O'Neill, Jim Wright, and Joseph McDade, Flood cosponsored many bills that rescued the Rust Belt economy of his district, which struggled to survive on a declining anthracite coal industry. Those measures created thousands of jobs by bringing a large, state-of-the-art hospital, an airport, new businesses and industries, and a modern interstate highway to Luzerne County, and rehabilitated its dilapidated neighborhoods with new residential and commercial buildings. But most of these projects were integrated into larger bills that benefited similar regions across the country and were at the core of the Johnson administration's Great Society programs of the 1960s. In fact, as the chair of the HEW Appropriations Subcommittee, Flood played an important role in engineering the Great Society programs through the House of Representatives.

Third, previous accounts portray Dan Flood as a jingoist whose unconditional support of the cold war resulted in the United States' protracted involvements in Vietnam and Panama. According to the argument, Flood's stance was firmly rooted in an unshakeable patriotism that ignored human or financial costs. He firmly believed that the United States had a responsibility to protect democracy wherever it was threatened and that the nation's foreign policy must be exercised from a base of strength, never capitulating to less powerful third-world nations.

Flood certainly did take a tough stand on communism. In the 1940s he was named to a special congressional committee charged with investigating the Katyn Forest massacre, the mass murder of eleven thousand Polish Army officers by the Russians during World War II. During the 1950s his activities grew even more prolific. Flood pushed for a resolution to require the Truman administration to explore ways to aid resistance movements behind the iron curtain, most notably in Hungary. He championed an amendment to the National Science Foundation Act to make an FBI security screening a prerequisite for the foundation's employment of a foreign national "in any capacity whatsoever." He constantly opposed the Eisenhower administration's efforts to control military spending in the interests of a balanced budget. But Flood was not ignorant of the fiscal concerns these involvements were creating.

While he publicly supported American involvement in the Vietnam conflict in the 1960s and 1970s, Flood scrutinized Defense Appropriations budgets and severely grilled Pentagon officials when they defended their budget requests in hearings. Flood was clearly concerned about having to compromise the quantity and quality of the Great Society legislation that was so important to him and to his district. Even his vehement opposition to a Panama Canal Zone independent of U.S. control cannot be divorced from the commercial benefits it created for this country.

Finally, Flood's resignation from Congress on bribery charges in 1980 has been grossly exaggerated in national press accounts, which portrayed him as a corrupt politician who traded his influence for money.[7] Accused of improprieties in arranging federal contracts, Flood became the subject of sweeping investigations by the U.S. attorney general and the House Ethics Committee and was charged, in September 1978, with taking sixty-five thousand dollars in bribes. In fact, Flood's administrative assistant Stephen Elko, who abused the trust of the congressman for his own financial gain, committed those crimes. If anything, Flood, who was in failing health, was guilty of giving too much responsibility to an untrustworthy aide and then failing to carefully monitor his activities. The court case ended in a mistrial when one juror claimed that he felt sorry for the aged congressman and couldn't bring himself to convict a seventy-four-year-old man.

Stripped of his congressional power, ravaged by illness, and facing a second bribery trial, Flood resigned from Congress on January 31, 1980. He subsequently pleaded guilty to federal charges that he accepted money from individuals seeking government contracts and was sentenced to one year of probation. But Flood insisted that he considered himself innocent, entering the guilty plea only to spare himself the ordeal of another trial. Flood's great misfortune was to be caught in the chasm between the old Machiavellian politics that once dominated Congress and the era of public cynicism that immediately followed Watergate. If Flood profited financially from influence peddling, there is certainly no evidence of it in his financial records. When he died, on May 28, 1994, he was living on a fifty-five-thousand-dollar pension from Congress and in the same modest residence he had called home since 1949.

The rise and fall of congressman Daniel J. Flood represents a political culture that no longer exists. It is a story of power, accomplishment, and, ultimately, failure and humiliation. He arrived on Capitol Hill at the beginning of the House's forty-year Democratic era, the longest period of single-party control in the nation's history. It was also a time when the House enjoyed a spirit of camaraderie and when congressmen did their job with little public attention. The most meaningful legislation was sponsored by a few indomitable old-timers whose seniority allowed them to control the most important committees and subcommittees. Flood listened and learned. What he learned was that successful legislative leadership relied on the time-honored practices of deal making and horse trading, both in Washington and back home in the district. In fact, he learned the lessons of the old politics so well that he became their most successful practitioner in Congress by the 1970s.

Flood's colorful personality, remarkable legislative success, and enigmatic background have made him a subject of endless fascination for me since the age of twelve, when I first met him. At that time I was spending my summers with a great-uncle, John "Dada" Kashatus, a tavern owner and former Democratic Party boss in Newport Township, Luzerne County, Pennsylvania. Flood first met my uncle as special counsel for the Pennsylvania Liquor Control Board and the two men quickly became friends. Dada was an active supporter of Flood during his many congressional campaigns, turning out the vote for him in Newport Township. In return, Flood often acted on my uncle's advice, whether for a construction project or a congressional appointment. On the few occasions when his counsel was ignored, Dada would dial the congressman's Washington office and shower him with a hailstorm of profanities. By the mid-1970s both men were in their seventies, their glory days behind them. Still, Flood indulged Dada, probably out of sentiment or the loyalty that comes with a cherished friendship. One summer afternoon, the congressman strolled into Dada's tavern and introduced himself to me. "The name's Dan Flood," he said, extending his right hand. "What's yours?"

Awestruck, I didn't know what to say. I certainly knew who he was, but I never anticipated the charismatic figure that stood before me. He was dressed in a white Edwardian suit, black shirt, and white tie. His handlebar mustache was impressively waxed to its mouse-tailed points. Somehow I managed to shake his hand, one so huge that it completely wrapped around mine.

"Hi," I blurted out. "I'm Billy Kashatus."

"Oh! The doctor's boy!" he exclaimed, referring to my father, who was one of Flood's physicians. He was pleasantly surprised to meet me and his demeanor softened.

"Your father is a great man," he added. "Please tell him that I asked for him."

Dada was much less impressed. Apparently he was angry with Flood over some issue and he motioned for the congressman to step into the kitchen to discuss the matter.

"Well, Dada beckons," he said, with the clipped accent of a vaudevillian actor. "Very nice to meet you, Billy, my boy." And off he went. I would not see him again until eight years later, when he awarded me an internship to serve on his House office staff.

When I entered graduate school for history in the mid-1980s, I was determined to write my doctoral dissertation on Flood, but my adviser refused to support me. He insisted that his political career was too recent and that an objective study could only be done in the distant future after sufficient time had passed. Disappointed, I moved on to another topic.

Once again, after Flood's death in 1994, I attempted to write his biography. I was living in Philadelphia at the time and made numerous trips to Wilkes-Barre in the hope of researching the necessary primary source materials and doing oral interviews. Although Judith Tierney, the director of the Daniel J. Flood Collection at King's College Library, was very encouraging and gave me unlimited access to the special collection, the FBI had already seized dozens of files that had been used to prosecute the congressman, and those files remained classified. Therefore it was difficult to gain a full understanding of the forces that led to his 1979 trial on bribery charges and his subsequent resignation from Congress. In addition, few of Flood's contemporaries agreed to be interviewed for the project. They were concerned about the legal implications of their remarks since Flood's congressional career was tainted by scandal. As a result, I abandoned the project.

Not until 2004, when I accepted a position to teach history at Luzerne County Community College, did I resurrect the idea of writing Flood's biography. Although many of his contemporaries were dead, I still had access to others who were now willing to discuss their relationship with the pork-barreling congressman. I was also privy to thousands of public documents that detailed Flood's activities, including the FBI records that I paid to have declassified. The research for his book is based on more than thirty interviews of Dan Flood's family members, friends, and congressional colleagues; public papers, photographs, audiotapes, and film stored at King's College Library in Wilkes-Barre; approximately seven thousand court and FBI documents relating to Flood's 1979 trial; and another two thousand newspaper articles that were carefully preserved and sealed away in scrapbooks by his widow until her death in 2005. These scrapbooks are now in the collections of the Luzerne County Historical Society in Wilkes-Barre, Pennsylvania.

During the last decade, I learned to balance the admiration I have for Dan Flood with the necessary detachment that a historian must maintain to do a critical examination of his subject. As my research unfolded, I became quite aware of Flood's shortcomings: a tendency to lie about or exaggerate his educational and political background; his influence-peddling and intimidation of congressional colleagues; a stubbornness that bordered on the mean-spirited, especially with local Democratic Party leaders and Pentagon officials; question-able connections to organized crime; an ongoing battle with alcoholism in his later years; and a huge ego that motivated all his activities, for better or for worse.

At the same time, I was saddened by the fact that most of my students had never heard of Flood, and I became determined to educate the millennial generation on his many contributions to northeastern Pennsylvania and to the nation. While they may not have agreed with Flood's hawkish views or old-style politics, my students came to understand the significant role he played in the cold war, the Great Society programs, and the transformation of a declining anthracite coal industry to a more prosperous service economy. With the publication of *Dapper Dan Flood*, others can now appreciate Flood's enduring legacy too.

1

ANTHRACITE ORIGINS

Coal was king in northeastern Pennsylvania at the turn of the nineteenth century. Beneath the surface of a near-five-hundred-square-mile area lay 95 percent of the nation's anthracite deposits, a source that fueled U.S. industrialization and provided warmth to the homes of a rapidly growing population.[1] This triangular region was bounded on the west by the Susquehanna River, on the east by the Lehigh River, and to the south by the Blue Mountains. Within this triangle were four coalfields: the Southern Field, located primarily in Schuylkill County; the Western Middle Field, which cut across Northumberland, Columbia, and Schuylkill counties; the Eastern Middle Field, at the southern end of Luzerne County; and the Northern Field, which extended from Susquehanna County in the north to Luzerne County in the south.

The "Kingdom of Coal" was controlled by a monopoly of seven large railroad companies joined by interlocking boards of directors and connected by joint stock ownership to New York and Philadelphia banking interests. Their subsidiary mining companies accounted for 70 percent of production and all the employment of northeastern Pennsylvania.[2] The numbers were prodigious. In 1880 these four coalfields produced 27,974,532 tons of coal and employed a total workforce of 73,373 men. Three decades later, annual production had nearly tripled to 83,683,994 tons and the total workforce was 168,175 men. By 1917, the peak year of production, the four anthracite fields turned out 100,445,299 tons of coal, with a total workforce of 156,148 men.[3] Of all the fields, however, the most significant production of coal occurred in the Northern Field. At six miles in width and fifty-five miles in length, the Northern Field was the largest and most productive coalfield of the anthracite region. It was also the lifeblood of Luzerne County. From 1910 to 1917, the Northern Field produced nearly thirty-five million tons of coal annually.[4] The tremendous success was due to two major advantages it had over its neighboring fields to the south. First, operators found it easier to extract coal from the Northern Field because the beds gradually dipped into the ground beginning in Forest City, reached a maximum depth at Wilkes-Barre, and outcropped again at the western end of the field around Nanticoke and Shickshinny. This horizontal pattern contained twenty coal beds that were more accessible to miners than the deeper beds in the fields to the south. Second, the coal that was mined out of the Northern Field was more marketable because it contained more carbon, making it much purer. These two advantages made the Northern Field a virtual treasure chest of the "black diamond."[5]

At the heart of the Northern Field was the Wyoming Valley, which enjoyed major operations at Pittston, Wilkes-Barre, Plymouth, Glen Lyon, and Nanticoke. Each of these were controlled by one of four companies: the Glen Alden Coal Company; the Delaware, Lackawanna & Western Railroad Company (DL & W); the Lehigh & Wilkes-Barre Coal Company; and the Susquehanna Coal Company. Of the four companies, the DL & W was the largest, dominating both the mining and transportation of anthracite coal in the region. By 1900 the company was producing approximately eight million tons of coal each year, employed about fifteen thousand workers, and accumulated assets totaling fifty million dollars. Its production and wealth was second only to the Philadelphia and Reading Coal and Iron Company, whose operations were primarily in the Middle and Southern fields.[6] But those benefits came at a price.

The anthracite industry violated a once-beautiful region of rolling hills, fertile meadowlands, and thick forests rich in evergreens, oaks, and pines and abundant with wildlife, leaving only mountainous black banks of refuse, waste piles of slate and rock, and scrawny little birch trees to dominate the region. It polluted the sparking streams and creeks, turning many of them black with coal dust and redolent with the stench of sulfur. Even the Susquehanna River, which once weaved its way through the valley like a silver thread, bore a permanent dark tinge. The industry also triggered labor conflict between the older, more established settlers from northern and western Europe and newly arrived immigrants from southern and eastern Europe.

While the "old immigrants"—primarily English and Welsh in origin—were skilled laborers, foremen, and colliery owners who settled in the anthracite region during the early nineteenth century and established the coal industry, the "new immigrants" were largely unskilled workers who came from Lithuania,

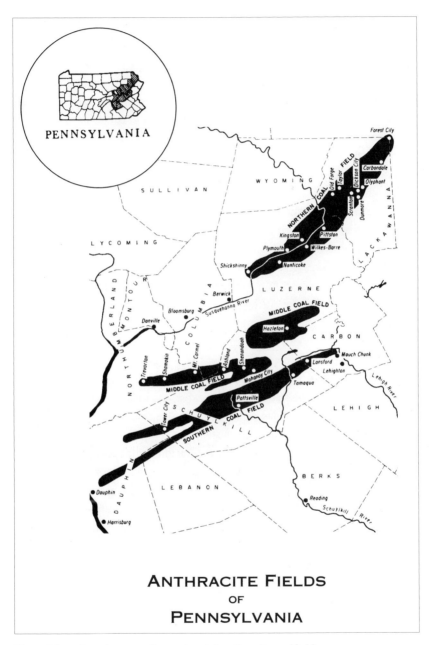

ANTHRACITE FIELDS
OF
PENNSYLVANIA

Fig. 1. Map of northeastern Pennsylvania's anthracite coalfields.

Russia, Italy, and Poland after the American Civil War. They had been drawn by the lure of the American Dream and a burgeoning anthracite industry, which they hoped would serve as their ticket to success. The Irish were caught between these two immigrant groups. They arrived in two large waves, first between 1845 and 1860 immediately following the Great Potato Famine, and later between the late 1870s and early 1880s as a series of crop failures and evictions by Protestant landlords foreshadowed another devastating famine.

The differences between the three groups were cultural, but they often manifested themselves in the living conditions, working relationships, patterns of mobility, and physical violence that characterized the life of the anthracite region. For example, the English and Welsh Protestants, who constituted the skilled labor force, discriminated against the Irish and the Slavic immigrants because of their Catholic faith and lack of skills. Similarly, the Slavic immigrants purposely kept their distance from the Irish as well as the English and Welsh because they found it difficult to trust any social group not of their own ethnicity. Under these circumstances, the English and Welsh established an "anthracite aristocracy" of mine operators and foremen, while the working Irish and the Slavs became the backbone of labor in the anthracite region.[7]

The profits of the coal companies (and the Protestant barons who operated them) came at the expense of the unskilled Catholic workforce. Wages were arbitrarily calculated, not by the hour but by the number of coal cars loaded by the miners. Earnings ranged from $0.75 to $1.25 per day. In the absence of child labor laws, a young male could go to work as a breaker boy as early as the age of eight. For $0.25 per day, he would sit on the ground floor of the breaker next to a coal chute and remove the slate, rock, and wood from the anthracite that had been siphoned into various sizes at the top of the breaker. By the age of ten many of these boys had permanently lost their fingernails, and it was not uncommon to find hunched backs among them.[8] Poor pay was surpassed only by the hazardous working conditions to which these immigrants were exposed.

Cave-ins were common, especially if wooden supports were improperly positioned when a coal vein was mined out. Flooding was also common because the mining was done hundreds of feet below the Susquehanna River bed. Runaway mine cars and unpredictable explosions were daily concerns for the miners. In fact, from 1890 to 1910 there were over five thousand deaths in Luzerne County that occurred as a result of these types of mining accidents. In 1904 alone, 595 men died in the county's mines, the worst accident being an explosion that occurred at the Auchincloss Colliery, claiming the lives of nearly one hundred men.[9] A coal miner faced the very real threat of death on a daily basis. If he were fortunate enough to escape these immediate dangers, the miner would eventually be forced to contend with "black lung," a respiratory disease caused by years of inhaling coal dust. The majority of these men would end up coughing themselves to death for less than subsistence wages.

The English and Welsh coal operators controlled even the simple pleasures of life. They owned the company stores, shops, and saloons in every small town in the anthracite region. Purchases would be deducted from the laborer's weekly salary, and there was no such thing as credit. No wonder the taverns were the most crowded establishments after working hours. Alcohol was the poor man's aphrodisiac. It provided him, in most instances, with the only release he had from the routine of his miserable existence. The only place a coal miner could express himself was among others who eked out a meager existence in the pits. When he finally returned home, often inebriated, his family made sure to stay clear of him or they would meet with a violent reception. Physical abuse of wives and children was a common reality in coal country.

High prices, low wages, and poor working conditions were not unique to the Slavic and Irish immigrants of the Northern Field. The Irish miners of the Middle and Southern fields also had to contend with these same problems during the 1860s and 1870s. They responded, at various times, with violence through organizations like the Molly Maguires, an alleged secret society that destroyed company property, or other groups that formed unions and called general strikes.[10] The most successful of these labor actions occurred in 1875 when the Welsh and Irish mine workers of the Middle and Southern anthracite fields banded together in a Workingman's Benevolent Association and refused to work for a five-month period. Unfortunately for them, the eastern European immigrants of the Northern Field continued to work and were able to meet the nationwide demand for hard coal, forcing their anthracite brethren to the south to return to the pits for a 20 percent reduction in wages. Embittered by this turn of events, the Welsh and Irish mineworkers developed a greater animosity toward the Lithuanians, Poles, and Russians of Luzerne County, denouncing them as "strikebreakers" who always seemed to "milk the cow" while the miners of the Middle and Southern fields "were left to hold the tail." Two years later, when these Slavic immigrants stopped work for three months and demanded a 24 percent increase in pay, the Irish and Welsh miners returned the favor by continuing to work.[11]

The struggle between the new immigrant miners of the Northern Field and the Irish and Welsh to the south continued throughout the 1880s and 1890s. Not only did the conflict prevent the unionization of the anthracite workers, but it also caused a great deal of ethnic animosity between the two groups. The Irish and Welsh considered the Lithuanians and Polish "stupid," "dirty," "ignorant," and willing to work for low wages, thereby preventing the establishment of a united mine workers union. The Slavs, on the other hand, considered the Irish and Welsh to be "lazy," "elitist," and unwilling to band together in a union with unskilled laborers. The Coal and Iron Police exacerbated the conflict whenever there was a strike by either group. Strikes were often marked by beatings, shootings, and sometimes by outright massacres, most notably in Lattimer, Pennsylvania, in 1897.[12] The stalemate continued until 1900.

Under the dynamic leadership of young John Mitchell, the United Mine Workers of America (UMW) succeeded in organizing all four anthracite fields. Mitchell united the anthracite miners by appealing to their common desire for economic justice, transcending the ethnic barriers that divided them. "The coal you dig," he reminded them, "isn't Slavish or Irish coal— it's just coal!" In August 1900 the UMW called a general strike to protest the arbitrary wage policies of the coal operators. After six weeks, the operators agreed to a 10 percent pay increase in all the fields and the miners returned to work. This event strengthened the bonds between miners of different ethnicities under UMW leadership and made possible an even more successful 1902 strike in which the mine owners formally recognized the union as a collective bargaining organization.[13]

The UMW's general counsel was Daniel John McCarthy, a prominent Wilkes-Barre attorney who was a member of the special commission appointed by president Theodore Roosevelt to settle the 1902 coal strike.[14] McCarthy's origins can be traced to the "shanty" or "working-class" Irish. Born in Ireland in 1851, he immigrated to the United States in 1866 at the age of fifteen.[15] Shortly thereafter, McCarthy settled in Freeland, Luzerne County, and secured employment as a laborer in the mines. He experienced firsthand the labor exploitation of the operators and the ethnic conflict among the rank and file. The poor wages and working conditions emboldened him to join the Knights of Labor—an early workingman's union committed to "securing to the workers the full enjoyment of the wealth they create"—and, later, to study law.[16] McCarthy's commitment to social and economic justice for the coal miners was only exceeded by his unshakeable patriotism. He quickly captured the attention of UMW president John Mitchell during the anthracite coal strike in 1902 and played an instrumental role in the settlement of that action.[17] When McCarthy retired from his legal practice, he invested his energies in cultivating his eldest grandson and namesake, Daniel John Francis Flood.

Born on November 26, 1903, in Hazleton, Luzerne County, Pennsylvania, Dan Flood was the eldest son of Patrick and Sarah McCarthy Flood. Patrick was the son of James and Bridget Flood, immigrants who relocated from Kilkenny, Ireland, to Wilkes-Barre sometime in the mid-1860s.[18] The surname "Flood" derives from the Gaelic designation for "Mac an Tuile," meaning "Son of the Flood." To this family belonged two noted politicians—Sir Frederick Flood (1741–1824) and Henry Flood (1732–91)—both of whom were staunch opponents of the union between Ireland and Great Britain. Another member of the family was slain by British soldiers during the unsuccessful 1916 Easter Rebellion in Dublin.[19] Such a pedigree anticipated a future in politics for young Daniel. But for the first American Floods, Capitol Hill was still two generations away.

Patrick, born in 1872 as one of seven children, left school at an early age to work in the mines of the Northern Field. Sometime in the mid-1890s he relocated to Hazleton, where he found employment as a laborer.[20] He also met and married Sarah McCarthy. After Dan's birth, the Irish Catholic couple moved to Wilkes-Barre, where they rented a double-block house at 77 Madison Street. Patrick, hoping to improve his lot in life, found employment as a tavern keeper.[21]

Between 1906 and 1911, Sarah McCarthy Flood gave birth to two more children, Gerald and Katherine. She died shortly thereafter, and her parents moved in with Patrick to help raise the three children.[22] McCarthy took a special interest in his eldest grandson, spending countless hours quizzing him on people, places, and events in American history. The memory of those sessions lingered well into the congressman's old age. "I can remember when I was five years old," Flood recalled, "and my grandfather asked me, 'Dan, what would you do if someone insulted the flag?' And I said, 'I'd stand tall in my sailor boy suit and say shoot him on the spot!'"[23]

During the winter months, McCarthy took the youngster with him and his wife, Catherine, to St. Augustine, Florida, where they took excursions across the Caribbean aboard small schooners. It was most likely on one of these trips that Flood rode across the Isthmus of Panama aboard the canal-side railroad and first laid eyes on the interoceanic passage that would later dominate his interest in foreign policy. McCarthy also allegedly enrolled young Dan at a "Florida Military Academy" to foster in him a strong sense of patriotism.[24] No such institution, however, can be found in the historical record. The closest military school to St. Augustine, Florida, in the early 1900s was the Kentucky Military Institute, which conducted a three-month winter session at Eau Gallie, now Melbourne.[25] Located on Florida's east coast, KMI was located 143 miles to the south of St. Augustine, about a two-hour train ride. It is doubtful, however,

Fig. 2. Patrick Flood and Sarah McCarthy were married in Hazleton, ca. 1900.

that young Dan attended the school, since KMI's enrollment was restricted to high-school- and college-aged students. Nor is there any record of his attendance. More likely, young Dan received his elementary education in the public schools of Wilkes-Barre and St. Augustine when he accompanied his grand-parents to Florida. Whatever the case, Daniel J. McCarthy exerted the greatest influence on his young grandson's life.

Many years later, Flood would admit that he was a "very lonely child," having spent so much time with adults. He never developed a close bond with his younger siblings either.[26] It is unknown whether that failure was due to the special attention his grandfather lavished on him or his own inability to cultivate a closer relationship with his brother and sister. What is certain is that his family had high expectations for him.

Flood's father enrolled him at Wilkes-Barre High School (now the James M. Coughlin High School) at the age of thirteen, nearly two years younger than most of the freshman class. In the anthracite region during the early twentieth century, just to attend high school was exceptional. Most families sent their sons off to work in the collieries as breaker boys once they completed grammar school, while girls remained at home to help their mothers raise younger siblings and assist with other household chores. Thus Flood's case was exceptional, both in terms of age and circumstance.

The youngster must have been in awe of the formidable-looking high school building when he entered it in September 1916. Located at the corner of Union and Washington streets, Wilkes-Barre High School, constructed in 1911, was one of the most attractive public buildings in the city. It was a impressive four-story structure of limestone, red brick, and marble conceived in the turn-of-the-century architecture style, which was characterized by a symmetrical design, large, plate-glass windows, and high ceilings. The building boasted a 1,554-seat auditorium with plaster frescoes, a stained-glass dome, and a balcony that spanned three-quarters of the room. The main floor also consisted of well-lighted library, administrative offices, science laboratories, and classrooms. Additional study, lecture, and recitation rooms were located on the upper floors. In the basement was a large gymnasium and locker rooms.

Students chose from one of three educational tracks—classical, traditional, and vocational—as well as courses in domestic science, physical education, laboratory science, commercial and mechanical drawing, and a plethora of extracurricular clubs.[27] Assisting them in choosing the appropriate course of study and monitoring their progress was Jacob P. Breidinger, the school's principal and a beloved figure among the students.[28] Breidinger helped the

Fig. 3. Dan Flood, age two, with his teddy bear on the
front porch of the family home at 77 Madison Street,
Wilkes-Barre.

adolescent Flood make the difficult adjustment to high school. "His great love
for our school, his keen understanding of young people, and his deep interest
in me allowed me to flourish," he recalled many years later.[29]

Despite the significant difference in age from his peers, Flood managed to
keep up academically. His transcript reveals that he struggled with mathe-
matics and the classics, earning grades in the 70s, but excelled in history,
geography, and literature, subjects in which he carried a 95 average, probably
due to his grandfather's encouragement.[30]

Surprisingly, Flood, for all his future oratorical and literary flamboyance,
only managed to earn a 79 in rhetoric and an 80 in public speaking. Still, he
graduated in June 1920 with an 86 cumulative grade point average, which
was very impressive for a sixteen-year-old. More remarkable was his election
as senior class president, an honor he later credited to the "political skill and

Fig. 4. Sarah McCarthy Flood in St. Augustine, Florida, with her three children (*left to right*): Dan, age twelve; Gerald, age eight; and Catherine, age two.

adroit handling of classmates Henry Smulowitz and Dick Williams." Both were among the most popular students in the senior class and went on to become successful in their own right. Smulowitz later owned and operated a brewery, and Williams became a prominent dentist.[31]

Even at a young age, Flood possessed the political and social skills necessary to make the "right" friends and influence others. With Principal Breidinger's encouragement, he joined the Glee Club and the Cliosophic Society, a debate club that familiarized students with parliamentary procedure and public speaking. Flood also wrote for *The Journal,* the high school's quarterly literary magazine. This particular activity is telling because his essays offer some important insight into his adolescent interests and self-perception.

One essay, titled "School Spirit," was a flagrant attempt at promoting greater student attendance at the school's football games, as well as a plug to establish a cheerleading squad. Flood writes of the fictional Milton High School football team that loses the first two games of the season. Despite their gutsy play, few students support them on the sidelines and they become discouraged. The team's spirits "hit rock bottom" after a 33–0 drubbing by archrival Phillipsburg. Then Jack, the team captain, makes a deal with the coach.

"Listen, Coach," he says. "If we can get some real live wire cheerleaders that are just full of pep, and get them out in front of about 1,000 of our schoolmates, and get them to lead some yells and sing the old Alma mater, you can't show me a fellow on the team that wouldn't fight his head off in a game."

The coach takes the request to the principal, "an old athlete himself," and the cheerleading squad is formed. Predictably, on Thanksgiving Day, 1,700 Milton students "madly cheered their varsity to a 72–0 victory of Phillipsburg, which fully repaid the previous defeat."[32]

Of course, readers recognized the parallels to Wilkes-Barre High School. The varsity football team posted a record of five wins and four losses in Flood's senior year, but they struggled early on. After losing the first two games, they suffered their worst defeat, a 72–0 whitewashing by Harrisburg Technical High School. The team had also gone through a series of coaches during the past year, due to a retirement and a resignation. Flood realized that the football players needed some encouragement and used his writing as a catalyst to rally student support. His essay prodded Jack Mangenella, the team captain and quarterback, to approach coach Bill Ganoposki and make the request for a cheerleading squad. Shortly thereafter, cheerleaders appeared on the sidelines and the Wilkes-Barre varsity squad earned three straight victories against Scranton Central (12–0), Scranton Tech (7–0), and Wyoming Seminary (33–0).[33]

Although Flood would love to have played high school football—and some accounts suggest that he did—another one of his essays offers an explanation for why he remained on the sidelines. "Preston's Hero" is about a student named Craig McCormack, "a tall, husky newcomer to Preston High School whose jet black hair, sparkling eyes, handsome features and solid frame were the envy of the boys." When approached by some classmates to try out for the football team, Craig refused. He was "too proud to offer any explanations," but was immediately branded as "yellow" by the boys, which "made his friendships with girls all the more welcome."

One day Craig overhears Marion Canova, one of his best friends and the most attractive girl in the high school, reveal her true feelings about him. "I did like Craig because he is so good looking," she confesses to a girlfriend. "I thought he would certainly show some spirit soon, but now I know he can't. He's simply yellow, there's not a bit of man in him. Before I ever like him again, he must prove himself a man."

Dazed by the suddenness of the attack, Craig flees the room. All the way home Marion's words keep cutting into his thoughts: "'So, she thinks I'm a sissy, huh?' he stewed. 'She's just like the rest of 'em. They all think I'm yellow.

If they only knew that Dad wouldn't let me try out for football! Well, they'd think different if they knew how much I wanted to play. I'll show 'em!'"

Craig finds the opportunity to "show 'em" when Congress declares war on Germany and enters World War I. Interestingly, his father, P. J. McCormack, "though afraid of football, would not refuse his son permission to enlist." Craig joins the Marines and finds himself in France fighting in the Allied offensive in the Argonne Forest. After "rescuing three wounded members of his company" and "successfully destroying an enemy machine gun nest," he is killed by shell fire and awarded the Congressional Medal of Honor posthumously for his heroism. "Thus," writes Flood, "Craig McCormack, once despised as a coward, became a hero in the eyes of every man, woman and child in Preston."[34]

If life imitates art, the adolescent Dan Flood felt more comfortable in the company of females than males. No doubt his own "jet black hair, sparkling eyes, handsome features and solid frame" held the same appeal for them as did Craig McCormack's. Perhaps Dan, like Craig, did not try out for the football team because his father, who also went by the initials "P. J.," disapproved. Football was not as valued as much as education by the Floods or the McCarthys. Dan was expected to advance himself in the classroom, not on the playing field. Finally, both Dan and Craig shared an intense patriotism that encouraged service to country. "Cowardice" or being considered "yellow" was the ultimate insult, whether it referred to sports or the military. Flood saw eight of his teachers go off to war by June 1918 and took seriously his own responsibility to aid in the war effort in whatever way possible.[35] As part of *The Journal's* staff, he helped to author editorials that promoted Liberty Bonds, war stamps, Red Cross drives, and growing produce for the war effort.[36] These activities helped to shape a fierce patriotism that later made Flood one of Capitol Hill's most hawkish congressmen during the cold war.

There was one other area of interest at which Dan Flood excelled: acting. His talent captured the attention of Mollie Weston Kent, who arrived at Wilkes-Barre High School in the fall of 1919. In addition to teaching public speaking, Kent, a graduate of the Boston School of Expression and the National School of Oratory, was responsible for the senior play.[37] Of the three hundred male students in the senior class, she recruited Dan for a male lead in Arthur W. Pinero's *The Amazons*, a farcical romantic comedy about three suitors competing for the affections of a single girl. He didn't disappoint her, either. The young thespian thrilled the audience with his quick-witted humor. "Say, which of the luggage has burnt cork in it?" Flood was asked at one point in the play. "Why, the soot case, of course!" he retorted. Afterward, Kent commended him

Fig. 5. Boys' Glee Club, Wilkes-Barre High School, 1919. Flood is seated at far right in the second row.

for acting with the "ease and grace of a professional."[38] He had discovered a passion in theater that would consume him for the rest of his life.

In 1921 Flood entered Syracuse University to pursue a course of study in the liberal arts.[39] Although his congressional biography states that he received bachelor's and master's degrees in history at Syracuse, university records indicate that Flood received only a bachelor's in business administration.[40] It is one of many discrepancies in the congressman's past that can be attributed, in part, to his desire for personal privacy and, in part, to strengthen his image on Capitol Hill. Flood's claim that he held bachelor's and master's degrees in history certainly validated his appointments as chair of the Health, Education, and Welfare Appropriations Subcommittee and vice chair of the Defense Appropriations Subcommittee. Such degrees would suggest that he had the academic background to inform his decisions on domestic welfare and defense. The purposeful obfuscation of his academic record and undergraduate activities allowed Flood to advance himself in Congress, which ultimately benefited his constituents. What's more, Flood, for most of his congressional tenure, escaped the scrutiny of an intrusive press, which never challenged his record or activities. Prior to Watergate and the era of public cynicism it triggered, Flood was a celebrity in Congress. His flamboyant style, colorful quotations, and rhetoric on the House floor endeared him to the Washington press corps. Similarly, the local press protected him, realizing that the economic welfare of the district depended on Flood's authority and influence on Capitol Hill. Thus the "secrets" of his early past remained safe.

Flood's fascination with acting grew stronger at Syracuse. He was just as committed to extracurricular activities in public speaking, debate, theater, and music as he was to his studies. While such extracurriculars might appear to be frivolous for a young man who hailed from the anthracite coal region of Pennsylvania, they were an important part of Flood's emerging identity. He belonged to a college generation referred to as "the damned and the beautiful" because of the popular misconception that they were "frivolous, rebellious and lost to social responsibility and traditional values." To be sure, as children of the white middle class, the college-going youth of the 1920s were socially and economically secure and enjoyed the luxuries of a higher education and considerable leisure time. But they also recognized that "individual merit came from group strength; that personal identity resulted from rigid conformity; and that social stratification bred the kind of community homogeneity" that their parents valued.[41] Accordingly, like the rest of his college generation, Flood adopted the fraternity and extracurricular clubs as vehicles not only for individual advancement, but also for social acceptance.

Flood joined the Janus Literary, Oratorical, and Dramatic Fraternity, founded at Cornell University in 1910 and established at Syracuse four years later. Among several activities, the fraternity sponsored an oratorical contest each semester. In his junior year, Flood captured first prize in that contest for his speech "Ireland's Struggle for Independence."[42] The following year he was elected president of the fraternity and won the Janus trophy, awarded to the "most representative Senior in the University in the activities for which Janus stands."[43] Indeed, Flood was a deserving winner.

During his senior year, the future congressman sang for the Glee Club, acted for Tambourines and Bones Drama Club, served as president of the Debate Union and the University's Social Cabinet, and won three of the most prestigious oratorical contests on campus.[44] But his greatest achievement was anchoring the debating team that defeated Oxford University on October 12, 1923, in the very first international debate held at Syracuse. The issue at hand was whether the United States should enter the League of Nations. The "cold overwhelming logic" of Flood and his teammates, C. Everett Shults and Achilles Catsonis, "overcame the emotional diplomacy of the Oxford team by a popular vote."[45] Many years later Flood identified the victory as the "highlight" of his

Fig. 6. Flood (*left*) poses with members of the Syracuse University debating team, which defeated Oxford University on October 12, 1923, in the very first international debate held at Syracuse. He would later identify the victory as the "highlight" of his college years.

college days and recalled one of the insightful one-liners he worked into the debate. "They buried the hatchet in the Middle East," he noted, "and struck oil."[46]

Although later accounts of Flood's college days claim that he was an "outstanding intercollegiate boxer in the 170-pound weight class," the only record of any athletic involvement was in track and cross-country.[47] Nevertheless, the repeated references to Flood's alleged athletic activities, first as a high school football player and later as an amateur boxer, indicate that he valued the hard-edged competition and physical prowess of those particular sports. These qualities became part of the image he would later craft for himself back in his congressional district.

After graduating from Syracuse in 1924, Flood briefly attended Harvard Law School. Tuition was paid through a savings account established by Daniel McCarthy for the purpose of putting his eldest grandson through law school. Required to take four courses—Civil Procedure, Contracts, Property Law, and Torts—Flood's academic performance was satisfactory, the equivalent of C work.[48] But his more inspirational experience with Harvard's Hasty Pudding club, a student theatrical group, convinced him that he should follow his true

Fig. 7. In the mid-1920s, Flood (*second row, fourth from left*) established himself as a matinee idol with the Manhattan Players Theater Company. He appeared in some fifty productions during a three-year span.

passion of acting. As a result, he abandoned his legal studies in the spring of 1925 for Broadway.[49]

Flood's success was immediate. He quickly established himself as a matinee idol with the Manhattan Players Theater Company, one of New York City's most renowned professional acting troupes. Landing roles as a leading man in droll, drawing room comedies and romantic melodramas, Flood appeared in some fifty productions during a three-year span. But the role that had the most enduring influence on his future was *White Cargo*, in which the young thespian starred as a British shipping merchant. He had to grow a handlebar mustache for the performance, a sartorial addition that would later become a trademark of his political career.[50]

By 1927 Flood realized that popular interest in the theater was waning and that whatever future he had in acting lay with the film industry. He made a screen test for Paramount Pictures in the hope of catching on, but it wasn't to be. While Flood projected a handsome appearance, the producers questioned whether he "truly possessed the full range of acting skills necessary for the silver screen." "I took the hint," he recalled many years later with a hint of bitterness in his voice. "So I enrolled at Dickinson to complete my legal studies."[51]

Flood went off to Dickinson Law School, in Carlisle, Pennsylvania, more focused than he was at Harvard, and his grades reflected that fact. He completed his second year of law studies with a 2.8 grade point average, and improved that average to 3.3 in his third and final year. Flood received A grades in Constitutional Law, Corporations, and Evidence, which anticipated his later success as a trial lawyer and legislator.[52] He graduated from Dickinson in 1929 and was admitted to the bar on September 4, 1931.[53]

The young lawyer began practicing in Wilkes-Barre with the firm of Charles B. Lenahan. According to Lenahan, Flood was "such a good trial lawyer" that he "won two cases that became 'name cases,'" or cases that set precedents so important that lawyers refer to them by colloquial names.[54] The first was the "Strip Mine Drowning case," in which Flood gained a judgment for the family of a boy who drowned in an unguarded strip mine hole filled with water.[55] The second, the "High Tension Wire case," involved a thirteen-year-old boy who lost his right arm and permanently disabled his left when he came into contact with a high-voltage transformer near his home in Sugar Notch. After Flood won that case, the Glen Alden Coal Company, which owned the transformer, appealed the verdict to the Pennsylvania Supreme Court.[56] Once again, Flood, this time overdressed in cutaway striped trousers and a formal four-in-hand tie, prevailed. The defense lawyer for the coal company congratulated Flood for his victory, duly noting that it was the very first time the company had paid on a case it had elected to appeal to the state supreme court.[57]

Others maintain that Lenahan exaggerated Flood's success at law. "Truthfully, Dan was not cut out to be a lawyer," said Harold Rosenn, a longtime Wilkes-Barre attorney and friend of Flood's. "He really didn't want to practice law. Dan just didn't see himself stuck in a library doing research and briefs. If he had remained a trial lawyer, he'd probably have been a good one, but even that wasn't his field. I watched him in court a few times. He was as astute and as brazen as he could be. He sounded good and presented himself well, but there was very little substance to his remarks. Truth is, that Dan Flood was acting all the time. So law served him well, but it certainly was not his profession."[58] Attorney Joseph Farrell agrees. Farrell, a partner in Flood's law firm in the 1960s, recalls that the congressman once told him that occasionally he "got a hankering to practice law," but then he would "slap [himself] and the urge quickly disappear[ed]." "He just had no interest in practicing law once he got into Congress," said Farrell. "I'd imagine that law would be pretty boring for him after he'd been such a powerful influence on Capitol Hill."[59]

Flood certainly could be brazen. One story that still circulates about his early law practice holds that he insulted one of Luzerne County's most respected judges during a petty theft case. This incident occurred sometime during the Great Depression. Flood was defending an elderly Polish immigrant who was arrested for stealing vegetables from a grocery store. It was a repeat offense because the old man had gone before the judge about a year earlier. Flood argued that the immigrant was unemployed and didn't have any money to purchase food for himself or his family. In addition, he didn't understand that he had to purchase the vegetables since the store owner placed them outside along the street. Naturally, the elderly foreigner thought the grocer was throwing spoiled produce away, so he just helped himself. But the argument didn't hold any weight with the judge, who told the immigrant that he was very disappointed to see him once again and on the very same charge.

"Well, Judge, I must say that I'm disappointed in you!" interrupted Flood.

"Why is that, counselor?" he asked.

"There you sit in the very same chair, the same black robe, and hearing the same type of case as the last time I came before you," explained the young lawyer. "I thought a man of your intellect would certainly be on the state supreme court by now!"

Shocked by the insolent remark, the judge was speechless and paused to regroup. He then turned to the defendant and asked, "Do you have anything to say for yourself?"

The immigrant, standing before the bench with his hat in his hand, looked up at the judge and said, in broken English, "Judge, I got you six votes last election."

Now the judge was straining to keep himself from laughing. "You and your counselor are quite a pair," he said. "Get the hell out of here, both of you! And I don't want to see either one of you before me again!"[60]

Flood's controversial—and colorful—style was already developing at this early stage of his career. He quickly became known for his theatrical manner, taste for the extravagant, and a willingness to use the outrageous to deliver his point. More important, the experience allowed him to refine the legal skills he would later need to become an effective legislator on Capitol Hill.

Despite his success as a trial lawyer, Flood still retained his passion for theater. He continued to act and, on occasion, direct a play. In fact, he met his future wife, Catherine Swank, through his involvement in local theater. Shortly after returning to Wilkes-Barre, Flood was coaxed into directing a play sponsored by his family's parish, St. John the Evangelist Church. The production was called *Princess Pat*, a romantic comedy about a princess who grows up among commoners. Eddie Gallagher, the playwright, asked Flood to help him with the auditions. Catherine, who was in her late teens and a student at College

Misericordia in nearby Dallas, immediately caught the young attorney's eye. One look at the aspiring actress with golden blonde hair, sparkling blue eyes, and a luminous smile, and he was smitten.[61] While she was clearly the best actress to audition, Catherine was not the best singer, something that was necessary to play the lead role. "Dan convinced Eddie to give me the part of Princess Pat by promising that he'd teach me how to sing," recalled Catherine. "We both knew right away that we were meant for each other."[62] Despite the thirteen-year difference in age, Catherine and Dan began a courtship that centered on their common interests in theater, history, and politics, and eventually led to their marriage in 1949.

Born on December 4, 1916, Catherine was the daughter of Anthony J. and Elizabeth Swank. Anthony was a German immigrant who settled in Wilkes-Barre in 1884. Shortly thereafter, he found employment as a weaver, and met and married Elizabeth Hogan. The couple had six children, Catherine being the youngest. She attended St. Mary's Parochial School, graduated from St. Mary's High School, and earned a bachelor's degree from College Misericordia in 1939.[63] Afterward, she taught civics, government, and business courses at James M. Coughlin High School until her marriage to Flood. "I taught long enough to really get enjoyment out of it," she admitted, "and not too long as to have it become a burden."[64] Throughout her teaching career, Catherine continued to act in a summer stock theater at Lake Nuangola and at Wilkes-Barre's Little Theater Company, the third longest continuously running community theater in the United States (organized in 1922).[65]

Although they never acted across from each other, Dan and Catherine were regulars in Little Theater productions. Flood's first performance for the community theater came on June 6, 1933, when he played Prince Albert in *The Swan*, a charming, sophisticated play that takes place in a castle in central Europe.[66] Other, more memorable performances followed, including a role as "Death" in the play *Death Takes A Holiday*. He seemed to excel in more dramatic rather than lighthearted roles. Catherine was just the opposite. "Where I was sort of a comedian, or a 'cutesy' actress, Dan could play any role," she explained. "Don't forget that he had already been on Broadway and had also done some Shakespeare. His background allowed him to be remarkably successful in dramatic shows. Dan was also a beautifully expressive and handsome man who invested all of himself in his performances."[67]

Roy Morgan, a former *Times Leader* drama critic, also remembers Flood's local theater career. "Dan was a brilliant actor," said Morgan. "He had personality and that allowed him to bluff his way right through. Once, the curtain lifted on him, alone on the stage, and Dan promptly forgot his lines. For the

Fig. 8. Catherine Swank, thirteen years Flood's junior, began a courtship with the future congressman that centered on their common interests in theater, history, and politics.

next five minutes he made up a new play. Then the cloud lifted and he went right into the play as rehearsed. I don't think he ever had stage fright. Dan was a natural as an actor."[68] At the same time, however, Flood also began planning for a career in public service.

During the 1930s Flood became active in local and state Democratic Party politics. His initial foray came in 1933 as campaign manager for Frederick Kirkendall, the Democratic candidate for Wilkes-Barre mayor. Kirkendall was a long shot in a heavily Republican area, but Flood's persistence made the campaign a close one.[69] It also captured the attention of state lawmakers, who brought Flood to Harrisburg, the state capital. Among the many positions he held with the Commonwealth of Pennsylvania was special deputy attorney general with the Liquor Control Board (LCB) from 1935 to 1939. Though he was paid an annual salary of just four thousand dollars, he gained some important local political contacts that would benefit him later.[70]

The Pennsylvania Liquor Control Board is an independent government agency that was established in conjunction with the Twenty-first Amendment and the repeal of Prohibition. Officially organized in 1933 just four days before the sale of alcohol became legal in Pennsylvania, the Board was originally composed of three members appointed by Governor George Earle to staggered four-year terms. Flood's appointment came on January 25, 1935, after E. W. Davis, a Stroudsburg attorney and one of the original members of the Board, resigned from the post. Flood was responsible for managing the beverage alcohol industry in thirty-five counties across eastern and central Pennsylvania. His specific duties included licensing the possession, sale, storage, transportation, importation, and manufacture of wine, spirits, and malt or brewed beverages in the Commonwealth, as well as operating a system of liquor distribution (retailing) and providing education about the harmful effects of alcohol consumption.[71]

His first series of cases was conducted in the spring of 1933 before three justices of the Berks County Court and anticipated the colorful performances that would later make him a storied legislator in Washington.

"Your honors," Flood began in a thunderous voice. "I am Daniel John Francis Flood, member of the bar of the Supreme Court of Pennsylvania. I have been retained as special counsel to the attorney general of the Commonwealth of Pennsylvania. I am here to represent the Commonwealth in these cases." His delivery was crisp and to the point. He presented a picture of confidence and a no-nonsense approach.

"Now I don't know if you've had any appeals from the Board's decision before or not, and I don't know how you've handled it," he continued. "But I'm going to tell you how to handle them right because they're going to be handled that way today."

Flood's patronizing tone suggested that he was either supremely experienced in these matters or an ignoramus for challenging the intelligence of the court. Apparently the three judges gave him the benefit of the doubt and allowed the thirty-year-old counselor to outline the procedure for them. Then he called his first witness, attorney Louis Feldman, whom he grilled for twenty minutes. Satisfied that he had proven the Board's case, he took his seat.

When the defense attorney began his cross-examination, Flood jumped to his feet, waving his arms wildly over his head and screaming, "Your honor, I object!"

"Why?" asked Judge Shaffer.

For the next five minutes, Flood, with his mastery of legal jargon and purposeful obfuscation, argued his point. Though his meaning wasn't clear to anyone but himself, he managed to convince the court and the witness was dismissed.

"When the court got around to the defense's case," recalled Feldman, "Flood would jump to his feet and object whenever they made a strong argument. Of course, Judge Shaffer would always ask him to explain his objection and Flood would give another persuasive speech. In fact, I don't think he was overruled once that morning."

By noon the three justices had heard all but one of the thirteen cases on the docket. Judge Shanaman suggested that the court adjourn for lunch. Once again, Flood got took to his feet. "No!" he boomed, angered by the thought of being inconvenienced. "You can't adjourn for lunch. I'm a busy man. I have to leave here by twelve fifteen if I'm to catch my train!"

Impressed by Flood's conscientiousness, the three judges briefly conferred and agreed to finish the hearing. When the final case ended, sometime around 12:10 P.M., Judge Shaffer turned to Flood and said, "Mr. Flood, we thank you for being here and in a few weeks we'll hand down our opinions."

"Your honor," Flood replied, "I see no reason to do that. We've had perfect cases here this morning and so I've taken the liberty of preparing the orders for your honors to sign." Reaching into his brief case, the LCB's attorney produced the orders, all of which either revoked or sustained the revocation of the two-thousand-dollar bond.

The three judges looked at one another, again impressed by Flood's conscientiousness. His request was highly unusual. "Would you object seriously if we took just five or ten minutes to consider these matters?" asked Judge Shaffer.

"Well, not if you're any longer than that, your honor," replied Flood, looking at his wristwatch. Ten minutes later, the three judges returned and rendered their verdict. They sustained every single case for the Liquor Control Board.[72]

Flood built an impressive record with the LCB. In 1937 alone he prosecuted thirty violators and won twenty-five of the cases, securing the revocation of the taproom owners' licenses.[73] There was at least one violator, however, who managed to escape Flood's scrutiny.

John "Dada" Kashatus was the proprietor of a candy store called Chinatown in Glen Lyon, Newport Township, which was actually a front for a speakeasy he operated in the basement. One summer afternoon, Flood meandered into the "candy store." Kashatus, who had lost his right leg in a coal mining accident years earlier, was sitting on the counter chipping ice off a large block that had recently been delivered. His artificial leg (made of wood) was propped up on the counter and concealed by his long denim pants.

Flood began questioning him, insinuating that he was operating an illegal taproom in the basement. Kashatus, a superb actor in his own right, listened with growing consternation, repeatedly denying the charge. Finally, when Flood asked to check the cellar, Kashatus, in a brilliant show of furor, rammed the ice pick into his wooden leg and exploded, "God damn it man! I told ya that I don't have booze in the place!"

Flood, having no previous knowledge of the store owner's artificial leg, reportedly went into shock. He turned "white as a ghost" and the tips of his

Fig. 9. John "Dada" Kashatus, a Newport Township tavern owner and Democratic Party leader, played an instrumental role in getting Flood elected to Congress in the 1940s.

mustache "sprang straight out on both sides like mouse tails" protruding from his nostrils. The LCB attorney then turned "crazed and ran out the door screaming, 'Wild man in Chinatown! Wild man in Chinatown!'"[74]

Five years later, Flood made his first run for Congress. Kashatus, then a prominent Democratic precinct leader and legitimate tavern owner, resolved his differences with the LCB attorney at the urging of the county's Democratic leaders and helped get out the vote for him in Newport Township. To return the favor, Flood, acting on Kashatus's advice, urged liquor dealers to organize in the face of a growing movement for a return to a "dry" nation and the quickly shifting wartime public opinion. "It is time for liquor dealers to take concerted action against the dry forces," he insisted. "You must put a halt to the rather general opinion that the tavern keeper is not in just as legitimate a business as the grocer, banker, or druggist."[75] It was Flood at his best, playing both sides of an issue to his benefit.

State treasurer G. Harold Wagner tapped Flood in 1941 to serve as executive assistant and director of the Pennsylvania Bureau of Public Assistance Disbursements. The position paid five thousand dollars a year and gave Flood the financial and budgetary experience that would make him an attractive candidate for the House Appropriations Committee when he was elected to Congress three years later.[76]

Dan Flood was born into privileges that the vast majority of people in northeastern Pennsylvania did not enjoy. His middle-class background, exceptional education, and training afforded him position, influence, and access to the highest level of government in the nation. As a college-going youth of the Roaring Twenties, he may have yielded briefly to a deep passion for acting, but a strong sense of social justice and personal responsibility for the less advantaged members of society prevailed. Flood realized that the advantages he enjoyed demanded that he give something back to society. He became the embodiment of noblesse oblige.

Afterward, he carefully crafted a career in public life, first as an attorney and eventually as a public servant. Throughout his journey, a flair for the dramatic and a love for theater were never far behind. As a result, he was able to blend politics and acting, and do so on the greatest stage in the nation—the floor of Congress. Ultimately, the beneficiaries of his success would be the people of Pennsylvania's Eleventh Congressional District.

2

* * * *

EARLY CAREER

Pennsylvania's Eleventh Congressional District was located in Luzerne County, the third most populated county in the state after Philadelphia and Pittsburgh. Once a prosperous and influential anthracite region populated by large numbers of immigrant workers from southern and eastern Europe, the district had fallen on hard times. The coal industry was in decline and miners were placed on a limited work schedule. Some left the region for jobs in New Jersey, Maryland, and southeastern Pennsylvania. Those who remained relied on their public officials to improve the worsening economic conditions, and they registered their approval or disapproval at the ballot box.

The Eleventh was organized into seven legislative districts, each consisting of six to sixteen wards. The largest districts were the City of Wilkes-Barre (sixteen wards) and the City of Hazleton (fifteen wards). Each ward was subdivided into precincts, where the polls were located. Luzerne County contained more than four hundred precincts in the 1940s.[1] Voting was controlled by a formidable Republican machine that influenced local, county, and state elections for thirty years beginning in 1922, when John S. Fine, a common pleas judge from Nanticoke, became chair of the county Republican organization.[2] Fine consolidated his power through patronage, voter fraud, and a strong connection to Pennsylvania governor Gifford Pinchot.[3] His influence was so complete that only three times did voters from the Eleventh send a Democrat to either house of Congress during the 1920s. That Democrat was John J. Casey of Wilkes-Barre, a former coal miner who won election to the House in 1922, 1926, and 1928.[4] Casey was a maverick during the Republican hegemony of the twenties. A pro-labor Democrat, he fought for child labor laws and the right of the UMW to strike, and against Prohibition and restrictive immigration legislation that discriminated against southern and eastern Europeans.[5] While the gregarious congressman experienced only limited legislative success, his pro-labor position attracted greater numbers of voters among the working class, paving the way for the Eleventh District's support of Franklin Delano Roosevelt for president in 1932.[6] But it was the Great Depression and Roosevelt's New Deal reforms that were most responsible for challenging the Fine machine and changing the political complexion of the district, if only briefly, from Republican to Democrat.

The Depression worsened an anthracite economy that was already in decline. In 1930 the region's anthracite industry produced eleven million tons of coal. Two years later the total production dropped to seven million tons. Seventy percent of Luzerne County's 445,109 residents who had been employed in the coal industry were placed on limited work schedules. Even Truesdale, located in the Hanover section of Nanticoke—the highest coal-producing operation in the Wyoming Valley—had its work schedule limited to 150 days and its workforce cut in half. Tensions increased when Slovak and Lithuanian miners rebelled against the UMW leadership, whom they believed were siding with the owners instead of acting for the welfare of the rank and file. A rash of strikes took place to protest the mine closings. In 1935 these dissident miners established a renegade union, the United Anthracite Miners of Pennsylvania (UAM), and demanded a policy of "job equalization." When the UMW refused to comply, the UAM went on strike.[7]

The Glen Alden Coal Company (formerly the Delaware, Lackawanna & Western Railroad) antagonized the UAM by replacing its members with strikebreakers (newly arrived immigrants who were immediately given membership in the UMW). When UAM leader Thomas Maloney was killed by a mail bomb in late May, the striking miners resorted to violence. UMW miners attempting to travel to work or return home were greeted with rocks, abusive language, and the gunfire of the strikers. Governor Gifford Pinchot sent in the National Guard to restore order. A month later, the UAM was forced to concede to the UMW's policy of selective work scheduling, and the strike ended.[8] The episode not only taught the rank and file that they could not challenge the UMW's authority, it convinced the operators to lease their mines to smaller, independent companies.

During the mid to late 1930s, the contract-leasing system was adopted by all of the region's large coal companies: Glen Alden, Pennsylvania, Hudson, Lehigh Valley, and Susquehanna. While these large companies still retained the mineral rights to the land and controlled the processing, transportation, and sale of the coal, they avoided the safety risks, high costs, and potential labor conflict that were now the responsibilities of the smaller, independent companies.[9] The Pennsylvania Coal Company, in particular, leased their lands to independent companies controlled by organized crime. Santo Volpe, considered the "first boss of the Northeast Pennsylvania crime family" by the Pennsylvania Crime Commission, purchased 56 leases between 1934 and 1948.[10] An Italian immigrant from the small Sicilian town of Montedoro, Volpe became a power in several UMW locals. Using his leverage, he extorted payoffs from mine owners to avoid labor problems. Another member of the crime family (and Volpe's successor), John Sciandra, secured several leases as a partner in the Saporito and Knox coal companies. Both Volpe and Sciandra maximized their profits by violating the union wage rate, changing work rules, mining coal in off-limits areas, and employing unsafe mining practices. Together with their control of several UMW locals, these illegal practices gave organized crime a huge competitive advantage over the other coal companies in the region.[11]

As organized crime strengthened its grip on the anthracite industry, unemployment increased and conditions became desperate. Some out-of-work miners resorted to "bootlegging," or stealing coal from company-owned land to exchange for goods and services or sell for a profit. As many as 1,600 people were homeless, living in makeshift shanties in the Heights section of Wilkes-Barre, or on the riverbank near the North Street Bridge.[12] The economic emergency forced Pinchot, the Republican governor, to turn to Roosevelt's New Deal, which ended up paying most of the Commonwealth's relief costs.[13] By 1934, 85,711 people were receiving direct or work relief, a number roughly equal to the population of Wilkes-Barre.[14]

While the New Deal did not end the Depression, it did create thousands of jobs, which were all controlled by local Democratic leaders. The Works Progress Administration, for example, employed more than sixteen thousand people in Luzerne County, while the Public Works Administration employed another thirteen thousand.[15] Pennsylvanians registered their approval at the ballot box in 1934 by electing George H. Earle III as the state's first Democratic governor since the 1890s. That same year Joseph F. Guffey became the state's first Democrat in the U.S. Senate since the 1870s. Pennsylvania's thirty-four-member delegation to the U.S. House of Representatives also boasted a majority of twenty-four Democrats as a result of the 1936 election.[16] Among their numbers was J. Harold Flannery, a West Pittston lawyer, who outpolled Republican incumbent C. Murray Turpin of Kingston by 14,159 votes.[17] Flannery responded by giving his unconditional support to New Deal legislation. Between 1937 and 1940, he supported every New Deal bill that came before the House, including such major legislation as the Housing (Wagner-Steagall) Act, the Fair Labor Standards (Minimum Wage) Act, the Bituminous Coal (Guffey-Vinson) Act, the Farm Tenancy (Bankhead-Jones) Act, and the Agricultural Adjustment Act of 1938. At the same time, Flannery fiercely opposed the conservative attempt both to slash funding for the Civilian Conservation Corps, the National Youth Administration, and the Works Progress Administration, as well as to restrict the jurisdiction of the National Labor Relations Board.[18]

The Roosevelt landslide of 1936 also had reverberations at the state level, where Democrats gained control of the Pennsylvania House by a margin of 116 to 90.[19] One of the newly elected members was Leo Mundy, a Wilkes-Barre physician who would become a powerful Democratic Party boss in Luzerne County. Born on June 2, 1887, Mundy was the son of Irish immigrants. He attended Wilkes-Barre's public schools and Wyoming Seminary, a local college preparatory school, before earning his medical degree at the University of Pennsylvania in 1908. Two years later he returned to Wilkes-Barre and opened a practice.

During World War I, Mundy was commissioned a captain and placed in command of a one-thousand-bed military hospital in France. In 1919 he was brevetted a lieutenant colonel and received the "distinguished service" citation from General John Pershing for heroism in treating and evacuating wounded soldiers under fire. Returning to Wilkes-Barre after the war, Mundy resumed his medical practice and entered politics, directing the campaign of his brother for city council. Intrigued by the political process, he gained the confidence of local Democratic leaders, who made him chair of Luzerne County's Democratic Committee, a position in which he exercised great patronage. More important, Mundy transformed the committee from a titular institution with little power or influence to an efficient party organization that successfully challenged Fine's more formidable Republican machine.

During the early 1930s, Mundy recruited the most promising young professionals to assume leadership of the subcommittees in charge of voter registration, fund-raising, public rallies, and publicity. He also worked at the grassroots level, in the wards, identifying the most politically savvy businessmen to appoint, train, and supervise the precinct workers, who, in turn, would call on voters, explain issues, and get Democrats to the polls. As his reputation grew, Mundy became more involved in national politics. In 1932, as a delegate to the Chicago convention, he actively campaigned for FDR's presidential nomination. Roosevelt thanked him by appointing the Wilkes-Barre physician collector of internal revenue for the Middle District of Pennsylvania. Not until

Fig. 10. Dr. Leo Mundy, chair of the Luzerne County Democratic Party in the 1930s and 1940s, promoted Dan Flood's early political career.

1936, however, did Mundy run for office, seeking to become a state senator. He handily won the election, defeating his Republican opponent by nearly eighteen thousand votes.[20]

It was Dan Flood's good fortune to be well connected to both Mundy and Flannery. Flannery, an attorney and novice actor, was a partner in the same Wilkes-Barre law firm as Flood, and both men had appeared together in Little Theater productions.[21] His relationship with Mundy was even stronger. The Democratic Party boss handpicked Flood to serve as legal counsel for the county's Democratic Committee and encouraged him to become the leader of the Seventh precinct. Impressed by Flood's youthful enthusiasm and energy, Mundy also persuaded him to serve as the Democratic National Committeeman for the Young Democratic Club of Pennsylvania.[22] When Flannery resigned from Congress in November 1941 to become a common pleas judge, Mundy reconciled the competing factions within the Democratic Party by proposing Flood as a compromise candidate.[23]

"Dan was a wonderful campaigner," recalled James Lenahan Brown, a fellow attorney who later became Flood's campaign manager. "He dutifully toured the area making speeches to phone-booth-sized party rallies."[24] Dozens of letters preserved in Flood's personal scrapbooks confirm Brown's assertion. It appears as if he spoke before any organization that made a request, including the Wilkes-Barre Lions Club, Friendly Sons of St. Patrick of Pittston, Order of the Owls, the Wyoming Valley Chapter of Disabled Veterans, Hazleton's Kiwanis

Club, Catholic Charities, Berwick Chamber of Commerce, Textile Workers Union, and the Knights of Columbus.

Flood's impressive campaigning was also due, in part, to Brown's influence. Born and raised in the Wyoming Valley, James Lenahan Brown was educated at Wyoming Seminary, Lafayette College, and the Dickinson School of Law. He met Flood in the mid-1930s and the two men instantly became close friends. They served as best man at each other's weddings and Flood was the godfather of Brown's eldest child, Karen. In 1937 they established Flood and Brown, a Wilkes-Barre law firm.[25] According to Joseph Farrell, who later joined the firm, Brown was "a very dogged, two-fisted fighter in legal circles. When Jim went into the battle, he went in wholeheartedly. He also prepared his cases in a very methodical fashion. I'd see him with sixteen chairs lined up in a row. Each chair had various parts of briefs on it and he could tell you exactly where certain information was. Jim was meticulous. He truly believed that law was a profession—not a business—and he conducted himself that way, too."[26]

Brown also had a strong interest in local Democratic Party politics. Instead of running for elective office, however, he devoted his energies to Flood's aspirations for Congress. "My father preferred working behind the scenes," said Larry Brown, the attorney's son, in a recent interview. "He felt that his greatest reward was building the county's Democratic Party from the grass roots. He used to joke that the party's earliest meetings used to take place in a phone booth, just big enough for him and Flood."[27]

Brown's influence was certainly formidable. He made the Republican Party accountable to the election laws. "Jim put a lot of heat on the Fine machine," said Farrell. "He was the one who insisted that all the Republican campaign signs be taken down at the courthouse—and they were. He also went after the Fine machine on the issue of voter fraud—and won. Jim covered every angle to get Flood those votes for Congress. It was just plain hard work. Dan was the same way. That's why the two of them worked together so well. In fact, I would say that the Democratic Party prevailed over the Fine machine in the late 1950s because of Dan Flood and Jim Brown."[28]

Flood had to be a strong campaigner, since he was widely considered the underdog. "While Mr. Flood is a very personable young man and a diligent worker for his party, his friends realize that he faces a stiff battle owing to the fact that the G.O.P. has an advantage of more than 20,000 in registrations," according to the February 1, 1942, edition of the Wilkes-Barre *Sunday Independent*. "It is admitted by the leading Democrats that Mr. Flood must be from 12,000 to 15,000 votes stronger than his party to capture the congressional seat."[29] Flood's performance in the May 1942 special election almost proved the pollsters wrong. Mundy had built an efficient party machine that turned out the vote for the thirty-nine-year-old Wilkes-Barre attorney. As a result, Flood lost the special election to his Republican opponent, Thomas B. Miller of Plymouth, by just ninety-three votes.[30] But he suffered a worse defeat in the general election six months later when Miller outpolled him 54,720 to 46,378.[31]

Despite the loss, Flood took heart in Mundy's encouraging words that the November election should "not be construed as a personal defeat" since "many of the factors transcended local issues," being "national in scope."[32] Democratic voter registration was down across the country as FDR shifted his attention to winning World War II and away from the New Deal. As relief agencies and jobs declined or disappeared altogether, so did support for the Democratic Party. Nevertheless, Mundy continued to back his protégé for another run at Congress in 1944, an election in which he would be vindicated. With Mundy's influence, Flood easily defeated Joseph M. Walsh for the party's nomination in the April primary and went on to beat Miller, the Republican nominee, in the November election, 71,843 to 65,922.[33]

During the campaign, Flood showed signs of the aggressive, and some would say ruthless, methods he would employ in future elections. He went on the attack against Miller almost immediately after winning the Democratic Party's nomination. He repeatedly asked the incumbent congressman to "debate in an open forum on current issues" so that the "average voter may have a better chance to make up his mind on the qualifications of the candidate before entering the polls."[34] Miller refused, realizing that Flood was an excellent debater. Undeterred by the rebuff, Flood proceeded to court the military vote by exploiting a controversial statement that the Republican candidate had made shortly after his election to Congress in 1942 about the soldiers fighting abroad. When asked how the army might be able to improve the fighting abilities of the U.S. soldier, Miller stated that "furloughs should be cancelled and discontinued." "Our boys forget the purpose for which they are in the Army," he contended. "They become soft and their military attitude is broken with each visit home. Packages are also unessential to the welfare of the fighting man. Therefore, all of these contacts should be eliminated."[35]

Flood printed up handbills that highlighted the quote along with the suggestion to "answer this statement by voting Daniel J. Flood for Congress." Wounded veterans, recently returned from the battlefront, were hired to distribute the advertisements throughout the district.[36] It was a sensitive point for Flood, whose brother Gerald, a naval combat officer, had been wounded while on duty in the Pacific earlier that year.[37] In fact, Flood himself had hoped to serve in the World War II but was exempted because of poor eyesight. "Dan was a frustrated soldier," insists John C. McKeown, a longtime friend and former personnel officer at the Wilkes-Barre Veterans Administration hospital. "I think he dedicated himself to military matters because he felt guilty about being unable to serve and he wanted to honor those who did make that sacrifice for their country."[38] Regardless of his intentions, the ploy worked. Flood's margin of victory over Miller in the 1944 election was 5,921 votes, just about the same number he tallied from soldiers fighting abroad.[39] He would remember that debt when he went to Capitol Hill, and never relinquish an opportunity to vote or sponsor legislation that benefited the military or its veterans.

If there was a sour note in the forty-one-year-old Flood's election to Congress, it was the death of his mentor, Leo Mundy, who died of a heart attack five months before the election. Mundy, age fifty-seven, was planning to run for his third term in the state senate when he passed away. Pete Margie, a West Pittston beer distributor, was nominated by the county Democratic Committee to replace him and won, defeating Republican candidate Robert A. Eyerman, a Wilkes-Barre architect.[40] Flood's election to Congress in the Roosevelt landslide of 1944 was Mundy's most important legacy to Luzerne County's political culture, though it wouldn't be recognized for many years. At the time, however, the voters of the Eleventh District were more concerned about the "obvious advantages that will accrue to Luzerne County" with Flood representing them during a Democratic administration.[41]

By 1944 the Eleventh District had fallen on hard times as the anthracite coal industry was in sharp decline. Competition from bituminous (or soft) coal—which is cheaper, easier to mine, and more abundant—as well as gas and oil, resulted in massive unemployment. With an aging population, decaying towns, and few prospects of gainful employment for the young, Flood's district was designated as a "depressed area." The fact that no major roads led into the region, and that the closest fully equipped hospital was over one hundred miles away in Philadelphia, made his quest for success in the nation's capital seem even more insurmountable.[42]

"When I came to Congress in 1944," Flood once recalled, "my district was exporting one thing—high school graduates. We had 19 percent unemployment. Coal mining was dead. People told me, 'Get us something big in here, like Lockheed or Boeing.' Well, nonsense! I didn't want any one-shot industry. I wanted diversity. I wanted companies that made shoes, brooms, whatever. But not any one-shot deal."[43] Flood's primary agenda when he was first elected to Congress was to reduce unemployment and to entice a host of new businesses into his district. Had he not made a positive impression with House

Speaker Sam Rayburn, who appointed him to the House Appropriations Committee, Flood would have struggled to secure any significant legislation or revenue for his district.[44] Membership on the Appropriations Committee is powerful because it distributes the spending money for each branch of government. Members also tend to be successful in securing projects for their own districts, a practice known as "pork-barreling." For a freshman representative like Flood to secure such an appointment was extremely rare. But Rayburn made it possible.

Sam Rayburn, a Democratic representative from Texas, was one of the most powerful Speakers in the history of the House of Representatives. He was first elected to Congress in 1912 and reelected to the twenty-four succeeding Congresses, serving continuously from March 4, 1913, until his death on November 16, 1961. Initially appointed to the Interstate and Foreign Commerce committees, Rayburn rose to Speaker in 1940 and quickly became the uncontested leader of the Democratic Party, both within the caucus and on the House floor. He had a remarkable talent for influencing policy making by choosing which members to speak and make motions, deciding points of order, and determining which bills should be presented to the House for a vote.[45] Rayburn brought to the Speakership a mixture of stern guidance, strict discipline, and care. Longtime representatives considered him a "whacker" because of his penchant for using the gavel. More discerning members understood that the manner in which Rayburn used the gavel often reflected his state of mind. A heavy thump, for example, meant anger. Repeated hollow tappings indicated weary impatience, and an echoing blast meant finality. In the process, he broke more gavels than did any of his predecessors. When necessary, Rayburn regulated activity on the House floor by stepping down from the Speaker's platform and circulating on the floor. If a congressman made a disagreeable motion, or refused to relinquish the floor, Rayburn, who favored brevity and forthrightness, would place a hand on his shoulder and whisper his advice into the offending member's ear before returning to the dais.[46]

When he needed votes, Rayburn became a backroom operator. By using persuasion, cajolery, or threats if necessary, he frequently snatched victory from seeming defeat. But he never asked a colleague to vote against personal conviction. While many of his opponents complained that Rayburn's leadership was "harsh," "arbitrary," and "dictatorial," they also conceded his fairness. As a result, he commanded the respect of eight different presidents, all of whom addressed Rayburn as "Mr. Speaker." Without his help, they were in trouble on Capitol Hill and they knew it. He never hesitated to speak his

Fig. 11. Sam Rayburn, a Democratic representative from Texas, was one of the most powerful Speakers in the history of the House of Representatives. Rayburn was Flood's mentor and secured for him membership on the House Appropriations Committee, one of the most powerful in Congress.

mind to a chief executive, and rarely was he challenged.[47] The same was true of his nominations for committee assignments.

When Rep. John B. Snyder (D-Pa.) passed away in 1945, there was a vacancy on the Appropriations Committee. Determined to hold onto the Appropriations seat, the Pennsylvania delegation spoke with Rep. Robert L. Doughton (D-N.C.), chair of Ways and Means (which made the nominations), and Speaker Sam Rayburn. Although Rep. Matthew M. Neely (D-W.Va.) was the leading candidate for the post, Flood received Rayburn's endorsement. The Speaker was immediately taken by the young congressman's forthrightness as well as his eccentricity. To mollify the West Virginia delegation, Rayburn introduced a resolution to increase the size of the Appropriations Committee from forty-three members to forty-five so that both Flood and Neely could be appointed.[48] "Mr. Rayburn was fond of Dan," recalled Rep. Jim Wright (D.-Tex.), who arrived on Capitol Hill in 1955 and later became Speaker of the House himself. "I think he liked Dan because he saw a fierce individualism that he admired. Both Flood and Rayburn shared that quality. Dan became one of his protégés and as such received advice and opportunities that few others enjoyed."[49] Flood admired Rayburn's example and realized how fortunate he was to have gained his personal attention. "Mr. Rayburn never feared to accept responsibility," he recalled shortly after the Speaker's death in 1961. "His words were honest and forthright, his reasoning was sound. I was truly fortunate to benefit from his sound advice as well as by his firm but courteous conduct when I first came to the House of Representatives."[50]

Armed with an appointment on the Appropriations Committee, Flood proceeded to promote Luzerne County as a "superb location" for the nation's growing military industry. He called his congressional district the "Shangri La of the war effort." "We have a great surplus of manpower and facilities that the government, for some reason, has never used for the war effort," he declared during the early weeks of the seventy-ninth Congress. "Some of the present war production shortages could be handled in the anthracite area simply by building a few factories up my way and putting people to work."[51] When he discovered a proposal that would reorganize the War Manpower area of northeastern Pennsylvania by diverting new industry to Lackawanna instead of Luzerne County, Flood took his case directly to the War Manpower commissioner, Paul V. McNutt. "Unbelievable neglect of the county's labor surplus by government agencies comes very close to discrimination," he fumed. "Such a division of our region's labor market would be another step in denying those constituents who cannot find jobs and who do not want to work in the mines an opportunity to contribute to the war effort. If you deny war and other industries opportunities to establish themselves in Luzerne County, you will do irreparable injury to the region's future."[52]

Within a month's time, Flood arranged to have two army engineers visit Luzerne County to determine the suitability of existing sites for available defense work.[53] Sufficiently convinced, the engineers reported their findings to the War Production Board, which agreed to spend five hundred thousand dollars for a county facility for mortar ammunition production.[54] In addition, Flood secured defense contracts for the production of metal ammunition cases for the Penn Metal Ware Company in Kingston, and for the manufacture of radio equipment by the Sylvania Corporation at the 109th Field Artillery's West Side Armory. These two contracts alone created more than a thousand jobs for constituents for the duration of the war, and they were secured by Flood within his first months in Congress.[55]

"Of all the congressmen Luzerne County has sent to Washington, none has advanced with the speed set by Dan Flood," editorialized the *Pittston (Pa.) Gazette* on February 23, 1945. "He's been in the national capitol slightly more than two months and has established contacts and prestige held by no predecessor. Most congressmen wait for their second term to make a speech on the floor of the House. Mr. Flood did not. Instead he seized the opportunity to speak on the 27th anniversary of Lithuania's independence, earning him high praise from many constituents in the district."[56] To be sure, Flood's address was one of hundreds of commemorative speeches given by legislators each year. But the twenty-minute discourse allowed him to showcase his flamboyant oratorical skill on the floor of the House and capture some rare exposure for a freshman representative.

"Lithuania is a land that commands our attention," he began. "I speak of this remarkable nation that has existed on the shores of the far distant Baltic Sea from time immemorial." "Lithuania is a land of surpassing beauty," Flood continued, speaking as if he had actually visited the Baltic nation when, in fact, he had never traveled to Europe. "It is resplendent with lakes, rivers and beautiful forests. Few hills are to be observed in the softly rolling country. It is little wonder that the people have a deep passion for their beloved homeland." The florid language struck an emotional chord with his audience, and the precision of his delivery was impressive. Flood proceeded to showcase his knowledge of European history by outlining the highlights of the small country's past, beginning with the "brave deeds of Vytautas the Great, Lithuania's first warrior king" in the fifteenth century to the day a quarter century ago when "that clear clarion call to awaken as a restored Republic was issued at Vilnius." Making a seamless transition to the Lithuanian American reverence for the Fourth of July, Flood noted that the Sons of Lithuania from his congressional district recently sent a replica of the Liberty Bell to their native land. "And on this bell appear the words, 'Forever toll the sons of Lithuania. Whoever fails to defend their liberty is unworthy of it,'" he concluded.[57]

Over the course of his first term, the energetic congressman would also introduce legislation granting sweeping income tax waivers to members of the armed forces and veterans, and lay the groundwork for the construction of a $4 million airport at Avoca as well as $2.6 million VA hospital along East End Boulevard on the outskirts of Wilkes-Barre.[58] The latter project was a major coup for Flood, who had to battle with neighboring Lackawanna County for federal support. Shortly after his election to Congress, Flood, in an effort to solidify his support among veterans, appeared at an American Legion meeting and proposed the building of a VA hospital and rehabilitation center in the Wyoming Valley. Appealing to the legionnaires to assume the lead role in such a plan, Flood promised to make it a priority when he arrived on Capitol Hill.[59] But he faced stiff competition from Pennsylvania Rep. John W. Murphy, a fellow Democrat, who made a similar promise to locate a VA hospital near Scranton in his Lackawanna County district.

Between January and May 1945, the two legislators jockeyed for advantage with secretary of war Henry Stimson, who considered such proposals and then made a recommendation to the president.[60] Flood supposedly convinced Stimson that Wilkes-Barre was a better location than Scranton for the hospital because it had greater accessibility to the communities it would serve by car, railway, and bus; the site offered greater possibilities for development, being away from the congested part of the city; and the Wyoming Valley had an ample labor force—many of whom were veterans—to maintain the hospital.[61] More probable, however, is that a deal was negotiated between the Truman administration and the two Pennsylvania congressmen. Specifically, whoever removed their district from consideration of the VA hospital would be named to a federal court judgeship. It appears that Murphy was more desirous of advancing his legal career than Flood because Truman, on May 7, appointed him to the Middle District of Pennsylvania to fill the vacancy created by judge Albert W. Johnson's resignation.[62] Accordingly, four months later, on September 19, Truman announced that Wilkes-Barre would be the site of a $2.65 million, 457-bed VA hospital. Flood called the announcement "one of the happiest moments of his career" and pledged that his first obligation would be "to the brave men who will be patients in this new institution."[63]

Flood was also named to the House Foreign Affairs Committee, another rare post for a freshman congressman because of the demanding responsibilities of the committee, especially in wartime.[64] As a member of the prestigious committee, Flood would play a role in determining the nature of the peace treaty ending World War II and shaping postwar Europe. Nor did he waste any time in expressing his sentiments on these matters to President Roosevelt. In late January 1945 Flood headed a group of fifty-seven freshman Democratic congresspeople who sent a letter to FDR pledging their "full aid in working for a world peace organization." The letter stressed that the United States should take the "lead among the Allied nations in insuring an enduring world peace." To that end, the congressmen expressed their "firm adherence to the principles of the Atlantic Charter" of 1941, which emphasized the necessity of all nations to honor freedom of thought, freedom from fear and want, economic cooperation, self-determination, and armament reduction. The letter ended by endorsing U.S. participation in "some strong international organization to preserve world peace," an intention that would be realized later that year with the establishment of the United Nations.[65]

Flood also endorsed a one-year extension of the Lend-Lease Act, which gave U.S. aid in supplies and armaments to her wartime allies, Great Britain, France, Russia, and China. The act, which was passed by Congress in March 1941, had already supplied the Allies with goods and services amounting to $35.4 billion. In return the four Allied nations supplied the United States with $4 billion worth of goods and services. But Flood saw Lend-Lease as more than a economic measure. He viewed the act as an "indispensable unifying force which has allowed the Allied coalition to be so effective."[66] After the war, Flood, on his very first trip to Europe, had the opportunity to meet British prime minister Winston Churchill, who was "most gracious" to him and "expressed his gratitude" for the congressman's strong support of Lend-Lease.[67]

The prosecution of German war criminals was another area in which the first-term congressman became involved. On April 20, 1945, Flood offered a resolution to authorize a joint committee of Senate and House members to "leave at once for Germany to visit the death houses and prison camps" to gain "first-hand information that would lead to the punishment of the war criminals."[68] The resolution passed, though Flood was not assigned to the committee. The following month, when Flood learned that Hitler's field marshal, the war criminal Hermann Goering, was receiving special privileges, he exploded in a fiery speech on the House floor. "Still pompous, strutting and arrogant," he said of Goering, "this obscenely obese buffoon and charlatan, demanded and was granted the privilege of a bath and a change to one of his grotesque musical comedy uniforms to have his picture taken with his captors."

Flood's voice grew more emphatic with each condescending adjective. "I protest this fantastic mockery of justice!" he thundered. "I protest in the name of the 100,000 peaceful citizens and the destroyed City of Rotterdam, wiped out in twenty minutes by this evil Bird of Prey Goering and his Luftwaffe— this was cold-blooded murder by order of this fat fiend."

His voice was at full volume, his temper controlled but rising. "I protest in the name of the dead of Warsaw—dominated by the orders of this devil from the hell that was Potsdam," Flood continued. "And I protest in the name of a long list of peoples, cities and nations done to death by this 'schweinehunde' and his evil crew."

It was classic Flood, exploiting both the English and German languages to vent his rage. He was, at once, intensely passionate yet colorful in his expression as well as in his animated delivery: "Instead of being wined and dined as a privileged character, this overstuffed museum piece should have been shot on sight as any other mad dog." Flood paused, taking a moment to collect his emotions and to prepare for the finale. His colleagues were spellbound by the performance. Some chuckled, while others whispered their assent. "This very day the joint committee of Congress sent to view the atrocity camps in Germany returned to the United States," said Flood, now more somber in his tone. "In statements to the press, they emphasized the revolting horrors of the Nazis and demanded punishment for war criminals. We must never forget what Goering and others of his ilk have done and punish him for his crimes rather than honor his requests."[69]

Flood gave a similar performance in early September when the first installment of the United Nations war criminal list was released. Near the top were Goering and former German diplomat Franz Von Papen. Von Papen had earned the Pennsylvania congressman's wrath when he defended his innocence by insisting that he was a "harmless old man who never liked Hitler anyway." Mustering all the venom in his literary arsenal, Flood excoriated Von Papen in the most insulting terms: "I now charge that evil old man with high crimes against God, humanity and society," he snorted. "I indict that mischief maker, that unregenerate scoundrel, as a war criminal in the classic meaning of the term. That jackal, sneak, liar, deceiver, must now answer to history as a war criminal!"[70]

While Flood followed the party line on Capitol Hill in regard to his support for the principles of the Atlantic Charter, the creation of a United Nations to preserve world peace, and the punishment of Nazi war criminals, he was not afraid to challenge the majority when he disagreed with it. The very first vote he cast in Congress, for example, was against a proposal to make the wartime Committee on Un-American Activities a permanent part of the House committee system, a measure that carried, 207 to 186.[71] Although Flood did not comment on his opposition to the measure, history proved that his reservations were justified. It was, after all, the Un-American Activities Committee that eventually gave Senator Joseph McCarthy a platform to launch the notorious Red Scare of the 1950s. Flood also challenged the Senate's exclusive treaty-making powers under the Constitution, whereby that house could consent or oppose a treaty by a two-thirds majority vote. "It is the House of Representatives—not the Senate—that speaks to the will of the people," Flood argued. "Members of the House must go to the people to seek election every two years, whereas senators are elected for six-year terms. I'd say that ninety percent of the people in my congressional district favor treaty approval by a majority vote of both the House and the Senate. I think that between seventy-five and eighty percent of all people in the country hold the same belief as well."[72] The jingoistic congressman would return to this argument time and again throughout his tenure on Capitol Hill, most famously during the late 1970s, when the Carter administration lobbied for a Panama Canal Zone independent of U.S. control.

Whether on domestic or foreign issues, Flood worked hard during his first term in Congress, but he lived frugally. His ten-thousand-dollar annual salary was about six thousand dollars short of his expenses. Legislators were not reimbursed for traveling costs, and Flood returned to Wilkes-Barre every weekend to meet with constituents. Nor did he receive a pension during those early years in Congress.[73] As a result, he cut costs wherever possible. He lived at the Mayflower Hotel on Capitol Hill, paying a reduced rate thanks to Cornelius Mack, the manager, who was also a native of Wilkes-Barre.[74] And he employed the customary bare-bones staff, which consisted of three people: an administrative assistant, a legislative assistant, and a caseworker.[75] Nevertheless, Flood didn't appear to spare much expense when came to his clothing or his constituents.

Back in the district on weekends, "Dapper Dan," as he was known for his stylish wardrobe, would attend as many social events as possible and always arrived dressed to the hilt for the occasion. That did not mean he refused to associate with the blue collars who voted him into office. One night, the freshman congressman was attending a formal dinner party in Wilkes-Barre and was summoned to subdue a wildcat miners' strike. Upon taking the union hall stage, dressed in a cerise-lined cape, white scarf, and opera hat, a drunken coal miner heckled Flood, bellowing, "Who's the pansy on stage?" Amid the catcalls and jeers, the mustachioed legislator carefully removed his top hat, leaped from the stage, and knocked the offending miner across four rows of chairs. "Then I proceeded to give my spiel," he recalled with a smile. "When you dress like I do, there's always some joker trying to start something, so you better be able to fight."[76]

Another popular story, probably apocryphal, involves Flood's generosity in sponsoring a local coal miner to play Santa Claus and entertain the children of Glen Lyon each Christmas eve. The congressman gave the willing miner a few dollars in advance and arranged for the local tavern keepers to give him a shot and a beer as he made his way across town talking with children and handing out candy canes, also purchased by Flood. Unfortunately, in the second year of this event the Santa Claus spent more time in the local bars than he did on the streets with the children. By the time he reached the west side of town he was so intoxicated that he found it difficult to stand up, and he fell asleep in an alleyway. A passerby, on his way to midnight mass, woke Santa from his drunken stupor and told him to "go home and sleep it off." Instead, Santa followed the man into St. Michael's Church. To the consternation of some female parishioners, he proceeded to stagger down the center aisle pointing at their husbands and yelling, "Give that guy a drink!"

When the priest, who was sitting in the confessional booth, pulled back the curtain to see what was happening, the drunken Santa spotted him and shouted out, "Give that guy in the shit house a drink too!" Fortunately, the attendants grabbed the offender by the arms and hustled him out of the church before he could cause any further embarrassment. Needless to say, Flood was more particular about the coal miner he chose to pose as Santa Claus in the future.[77]

Flood's reelection to Congress in 1946 seemed to be a forgone conclusion. His voting record placed him squarely in the camp of the New Dealers and was highly favorable to the Democrats back in his home district. At the same time, Flood's efforts at creating jobs and securing a VA hospital and airport for Luzerne County impressed many of the Republican voters. In fact, the Fine machine was hard-pressed to find a candidate to oppose him. But the Republican Party boss managed to convince Mitchell Jenkins, assistant district attorney of Luzerne County, to enter the campaign. Jenkins, who was hoping to run for common pleas judge, reluctantly agreed.[78]

In May, Flood won the Democratic Party primary easily over Ambrose Nowak of Jenkins Township, outpolling him 10,190 to 2,052.[79] But two weeks later he made a critical mistake by voting for strike curb legislation proposed by President Truman, who was attempting to prevent a soft-coal strike by the United Mine Workers. The measure was a precursor to the 1947 Taft-Hartley Act, which banned the closed shop, allowed employers to sue unions for broken contracts or damages inflicted during strikes, and authorized a government-imposed cooling-off period of eighty days for strikes that might endanger the national welfare.

It's not clear why Flood voted for the antilabor legislation. Unions had for twelve years enjoyed the protections of the pro-labor Wagner Act. He might have believed, like many members of the House, that the massive wave of postwar strikes that had gripped the nation was instigated by Communist influence, or perhaps he was simply following the lead of the House's thirty-five-member Pennsylvania delegation in voting for the proposal (only William Green, a Democrat from Philadelphia, voted against it).[80] Regardless, Flood made a crucial mistake. Two days after the vote, he received a vitriolic letter from the UMW's Local 2444 based at the Loomis Colliery. "You have been doing a pretty good job in behalf of the workingman up until Saturday when you voted for the strike curb legislation proposed by the President," began the letter:

> You have now betrayed labor by this "yes-man" vote for the anti-labor bill. If Hitler is alive, he is pleased with the way you voted to give the President Nazi powers. One point alone in the bill should have caused you to vote against it: the U.S. Treasury would get all the profits from an industry seized by the government. That's Fascism, that's Nazism, that's Communism! Whom do you represent? Do you not realize that the bill would forbid benefit funds for the poor miner's orphans, the widows, or for his health's sake? We will remember in November what you did in May.[81]

The following month, Flood tried to rectify his mistake by urging Truman to veto the very same bill he had recently proposed. "H.R. 4908 is a vicious hate labor bill," he now insisted. "It is labor baiting at its worst, born in the tempest and turmoil of this time of industrial unrest. I will fight this bill if I am the only man in the House to do so." Flood's efforts proved to be in vain. Truman stood firm and the legislation went into effect.[82]

Flood ran himself ragged campaigning for reelection that summer and fall. "He was an indefatigable campaigner," recalled Mitchell Jenkins, his Republican opponent. "I thought that I had made every stop in the county where, as the phrase goes, 'two or three were gathered together in my name.' But everywhere I campaigned Flood had either been there or was scheduled to speak. His energy was unbelievable."[83] But Flood couldn't do it alone. Stephen Farris, the new Democratic County chair, was well-intentioned but not nearly as experienced as the late Leo Mundy. In addition, the Fine machine launched a strong assault against Flood's voting record to unseat him. Not only did the Republicans exploit the antilabor gaffe, but they also highlighted three other measures that would have benefited the county's farmers that Flood voted against.[84]

On election day the voters turned Dan Flood out of office by just 1,849 votes.[85] When Flood lost his second election in six years, a pattern seemed to be emerging. Like the 1942 election, when he suffered his first defeat, 1946 was another bad year at the polls for the Democratic Party nationwide. Rising prices, anger toward organized labor, and the perception that Communists had infiltrated American labor unions led to popular discontent. Voters repudiated Truman and the Democrats, giving Republicans majorities in both houses of Congress and in the state capitols. Once in office, the Republicans set out to turn back the New Deal.[86] Flood would lose again, in 1952, during the Eisenhower landslide that swept another majority of Republicans into Congress. But that would be his last defeat. Dan Flood made himself independent of the fickle national voting trends by securing bipartisan support in his district.

3

TRUMPING THE FINE MACHINE

"John Fine was the best party leader Luzerne County ever had and the only class act that ever opposed me," insisted Dan Flood near the end of his own storied political career. "His Republican machine was magnificent and accounted for the only defeats of my Congressional career, in 1942, '46 and '52."[1] At the time of those defeats, however, Flood was anything but complimentary to Luzerne County's Republican Party boss. There was no love lost on either side as Fine, increasingly jealous of Flood's voter strength, employed every weapon in his political arsenal to unseat the county's leading Democrat during the 1940s and early 1950s.

John S. Fine, a small, bald, and colorless little man, was the dominant political force in Luzerne County for more than a generation. Although he served a single term as Pennsylvania's governor, Fine claimed that his proudest accomplishment was "throwing together a [Republican Party] organization that was in control of Luzerne County for some thirty years."[2]

Born on April 10, 1893, in Alden, Newport Township, Fine was the next to youngest of eleven children. He attended Nanticoke High School and spent the summers of his youth working either on his family's farm or in the coal mines until he went off to attend Dickinson School of Law in Carlisle, Pennsylvania. Fine returned to the Wyoming Valley in 1915 to open a law practice in Nanticoke. With the outbreak of World War I, he abandoned the practice to enlist in the Twenty-third U.S. Army Engineers and served in France as a sergeant. In 1919, while stationed in Ireland, Fine completed postgraduate work at the University of Dublin's Trinity College. After the war, he entered local politics as Republican chair of Luzerne County's Fourth Legislative District.

Fine rose to prominence in the Republican Party during the early 1920s when he was named secretary of the county executive committee and, later, county chair. When Governor Gifford Pinchot in 1927 appointed him judge of common pleas, Fine, just twenty-nine years old, was the youngest justice ever named to the bench in Luzerne County. Two years later he was elected to a full term on the Republican, Democratic, Socialist, and Prohibition tickets, and was reelected in 1939 for another ten-year term. In 1947 Governor James Duff appointed Fine to the state Superior Court, a position he held until March 1950 when he resigned to run for governor.[3]

Although he had been allied with Pinchot, Fine was no progressive.[4] He did not view reform as a high priority and ran his Republican machine like a traditional party boss. His main objective was to expand the influence of the organization for the sake of controlling patronage and votes—and thus, political power—in the county.[5] "I like to give good government where I can," Fine once admitted, in the most succinct statement of his political philosophy. "But I am most dedicated to building up my organization, keeping the confidence of the people, keeping down the gripes, and refreshing the organization with new blood."[6] In the process, Fine was known to distance himself from previous loyalties when they didn't suit his political needs, as well as to employ such scandalous tactics as voting fraud and intimidation at the polls to secure the election of his party's candidates. Flood was often the target of these practices.

After losing his congressional seat in 1946, Flood, who had recently been admitted to practice before the United States Supreme Court, resumed his law practice in Wilkes-Barre with his partner, James Lenahan Brown.[7] Although he was bitterly disappointed by the defeat, the time away from Capitol Hill allowed him to prepare for reelection to Congress and bask in the local spotlight for some of his legislative achievements. On June 2, 1947, for example, Flood spoke at the dedication ceremonies of the new Scranton Wilkes-Barre International Airport at Avoca. The former congressman's position on the House Appropriations Committee allowed him to secure a significant portion of the $6 million cost for the project. Flood, speaking before some twenty-five thousand people, reminded his audience that the 720-acre airfield was "more spacious than New York's LaGuardia Airport," and appealed to them to "make good use of the facility by patronizing the airlines."[8] Later that year, he attended dedication ceremonies for a new $1.2 million VA building that he helped bring to Wilkes-Barre, a facility that would create more than one

Fig. 12. John S. Fine, the powerful party boss of Luzerne County's Republican machine, ran candidates who defeated Flood for Congress in 1942, 1946, and 1952. He would be elected governor of Pennsylvania in 1950.

thousand new jobs for local residents.[9] A similar plaudit came the following year when Flood spoke at the groundbreaking ceremonies for the VA hospital along East End Boulevard on the outskirts of Wilkes-Barre. He was responsible not only for having the hospital located in his congressional district, but also for securing most of the $11 million cost.[10] He also enjoyed the privilege of hosting former First Lady Eleanor Roosevelt when she visited Sugar Notch in July 1948 to unveil a memorial to her late husband and those soldiers from the borough who died in battle.[11] But Flood's primary concern was his return to Capitol Hill.

The mid to late 1940s was a critical period for the Democratic Party, not only in Luzerne County but also in Pennsylvania and in the nation as a whole. On the national level, Democrats were divided over president Harry S. Truman's leadership. One group of liberals, who had come to power during the Roosevelt administration, criticized the president for distancing himself from the New Deal policies of his predecessor. They also opposed his efforts at deviating from the concept of a "Popular Front" with communism, predominant during the war years when the major threat to liberal values was fascism. Unable to overcome their need for the type of charismatic leadership that Roosevelt had provided, the New Dealers hoped that Truman would step aside for a more liberal candidate like justice William O. Douglas. Another group, consisting of Southern conservatives, Western progressives, and urban labor advocates, also believed that Truman had abandoned their interests. Unlike the New

Dealers, however, this liberal coalition rejected all types of totalitarianism and was ready to draft General Dwight D. Eisenhower as the Democratic Party's presidential candidate.[12]

On the state level, Pennsylvanians had registered their approval of the Republican Party in 1946 by electing James H. Duff as governor by a 557,000-vote margin, while the Democrats were floundering to find a candidate who could compete with the GOP in 1948.[13] Finally, in Luzerne County, where the Fine machine held sway, voter registration favored the Republicans 135,280 to 50,093. After the death of Dr. Leo Mundy, the management of Democratic organization drifted into the hands of county commissioner John A. Riley and Mundy's lieutenant, James J. Law, neither of whom was very aggressive in increasing voter registration. Nor did Flood have a high opinion of either man. Pennsylvania's Democratic leaders were deeply concerned about the situation, realizing that the Commonwealth would be a battleground state in the upcoming presidential election.[14]

Flood's candidacy would play an instrumental role in defeating the Fine machine in 1948. He ran unopposed in the primaries, persuading Democratic officials that he could defeat any Republican opponent in the general election.[15] "I do not believe that the party leaders took my candidacy very seriously at first," he recalled years later. "But I convinced them that I had the experience from my first term in Congress to defeat anyone who ran against me. Besides, after I drank some of that Potomac River water, I decided, as many first-term congressmen do, that I wanted to stay in Washington."[16]

Flood gave his unconditional support to Truman's candidacy and actively campaigned for the president in the Wyoming Valley. He also asked for a federal investigation of voter registration in Luzerne County. In an August 15 letter to U.S. attorney general Tom Clark, Flood asserted that there were forty thousand illegal voters in Luzerne County and requested that an investigation be held to find out "who are the quick and who are the dead" among those citizens who would vote in November's general election. Upon learning of the allegations, John Watro, Republican chair of the First Legislative District, responded that "purging the voters' lists will not prevent Democratic frauds as Mr. Flood well knows." "Go ahead!" he snapped. "Bring on Clark!"[17]

Flood took the high ground. "The false and fraudulent registrations of Republican voters in Luzerne County is an open and notorious scandal and has been for years," he replied. "It is an affront to thousands of decent, law-abiding and respectable independent Republicans as well as Democrats who abhor the practice." Flood, striking a conciliatory note, suggested that the investigation of registration fraud be conducted on a "non-partisan basis." "Let the chairmen of both the Republicans and Democrats ask the United States District Court to empanel a special grand jury to appoint prosecutors for a grand jury investigation," he added. "Then, let the chips fall as they may."[18]

Flood certainly had no intention of "letting the chips fall as they may." He realized that the county's Democratic leaders, John Riley and James Law, didn't give him much of a chance to win, especially when he tied his success to Truman's reelection. In addition, the only county newspaper that endorsed Flood's candidacy was the *Pittston Gazette*.[19] Flood's chances for victory in the fall election depended on his ability to court both the Democratic and the labor voters. To that end, he became an indefatigable campaigner, traveling to every town in the county and speaking to every conceivable group. He made friends with labor as well as capital. Business owners seemed to be just as enthusiastic about Flood's candidacy as the rank and file. He championed the cause of the miners as well as the dressmakers. If there was a movement or drive, he took part in it. Noting that his Republican opponent, Dr. Robert Stroh, had very little political experience, Flood focused on his own legislative background and his excellent record for constituent service, especially for the workingman. He detailed his special qualifications for Congress as being an "outstanding public speaker, skilled parliamentarian and a man trained in the law." Above all, Flood promised to be "an ambassador without portfolio" for the Eleventh District, being "available at all times" for his constituents' needs. Stroh, on the other hand, emphasized his intent to secure more federal revenue for the district. As a former Luzerne County auditor, the physician tied his candidacy to "getting the most service at the least [county] expense." He insisted that the Truman administration had "hurt the local agricultural economy by fixing farm and poultry prices" and that he would "work to make more federal funds available for the county."[20] Stroh's constituency was too small and his message was too similar to Flood's, who had already secured millions of federal dollars for the district during his first term on Capitol Hill. It would be difficult for the physician to outpoll a former congressman, especially one as successful and colorful as his Democratic opponent. Still, Flood left nothing to chance.

By guarding against voter fraud the Democratic candidate made sure that the Fine machine wouldn't steal the election. Those ward leaders loyal to Flood hired poll watchers to scrutinize the activities of Republican precinct leaders suspected of robbing votes. In Newport Township, the contest for votes was especially acrimonious, nearly coming to fisticuffs. Ward leader John "Dada" Kashatus was responsible for turning out the Democrat vote in the township. His success in previous elections caught the attention of

Republican ward leaders, who sought to neutralize the tavern keeper by offering him a job as township fire commissioner, a patronage position.[21] Kashatus took the job in the spring of 1948 but had no intention of abandoning the Democratic Party. "The Republicans thought they were going to buy me by giving me that job," he recalled years later. "Well, I contacted [Democratic county commissioner] Johnny Riley and Dan Flood and told them to let me register Republican, but give me the Democratic Party's overseers so I can place them at every polling place to watch the voting machines. I knew that the Republicans were placing votes for dead people and scaring other Democrat voters away from the polls and I wanted to catch those bastards in the act."

On election day, November 2, 1948, Kashatus received a phone call from a poll watcher at the Glen Lyon Fire House informing him that the Republicans were trying to steal the election by bribing registered Democrats. According to the informer, the Republicans had already cost Flood some sixty votes. Kashatus and a group of burly coal miners—all Democrats—piled into cars and sped to the polling place to put a stop to the scandal. Tempers flared. One miner threw a punch at a Republican Party boss, but the two men were separated before a fight broke out. "Didn't matter in the end," admitted Kashatus. "Flood won the election anyway because the Democrats were slicker. One of our guys told me he voted for Dan four times that day. Another one told me that he cast ten votes for Flood. And another guy somehow managed to vote for Dan fourteen times!"[22]

Predictably, Flood won the election, defeating Stroh 68,646 to 63,836.[23] It was an impressive triumph considering that Republican voter registration (135,280) in Luzerne County outnumbered the Democrats (50,093) almost three to one. In other words, Flood not only garnered every Democratic vote in the county but also 18,553 Republican votes.[24] What's more, Flood's victory embarrassed the Fine machine, which used all the money, jobs, power, and threats in its power to stifle his candidacy. "Flying in the face of a ruthless Republican machine was Dan Flood," editorialized the *Wilkes-Barre Sunday Independent.* "Mr. Flood had no strong party organization, no money, no nothing. But he managed to defeat the Republican machine by aggressive campaigning and by getting out the vote. Mr. Flood's victory has given new heart to the thousands of good people of the county who are tired and ashamed of control by politicians who have grown so brazen that they would strangle democracy in Luzerne County."[25]

Dan Flood had become a formidable political force in Luzerne County. Usually a congressperson is swept into office on the coattails of the president, especially an incumbent. Instead, Flood polled more votes than Truman during the 1948 election, running ahead of the president by 6,859 votes.[26] The strong turnout at the polls for the congressional candidate probably gave Truman more Luzerne County votes than he would have otherwise enjoyed. Such remarkable influence among the voters instilled in Flood a greater confidence, allowing him to distance himself from the county's weak Democratic organization and its suspect leaders, who had given him limited support in the election. Now reelected to Congress, Flood assumed the role of a maverick. Appointments for federal and state jobs were guided by his own judgment instead of that of the County Democratic Executive Committee.

Flood ignored the advice of Democratic county chair John Riley and appointed Clara Mancini Democratic state committeewoman of the Twenty-first Senatorial District. He also went ahead and appointed two of his own candidates from each of the county's seven legislative districts for federal census jobs.[27] Furious over the rebuffs, Riley attempted to install his own candidate as postmaster in Pittston. When Flood heard of the appointment, he quickly replaced Riley's selection with his own.[28] Riley was "up in arms," having been "completely ignored" by Flood. "This situation has got to be straightened out," he insisted. "I have been in politics a number of years and have never encountered a situation like this before. Everyone knows that all appointments must come through the county's Democratic organization. But I've been ignored all together as county chairman."[29]

Although Riley appealed to Philip Matthews, state Democratic chair, Flood's appointments stood, probably because Pennsylvania's Democratic leaders realized that his influence far surpassed the tentative leadership of the local party machine.[30] Flood's impressive reputation among the state's Democratic leaders extended well beyond northeastern Pennsylvania too. His connections were becoming more powerful, as evidenced by the congratulatory letter he received from John B. Kelly, patriarch of one of Philadelphia's most prominent families and a leading Pennsylvania Democrat. "I think you could run on a laundry ticket and win," wrote Kelly, "at least you would have my vote!"[31]

Flood made one other appointment upon his return to Congress that would strengthen his House office staff: Eugene D. Hegarty, a Forty Fort real estate agent, was made his new administrative assistant. Hegarty replaced Joseph Gillespie, who had taken a job with the U.S. attorney general's office after Flood lost the 1946 election. Hegarty, age thirty-seven, was a former marine who saw combat in World War II. Discharged with the rank of major in December 1945, the ex-marine served briefly as a landscape engineer with the Pennsylvania Department of Highways before Flood appointed him housing expediter for Luzerne County.[32] Hegarty was a colorful individual,

Fig. 13. Eugene Hegarty, a former marine who saw combat in World War II, served as Flood's administrative assistant from 1949 to 1970. Hegarty served the Pennsylvania congressman with unconditional loyalty.

cut from the same mold as Flood himself. More important, he was a "straight arrow" who quickly learned the political culture of Capitol Hill. His genius for political gamesmanship was exceeded only by his dedication to Flood. While Hegarty was a personable individual, he could also be a tough administrator, and he ran the office with a tight fist. He did all the hiring and firing, assigned staffers their specific responsibilities and made them accountable, maintained good relations with the various executive departments, and scrutinized campaign contributions as well as the operating budget. In short, Hegarty was the anchor of Flood's staff and enjoyed the congressman's complete and unconditional trust.[33]

Flood also continued to build trust with his constituents by returning to his previous assignment on the House Appropriations Committee. Flood realized the importance of that particular committee since it gave him some influence, no matter how small at first, over the federal government's purse strings. His ambitions were intimately tied to the House of Representatives, unlike some of his contemporaries who had their eye on the Senate and beyond. One of those colleagues was John F. Kennedy, another Irish Democrat, who represented the working-class neighborhoods of Boston. Flood and Kennedy became fast friends not only because of the similarities of their constituents and their common bond as Irish Democrats, but also because they had neighboring offices at the Cannon House Office Building and frequently consulted with each other.[34] Kennedy came from a wealthier background, however, and he carried the burden of extremely high expectations from his father, who was already planning his son's run for the presidency.[35] Flood, on the other hand, had a less lofty career goal. He understood that the most important position in Congress was that of Speaker of the House. It ranked only two notches below the presidency itself. To become Speaker a lawmaker had to fashion a reputation for himself on one of the House's top committees and simultaneously climb the ladder of power within his party. Flood realized that seniority would take care of itself as long as he had the ability to be reelected. Seniority and ability would result in power. The important thing now was to secure an assignment on one of the premier committees, such as Appropriations, with the duty of appropriating the money needed to run the federal government; Ways and Means, with its responsibility for writing tax laws; and Rules, with its authority to decide which measures would go to the floor for debate. It was an opportunity to serve on Appropriations that came Flood's way.

Of the five Pennsylvania Democrats who were reelected, all were happy to retain their previous committee assignments. That left the Pennsylvania delegation with two Republicans and no Democrats on Appropriations. Under those circumstances, Flood's appointment to the committee was a forgone conclusion, especially since he enjoyed the unconditional support of House Speaker Sam Rayburn. Most important, however, was the fact that the assignment would allow him to pork-barrel even more federal money into the Eleventh District.[36]

During the next two years, Flood channeled more than one hundred million dollars in federal revenue into Luzerne County through legislation that created new industries and jobs, as well as through an ongoing commitment by the government to purchase and export coal for heating the barracks on U.S. military bases in Europe.[37] In addition, the second-term congressman introduced bills that would provide federal grants to municipal government for public works; for the federal government's purchase and stockpiling of coal, which would guarantee full employment for miners and reasonable profits for the coal companies; and for the establishment of a watershed commission to conduct flood control, navigation, reforestation, and industrial development of the Susquehanna Valley.[38] Flood was careful to stipulate that none of these measures included the "dole" or any direct relief that would "encourage pauperism." Instead, they were designed to boost the industry and incentive of those individuals and businesses that would contribute to the fiscal welfare of the community in which they lived and worked. The legislation was, as Flood said, "intended to help those who seek to help themselves and the community."[39]

Such legislative achievements did not come without considerable effort. Flood was a workaholic, and his days on Capitol Hill began early in the morning and ended late at night. Though he made several important friendships that would allow him to advance his congressional career, he was still lonely for the one person who mattered most in his life—Catherine Swank. That changed on September 24, 1949, when the couple was married at St. John the Evangelist Roman Catholic Church in Wilkes-Barre.[40] She was thirty-three years old and he was forty-six. The thirteen-year difference in age, which had once prevented them from dating each other, now meant very little. "Catherine fell in love with Dan the first time she met him at age thirteen," said Bill Breslin, her nephew.

> She remained madly in love with him for the rest of her life. And I believe those feelings were mutual. They complemented each other quite well. Catherine was very demonstrative of her feelings, especially to those she was close to. Her emotions came strictly from the heart. Dan, on the other hand, wasn't demonstrative at all. His affection was more from an intellectual standpoint. He simply didn't approve of any public displays of affection. In fact, at their wedding, Dan kissed Catherine on the hand— not on the lips—after the priest pronounced them man and wife. That was as much emotion as he was capable of showing in public. I just don't think that he was used to a great deal of affection, except from her.[41]

Since their father was deceased, her brother, Joseph Anthony Swank, gave Catherine in marriage. Her sister, Anna, served as maid of honor. Bridesmaids were Mrs. Thomas Herbert, sister of the groom; Mrs. Millard Glowacki, Nanticoke; Mrs. David Kelly, Forty Fort; and Mrs. William Wasnick, Lee Park. Attorney James Lenahan Brown, Flood's law partner, was best man. Ushers included U.S. Senator Francis J. Myers, Philadelphia; Rep. John J. Rooney, New York; judge J. Harold Flannery, West Pittston; Commander Gerald P. Flood, brother of the groom; attorney Cletus Lyman, Hazleton; attorney Neville Shea, Nanticoke; attorney Thomas Farrell, Jr., Ashley; and attorney Michael Sheridan, Nanticoke. Reverend Raymond E. Larking presided over the ceremony.[42]

A reception at the Hotel Sterling followed the wedding and was attended by more than five hundred guests, including ambassador to Venezuela Frank Corrigan, undersecretary of state John E. Peurifoy, assistant U.S. attorney Edward L. Carey, several members of the House of Representatives, as well as state and local officials.[43] "That reception ranked among the biggest social events of the twentieth century in the Wyoming Valley," recalled Breslin, who attended with his parents. "The wedding party and their guests took over the entire Sterling Hotel. Lee Vincent's complete orchestra played on the balcony, and the lobby served as the dance floor. The receiving line and the food were located in the General Sullivan Room, while the champagne and other drinks were served in the cocktail lounge. Anybody who was anybody in the eastern United States was there. It was a very glamorous affair."[44] Afterward, the couple flew out of the Avoca Airport to their honeymoon in Bermuda.

When the Floods returned, they established a dual residency on Capitol Hill and in Wilkes-Barre. Dan moved out of the family homestead he shared with his sister and brother-in-law at 77 Madison Street and into Catherine's family home, which was bequeathed to her by her parents. It was a modest, two-story house located at 460 North Pennsylvania Avenue. The Floods also joined the "Tuesday-to-Thursday club," which comprised those East Coast representatives who arrived in Washington on Tuesday and left for their home district after the last vote on Thursday. Even when he traveled back to Wilkes-Barre, though, Dan was constantly working. He spent Fridays and Saturday mornings at his district office at the Miners' National Bank Building on public square meeting with constituents. Catherine joined him for the heavy schedule of social events and public appearances that consumed the remainder of weekend. But the more glamorous side of the Floods' life was spent in the nation's capital.[45]

Capitol Hill was a more congenial place in the 1940s and 1950s than it is today. Representatives enjoyed a spirit of bipartisan camaraderie and did their jobs with little public attention. When the day's votes ended, the legislators gathered in someone's office to trade stories and drink bourbon. A few indomitable old-timers whose seniority allowed them to control the most important committees and subcommittees sponsored the most meaningful legislation. Freshmen listened and learned. Those who demonstrated staying power were enthusiastically welcomed by the old guard, regardless of party. Bachelors could expect free dinners, compliments of their colleagues' wives. Families knew each other well. Wives saw one another at the congressional club for spouses, volunteered their time for charitable organizations, and joined their spouses for the many social functions that occurred during the session. Congressional children went to school with one another, met at after-school events, and roamed the Capitol building looking for secret hiding places or enjoying the stories of the guards. It was a more intimate environment than today and one into which the Floods settled with ease.

The couple lived at the Mayflower Hotel during their early years on Capitol Hill. They had a comfortable one-bedroom apartment with a living room and a small kitchenette, but they did so much entertaining that they soon relocated to the Congressional Hotel, across the street from the Cannon House Office

Fig. 14. Dan and Catherine Flood made this modest Dutch Colonial at 460 North Pennsylvania Avenue in Wilkes-Barre their home shortly after their marriage, spending their weekends there during his years in Congress.

Building, where Dan worked. Their apartment had a very large living room overlooking the Washington Mall. In the evening, there was a breathtaking view of the spotlighted Lincoln Memorial. The apartment also had a sizeable kitchen and bathroom as well as a large dressing room. Hugh Auchincloss, Jacqueline Kennedy's stepfather, lived in the apartment next door, which strengthened the Floods' friendship with the young Massachusetts congressman and his wife.[46] "It was heavenly living in Washington," recalled Catherine. "We entertained everyone at our apartment from congressmen and their wives to family and friends from the district. Jerry and Betty Ford were dear friends. It didn't matter that Dan was a Democrat and Jerry was a Republican. They served on Appropriations together and had a lot in common with each other. Betty and I were very active in the Congressional Wives Club with charity work, things like raising money for literacy programs or giving monetary donations to needy groups."[47]

To be sure, the Floods loved to entertain as well as be entertained. "Dan and Catherine were regulars on the cocktail circuit," said John Cosgrove, a former Associated Press journalist. "Both of them were very flamboyant. In fact, Catherine, a very attractive woman in her day, often made the fashion pages of the Washington newspapers for her wardrobe and good looks. Even the national gossip columns covered her."[48] One of those tabloids was the *New York Daily News*, which ran a photo of Catherine dressed as the biblical Eve during a fashion show celebrating the fiftieth anniversary of the Congressional Wives Club. Wearing a skintight, flesh-colored leotard adorned with an oversized fig leaf and an imitation snake hugging her bust line, Catherine raised a few eyebrows as she paraded before a rather staid audience of legislators and their spouses. While other congressional wives also portrayed prominent historical females, none had the courage—or figure—to don skintight leotards like Catherine.[49]

During congressional recesses, the Floods returned to Wilkes-Barre, where they kept up a full schedule of events. A constant stream of family, friends, and constituents visited with the congressman on the porch of his home. "Dan would listen to their concerns and, if he could, he'd help them right there on the spot," recalled Catherine.[50] For her, the recesses also provided a chance to catch up with friends. "Home was most important to Catherine," said Bill Breslin. "She never high-handed anyone, including the neighbors back home. She could be in the White House eating caviar and champagne with Winston Churchill or Queen Elizabeth II one night and back here in Wilkes-Barre in the kitchen eating pickled pigs feet with a neighbor the next. Both sets of people were equally important to her."[51] Catherine also enjoyed the opportunity to do some acting before local women's organizations whenever she came home for recesses. Usually these were dramatic readings of scenes from her favorite plays, like *The Women* by Clare Booth Luce; *Born Yesterday*, featuring the Billie Dawn role made famous by Judy Holliday; and George Bernard Shaw's *Pygmalion*, featuring the Eliza Doolittle character (later popularized on Broadway as *My Fair Lady*). Catherine was also active in the Luzerne County League of Women Voters and in fund-raising for the Little Theater and her alma mater, College Misericordia.[52] Yet she would have given up all the glamour of being a congressman's wife for motherhood.

"Both Dan and I would love to have been parents," she admitted near the end of her life. "We just couldn't have children. We tried many times, but I'd be

Fig. 15. Catherine Flood dressed as the biblical Eve for a fashion show celebrating the fiftieth anniversary of the Congressional Wives Club. Her skintight, flesh-colored leotard and imitation snake raised a few eyebrows among the legislators and their spouses.

pregnant for a short time and lose them."[53] Instead, Catherine lavished her attention on surrogates. "She would have been a marvelous mother," said Breslin. "Catherine absolutely loved children. But when she couldn't have any, she gave her affections to her nieces and nephews. I was very fortunate for that because we had a special relationship. Dan was different. He guarded very carefully about doing anything for the family. He never wanted to be charged with nepotism. Strangers were far better off to ask Dan for favors than a family member was. We came to accept that, though. We understood politics."[54]

Flood was correct in avoiding charges of nepotism. He quickly learned that the Fine machine was not above personal attacks. During his 1950 bid for reelection, the Republicans printed a circular positing a honeymoon photo of him and Catherine in Bermuda against a portrait of GOP candidate Elwood H. Jones in the uniform of a navy ensign. Sponsored by the "Veterans Committee to Elect Jones to Congress," the circular posed the question: "Who would you vote for?" Voters of both parties were shocked by the tactic, viewing it as an invasion of Congressman Flood's personal life and privacy. While the County Republican Committee denied any responsibility for the circular, Judge Fine, inundated with complaints from an indignant electorate, ordered all remaining circulars impounded. The incident proved especially embarrassing for Fine, who was the Republican candidate for governor that year.[55] The ploy was a desperate attempt by the GOP to return one of its members to Congress in a critical election year.

Control of the U.S. House of Representatives was at stake in the 1950 election with 102 congressional districts across 25 states up for grabs. These "battleground" districts demanded special attention because of their tendency to shift from one party to the other during the previous three elections, while the same party had held the remaining 333 "safe" districts continuously. Of these "safe" districts, 149 were held by Republicans, 183 by Democrats, and one by the American Labor Party. Pennsylvania would be a critical state in the 1950 election because it was home to 13 of the "battleground" districts, including the Eleventh of Luzerne County.[56]

Historical circumstances favored the Republicans in off-year elections. Only once during the previous half century (1934, the high-water mark of the New Deal) did the GOP fail to carry the Keystone State in an off year. In 1950 history looked to repeat itself as the formidable James H. Duff led the Pennsylvania State Republican Committee. Barred by the state constitution from succeeding himself as governor, Duff sought the Senate seat of Francis J. Myers, the Democratic whip. Duff's gubernatorial record was impressive. During his two terms in Harrisburg he was credited with cleaning up Pennsylvania's rivers, improving public transportation, building an impressive highway system, and increasing state aid to schools. He also amassed goodwill among members of the Republican State Committee, which helped him trounce the old party boss, Joseph R. Grundy, in the primaries. Duff's gubernatorial choice was Fine, who was running against Richardson Dilworth, Philadelphia's charismatic city treasurer. One of four liberal reform Democrats who routed Philadelphia's

Fig. 16. Newlyweds Dan and Catherine Flood honeymooned in Bermuda in September 1949. During the 1950 campaign, Luzerne County's Republican Committee reprinted the photograph on circulars, suggesting that he was shirking his congressional responsibilities.

Republican machine in the most recent election of city officials, Dilworth, who graduate cum laude from Yale University, was a patrician and former marine with a Purple Heart from World War I and a Silver Star from World War II. He was considered "the most dynamic figure to come to the fore in Pennsylvania politics in a generation" and a much more colorful candidate than Fine, a highly practical politician. Though relatively unknown outside of Philadelphia, Dilworth's talent as a campaigner, combined with the infighting the Duff-Fine campaign had caused among Pennsylvania's Republican leaders, held out the possibility of an upset.[57]

The Republican Party was divided throughout the election. Most damning was a statement published by John Kunkel, who had lost the party's senatorial nomination to Duff. "During Fine's reign, racketeering in Luzerne County has turned into a big business," alleged Kunkel. "There is a take of about a million dollars a year with a certain percentage going into a boodle chest controlled by Fine's political machine."[58] In late October, Morgan Bird, one of Fine's chief lieutenants, was indicted on charges of fraud, giving credibility to Kunkel's assertion.[59] Fine himself was engaged in a double-cross of Duff by courting the support of his enemy, former party boss Joseph Grundy. After securing the former governor's support for his own candidacy, Fine began secretly meeting with Grundy's chief adviser, G. Mason Owlett, president of the Pennsylvania Manufacturers' Association and an influential figure in the state's Republican Party organization. While Duff criticized Grundy for all of Pennsylvania's ills during his campaign, Fine continued to seek reconciliation with him. Though hypocritical, Fine's actions were also very practical. He realized that if elected governor, his own success would depend on his ability to work with the state legislature, where Grundy controlled many seats.[60] Thus if the Republicans lost in the 1950 elections it would be nobody's fault but their own.

In Luzerne County the Democrats were having problems of their own. Voter registration still lagged far behind the Republicans, 51,828 to 142,642.[61] Worse, county chair John Riley was engaged in a battle for control of the organization against Flood and state senator Patrick Toole, the two leading Democrat vote getters. Flood and Toole demanded the selection of a new party chair, Stephen Farris, owner of a Swoyersville plating company. After months of wrangling, state Democratic leaders interceded, demanding that Riley issue a call for a county convention to name a new chair. Deferring to their authority, Riley agreed; on July 21, the convention unanimously elected Farris as party chair.[62]

With Farris at the helm to increase Democratic voter strength, Flood began to launch his own assault against the Republican machine. He ran an exhausting campaign covering every town in the district and actively courted potential swing voters, especially those connected to labor. Farris played an instrumental role in courting the labor vote by writing and collecting money to pay for newspaper endorsements that both attacked the Republican machine and highlighted Flood's achievements. The endorsements charged Fine with supporting the antilabor legislation of former governor James Duff, including bills that prevented union members from taking part in sympathy strikes; reduced employee contributions to the unemployment compensation fund and made it difficult to collect in the event of a layoff; and denied collective bargaining rights to public employees, teachers, and public utilities workers.[63]

Flood, on the other hand, was endorsed for the strength of his labor record, which included the fight to repeal the Taft-Hartley law and his sponsorship of legislation supporting the federal government's purchase and stockpiling of anthracite coal.[64] Flood also tapped his powerful contacts on Capitol Hill. He secured the support of Speaker Sam Rayburn and majority leader John McCormack, both of whom also contributed $250 to the Flood campaign.[65]

Fig. 17. Flood campaigns in Newport Township, October 1950. Reelected to Congress over Republican candidate Elwood Jones by a twelve-thousand-vote margin, Pennsylvania's Democratic leaders encouraged him to run for the U.S. Senate in 1952.

Finally, the Democratic congressman directed his campaign manager, law partner James Lenahan Brown, to organize a group of loyal inspectors across the county to watch the polling places.[66]

The strategy worked. On election day, November 7, 1950, Flood was reelected to Congress over Elwood Jones, 74,593 to 62,694. Fine also won his bid for the governorship over Dilworth by the narrow margin of 85,764 votes. But the close election suggested that the long era of Republican dominance in Pennsylvania was coming to an end. Although Fine was now entrenched in Harrisburg, he would still try to continue his control of the Luzerne County Republican machine through Olin Evans, his chief lieutenant.[67]

Flood's strong showing in the election captured the attention of state Democratic leaders, who encouraged him to run for the U.S. Senate in 1952. Duff had defeated the incumbent, Francis Myers, in the 1950 campaign, and they were eager to find a Democrat with staying power. But Flood demurred, stating that it was "a little early to make a decision." "However," he added, "if my good friend Francis Myers is a candidate, you can be sure I will support him wholeheartedly."[68] Catherine Flood insists, however, that her husband was never very serious about making a run for the Senate. "I think it's important to understand that Dan was extremely loyal to his constituents in the Eleventh Congressional District," she said. "That's just the way he was. He refused to run for the United States Senate because he felt that he wouldn't be able to serve the people who were most important to him. Dan also had a lot of friends in the House of Representatives and held a very powerful position on the Appropriations Committee that would allow him to serve the district much better than if he went over to the Senate and had to start at the bottom."[69]

In 1952 Flood could care less about running for the Senate; he would be too busy fighting to hold on to his congressional seat. The mustachioed legislator had become the target of national tabloid journalism to the advantage of the Fine machine. Ruth Montgomery, who worked out of the *New York Daily News's* Washington Bureau, reported, in December 1951, that Flood "accepted 109 free trips from Colonial Airlines," which included regular excursions between Washington and his congressional district, three round trips to Bermuda, and others to New York and Baltimore. Montgomery pointed out that such trips were "in violation of House ethics rules" since airlines, which benefit from government-subsidized mail pay, "are forbidden by law to give free transportation to public officials on such scheduled runs."[70] When asked about the allegation, Flood insisted that his Wilkes-Barre law office had been "retained as local counsel by Colonial Airlines and in that capacity a pass was issued by the airlines for [his] use." He dismissed any notion of impropriety, stating that "a retainer fee of $100 was paid annually during the previous two years of [his travel]" and that this was "not an unusual practice." Flood added that "at no time did [he] represent Colonial Airlines before any federal body, agency, or intercede in its behalf."[71] While the explanation seemed to clear the congressman of any wrongdoing, the circumstantial evidence against him was damning. The Civil Aeronautics Board, the smallest federal agency, was a prime candidate for influence peddling. When CAB chair Joseph J. O'Connell, Jr., went before the House Appropriations Committee during its November 1951 hearings, Flood harassed and berated O'Connell for not granting Colonial Airlines' request for a financially lucrative route between Washington and New York. He also demanded that Colonial be permitted to fly from Wilkes-Barre to Philadelphia and to Atlantic City. Flood opposed any increased appropriations that would allow the CAB to expand its tiny staff of enforcement officers.[72] It was at this same time, according to the *New York Daily News*, that Flood and his wife enjoyed a round trip honeymoon to Bermuda, which was listed on

Colonial records as a "holiday," and also twelve other trips between Washington and Wilkes-Barre. CAB files also indicated that Flood enjoyed a total of 109 free trips on Colonial Airlines beginning in January 1950. These free trips stopped just before the CAB investigated Colonial Airlines in June 1951. As a result of the investigation, Colonial's president, Sigmund Janas, was fined seventy-five thousand dollars and charged with forty counts of evading Federal Civil Service Act regulations.[73]

Just three days after the influence peddling allegations broke, Montgomery wrote another story, charging that Catherine Flood was listed on her husband's payroll as "a $382.81 clerk, although she does not work on his staff and spends much of her time at winter and summer resorts."[74] When Flood learned of the new allegations he was furious. "My wife works all hours of the day and late into the evening whenever I feel it necessary for her to help me in my Congressional duties," he fumed. "It would be impossible for me to operate without her and I thank God for her every hour of the day and night."[75] Although both allegations were later proved to be unfounded, Flood was investigated by the Internal Revenue Service for income tax evasion.[76] The Fine machine would use the allegations to embarrass Flood during the 1952 campaign.

The Republican candidate for Congress was Edward J. Bonin, Hazleton's forty-seven-year-old mayor. Bonin had an impressive background. After serving in the U.S. Navy from 1922 to 1926, he attended Wyoming Seminary in Kingston, one of the very few private schools in northeastern Pennsylvania. He graduated from the prep school in 1929 and matriculated to Dickinson College, where he earned a bachelor's degree in 1933. Bonin went on to earn a law degree from Temple University in Philadelphia and began practicing law in the Wyoming Valley. During World War II he volunteered to serve in the U.S. Army before returning to his law practice. Bonin also served as an assistant district attorney before he became the mayor of Hazleton in 1951.[77]

Interestingly, the GOP candidate's platform was not very different from Flood's. Both men supported U.S. cooperation with the United Nations within the scope of the federal constitution, the need to halt inflation by balancing the national budget, and cutting federal expenditures by eliminating useless government agencies and mismanagement of the armed services. Most important, the two candidates agreed on the need to generate jobs and new industries through legislation that would stabilize the coal industry, eliminate competition from alternative fuel sources, and bring federal dollars into the district. The only discernable difference between Flood and Bonin dealt with U.S. policy toward third-world nations. While Flood viewed U.S. financial and military aid as "the most effective weapon against a communist takeover" of those countries, Bonin was more guarded, insisting that any assistance "be rendered without jeopardizing the financial welfare of our country."[78]

With such similar platforms, Flood chose to emphasize his congressional experience and the importance of seniority. He pointed to his legislative achievements as a member of the Appropriations Committee, including the creation of the $11 million VA hospital, with an annual payroll of $2.5 million; the $1.2 million VA regional office, with an annual payroll of $4 million; the $6 million Avoca Airport; and the $5 million Swoyersville–Forty Fort dyke project slated to begin in April 1953. "For the first time in the history of Luzerne County, the residents are represented on the Appropriations Committee through me," said Flood, reinforcing the importance of his position on one of Congress's most powerful committees. "I cannot emphasize adequately the importance of this advantage, especially in view of all our efforts to revitalize the industrial development of the county. Because of this our labor force has been afforded opportunities to use their skills to the fullest advantage. With God's help and the combined efforts of the good citizens of Luzerne County, I shall continue to go forward and make our beloved county a better place in which to work and live."[79]

Bonin eliminated Flood's advantage, however, by running a negative campaign. He marginalized his Democratic opponent's efforts to bring the VA hospital and administration building to Wilkes-Barre by crediting those projects to the "subscription of several hundred thousand dollars by public-spirited men of the community." "Mr. Flood did nothing more than make some contacts for the Wyoming Valley," insisted Bonin, "and that's what every congressman should be doing for his constituents."[80] More damaging was the Hazleton mayor's accusation that Flood made several promises during his last campaign that he never kept. Among those promises were sponsoring a bill for the federal government's stockpiling of coal to create full employment for the region's miners; the building of a new $750,000 federal armory at Wilkes-Barre; and the construction of an $8 million steel mill at Hazleton. Capitalizing on earlier allegations about Flood's free travel on Colonial Airlines, Bonin portrayed his opponent as an "opportunist" who was absent for 55 percent of the roll calls taken in Congress because he was "using taxpayer dollars touring the world." "What we need here," Bonin said before a rally of two thousand VFW members, "is a little bit of performance rather than a lot of empty promises."[81]

Flood was quick to respond to his opponent's criticisms. "My overseas trips were undertaken to fulfill my obligation to Congress," he shot back. "I have a

responsibility as a member of the House Appropriations Committee to supervise and inspect where federal funds are being expended in war-torn countries
which have asked the United States for financial assistance." As for "broken
promises," Flood insisted that he had set "no timetable for the various projects
he proposed and that at least in one case—the Hazleton Steel Mill—he had
already secured federal money for the project."[82]

Despite major endorsements from Thomas Kennedy, president of the
United Mine Workers of America, and Min Matheson, manager of the local
International Ladies Garment Workers' Union—the two largest labor unions
in the Eleventh District—Flood lost the 1952 election to Bonin by less than
six hundred votes.[83] Flood appealed to the Pennsylvania Supreme Court for a
recanvass, but the slim margin held up. The final vote was 80,310 for Bonin
and 79,722 for Flood, a fifty-fifty percentage split.[84] "I would have won that
election," insisted Flood more than twenty years later. "But a voting machine
fell off a truck going around a mountain near Hazleton, not far from my
opponent's place of residence. You know how that works!"[85] Catherine Flood
disagreed. "The New York Daily News gossip columns won that election for
Bonin," she said. "People who knew Dan realized how hard he worked for
the district, but those columns gave the perception that he was a bum who
used taxpayer dollars for his own good times. It was the kind of image the
Fine machine wanted the voters to have and the Republicans manipulated
those two columns to their own advantage. There's no question in my mind
that those columns lost the election for us."[86]

Afterward Flood became obsessive about avoiding even the appearance of
a conflict of interest. He was careful, for example, to keep his congressional
duties independent of his law practice. "After Dan was re-elected to Congress,
he moved out of our law office on the tenth floor of the Miners' Bank Building
and set up his district office next door," recalled Joseph Farrell, a partner in
Flood's law firm. "It had a big sign, 'Congressional Office,' and there was no
law practiced there. He was somewhat compulsive about separating the two.
Once he was trying to help a constituent get unemployment compensation,
something I handled at the law office. Instead of walking across the hall to
discuss the matter with me, he wrote a letter and sent it to me at the unemployment office just to keep his affairs separate. I used to laugh about it. But
I understood why he did it after the bad press he received over his relationship
with Colonial Airlines."[87]

While the negative perception of Flood among the voters certainly played
a role in his defeat, the 1952 presidential election was a more significant factor.

Republican Dwight D. Eisenhower soundly defeated his Democratic opponent, Adlai Stevenson. Ike garnered 442 electoral votes to Stevenson's 89.
The popular vote was 34,075,529 to 27,375,090 in favor of Eisenhower, who
easily carried a Republican majority into Congress with his landslide victory.

Republican candidates throughout the nation emphasized the necessity of
giving Eisenhower a majority to work with in Congress if the American people
expected constructive change, and apparently the voters listened. A bitterly
disillusioned Sam Rayburn was forced to surrender the Speaker's gavel to
Republican Joseph Martin of Massachusetts.[88] Once again, Dan Flood returned
to his Wilkes-Barre law practice. It would be the last election he ever lost.

Flood regained his House seat in 1954. His indefatigable campaigning and
effort to keep the election clean of voter fraud were only part of the reason for
his success. Infighting among the local Republican leaders also contributed to
his victory. When state senator Newell Wood was narrowly defeated in the
Republican primary by Harold Flack, he initiated an investigation of the vote
totals. "Those who checked the voting for me report indications of fraud,"
Wood told the *Sunday Independent.* "A large portion of the voters in some areas
were illiterate or incapacitated and had to have assistance in casting their
votes." Wood also insisted that he was not pursuing the investigation to be
reelected to the state senate, but rather to "restore some semblance of the
democratic process in Luzerne County and to remind those who would be
party bosses that any citizens has a right to run for office at it's party's primary
election."[89] Wood's investigation exposed not only the intraparty squabble, but
also the overt corruption of the Fine machine. Many Republican leaders, disappointed with the results of the May 18 primary election, stated that they
would "vote for Flood in the general election."[90] These individuals were also
angered by Fine's imposition of Olin W. Evans, his self-appointed Republican
county chair, on the local organization. They believed that Evans had divided
the party apparatus by "meddling in ward matters" and by taking a "lucrative
venture into the insurance business."[91]

The Democrats, on the other hand, were enjoying the sideshow. Their
party organization was strongly unified under the leadership of Dr. John Dorris,
who was easily reelected county chair, and Flood, who ran unopposed for the
Democratic nomination for Congress.[92] "Any time a party chairman gets in
such bad graces with the voters that he becomes the main issue of his own
party's primary election," mused Flood, "something is definitely wrong within
the party. If they continue to battle like that 1954 will be a bigger year for the
Democrats than we anticipated."[93]

To insure that 1954 would be the Democrats' year, Flood filed a mandamus petition at the Luzerne County Courthouse to compel the county commissioners, acting as the Board of Elections, to clean up voter fraud. The action was a continuation of the same campaign waged the last several years by the county's Democratic Party organization and Flood's attorney, James Lenahan Brown. These previous efforts were thwarted when the U.S. Supreme Court upheld the Board of Elections contention that a political party has no rights under the state election laws to bring about such an action. This time, however, the candidate himself was filing the petition, which was legal. Flood's petition charged that the Board of Elections never complied with certain provisions of the election laws and that other sections were ignored in the past. He contended that "such non-compliance with the law deprived him of guaranteed rights under the federal and state constitutions" and "did [him] harm in the November election." To rectify these problems, Flood requested that the county court require the Board of Elections to "instruct all judges and inspectors of elections in the operation of voting machines and the recording of votes" so that "all provisions of Pennsylvania's election laws will be complied with."[94] Flood followed up by taking his case to the voters themselves in a television address three days before the general election. In that speech, he pointed out that in the past some judges of elections had "opened the election board box and passed out slips for people to sign so they wouldn't even have to go to the polls." Some of these were "forgeries" and amounted to "several thousand votes." Flood reminded voters that such practices constituted a "crime" and that there would be "250 overseers at the polls this year to prevent voter fraud." "I have an old-fashioned American belief that the Congressman from this county should represent the people of this county, not the whims, prejudices and self-serving purposes of a very small band of political adventurers gathered around Olin Evans," he concluded.[95]

On election day 1954, Flood got his revenge on Edward Bonin, defeating the incumbent 70,254 to 67,682. It would be the first of twelve straight victories for him.[96] George M. Leader, another Democrat, was also elected governor, replacing Fine. Flood and Leader carried each other on their coattails as the political climate of Pennsylvania was changing to favor the Democrats. Leader was only the second member of the party to be elected governor since 1891, and he would be succeeded by David L. Lawrence, another Democrat, in 1958.[97] What's more, Flood's reelection to Congress spelled the end of the Fine machine's dominance in Luzerne County politics. Bonin, embittered by the loss, insisted that he was the "victim" of a "desperate offer Governor Fine made to defeat state senator Newell Wood in the primary election." "Apparently, the governor believed that it was more important to elect his own state senator than it was to re-elect a United States Congressman," he said. "I was given very little support or campaign money from the county's Republican organization. Its efforts amounted to nothing more than a little eye wash." Taking his case all the way to the White House, Bonin met with President Eisenhower and told him that the leaders of the GOP in Luzerne County had "fallen into disrepute with the voters" and that "its leaders were too long entrenched."[98]

Bonin's outburst represented the very first time in the twenty-five-year history of the Fine organization that any of its members or officeholders spoke out against its leader. It was also the only time that Fine had been accused of duplicity by an individual he had chosen as a candidate. When asked about the former congressman's scathing criticism, Fine passively replied, "No comment." He realized that the days of his once-powerful machine were numbered. Dan Flood and the Democrats had taken control of Luzerne County politics.

4

THE FIGHT TO SAVE ANTHRACITE

After establishing his seat in Congress and earning seniority on the House Appropriations Committee in the 1950s, Dan Flood seized every opportunity to promote the economic interests of the Eleventh District. He faced a formidable challenge.

Luzerne County was home to decaying cities and towns, an aging population, and a declining economy. Coal was being displaced by oil and gas for industrial use and home heating. Annual coal production, which increased slightly during World War II, had dropped below fifty million tons in 1950, and unemployment was at 19 percent and rising. Ten years later, the industry yielded an output of eighteen million tons, down 72 percent since World War I, and employment was at twenty thousand workers, down almost 90 percent since 1914.[1] The declining fortunes of the Glen Alden Coal Company, the largest producer of anthracite in the Eleventh Congressional District, is most indicative of the problem. In 1950 Glen Alden's coal production was just five million tons, less than half of what it was in the 1920s. To remain financially solvent, the company consolidated its operation by laying off miners and shutting down many of its collieries. It also sold off its coal lands in the Scranton area to concentrate its operations in the Wyoming Valley, and diversified its production line to avoid complete dependency on the anthracite heating market. By 1958 Glen Alden secured more than 40 percent of its sales revenues from air conditioners and truck sales.[2] The coal industry created environmental problems as well.

Mine subsidence, or the depression of the earth's surface above old mining veins, became a serious concern. More commonly known as "mine squeezes" or "sink holes," these surface depressions occurred in areas where underground pillars of coal, left to support the surface, had been robbed by miners looking for a quick and easy carload of anthracite. Squeezes often consumed the concrete foundations of houses and commercial buildings, twisted and damaged highways and roads, and broke underground utilities. Some of the holes were as large as twelve feet in diameter and twenty feet deep. Perhaps the worst cases of subsidence occurred in February 1954, when a mine squeeze damaged some five hundred homes in the Old River Road section of Wilkes-Barre.[3] There was also a critical need for drainage in abandoned mines. Some of those mines were connected to veins that were still operational and the water blocked off valuable coal reserves. In other inundated mines the acidic overflow polluted streams and creeks in the region.[4]

Dan Flood would have to find ways to not only remedy these environmental problems, but also stem the decline of the anthracite industry and attract new, more profitable industries. He was able to do so by melding together the three sometimes-conflicting responsibilities of a U.S. congressperson. To be sure, every member of Congress has three distinct responsibilities: to represent each of his individual constituents, especially with any problem they might experience with any agency of the federal government; to serve his congressional district, or the unique piece of geography he was elected to represent; and, most important, to help decide the many issues that confront the entire nation, regardless of whether they affect his particular district. While effective constituent service is extremely important if a representative hopes to be reelected, it will not gain him much influence on Capitol Hill. Each member of Congress must decide the extent to which he will compromise the comparatively provincial interests of his own congressional district to achieve the greater exposure that comes with acting on broader national issues.[5]

Flood's special genius was his ability to make the particular interests of his own congressional district synonymous with the larger interests of the nation itself. He was able to do this because he possessed both the ability to anticipate future developments within his district and apply them to the larger needs of the postwar United States. John Cosgrove, a Pittston native who worked for the Associated Press in Washington, D.C., in the 1930s and 1940s, called Flood a "quick study." "Dan learned the ways of the House very quickly," said Cosgrove. "Initially, it was his charismatic personality and his flamboyant dress that caught the attention of his colleagues. But as his seniority increased, people began to listen to his ideas more carefully. When he presented legislation in his early years in Congress, it was almost always proposed in a manner that would benefit both the national as well as his district's needs."[6]

Fig. 18. Aerial view of Glen Lyon, located in the Northern Field. Like many of the small towns that dotted Pennsylvania's anthracite region, Glen Lyon's landscape was dominated by the Susquehanna Coal Company's coal breaker.

The Seventy-ninth Congress, to which Flood was first elected in 1944, was a "victory and reconversion" Congress, with a Democratic majority. It was forced to dismantle wartime controls while also addressing the unmet needs that had accumulated during the war years.[7] Among those needs was a program to provide federal funds for additional hospitals, funds that Flood jettisoned to secure the Veterans Administration hospital in Wilkes-Barre. Another need was a federally assisted program for airport construction as commercial aviation entered its postwar boom. Similarly, Flood capitalized on this program to divert federal funds into his district for the Avoca Airport. Yet another need was internal improvements, specifically the repair and construction of bridges, roads, and highways. Again, Flood secured federal funding to extend the dike system for Forty Fort and Swoyersville, to build a dam at Bear Creek, and to construct the Luzerne-Dallas Highway, connecting downtown Wilkes-Barre to the more rural Back Mountain.[8]

The three congresses to which he was elected during the Eisenhower administration—the Eighty-fourth, Eighty-fifth, and Eighty-sixth—consisted of a largely Democratic bipartisan coalition that favored improvements in health, education, and welfare.[9] Eisenhower himself believed in a philosophy of "dynamic conservatism," which, as he put it, meant "in all those things which deal with people, be liberal, be human. In all those things that deal with the people's money, or their form of government, be conservative." Accordingly, Ike accepted the New Deal legacy of greater federal responsibility for social welfare. Rejecting calls from conservative Republicans to dismantle the Social Security system, the Eisenhower administration agreed to a modest expansion of Social Security and unemployment insurance. Ike also established the Department of Health, Education, and Welfare, which would play a critical role in subsidizing programs that helped millions of Americans achieve middle-class status. At the same time, Eisenhower did very little to support area redevelopment programs in declining industrial and rural areas, in keeping with his domestic agenda to balance the budget, reduce taxes, prevent inflation, and increase the gross national product.[10]

Flood, as a rising member of the House Appropriations Committee, achieved great prominence on Capitol Hill during the 1950s. Not only was he a Democrat in a Congress with a Democratic majority, but his masterful manipulation of the legislative process and his position on the Appropriations Committee at a time when the federal government was taking an active role in building a strong and prosperous economy gave him great leverage in saving the anthracite industry. Flood concentrated his legislative efforts on maintaining coal production while opposing oil and natural gas as fuel alternatives. He embraced the mission with the fervor of a camp revival preacher. "The God-given natural resources upon which this great country has so long depended, cannot be cast aside and tragically ignored," he declared in a May 2, 1955, speech on the House floor. "It must be cared for and appreciated as anything of value in this world should. Anthracite coal has served this country well in times of peace and most certainly war. We cannot permit it to perish. That would not only be sinful but a national economic disgrace."[11] Flood was vehement in his insistence that the federal government had a "significant responsibility" to address the "chronic unemployment condition" and "declining coal industry" in northeastern Pennsylvania, and that until it did the United States "cannot be considered a prosperous country."[12]

Of principal concern was his proposal that the federal government purchase and stockpile anthracite coal. Flood first proposed the measure in 1950 as a means of maintaining normal production levels and employment in the anthracite region. According to the legislation, a three-person board would be established to set, on a monthly basis, the amount of coal to be purchased, as well as the price, and to determine which coal companies would be patronized. The bill also authorized that the federal government's annual purchase of coal would "not exceed more than ten million tons," which was less than 25 percent of the 42.6 million tons produced in 1949. Flood explained that the 1949 tonnage represented a drop in anthracite coal production lower than at any time since 1902 because of competition from petroleum, natural gas, and hydroelectric power. "Within recent years a definite trend has been established toward a petroleum and natural gas economy," he indicated:

> Unfortunately, this represents a great national dependence upon two fuels of limited reserve. But more importantly, anthracite is of special strategic significance to direct military security and defense. Total reserves of anthracite are estimated at between 160 and 180 years of expected life. For petroleum and natural gas, comparative figures are 12 to 30 years, respectively. Yet in 1947, fuel oil for the first time surpassed anthracite consumption in the primary anthracite market area, and in 1948 accounted for 52% of the total consumption of fuels in that same area. We cannot afford to do this at a regional or national level.[13]

Flood's proposal was defeated easily, as was a similar proposal he made the following year.[14] Nor were his proposals for alternative uses of anthracite in the steel-making and fertilizer industries very successful.[15] As a result, he explored other ways to salvage the industry.

Flood often manipulated the debate on the House floor to press for anthracite legislation he was sponsoring. One of his finest performances came in a 1952 debate on a Republican amendment that proposed to remove peanuts from the list of "basic" commodities so that peanut producers would be ineligible for price supports. The Republicans intended to use the amendment to drive a wedge between the labor and agrarian wings of the Democratic majority. Flood seized the opportunity to promote party support among both wings for a mine-safety bill that was stalled before the Committee on Rules. "I bow to the opinion and the experience of the Agriculture Committee on the subject of peanuts," he began. "But this is their problem, and because of the procedure of this House and the way we operate here and because the work is left to the committee, perforce we must follow their advice."

"Now the number of peanuts we get from the coal mines in my district would not fill your hat," said Flood, addressing the southern Democrats and shrewdly shifting the subject of the debate. "The number of bales of cotton yielded per acre and the pounds of tobacco produced in my district are very,

very small, believe me. Yet I come here year after year baring my breast to the slings and arrows of the outraged farm districts, and vote for them. But it is a one-way street." Calling on his colleagues who represented the farming districts, the mustachioed Pennsylvanian continued:

> Why do you otherwise charming, gracious, intelligent, patriotic and learned gentlemen tell us how to run the coal mines, tell us how to house our poor, the starving in our cities? Why do you not reciprocate and take our advice on matters affecting our areas which at least are equally important to the general welfare as your farm areas—for we are the consumers—we must also live.
>
> You point to me in the great debates on the control bill for years and you get down and thunder at me that I am a Socialist if I support liberal legislation. Daniel John Francis Flood a Socialist. What double-barreled nonsense. I would never vote for any Socialist legislation, and you know it. Housing for the poor in great cities. That is not Socialism—that is Americanism . . .
>
> We need your help badly for work and safety. My friends have gone through this aisle shoulder to shoulder for you year after year. We ask you for bread, you farmers, and you give us stone.[16]

Flood's theatrics appeared to sway at least one member, Rep. Price Preston, a Democrat of Savannah, Georgia, whose district bordered on a major peanut-producing region. "The gentleman from Pennsylvania made some slight, very courteous reference to the fact that certain Members from the South sometimes do not vote on measures that are important to his area in a manner that would be pleasing to his people," Preston said. "But may I say that the majority of the Members of the House of Representatives from the South have supported public housing. We feel for you and your problems, and hope to reciprocate for the generosity you have shown."[17]

Capitalizing on the sympathy, Flood drove his point home. "I have just come from testifying before the Committee on Rules with many of your Members on both sides of the aisle in behalf of that vital and important legislation, the mine-safety bill," he said. "Now will you look into your hearts and vote, and will the gentleman from Georgia preach the gospel in the ears of all our friends from the South to support that mine-safety legislation when it comes on this floor as we are going to support you today? Now this is a ball game—let us play it."[18]

Flood's exhortation was followed by assurance from Rep. Edward Cox of Georgia, chair of the Rules Committee, that "due and proper consideration was being given to the mine safety bill." Since Cox's district was located in southwestern Georgia, one of the most important peanut-producing regions in the country, his word was good enough for Flood. Hoping to bring the debate to a close on a harmonious note, Democratic majority leader John McCormack of Massachusetts committed the party leadership to prompt passage of the mine safety bill.[19] Flood had prevailed.

Similarly, he was successful in discouraging the powerful Ways and Means Committee from collecting additional revenue by abolishing the depletion allowance on coal taxes, thereby saving millions of dollars for the industry.[20] In 1955 Flood successfully sponsored HR 7066, a mine drainage bill that called on the federal government to provide $8.5 million on a matching basis with Pennsylvania for pumping water out of the anthracite mines. The measure would also create more than 2,630 jobs for northeastern Pennsylvanians.[21] Passage of the bill can be credited to Flood's ingenuity. Realizing that Congress was nearing the end of its session, he bypassed the Rules Committee— which decides whether a bill will go before the House for a vote—and secured passage on a voice vote of two-thirds majority. President Eisenhower signed the bill into law a week later. Flood also enlisted the support of the Army Corps of Engineers and secured $495,000 to "alleviate the chronic and terribly serious problem of mine subsidence" in his district.[22] But the congressman's greatest coup was securing a continuous market for anthracite coal through export to U.S. military bases in Europe.

During the late 1940s and early 1950s, Flood began to consider the exportation of Pennsylvania anthracite to Europe as a possible solution to his dilemma. He explored the idea with the Office of International Trade and the Munitions Board. Both of these federal agencies emphasized that the "need for coal in Europe will only grow as the United States is assuming a greater role abroad in the Cold War." But there were "no European funds being made available by participating countries to procure coal from the United States."[23] After World War II, U.S. coal was purchased by individual European countries through a "controlled procurement" negotiated through bids and awarded to the lowest bidder, or through a "direct procurement" by the European consumer negotiated with the American supplier.[24] No organized arrangement existed between American coal operators, the federal government, and its allies in western Europe. Flood would first have to determine whether there was a need for U.S. anthracite and then explore ways bring the various parties together in a mutually beneficial enterprise. To that end, he contacted the State Department and asked for "any information on the coal requirement situation in Europe and whether European production will satisfy needs of the NATO allies or if there would be any need for imports from the United States."[25] He was informed that the European needs of U.S. anthracite coal "will amount to approximately 36,000,000 tons in the year ending June 30, 1952."[26] Next, he entertained the idea of a joint United Mine Workers–coal operators shipping pool proposed, in January 1952, by UMW president John L. Lewis.

The shipping pool would lease and operate government surplus ships to relieve Europe's critical coal shortage at a cost-effective rate, and to develop an American export market for coal. At the time, the delivery price of American coal at European ports was $25 a ton. Approximately $14.50 of that amount was for ocean freight charges. "Excessive ocean freight rates on coal shipments are largely due to high insurance rates imposed by Lloyds' of London, and those high rates have acted as a deterrent to the export of American coal," argued Lewis. "But under this proposal, the coal would be delivered virtually at cost since there would be no profit on the shipping operation. The insurance angle would be handled through an arrangement whereby the government carried insurance on the empty boats and the shipping pool to be organized would set aside a reserve to take care of any loss of cargo. This would eliminate the private insurance firms with their high rates." Lewis also stressed that the shipping pool would allow American coal to compete more effectively with "Russia's satellite nations, which are now a source of coal for both Europe and the Orient." Ironically, many European nations had resorted to purchasing coal from Poland and East Germany with American dollars received under the Marshall Plan. Thus U.S. funding indirectly went toward assisting the Soviet economy. "The shipping pool is not only a sensible, constructive way to boost the sale of American coal," concluded Lewis, "but would result in more employment, more sales, more railroad tonnage and more taxes for the government."[27]

Because the Eisenhower administration had abandoned its emergency program of buying domestic coal for use overseas, the UMW plan lay dormant through 1955. During that three-year span, Flood began to build a network of like-minded legislators from the coal states of Pennsylvania and West Virginia to promote the export of coal abroad. Exasperated by the president's refusal to implement the plan, Flood and Rep. Robert H. Mollohan (D-W.Va.) accused the Eisenhower administration of "political duplicity." "Before [the 1954] elections, the Administration promised to purchase 10 million tons of coal from West Virginia and Pennsylvania where thousands of miners are jobless and ship the coal abroad for foreign aid," argued the two congressmen. "It is now clear that the Administration's promise was nothing more than a vote-getting ploy directed at the principal coal-producing states and that no honest effort was ever made to implement it."[28]

Flood also criticized the Eisenhower administration on its trade program, which catered to oil imports from the Middle East. "The President's message to Congress on his foreign economic policy is totally unacceptable to the coal industry," Flood complained to the *Philadelphia Inquirer*. "The anthracite industry realizes that its only hope for protection against cheap foreign competition lies with Congress and I intend to fight the battle there." Calling on the House Ways and Means Committee to impose quota restrictions on residual fuel oil imports, Flood argued that the 128 million barrels of foreign oil that were imported by the United States in 1953 translated into 31 million tons of coal. Accordingly, he proposed a bill that would limit such imports to 5 percent of the domestic demand for the corresponding quarter of the previous year. The bill, along with others that proposed protective tariffs, went down in defeat. Instead, Congress gave the administration a three-year extension on its trade program.[29]

Oil was the nation's fuel source of the future, regardless of how hard Flood tried to deny the inevitable. Since 1945, he had opposed the government's plan for the construction of the St. Lawrence Seaway, a two-billion-dollar project that would open up the Great Lakes to larger oceangoing vessels, including oil tankers. He focused on every conceivable downside to the project, including: the exorbitant cost of the undertaking to the United States; the need for heightened national defense; the diversion of labor that was needed for defense; and the impracticality of a treaty between Canada and the United States. Flood's ultimate concern, however, was that the Seaway would cause "such economic dislocation in the anthracite region that it would bewilder the imagination."[30] The Seaway was finally approved in 1954 as a joint U.S.-Canadian undertaking. Traffic on the route rose dramatically as foreign oil flowed into the United States, contributing, in part, to the decline of anthracite.[31]

But when military installations in the United States began replacing coal-fired furnaces with oil, Flood experienced an epiphany. Why not use his leverage on the Defense Appropriations Subcommittee to secure a foreign market for American coal by imposing the fuel source on U.S. military installations abroad? As a senior member of Defense Appropriations, for years the Pennsylvania legislator had vented his wrath against the military establishment whenever they tried to convert to oil heating in their domestic facilities. One of the most storied occasions occurred in June 1954 when he discovered that an armory planned for his own congressional district was to have oil furnaces installed. Flood had previously been assured by the army engineers that the facility would be equipped with *coal-burning* furnaces. Upon learning of the "double-cross," as he called it, Flood phoned Colonel Robert Whittaker, the district engineer in charge of the construction. Whittaker explained to Flood that the change of plans had come from his superiors in Washington and he did not "have the authority to intercede." Besides, added the Colonel, "it will take months to make such a change."

Flood exploded. "I obtained the authorization for this building three years ago as a member of the Appropriations Committee!" he boomed. "I discussed the plans for this building in great detail with the Army Engineers in Washington and was assured by them that anthracite would be the fuel!"

"But, sir . . . " interrupted Whittaker.

"The only 'butt' there's going to be is yours if I don't get what I want!"

Flood slammed down the receiver. Infuriated, he phoned Eisenhower to protest. When he was told that the president was not available, Flood told the president's secretary to "make sure he gets back to me. I'll be waiting for his call."

Still unsatisfied, the irate congressman phoned Brigadier General David Tulley, assistant chief of army engineers in Washington, and gave him a sound verbal lashing. By the afternoon's end, Flood was assured that the plans would be changed to "accommodate his desire for coal furnaces."[32]

When asked about the incident years later, Flood defended his actions by citing his seniority. "By the time you get on the Appropriations Committee you're not supposed to be an amateur," he explained. "You're supposed to be an SOB in your own right. That's the idea of waiting around for a while. Besides, the Defense Subcommittee needed me at that time. The whole damn membership was from the South. They had to have at least one Northerner in case there was another Civil War."[33]

By 1961 Flood, then a ranking Democrat on the Defense Appropriations Subcommittee, was convinced that the management of the U.S. defense program could be turned to the advantage of the declining anthracite industry. He realized that the United States had hundreds of thousands of troops stationed in Europe and that their barracks were heated by bituminous coal and coke purchased from European suppliers. It was his intention to replace German coke with Pennsylvania anthracite. Working together with Harry W. Bradbury of the Glen Alden Coal Company and James J. Tedesco of the Pagnotti Coal Company, Flood lobbied Pennsylvania's congressional delegation and the Kennedy administration to implement their plan.

In May 1961 Flood arranged a meeting in Washington of all the congresspeople who had constituents in the hard coal region. It was a bipartisan group, consisting of Pennsylvania's Senators Joseph S. Clark, a Democrat, and Hugh Scott, a Republican. The representatives were Republicans Ivor D. Fenton and William W. Scranton and Democrats Flood and Francis E. Walter. Also in attendance were Edward J. Sheridan, deputy assistant secretary of defense, General J. B. Lampert, director of military construction, and other high officials of the Department of Defense, representatives of the UMW, and the coal producers.[34] The congressmen, coal producers, and UMW representatives voiced their strong opposition to conversions from anthracite to alternative fuels by the army at home and abroad. They also proposed that the army switch from German coke to Pennsylvania anthracite at its European installations, a transition that would create a market for some 700,000 tons of coal.

"It was a very critical meeting," recalled Rep. Bill Scranton, who served in the House from 1961 to 1963. "We were desperate to bolster the economy of the anthracite region. In fact, Dan and I had worked on several pieces of legislation that would have increased coal production and employment in the anthracite industry, as well as dealt with the environment pollution caused by the mines. We knew if we could convince the army of our need that the arrangement could save the entire industry."[35] To be sure, the exportation of 700,000 tons of Pennsylvania coal to Europe had the potential to create as many as 318,700 man-days of work, $6.7 million in wages, and $7.7 million in sales.[36] As a result of the meeting, Paul A. Mulcey, a consulting engineer connected with the Pennsylvania Coal Research Board, was sent to West Germany to "inspect and investigate the plants in question to ascertain whether there is any valid reason why Pennsylvania anthracite cannot be used as economically and efficiently as German coke."

Mulcey's investigation proved favorable to the coal interests.[37] In addition, Flood appealed to President Kennedy to intercede with the Defense Department to secure the purchase of American-produced coal instead of German coke at the U.S. military installations in that country. Kennedy's intercession led to another meeting between representatives of the anthracite industry, Flood and the other Pennsylvania congressmen, and Pentagon officials in July. At that meeting it was determined that the anthracite industry met the Defense Department's requirements for bidding on the U.S. Army fuel needs for its West German installations. Shortly thereafter, the coal operators cast their bids on German fuel. Not until October, however, did the Pentagon announce that its military forces in West Germany would purchase more than 485,000 tons of Pennsylvania coal over the next eight months and would, more than likely, obtain an "even greater tonnage in the year beginning July 1, 1962."[38]

The announcement was hailed as the "most exhilarating news the anthracite industry has received in a long time."[39]

Flood and his congressional colleagues from northeastern Pennsylvania had registered a masterstroke. For the next few years they would cloak their anthracite legislation in rhetoric that emphasized the Kennedy administration's interests in improving the nation's balance of payments, raising the gross national product, aiding economically distressed areas, and decreasing unemployment. In so doing, they wedded the anthracite region's needs to the national interest. Flood, in particular, was a genius at this strategy. He improvised package deals with other members of Congress by attaching riders— substantially unrelated provisions—to a comprehensive labor bill to secure his own programs. Predictably, in July 1962 the Department of Defense announced that it would award contracts to Pennsylvania anthracite companies for about five hundred thousand tons of coal for shipment to West Germany. Throughout the 1960s, the tonnage was extended each year and the additional government revenues needed to conduct the program were never challenged.[40]

"The 'Army Contract' was a good shot in the arm for us," said James Tedesco, president of the Pagnotti Coal Company:

> Anthracite production was in decline. The smaller mines were going out of business because they couldn't compete economically. Then the condition started to snowball and affect the larger companies. It was difficult to meet the costs of production because we were losing our volume. I believe that the credit has to go to Dan Flood. He knew that unless he could tie our local interest here in the anthracite region to the national interest, that there would be no way to save the industry. When he persuaded the army that there was a clear and necessary relationship between the coal and defense industries, he secured an extremely valuable market for us.[41]

In the late 1960s, when the army attempted to convert its European furnaces from coal to oil, Flood used his leverage on Defense Appropriations to block the budget authority required for the conversion. "Hell, yes, I stopped it," he boasted. "I did it by twisting arms and hammering heads. I'd break a few arms if I had to."[42] Melvin Laird, a Republican member from Wisconsin, sat on the Defense Appropriations Subcommittee with Flood and was both impressed and amused by the Pennsylvanian's hyperbole. "Oh, we had a lot of fun together on that subcommittee," recalled Laird. "Our chairman was George Mahon of Texas, but Dan was the second-ranking Democrat and the most amusing member. Some four-star general would come into the hearings and inform Dan of the army's plan to convert from coal to oil and how much of a savings it would be. Dan would demote him three or four ranks and that general couldn't say a word. Dan had him over a barrel. He just loved to do that!"[43]

Once, when asked why the Defense Department and the Pentagon allowed him to get away with such obstructionist tactics, Flood replied, "They can't be blamed. After all, here's Flood, a nice fellow, and he's got a great reputation for supporting defense appropriations—bang, bang, bang, and all that. Jesus Christ! Suppose you were one of those goddamn generals or secretaries or deputy secretaries. What are you going to do? Jeopardize the army materiel command with a son of a bitch like me for a couple million dollars, for a couple tons of coal? Bullshit!"[44]

In 1972 Flood strengthened his control of the already-captive military market by adding a limitation rider to the Defense Appropriation Act for fiscal year 1973. According to the rider, "None of the funds available to the Department of Defense shall be utilized for the conversion of heating plants from coal to oil at defense facilities in Europe." Thereafter, the same provision appeared year after year, tucked away into an omnibus bill. "There's no question that Dan was a shrewd legislator," said Laird. "He knew how to secure that West German market for the coal industry by using the limitation rider in an omnibus bill. He never had to do that on the floor of the House because we always took care of it for him in committee." Flood had guaranteed an ongoing market and employment for his district.[45] It was his most successful boondoggle.

The "Army Contract" led to other legislative successes, thanks to Flood's efforts at strengthening Pennsylvania's anthracite coalition in Congress. He made sure to cultivate his younger colleagues from the anthracite region, regardless of their party affiliation. His greatest acolyte was Joseph M. McDade, a Republican representative from Lackawanna County. Lacking Flood's charisma and hyperbole, McDade, who was first elected to Congress in 1963, preferred to work behind the scenes. He was a classic "home-style politician," devoted to the needs of his constituents. McDade was appointed to the Interior Appropriations Subcommittee and, like Flood, worked hard for the interests of coal.[46] "When I first came to Congress, I was deeply concerned about mine subsidence in my district," recalled McDade:

> People were losing their homes and the coal companies refused to pay anything for the loss. I sat on the Housing Subcommittee that was to draft legislation on this issue. But Bill Barrett of Philadelphia and other ranking members ignored the issue of compensation. I was appalled. I

asked, "Don't the victims, as citizens of this country, have a right to decent housing after they've worked so hard over the years to purchase a home?" Still, there was no action taken on compensation. So I went to Dan. "Floody," as I referred to him, told me that he would take care of me.[47]

Flood phoned Barrett and told him he wanted a clause on compensation in the legislation. When the subcommittee chair tried to defend his position, Flood snapped: "Now look, goddamn it, I've taken care of you before, now you get in line!"[48] McDade got the compensation clause he asked for. Flood's "we take care of our own" attitude became a trademark of the anthracite coalition in the House. Nor did any of the members of the bloc apologize for the patronage, favoritism, and influence peddling that directed it.

Despite these legislative successes, Flood and his congressional colleagues were unable to stem the decline of the anthracite industry. That reality became evident on January 22, 1959, when the Susquehanna River gouged a huge hole into the River Slope Mine near Pittston. Tons of water swirled into the cavern, which was 150 feet in diameter. The tracks of the Lehigh Valley Railroad, which ran along the easy bank, were cut and extended toward the river so that ninety-eight gondola cars could be pushed into the whirlpool in the hope of plugging it. But the effort proved futile. The gondolas, like the huge chunks of ice floating down river, were swallowed by the massive whirling funnel. Crews fought to locate and rescue the fifty-seven miners trapped below ground and destined to drown unless they could find an escape.[49]

"The river had entered the mine just down slope of the chamber where the survivors had been working," recalled Bill Hastie, a laborer for the Knox Coal Company, which leased the mine. "Of course, the water went down slope. But by the time I entered the slope, which was around 2:00 P.M., the river was coming in with such force that the water had backwashed up the slope about 100 feet higher near the entrance, and it was violent." Hastie, who was scheduled to work the middle shift, was assigned to patrol the Lehigh Valley Railroad tracks and halt all traffic. The break-in of the river had occurred right near the bank and was threatening to wash out the remaining eastbound tracks.[50]

State and federal mining officials arrived on the scene, along with Governor David L. Lawrence, who dispatched telegrams to the Civil Defense office in Washington urging that a federal disaster proclamation be issued. Navy engineer Captain Norman Drustrup and Colonel Stanley T. B. Johnson, district engineer of the Baltimore District, U.S. Army Corps of Engineers, along with George Gushanas, superintendent of the Glen Alden Coal Company, coordinated a plan to seal the site of the river breach. Meanwhile Dan Connolly, deputy secretary of Pennsylvania's Department of the Mines, assumed leadership of the rescue operation. Congressman Flood set up his own headquarters outside the engine house near the Eagle Air Shaft, where the families of the trapped miners gathered. He maintained contact with Washington, attempting to find a solution to fill the riverbed cave-in.[51]

"Flood was putting on a big show for everyone," said Bill Hastie, who made his way to the engine house around 9:00 P.M. "He was in there making phone calls to Washington, supposedly to get federal assistance for the recovery. After he'd hang up the phone, he'd go outside and inform everyone that he was encountering resistance but that he wouldn't stop until he saw the trapped miners safely above ground. Yeah, Flood gave the appearance that he was in charge. But to tell you the truth, he didn't know his ass from a hole in the ground when it came to that operation. The state mine inspectors and officials from the Glen Alden Coal Company managed the rescue effort."[52] Of the fifty-seven miners who were trapped, forty-five were eventually rescued. Tragically, when water engulfed the River Slope the following day, the remaining twelve miners were given up for dead.[53]

The Knox Mine disaster exposed the scandalous nature of the contract-leasing system established in the 1930s. The arrangement was created by the much larger coal companies that had mined the region since the early twentieth century and continued to own the mineral rights. One of those original firms was the Pennsylvania Coal Company, which leased the River Slope to the smaller, independent Knox Coal Company. The Pennsylvania Coal Company controlled the processing, transportation, and sale of coal, but contracted out the actual mining to avoid safety risks, high costs, and potential labor conflict. Knox hired and paid small work crews of up to thirty men, and made profits by violating the union wage rate, changing work rules, mining coal in off-limits areas, and employing unsafe mining practices.[54] The most heinous violation was ignoring the thirty-five-foot regulation for mining under the Susquehanna River.

Knox Company officials allowed drilling under the river until the roof of the mine shrank to just a few feet, despite the known existence of a hidden valley of thick, heavy sand, clay, and gravel between the river bottom and the ceiling of the mine. In addition, the Wyoming basin's coal seams slanted sharply toward the surface, topping out at a point dangerously close to the hidden valley. Therefore, when Knox miners quarried the chamber in the Pittston vein to connect two other tunnels, they followed the steeply climbing chamber toward the riverbed to a point where the ceiling had only six to eight feet of rock topped by seventy-three feet of hidden valley. On January 22, 1959, the massive weight of the sand, clay, and gravel deposits in the hidden valley broke through and the Susquehanna's waters emptied into the River Slope mine.[55]

Subsequent state and federal investigations uncovered a corrupt sweetheart deal between Knox officials and United Mine Workers District One president August J. Lippi, who had ties to organized crime. The bribing of UMW officials allowed the Knox Coal Company to violate the labor-management contract regarding pay, safety, and other work conditions, leading directly to the January 22 mine disaster. Lippi's involvement, however, went even deeper than bribery. Another investigation revealed that he was one of the owners of the Knox Coal Company, a clear violation of the Taft-Hartley Act. Although he was never convicted on that charge, Lippi was found guilty of corporate and personal tax evasion for failing to report and pay taxes on his income as an owner of the firm; after several unsuccessful appeals, he entered federal prison in November 1965.[56]

Flood's grandstanding in the recovery effort also raises questions. Was he aware that the Knox Coal Company was mining too close to the Susquehanna River in violation of federal and state laws? Did he know about the bribing of UMW officials in violation of the labor-management contract? Did he choose to look the other way because of possible connections to organized crime? To be sure, Flood was no stranger to northeastern Pennsylvania's crime family. He maintained friendly relations with one of the earliest dons, Santo A. Volpe, a mine owner who once exercised tremendous power in several UMW locals, including Lippi's District One. Using this leverage, Volpe extorted payoffs from other operators to avoid labor problems, and maximized his own profits by violating the union wage rate, changing work rules, mining coal in off-limits areas, and employing unsafe mining practices. He also directed the crime family's bootlegging operations during Prohibition and was eventually implicated in the murder of a competitor.[57] Flood's relationship with Volpe appears to date back at least to the late 1940s, when he was one of the more prominent guests at the congressman's wedding. The Mafia boss considered the congressman a "friend" and suggested to other members of his family that they "afford him the hospitality and consideration of a friend in a new country."[58] Flood also served as a keynote speaker for Volpe's Montedora Society in the 1950s.[59]

In addition, Justice Department records indicate that in the 1960s Flood's personal intervention halted an Internal Revenue Service investigation of James Tedesco, president of Pagnotti Coal Company, who had ties to organized crime.

Fig. 19. Organized crime boss Santo A. Volpe was a mine owner who extorted payoffs from other operators to avoid labor problems and maximized his own profits by violating the union wage rate, changing work rules, and mining coal in off-limits areas. Flood's relationship with Volpe dated to the late 1940s; he was one of the more prominent guests at the congressman's wedding.

Tedesco was linked to Joseph Barbara, host of the infamous Apalachin, New York, meeting of Mafia bosses, as well as to Russell Bufalino, the don of Cosa Nostra activities in northeastern Pennsylvania. Tedesco, as heir apparent to the Pagnotti Enterprises, controlled sixty business firms that marketed more than seventy million dollars in coal by the mid-1970s. The IRS investigation charged the coal operator with nonrecognition of Pagnotti Enterprises Inc. as a corporation, transfer of operations to a new entity, accruals of payments due and unpaid to the Anthracite Health and Welfare Fund, travel and entertaining expenses, and checks drawn to cash.

Appealing to Flood for assistance in the IRS investigation, Tedesco wrote that "any action of this kind would seriously affect us in our business activities, which are all located in the anthracite area. Extensive bank credit accommodations are required to conduct our business and any action [by the IRS] would be sure to cancel our credit." It was the "charge of fraud," however, that most concerned Tedesco because it would "seriously affect our business and payroll." Since Pagnotti employed a significant portion of the anthracite coal workforce, Tedesco knew that this last remark would secure Flood's help.

In response, Flood telephoned assistant U.S. attorney general Louis Oberdorfer. Shortly thereafter, the IRS investigation was halted and no criminal indictments were filed against Pagnotti Enterprises.[60]

If the congressman knew about the Mafia's illegal involvements beforehand, why didn't he blow the whistle on the Knox Coal Company, possibly preventing the disaster? Was Flood being paid hush money? Was he receiving kickbacks? Or did he simply realize that his political influence was no match for the kind of power the Mafia exercised in his congressional district? Public records and recently declassified FBI documents are silent on these issues.

Whatever the case, the Knox Mine disaster ended mining in the middle section of the Wyoming Valley basin, in the heart of the Northern Field. The river cave-in flooded out the network of tunnels that once boasted some of the region's deepest and highest quality coal. It did not, however, spell the end of the anthracite industry as a whole. As a result, Flood continued to promote the coal industry while also supporting state efforts to diversify the regional economy. His major efforts focused on reducing unemployment in his district, which had risen to 16 percent by 1959, and encouraging new businesses through a series of federal regional redevelopment programs.[61]

Since the mid-1950s, advocates for the anthracite region had been making their case for federal assistance. Flood answered their call in 1955 when he sponsored the Depressed Areas Act to provide federal grants and loans to improve the infrastructure of such distressed communities. But the Eisenhower administration, intent on limiting federal aid for industrial decline, countered with a more modest alternative and vetoed the measure.[62] Undeterred, Flood in 1956 joined forces with Democratic Senator Paul Douglas of Illinois, who sponsored a similar bill. Flood mobilized a contingent of officials from the Eleventh District to testify before the Subcommittee on Labor of the Senate's Committee of Labor and Public Welfare when it held hearings on Douglas's area redevelopment legislation. At the opening session of the Eighty-fifth Congress in January 1957, Flood introduced the Area Redevelopment Act, which aimed to provide $275 million for alleviating unemployment conditions in economically depressed areas.[63] Serving as chair of a bipartisan steering committee on the issue, Flood again joined forces with Douglas, who introduced a companion bill (S 3683) in the Senate.[64] Flood was tireless in his effort to promote the measure, making sure to put it before the House Rules Committee to insure consideration by the full House. The first hurdle was cleared in early August 1958 when the Rules Committee placed the bill on the House calendar before the summer adjournment. "I feel confident that we have sufficient bipartisan support for this bill to bring it before the House for debate," said

Flood. "As is the case with most far-reaching legislation, it is not possible at this time to determine what the final outcome will be, but nevertheless, assurance can be made that when the debate is held an extremely strong case will be made by me and others from both sides of the aisle stressing the dire need for passage of this distressed areas legislation."[65]

"Dan was very successful in promoting the bill," recalled Rep. Bob Michel (R-Ill.). "His success was due, in part, to the greater spirit of bipartisanship on Capitol Hill in those days. Members were of a mind to work together. That was our job. Unless you had a vendetta against the other individual, you cooperated with your colleagues, especially those who enjoyed seniority like Dan. My modus operandi was to make friends and get along with as many members as possible. I supported area redevelopment not only because I came from a state that would benefit from it, but because Senator Paul Douglas, who belonged to the Illinois delegation, cosponsored the bill."[66] Predictably, both houses passed the Flood-Douglas area redevelopment legislation, and once again the measure was vetoed by Eisenhower, who believed that the bill was "excessive" and would merely establish another federal agency that would waste the taxpayers' money without accomplishing much. Ike also believed that the rise in real wages, combined with low inflation and steady economic growth, made the Flood-Douglas measure unnecessary.[67]

Flood was incensed by the action. "An increase in the economy of the nation will not necessarily benefit the chronically distressed interested," he snapped, "especially those areas that are dependent on a single industry, which is depressed or has moved away. Experts say that if there is 4 to 5% unemployment, the condition is serious, but in my district 16% are without jobs, and they've been without them for a long time." Noting that local and state funds for the distressed areas had been exhausted, Flood added that "federal assistance was absolutely necessary to resolve the problem."[68]

Flood and Douglas resumed their efforts at the opening of the Eighty-sixth Congress in January 1959, believing that the chances of overriding a presidential veto were "at least even," though they "hoped it would not be necessary." The new version of the bill would create a federal Area Redevelopment Administration to provide two hundred million dollars in low interest loans and fifty million dollars in grants to help distressed areas build new plants and attract new industry. In July the bill passed the Senate, where Douglas served as floor leader. Shortly thereafter, Flood called on Governor David L. Lawrence and the entire Pennsylvania delegation, both Democrats and Republicans, for joint support of the Flood-Douglas bill in the House. In a meeting on Capitol Hill, Governor Lawrence told members of the state delegation that "this job development legislation is the most important piece of legislation now before Congress." He pointed out that Pennsylvania "suffered severely during the recent recession and continues to suffer." "The most recent figures indicate that unemployment in the Commonwealth stands at 364,000," said Lawrence. "That is 10.7% of all the unemployed in the United States, but we have only 6.3% of the nation's population." Intent on registering the severity of the problem, Flood added that "unless the federal government steps in now and assists us, our district will become a ghost town, an object of pity and despair."[69] Once again, the measure passed the House and was vetoed by Eisenhower, who insisted that the bill would "squander the taxpayers' money where there is only temporary economic difficulty." He claimed to favor a scaled-back, fifty-three-million-dollar redevelopment program.[70]

Flood was furious. "The President says we must 'pull in our belts a little tighter,' though in our area we have pulled in our belly buttons until they are against our backbones!" he fumed.

> It would be impossible to make a $53 million program work to do the job that must be done. It took two years to get our bill through Congress and he fought us every inch of the way. Well, on the first minute of the first hour of the first day of the first Session of the next Congress in January, the many Democratic and Republican members, who come from the depressed areas where the bill is meant to serve, will join together and will pass a good Depressed Areas Bill, a proper Depressed Areas Bill, an honest Depressed Areas Bill for the greatest good of the greatest number of all the people in this nation who need help. And with God's help, the next President, no matter who he is, will sign our bill into law before Easter Sunday.[71]

Flood got his wish when his former House colleague John F. Kennedy was elected to the presidency in 1960. Flood had developed a friendship with the Massachusetts congressman beginning in 1948 when Kennedy was first elected to the House. Their offices were next door to each other and Kennedy, bored by the drudgery of constituent service, often visited with Flood, who shared his keen interest in foreign affairs. They occasionally ate together in the House cafeteria, where Flood introduced Kennedy to other senior members of Congress.[72] "Dan taught John Kennedy the 'ropes' so to speak," according to Rep. Jim Wright of Texas, who was also mentored by Flood. "Kennedy would often seek out Dan for advice because he was a more senior member of the House. They remained friends after Kennedy was elected to the Senate in the 1950s."[73]

One of the humorous stories that circulated on Capitol Hill in the fifties involved Flood's reaction to Senator Kennedy's authorship of *Profiles in Courage*, a highly acclaimed book about the moral courage of various senators throughout history to act on principle despite the personal consequences. Drew Pearson, a powerful nationally syndicated columnist for the *Washington Post*, accused Kennedy of having the book ghostwritten.[74] Flood, also a favorite target of Pearson's, saw an opportunity to tease his old friend. He approached Kennedy, congratulated him, and remarked, "Senator, that is a fascinating book." There was a mischievous twinkle in Flood's eye that revealed a hint of sarcasm. Kennedy, quick to recognize the Irish humor, braced himself for the punch line.

"Who did you get to write it for you?" Flood smirked.

"I wrote it myself," insisted the Massachusetts senator, enjoying the repartee.

"Well, then, Senator, who did you get to *dictate* it to you?"[75]

"Only Dan could get away with something like that," said Jim Wright in a recent interview. "Dan was, spiritually, part of Kennedy's group. And I don't mean just as an Irish Catholic. Both of them had compassion for the workingman. Both of them admired strength of character, whether it was of a political or a personal nature. They were also very charismatic individuals, each in their own ways. They enjoyed each other and would support each other after Kennedy became president."[76]

When Kennedy ran for the presidency in 1960, Flood brought him to Luzerne County, where he made stops at Hazleton, Ashley, Nanticoke, Plymouth, and Wilkes-Barre. Traveling en route to Wilkes-Barre in a twenty-car motorcade, Kennedy noticed a huge billboard that announced, "Flood for Congress," and asked why his name wasn't listed as well. The quick-thinking Flood turned to state senator Martin Murray, who was in charge of the local Democratic campaign, and snapped, "Get Kennedy's name on those damn signs, will you, Marty!"[77]

Thousands of Wyoming Valley residents converged on Wilkes-Barre's Public Square to hear the handsome young senator deliver a fifteen-minute address before being whisked away for another stop at Scranton.[78] The November election was a triumph for both candidates. Kennedy won the presidency, narrowly defeating Republican candidate Richard Nixon, 34,221,531 to 34,108,474 nationally, and 99,737 to 68,046 in Luzerne County. Flood was elected to his seventh term by an almost-incredible 56,000-vote margin over his Republican rival, Donald Ayers, a Wilkes-Barre chiropractor. His 112,000 votes also placed him about 11,000 ahead of Kennedy. More remarkable, Flood and Kennedy amassed their majorities in a county where the GOP had a 33,000 lead in registrations.[79]

Flood's friendship and support of John F. Kennedy were certainly instrumental in securing the Area Redevelopment Act. But the president also favored the legislation to begin with. Kennedy had been a cosponsor of Douglas's area redevelopment legislation in the Senate. He had also seen firsthand the poverty of West Virginia during the 1960 presidential campaign and vowed to "assist West Virginia to move forward" if elected president. Determined to honor his commitment, the president-elect stated his hope that "the Flood-Douglas legislation would be one of the first bills passed by Congress" and that he would "give it [his] full support."[80]

On March 15, 1961, the Senate passed the Area Redevelopment Act and the House followed, passing the measure on April 26 by a vote of 223 to 193.[81] "This is one of the happiest moments of my life," said Flood after the passage of the legislation. "It has been many years since anything of such great significance to Luzerne County has occurred in Congress."[82]

Signed into law on May 1, 1961, by President Kennedy, the Flood-Douglas bill established an Area Redevelopment Administration in the Commerce Department. The new federal agency had an appropriation of $451 million to be spent over a four-year period, much of it in grants and long-term, low-interest loans for businesses in depressed urban areas and in economically distressed regions of Appalachia. "This bill will help make it possible for thousands of Americans who want to work to work," said the president. "No other piece of legislation has given me greater satisfaction."[83] Kennedy immediately appointed William Batt, Jr., Pennsylvania labor commissioner and a veteran labor expert, to administer the program under commerce secretary Luther H. Hodges. Wilkes-Barre was one of eighteen cities immediately eligible for help. Among the others were Altoona, Erie, Hazleton, Johnstown, Pittsburgh, and Scranton, Pennsylvania; Pawtucket and Providence, Rhode Island; Charleston, Huntington, and Wheeling, West Virginia; Fall River, Lowell, and New Bedford, Massachusetts; and Atlantic City, New Jersey.

The measure, set to expire on June 30, 1965, gave to the depressed communities the task of initiating, planning, carrying out, and partially funding projects to attract new plants. Among the major features of the program were: urban and rural renewal loans of $100 million to clear land and build factories or canning and food processing plants; public facility loans of $100 million to improve industrial water supplies, sewer connections, railroad spurs, and similar projects; technical assistance grants of $4.5 million a year; and occupational retraining grants of $4.5 million a year to help unemployed workers and farmers learn a new trade.[84]

Shortly after signing the measure into law, Kennedy met with the governors of Pennsylvania, Maryland, Kentucky, Virginia, West Virginia, North Carolina, and Tennessee, and directed that the Area Redevelopment Administration (ARA) "focus particular attention upon the opportunities—and problems—of the Appalachian region." He also insisted that the retraining program for workers be expanded, that the Defense Department "review its policies with regard to the placement of contracts in areas of substantial employment," and that a special liaison be established within the ARA "to evaluate and implement suggestions by the Conference of Appalachian governors."[85]

The Area Redevelopment Act represented a sharp departure from the federal government's indifference to industrial decline in the 1950s. As a result, the agency quickly had a responsibility to fund programs in nearly one thousand counties that met fairly loose eligibility requirements as "economically distressed areas." Federal aid to the anthracite region included a loan to establish a mine tour in an abandoned mine in Ashland, loans to various businesses, and research to control culm bank fires. By 1965, however, the appropriated funds were exhausted and, with the launching of Lyndon Johnson's Great Society programs, Flood sponsored legislation that replaced the ARA with the Appalachian Regional Commission.[86]

In addition to the area redevelopment program, Flood used his leverage on the Defense Appropriations Subcommittee to secure both jobs and money for his district through prime defense contracts. In March 1958, for example, Flood queried the Defense Department about the Eisenhower administration's directive to "channel government contracts into distressed economic areas," especially those like his congressional district, which had "suffered chronic economic difficulties for several years." He pointed out that "unless the directive was given substance by delegating proper authority" to the contracting officers of the army, navy, and air force, the "entire program will be meaningless."

Flood also urged the Defense Department to monitor the contracting officers to prevent their traditional practice of "doing business with just certain firms in certain areas." He closed the letter by suggesting that the most satisfactory way to channel government contracts into distressed economic areas is by the "matching bid procedure" whereby bidders from distressed areas have "the privilege of obtaining a contract provided that they can meet the lowest quality bid and qualify as a government supplier."[87] McNeil, in his reply, stated that "without fundamentally changing the Department's basic policy of awarding

Fig. 20. President John F. Kennedy signs the Flood-Douglas bill into law on May 1, 1961. The measure was the first of several redevelopment acts sponsored by the Pennsylvania congressman. Flood stands to the president's right, and cosponsor Sen. Paul Douglas of Illinois stands to Kennedy's immediate left.

contracts to firms in labor surplus areas," the military departments have been directed "to give preference to small business firms in labor surplus areas." McNeil also explained that the "matching bid procedure," which had been in effect prior to 1953, was "eliminated by the Office of Defense Mobilization because it created serious procurement inequities."[88]

Dissatisfied with the response, Flood introduced legislation to repeal a law that specifically prohibited the payment of price differentials to relieve economically distressed areas so that the small business firms in labor surplus areas would be able to meet the competition of firms in more economically prosperous regions of the country.[89] As a result of Flood's maneuvering, Luzerne County was awarded a total of $4.6 million in prime defense contracts of $10,000 or more from the army and the navy in the two-year period 1957 to 1958.[90] Flood also landed a host of military reserve centers and armories for his district. In addition, the remote Tobyhanna Army Base was converted from a little-used shooting range to a principal East Coast center for repairing military communications equipment, and employed nearly four thousand workers.[91] He was much less successful, however, in convincing the federal government to use the abandoned mines in his district for national security purposes.

Between 1945 and 1950, Flood made repeated requests to President Truman, secretary of defense Louis Johnson, and David Lilienthal, chair of the Atomic Energy Commission, to consider northeastern Pennsylvania's abandoned mines as "underground facilities that would best lend themselves to defense from an atomic attack by the Soviet Union." He stated that Luzerne County, in particular, would be "an especially attractive alternative command post in the event of an atomic attack on Washington D.C." because of its "numerous mines, a fine system of highways and railroad lines, efficient power and telephone service, an abundance of pure water, adequate room for the dispersion and concealment of surface facilities, as well as a loyal population."[92] None of the requests, however, were given serious consideration.

Flood's efforts at reindustrialization also involved promoting the needs and interests of the region's growing garment industry. During the 1930s, garment factories abandoned New York City in droves. Operators were attracted to the Wyoming Valley, where they could secure cheap labor and avoid union battles. With the anthracite industry in steep decline, thousands of wives and daughters of unemployed miners went to work in these sweatshops. Married men, unable to find work, stayed at home performing chores traditionally done by their wives. "Men are in the kitchen, washing dishes, preparing meals and wearing aprons," Flood told a Senate committee in 1959, seeking to attract federal funds for his Area Redevelopment Act. "Do not tell me that is where they belong. Thousands and dozens of thousands of the best workers in the world are housekeepers."[93] While the Pennsylvania congressman decried the "feminization" of the coal miner, he realized that the garment industry had become the economic lifeline for many families in his district and became a champion of the International Ladies' Garment Workers' Union (ILGWU).

Garment workers often put in fourteen-hour days and were paid less than two dollars a day. Many of the factories were controlled by organized crime, and the gangster employers who operated them were staunchly anti-union. They engaged in intimidation, threats, and physical violence to undermine union efforts to organize workers. Min Matheson, the president of the ILGWU's Wyoming Valley District, made considerable progress in addressing these injustices during the 1950s. Unlike most union leaders, who saw their role as limited to securing higher wages and better working conditions for the rank and file, Matheson worked hard to build camaraderie and a "union way of life" in the Wyoming Valley. When she arrived in the anthracite region in

1944, there were only 650 union members in six organized shops. But by the time she left in 1972, the district could boast of 11,000 members in 168 organized factories with locals at Pittston, Nanticoke, and Wilkes-Barre. Just as impressive was Matheson's commitment to "social unionism," which resulted in the establishment of a strong union infrastructure that included educational programs, a sprawling Pocono Mountains vacation and conference center, and a health care center that, in its first decade of service, provided services to over 20,000 district members.[94]

Matheson's success was due, in part, to cultivating close relations with political officials at the local, state, and national levels. Flood was among her closest allies. "We support Dan Flood because he voted to raise the minimum wage from 40 cents to 75 cents, from 75 cents to $1, and from $1 to $1.15, and to $1.25," said Matheson when asked about her active endorsement of Flood. "Each of those raises put money in the pocket of garment workers. Each of them was won through political action. We know that the higher minimum wage helped the garment workers and that's the purpose of our union—helping garment workers."[95] The ILGWU's support for Flood not only reflected a growing awareness among its members that congressional action could have a direct influence on their lives, but also resulted in the political realignment of the anthracite region toward the Democratic Party in the 1950s. Matheson and the ILGWU joined the Committee of 100, a reindustrialization group composed of local labor, business, academic, and civic leaders that raised economic development funds and lobbied Congress on behalf of Flood's area redevelopment program. Their active participation in congressional hearings for the Flood-Douglas bill was an important factor in the passage of that legislation. It was just one of many Flood-initiated measures that enjoyed the full support of the ILGWU.[96]

"Dan Flood helped us all the time and we helped him," explained Matheson. "He's an actor. He became part of our performance. With his mustache and his mannerisms, he fit just perfectly into what we were doing. Just perfectly. When he became an influential congressman, we helped to elect him. We worked very hard for him from one end of this valley to the other. And he always gave us credit for sending him to Congress. He never voted wrong on any bill that would help this area, help the unemployed, do some good. He always voted right."[97]

Flood's loyalty to his district was acknowledged on June 6, 1959, when nearly one thousand persons attended a testimonial dinner in his honor at the Wilkes College gymnasium. Among the attendees were high government officials, including Speaker of the House Sam Rayburn, who served as the principal speaker. Rayburn, pointing to the aggressive expansion of Soviet communism, stressed that the "price for freedom is staggering," but that "it must be paid." "In doing our work in Washington, the burden is made easier by having someone of the type and ability of Congressman Flood," he said, lauding his junior colleague. "We need experts in government, men of character, integrity, ability and industry. Dan Flood has lived up to the highest standards. In the years since I have first met him, he has grown in stature, knowledge and popularity." Flood, in acknowledging the tribute, dedicated the evening to "the cause of helping this area to the fulfillment of its historic destiny." While he admitted that "we cannot restore the rich past of our [anthracite] region, we can build a prosperous future because of the dynamism that exists in the Wyoming Valley." He concluded his remarks with an expression of his "heartfelt appreciation" for the "friendship and demonstrated confidence" of his constituents.[98]

For all the influence he wielded in Congress, Flood certainly understood that his power came from a strong commitment to his constituency back home in the Eleventh District. As the district became transformed into a Democratic stronghold in the 1950s, Flood became more independent of the party organization and strengthened his relationship with constituents from both parties. His decision was made, in part, because of a growing division over leadership in Luzerne County's Democratic Party. Much of the controversy surrounded chair Dr. John L. Dorris, a Nanticoke ear, nose, and throat specialist who had assumed the role of party boss in 1952. Since that time he had been accused of conflicts of interest and supporting candidates who were "out of touch" with the "needs of the working man."[99] Specific complaints were brought to the attention of Governor George M. Leader and Joseph M. Barr, Pennsylvania's Democratic chair, including charges that Dorris:

- failed to convene the legislative candidates for a county-wide strategy during or since primary elections;
- repeatedly attempted to appoint or retain supporters of former Republican governor John S. Fine on the county payroll, discouraging Democrats and independent Republicans who had constantly called for reform since the election of the new Democratic governor, George M. Leader;
- ignored several meetings with ward workers and others having legitimate business with the party;
- forced the resignation of James L. Brown as counsel for the county's Democratic Party, a post he had held for ten years (during which time he was successful in litigating thirteen of the fifteen major proceedings on behalf of the party).[100]

Fig. 21. On June 6, 1959, nearly one thousand persons attended a testimonial dinner in Dan Flood's honor at the Wilkes College gymnasium. *Seated left to right:* Judge J. Harold Flannery, toastmaster; Reuben Levy, dinner chairman; Flood; and Speaker of the House of Representatives Sam Rayburn, who served as the principal dinner speaker.

Several ward leaders attempted to oust Dorris before the 1956 presidential election, claiming that they would not support any of Dorris's candidates for state or local offices. The movement was led by John "Dada" Kashatus of Glen Lyon, Joseph X. Lokuta of Dupont, Robert Gillespie of Hazleton, and Harry Lieberman of Kingston. Collectively known as the "Democratic Minute Men," the group had been instrumental in Flood's success in the district since his first run for Congress in 1942. Kashatus, acting as spokesman for the group, listed multiple grievances that had been ignored by Dorris over the last two years.

Prior to the primary elections in May, Kashatus called for a showdown meeting between Governor Leader and Dorris, insisting that it was "time for the governor to step into the picture and help those who were loyal to his cause two years ago." The fiery Newport Township ward leader pointed out that Dorris had repeatedly ignored the wishes of party leaders, including the late state senator Patrick J. Toole, one of the most revered public servants from the region. "I can't understand why Dr. Dorris has assumed the role of a czar," Kashatus continued. "I'm counting on the governor to clean up this mess if Congressman Flood and the rest of the Democratic ticket are to win."[101] But no meeting between the embattled county chair and the governor took place. Instead, Dorris, protected by his own faction within the party, continued to ignore the Minute Men's calls for his resignation. "If Dr. Dorris loses his candidates, his political head will fall," warned Kashatus shortly before the November general election. He also promised that the ward leaders would prevail in the battle and "dig a new, revitalized Democratic Party out of the wreckage."[102]

During the next few years, the Democratic Minute Men would promote Martin Murray, a Democratic state senator, as Dorris's replacement. As Murray ascended the ladder within the local party apparatus, first becoming secretary and then treasurer, the battle to remove Dorris became more antagonistic.[103] On June 16, 1964, for example, the county Democratic Party's district committeemen and -women were scheduled to hold elections for the party chair at the Nanticoke Armory. When Kashatus and the other Democratic Minute Men arrived, intending to lead the opposition against Dorris, the armory doors were locked and the committee members were prevented from voting. As a result, Dorris retained his position and the rift between the two factions continued.[104]

Flood wisely remained above the fray. He realized that he could not afford to lose bipartisan support in the district if he intended to retain his congressional seat. While the Democratic Party's rank and file consisted primarily of the elderly living on fixed incomes and the working class, Flood relied on the county's moderate Republicans for campaign contributions and political support among the wealthier sector of his constituency. Accordingly, he established one of the smoothest constituent service networks on Capitol Hill.

Gene Hegarty, Flood's administrative assistant, anchored the office staff, undertaking a variety of tasks for the congressman. He kept records of Flood's personal and political expenses and maintained an open channel of communication with other members and their staffs on legislation, especially on matters that would affect the anthracite region. He was in charge of all the hiring and firing of office staff. He provided a sympathetic ear as well as a candid lecture. And he protected the congressman from the intrusiveness of the press, running interference whenever necessary.

Flood took special care of constituents seeking government jobs or appointments to the service academies. He was always quick to write a letter of recommendation to the appropriate official. Of course, his membership on the House Appropriations Committee assured that the applicant would receive prompt attention, assuming that he possessed the necessary qualifications. Lesser requests were also honored and momentous occasions, achievements, and personal tragedies acknowledged.

Larry Casey, the press aide, scanned the district dailies regularly for announcements of weddings, births, deaths, and school, business, and civic awards. Letters of congratulations or condolence went out regularly over Flood's personal

Fig. 22. Pennsylvania state senator Martin Murray was part of an ongoing power struggle within the Luzerne County Democratic Party during the 1960s.

signature. Most of the letters were typewritten by Helen Tomascik, the executive secretary, but Flood often penned personal notes at the bottom. It was a small but effective touch. Many constituents who questioned Flood's vote on some bill would remember the letter they had received and vote for him in the next election after all.

The mail was voluminous and, sometimes, humorous. One constituent asked the congressman how to raise goats because he needed goat's milk for his child. Flood contacted the Agriculture Department and had them send the man instructions on how to raise goats. Similarly, Flood responded to many letters by sending constituents helpful Government Printing Office publications, always under his free mailing privilege and engrossed with the stamp, "Compliments of Representative Dan Flood, Eleventh Congressional District, Pennsylvania."

Another letter came from a constituent, a former coal miner, who lost his leg in a rockslide. He complained that his artificial leg of thirty-two years "no longer fits" and that he could "use some help getting a new one." Flood arranged for the man to be refitted with a new prosthetic at the Wilkes-Barre Rehabilitation Center. Yet another letter came from an applicant for a job with Washington's metropolitan police force. He reported that he was rejected because of "flat feet" and wanted to know if that problem could be "waived." Flood, perplexed, wrote back informing the man of the impossibility of fulfilling his request. "Why they won't even waive dandruff!" he replied.[105]

Flood's willingness to answer even the most trivial request and treat every visitor as if he mattered earned him the undying respect of the voters back home. Such "home-style" politics validated his position in Congress.[106] It showed his constituents that he was using the power they vested in him for their own welfare. The more Flood legitimized his power, the more the voters trusted him. As a result, he did not always have to explain a particular vote, or even a controversial action. This was especially true in foreign policy matters, where Flood was given nearly free rein by his constituents. The flexibility, along with his seniority on the Defense Appropriations Subcommittee, allowed him to become a major actor in foreign affairs and one of the House's most prominent hawks during the cold war era.

5

★　　★　　★　　★　　★

EDUCATION OF A COLD WARRIOR

Dan Flood was a steadfast liberal on domestic issues, but he endeared himself to conservatives with his hard-line positions on defense and foreign policy issues. Flood's understanding of foreign affairs was forged during the mid to late 1940s and 1950s. It was a period that coincided with the beginnings of the cold war, the ongoing ideological conflict between the United States and the Soviet Union based on the opposing political systems of democracy and communism, and the opposing economic systems of capitalism and socialism.

While the cold war was fought primarily in the diplomatic arena, it sometimes erupted into military conflict. Many of the "hot" wars were nationalist movements in third-world countries, like Cuba, Korea and Vietnam, where Soviet-supported rebels tried to overthrow a U.S.-supported regime. In response to Soviet expansion in these small, poverty-stricken countries, the United States developed a "containment policy" geared toward limiting the spread of communism wherever it appeared in the world, viewing that system of government as a national security threat.

Mutual distrust between the United States and the Soviet Union grew out of the settlement of World War II. In the early phases of the war, the British and the Americans put more emphasis on military victory than on war aims. By 1943, however, delaying discussion of the shape of the postwar world had become impossible. Britain and the United States realized that the task of making a lasting peace would not be easy because of their common distrust of Soviet communism. Of greatest concern was the future treatment of Europe in general, and Germany in particular. The fate of the region was to be determined by the "Big Three": U.S. president Franklin Roosevelt; Winston Churchill, prime minister of Great Britain; and Joseph Stalin, general secretary of the Soviet Union.

The first major conference between the Allied leaders was convened at Tehran, Iran, on November 28, 1943. Churchill and Roosevelt told Stalin of the May 1944 date for the planned invasion of Normandy. In turn, Stalin made a pledge that Russia would enter the war against Japan after the war against Germany was concluded. The Big Three also decided that until they could work out the details of a peace settlement, each country should temporarily control the territory it held at the end of the war. Armed with this incentive, Stalin ordered the Soviet armies to race westward so they could liberate and control as much of Eastern Europe as possible. After driving the Germans from Poland, Czechoslovakia, Romania, Hungary, and the Baltic countries, the Soviet Army was firmly in control of all Europe from the Ural Mountains to the Elbe River.

Fifteen months later, at the Yalta Conference, the Big Three resumed their discussions on the shape of postwar Europe. They agreed to divide Germany into four zones, with the United States, Britain, the Soviet Union, and France each occupying one region. Berlin, which lay in the Soviet zone, was also divided into four occupation regions, though access to Berlin by the western Allies was not as clearly worked out as it should have been. The Allied leaders also agreed that free democratic elections would eventually be held in all areas reconquered from the enemy. Finally, arrangements were made for a United Nations to monitor international relations and guarantee a lasting peace.

These temporary arrangements became permanent after the war ended in August 1945. The Soviet Union refused to relinquish its hold on or allow free elections in the countries it occupied in Eastern and Central Europe. Hardened by the severe losses they suffered in two world wars, the Soviet Union resolved to secure its borders to insure that Germany could never again be a threat to the homeland. To achieve this security, and at the same time to promote the goal of world communism, Stalin intended to push his nation's boundaries farther west and to establish "friendly" governments on Soviet borders. He achieved this aim with astonishing speed. Sending in the Soviet Army, Stalin squelched the democratic elements in the neighboring countries of Bulgaria, Romania, East Germany, Poland, Hungary, and Czechoslovakia, and took control of the police, radio, and press.

Increasingly alarmed by the expansion of communism and Soviet influence, president Harry Truman, in 1947, pledged support of "free peoples who are resisting subjugation by armed minorities or by outside pressures."

The Truman Doctrine was reinforced by extensive economic and military aid to Greece and Turkey, both of which had been threatened by internal Communist uprisings and external pressure from the Soviet Union. This action marked the beginning of a new American policy of containment and indicated that the United States was determined to stop Russian expansion in Europe. Shortly thereafter, U.S. Secretary of State George C. Marshall announced a bold program to provide relief for the war-torn countries of Europe and to assist in their economic recovery. The Marshall Plan was also meant to stifle the growth of communism, which was thriving on the poverty and unrest of western Europe.

Stalin denounced the Marshall Plan as a new instrument of "capitalist imperialism" and an attempt to form an anti-Communist alliance against the Soviet Union. He retaliated by establishing the Communist Information Bureau, or Cominform, to coordinate the activities of Communist parties throughout the world, bringing them more closely under the control of Moscow. He also provoked a crisis in Berlin. Hoping to force Western powers out of the city, Soviet authorities in 1948 imposed a blockade on West Berlin, cutting off all land and water routes by which supplies reached the Western garrisons in the city from their distant bases in West Germany. The Allies responded with a massive airlift, which brought food and supplies to both the Western occupation troops and the three thousand inhabitants of West Berlin. While Berlin survived the Communist attempt to take it over, the incident sharpened the division on the European continent.

Confronted with the continuing threat of Soviet expansion, the United States and its Western allies made defensive arrangements against the Soviet Union. In 1947 France and Britain signed a military alliance that, in early 1948, was extended to include Belgium, Holland, and Luxembourg. In 1949 this European mutual defense alliance was enlarged by the inclusion of the United States and Canada as well as Italy, Portugal, Norway, Denmark, and Iceland. By the North American Treaty, signed in April 1949, the twelve nations pledged to help one another against attack. In 1951 the North Atlantic Treaty Organization, or NATO, was expanded beyond the North Atlantic region to include Greece and Turkey. A few years later, in 1955, the NATO allies were joined by West Germany. The Soviet Union responded to the formation of NATO by organizing the Eastern European countries under its control into a similar military alliance, known as the Warsaw Pact. These two rival alliances faced each other in an increasingly divided Europe. Across the iron curtain, they matched insult with insult, threat with threat, always near the brink of a hot military conflict.[1]

Dan Flood was both a product and instigator of the cold war. His speeches were delivered with vitriolic anti-Communist rhetoric, his activities in foreign affairs pursued with the vengeance of a hawk. Whether on the floor of the House or before the general public, Flood constantly expressed unshakable beliefs in containing the Communist threat, the necessity of the Truman Doctrine and Marshall Plan in securing democracy in war-torn Europe, and that the United States could only guarantee worldwide peace through a strong military-industrial complex and a fierce allegiance to other democratic nations around the globe. "Communism is a worldwide conspiratorial movement," Flood insisted in one of his many impassioned speeches on the House floor. "The ultimate aim of this movement is the destruction of all non-Communist governments and the establishment in their place of Communist states subservient to the Soviet Union. In driving toward world domination, communism has advocated the abolition of religion, private property, and inheritance. Wherever communism has triumphed, it has suppressed all forms of representative government and destroyed freedom of speech, freedom of press, and the right to assemblage."

"Communism advocates the employment of all persons in a state-planned, state-owned, and state-controlled economy," he added, drawing a sharp distinction to American capitalism. "In such a state, individual initiative, ambition, and effort are replaced by economic security of collectivism, which amounts to the security of a prison. Communist revolutionaries had dedicated their lives and every waking moment of the day to one single goal—the advancement of a world revolution and the seizure of power by the Soviet Union."[2]

Viewed from the standpoint of the twenty-first century, Flood's remarks appear like more of an emotional rant than a careful analysis of Marxism-Leninism and its various objectives. But his comments serve as an accurate reading of the prevailing U.S. attitude toward the Soviet Union and its socialist political system. The American people and the federal government viewed communism as monolithic. They made no distinction between the socialist regimes established by Mao Tse-tung in China, the Bolsheviks in Russia, or even the nationalist movements that embraced socialism in smaller, third-world countries. Predictably, Flood, intensely patriotic and obsessed with the military, embraced the fight against communism, becoming one of the most prominent hawks on Capitol Hill. He could always be counted on to lead a fight for strong defense budgets and a powerful U.S. military establishment, as well as foreign assistance to friendly countries.

When asked about his views on the best method of preserving international peace, Flood replied that he was "a firm believer in the United Nations and as the vehicle for maintaining and securing world peace," but that he would "like to see the U.N. strengthened through the elimination of the veto in procedural and administrative questions in the Security Council in which Communist Russia is a member." He also emphasized his "unconditional support for the Marshall Plan and the North Atlantic Pact and the arms provisions implementing the pact," and expressed his hope that a "similar Pacific defense pact" would be created.[3]

By 1949 Flood had established himself as one of the most outspoken representatives on national security matters. He was appointed to a special delegation from the House Appropriations Committee to inspect U.S. State Department facilities in Europe to insure that U.S. economic aid to the war-torn nations was being spent constructively. The delegation consisted of Flood, John J. Rooney (D-N.Y.), Michael Kirwan (D-Ohio), John E. Fogerty (D-R.I.), Lowell Stockman (R-Ore.), E. H. Hendrick (D-W.Va.), Christopher McGrath (D-N.Y.), and Leon H. Gavin (R-Pa.). The two-month tour visited the cities of Palermo, Naples, Rome, Vienna, Munich, Berlin, Oslo, Copenhagen, Dublin, Paris, and London.[4] It was the very first time that Flood had traveled to Europe and, in the future, he would take advantage of every opportunity to return. He became so comfortable, in fact, that he took the liberty of correcting Pope Pius XII on his view of the United States' international responsibility.

During the delegation's audience, the pontiff stressed the mission of "responsible statesmanship" that the United States had undertaken. "It is a sacred duty bestowed by God and one that implies sensitivity, a delicate and determined adjustment of mind and heart to the divine as well as to other peoples who press for recognition and protection."[5] Apparently, Flood interpreted the mention of "other peoples who press for recognition and protection" as a veiled reference to the Soviet Union, which had taken control of many Eastern European countries to secure its borders from any possibility of invasion by Germany in the future. "I stated to the Holy Father that, in my opinion, the chief objective of the atheist-communist countries like Russia was the destruction of Christianity," he explained later to a reporter from the *Catholic Weekly*. "That only if Christianity were destroyed could the Soviets have any hope of world-wide communism. Under the circumstances, the United States' chief objective was to stop the spread of atheistic-communism."[6] Pope Pius quickly clarified his previous remarks, paying a "deep and heartfelt tribute to the United States" and urged the delegation to "convey to the people of America [his] love and affection for their great democracy."[7]

Of special concern for Flood was the future of Eastern Europe. Nearly 60 percent of his constituents hailed from Eastern bloc nations—especially

Poland, Lithuania, and Czechoslovakia—or still had family members living there. The plight of these people behind the iron curtain resonated with the voters of the Eleventh District, and Flood made sure that he acted on their concerns. During the late 1940s and early 1950s, he pushed for a resolution to require the Truman administration to explore ways to aid resistance movements in Eastern Europe, most notably in Hungary.[8] He petitioned President Eisenhower not to invite Marshal Tito, the Socialist dictator of Yugoslavia, to the United States.[9] He inserted editorials from various ethnic publications criticizing the deplorable living conditions in the Eastern bloc into the *Congressional Record*, or was quoted himself on the same subject.[10] He also made repeated requests to Congress and the White House for helping Lithuania regain its independence from Moscow.[11] Pointing to U.S. policy as expressed in the Atlantic Charter, Flood urged President Truman to "give active support to those principles before the United Nations to restore Lithuanian independence."[12] "Dan believed that Eastern Europe was sold down the river at Yalta," said Melvin Laird, who served on the Defense Appropriations Subcommittee with Flood in the 1950s. "He preached on that topic whenever he had a chance to take the House floor. He was a fierce advocate of an independent Poland, Lithuania, Latvia, and Estonia because so many of his constituents came from those countries. I think the action that spoke loudest for his constituents, though, was Dan's investigation of the Katyn Forest massacre."[13]

The Katyn massacre of 1940 was the mass murder of 4,243 Polish Army officers and intellectual leaders (with another 11,000 unaccounted for). The Soviets insisted that the Nazis had committed the atrocity after their invasion of Poland in September of the previous year. But the United States remained apprehensive because of the Soviets' longtime desire to squelch Polish independence. The nonaggression pact Stalin signed with Hitler in 1939 reinforced American distrust of the Soviet claim.[14]

On April 13, 1943, the Nazis made public their discovery of mass graves of Polish officers at Katyn and accused the Soviets of committing the atrocity. The United States, in the interests of Allied solidarity, dismissed the accusation as "propaganda," insisting that the Nazis had committed the massacre. Shortly thereafter, the International Red Cross requested Soviet permission to conduct a neutral investigation, but their request was ignored by Moscow.[15] To address international suspicions of Soviet guilt, *Pravda*, the official Soviet newspaper, on April 29 published a long tirade of abuse against the Polish government. It charged that the "whole campaign of slander against Russia" in connection with the Katyn murders was "only an excuse of Polish imperialists to encroach on the sovereign rights of the Soviet State and its people and wrest from it territory that was Russian."[16] Nine months passed with no further mention of the massacre in the international press, and the Polish government in exile in London dropped the issue in the interests of Allied solidarity.

The controversy was renewed on January 22, 1944, when Soviet authorities announced that they had investigated the Katyn incident and had "established once and for all that the Polish officers were killed by the Germans in August and September 1941." They cited as "irrefutable proof" letters found in the uniforms of the murdered Poles "written after the spring of 1940," the most important piece of evidence being a letter dated June 20, 1941.[17] Unwilling to accept the verdict, several Polish American groups began to lobby the U.S. government to investigate the massacre.[18]

For more than five years, the federal government dragged its heels. Finally, frustrated by the reluctance of Congress to appoint a select committee to investigate the atrocity, Flood took to the floor of the House in early October 1951. Reminding his colleagues he had "been bringing this matter to [their] attention for several years," the anthracite congressman introduced a resolution for the establishment of a select investigative committee. Katyn was "genocide if there was ever such a crime," he boomed, pounding his fist on the podium for emphasis. "There are several million American citizens in whose veins flow the proud blood of their Polish ancestry and they have a right to know the facts in this case."[19] Flood got his wish later that week when he was named to a special congressional committee charged with investigating the Katyn massacre. The other members of the bipartisan committee were: chair Ray Madden (D-Ind.); George Dondero (R-Mich.); Foster Furcolo (D-Mass.); Alvin O'Konski (R-Wis.); Thaddeus Machrowicz (D-Mass.); and Timothy Sheehan (R-Ill.).[20]

The committee traveled abroad to conduct a series of eight hearings that took place over a period of twenty-one days between October 11, 1951, and June 4, 1952. The testimony of eighty-one witnesses was taken in Washington, D.C.; Chicago; London; Naples, Italy; and Berlin and Frankfurt, Germany. Another one hundred depositions were taken from witnesses who could not appear at the hearings. Although the committee issued formal and public invitations to Soviet government officials to present any evidence pertaining to the Katyn massacre, they refused to participate in any part of the investigation.

At the end of the investigation, the House Select Committee concluded that the "Soviets had plotted this criminal extermination of Poland's intellectual leadership as early as the fall of 1939, shortly after Russia's treacherous invasion of the Polish nation's borders. There can be no doubt that the massacre was a calculated plot to eliminate all Polish leaders who subsequently would have opposed the Soviet plan for communizing Poland." Among the other findings

Fig. 23. The special congressional committee to investigate the Katyn massacre. Flood is seated second from left.

of the report were that the Soviets: refused to allow the International Red Cross to make a neutral investigation of the German charges against them in 1943; failed to invite any neutral observers to participate in their own investigation in 1944; and failed to produce sufficient evidence at the Nuremberg War Crimes Trials—even though they were in charge of the prosecution—to obtain a ruling on the German guilt for Katyn by the International Military Tribunal. These findings were confirmed by prisoners formerly interned at the three camps, medical experts who performed autopsies on the massacred bodies, and observers taken to the scene of the crime.

As a result of the findings, the investigative committee unanimously recommended that the House of Representatives take the following actions:

- Request that the President of the United States forward the testimony, evidence and findings of the committee to the United States delegates at the United Nations.
- Request that the President of the United States issue instructions to the United States delegates to present the Katyn case to the General Assembly of the United Nations.
- Request that appropriate steps be taken by the General Assembly to seek action before the International World Court of Justice against the Union of Soviet Socialist Republics for committing a crime at Katyn,

which was in violation of the general principles of law recognized by civ-
ilized nations.

- Request that the President of the United States instruct the United
States delegation to seek the establishment of an international commission which would investigate other mass murders and crimes against
humanity, especially the events now taking place in Korea.[21]

The final recommendation, urging the investigation of "other mass murders
and crimes against humanity, especially . . . in Korea," is instructive. The Katyn
investigation took place at the time of the Korean conflict—the first undeclared
U.S. war, termed a "police action." The U.S. belief that communism was monolithic and bent on world domination fueled speculation that Socialist North
Korea was employing the same tactics as the Russians at Katyn. The theory was
reinforced at the Panmunjom truce negotiations when North Korean authorities
evaded the issue of the whereabouts of missing UN troops.[22] Still, Congress and
the United Nations ignored the recommendations of the Select Committee for
the next four years. Throughout this span, Flood continued to press for action.

After Stalin's death in 1953, the Pennsylvania congressman had reason to
be optimistic. The leadership of the Soviet Union gradually passed to Nikita
Khrushchev, the first secretary of the Communist Party, who was committed to
eliminating Stalin's chief advisers. Speaking before the Twentieth Communist
Party Congress at Moscow in February 1956, the new Soviet premier criticized
Stalin as a "mass murderer" and a "torturer." But he did not mention the Katyn
massacre among the several atrocities committed under Stalin's rule.[23]

"I say it is not enough to have probed for the truth about Katyn, unearthed
it, exposed it, and proclaimed it," Flood insisted in an impassioned speech to
the Polish American Congress after learning of Khrushchev's remarks:

> For what is involved here is the very heart of the moral values for which
> World War II was fought, a war that cost mankind 40,000,000 lives and
> two trillion dollars. If we merely find the truth, tell it and let it pass into
> history we shall have performed a disservice to Western civilization and
> the free world. For that is only half the task. We shall have acted weakly
> and in a manner destined to make us look vapid and hypocritical in the
> eyes of posterity and pusillanimous before the bar of world opinion. It
> is one of the major prides of my career in the Congress of the United
> States that I have not permitted this matter to sleep in the archives of
> government. Nor could I rest comfortably in my conscience knowing
> that the job of the Select Committee, magnificently accomplished both

on American soil and in Europe, might evaporate without a fixed result. If there is genuinely a new policy in the Kremlin since the death of Stalin, I am determined to put it to the acid test.[24]

Flood was good to his word. On May 2, 1956, he wrote to Secretary of State John Foster Dulles and asked that he send copies of the Select Committee's report of Katyn to "the Polish Red Government in Warsaw, the Russian Government at Moscow, and the United States Delegation of the United Nations and to place the report in all our embassies and libraries overseas." In addition, Flood requested that Dulles urge Khrushchev to "admit Stalin's guilt in the massacre of 15,000 Polish officers at Katyn."[25] Two months later, Flood himself wrote to Khrushchev asking why he had not yet admitted to Stalin's guilt in the Katyn massacre, especially since he had "already blamed [him] for so many crimes against humanity."[26] Finally, on May 6, 1957, realizing that no admission of guilt from Khrushchev was forthcoming, Flood made a resolution that the "House of Representatives express its continued opposition to the international Communist conspiracy to enslave the world by recognizing Poland's advances against the Soviets and to continue to offer support to the Polish people."[27] He would continue to oppose communism in the Eastern bloc at every opportunity.

To be sure, Flood viewed his involvement in foreign affairs as a way to capture the spotlight, and he remained active in that domain throughout his political career. The tendency first emerged in 1946 when President Harry Truman selected him to represent the United States at the funeral of former Peruvian president Óscar Raymundo Benavides Larrea in July 1945. Flood not only exaggerated his role, later referring to himself as a "special ambassador to Peru," but ingratiated himself with Assistant Secretary of State for Latin America Nelson Rockefeller to gain more influence in the foreign policy of that region. The pattern was typical of Flood's largesse over the years in describing his own diplomatic skills and placing himself as a major figure in historic developments of the times. In fact, his diplomatic undertakings were few and far between, which is probably why he secretly detested other members of Congress who pursued unauthorized negotiations abroad under the guise of being deputized by the secretary of state.[28] Simply put, Flood was often given to convenient exaggeration time and time again when it served his purposes, but he was also extremely careful to keep his distance from certain events, such as the Red Scare of the 1950s.

Triggered by Mao Tse-tung's Communist takeover of China, the Korean conflict, and the Soviet Union's development of an atomic bomb, the Red Scare was a sensationalist movement to identify American Communists and purge them from the federal government as well as the nation's major industries. It began with a series of hearings by the House Un-American Activities Committee (HUAC). The hysteria was exploited by Joseph McCarthy, a little-known Wisconsin senator hungry for the spotlight, who announced that he had a list of dozens of Communists working for the State Department. The wild charges of Communist infiltration remained unproved, and undocumented claims of "proof" became a trademark of later charges. The inflammatory rhetoric of the Truman Doctrine and the accompanying fears of Soviet aggression promoted the hysteria. Playing on popular fears of a Red conspiracy, McCarthy soon spread his accusations to include Hollywood, the nation's universities, television networks, and the Truman administration itself as the tools of a Communist takeover. After his appointment as chair of the Permanent Subcommittee on Investigations, the Wisconsin senator began probing for Communism in the U.S. Army. The Army-McCarthy Hearings, televised in 1954, gave him even greater national exposure. But his charges went unsupported and his abrasive "guilt-by-association" tactics brought a Senate investigation that ended with his censure for breach of constitutional privilege on December 2, 1954.[29]

Flood was silent on the subject of McCarthyism, which is conspicuous considering his vehement anti-Communist rhetoric. It's difficult to accuse him of the same cowardice displayed by other politicians, who recognized McCarthy for what he was but refused to stand up to him. Democrats as well as Republicans lined up behind McCarthy, or at least refused to call his bluff. Flood, however, failed to win reelection in 1952 and was absent from Capitol Hill during the height of the Red Scare. But Melvin Laird, who did serve in Congress during those years, insists that "Dan purposely kept his distance from McCarthy." "In fact, we used to joke about him," recalled Laird. "Dan once told me that he was a little jealous of McCarthy because he was a better actor. It was a tongue-in-cheek remark, but there was some truth to it."

"McCarthy played to the press every day," Laird continued. "It was just sickening to see. Instead of making him accountable, the Washington press corps gave McCarthy a forum for his craziness. He loved it. He'd have something new for them every day and they'd print it. Dan had no tolerance for Joe McCarthy. But he also realized how dangerous it was to speak out against him because of his popularity. McCarthy was an egomaniac and you had to understand that in order to live with him. But he had no close friends in either house of Congress."[30]

That Flood didn't trust McCarthy was clear by the joint resolution he proposed in 1955 to establish a Congressional Commission on Communism. Although McCarthy had been censured by that time, Flood's intention in proposing the commission was to prevent the emergence of another dema-gogue. The commission was to "make available information as to the basic differences between the American way of life and the theories and practices of Atheistic Communism." It was no coincidence that the members would have access to all testimony given under oath before the Internal Security Sub-committee of the Senate Judiciary Committee and the House Committee on Un-American Activities. Though Flood was careful not to criticize the conduct of either committee, he did acknowledge that such testimony was "taken many times at great personal risk for the witnesses' lives or those of his relatives." He also underscored the necessity of having the "work of this commission to be made available for future action by the Congress if deemed necessary."[31]

Flood also found other ways to combat communism at home. He champi-oned an amendment to the National Science Foundation Act to make an FBI security screening a prerequisite for the foundation's employment of a foreign national "in any capacity whatsoever."[32] In testimony before the House Labor Subcommittee in 1949, Flood urged Congress to outlaw the Communist Party in the United States. Stating his opposition to the inclusion of a provision in the Taft-Hartley labor law requiring union officials to present anti-Communist affidavits, Flood stated that the provision "only serves to cast aspersions on the Americanism of loyal union leaders," and that "the Communist Party should be abolished altogether."[33] He constantly opposed the Eisenhower administra-tion's efforts to control military spending in the interests of a balanced budget, insisting that "America's leadership has placed her in a position of great financial responsibility abroad." Accordingly, he refused "to vote for a tax reduction when the revenue was necessary for the U.S. military build-up." "Anyone who tells you that America can ignore the people in other parts of the world is a knave, a fool, or a demagogue," he added.[34] Finally, Flood was convinced that the Soviet Union was threatening U.S. national security in the Panama Canal Zone and took an active role in protecting American sovereignty there.[35]

The United States obtained the Canal Zone in 1903 by payment of $10 million to Panama. In addition, Washington agreed to an annual payment of $250,000 for assuming ownership of the Panama railroad. According to the Hay-Bunau-Varilla Treaty, which secured the agreement, the United States was granted "sovereign right" to the ten-mile-wide Canal Zone for ninety-nine years, as well as the right to build and operate a canal.[36] The military signifi-cance of the canal became clear during World War II when the U.S. Navy was able to move more than five thousand vessels through the canal in half the time it would have taken to sail around the tip of South America en route to the Atlantic or Pacific Ocean (a factor critical to winning a large-scale war). Similarly, during the Korean conflict one thousand ships passed through the canal, reinforcing the military significance of the region to the United States.[37] But the worldwide rise of nationalism and the revolt against colonial control that erupted in the post–World War II era resulted in a challenge to U.S. sovereignty of the Canal Zone. Although the U.S. State Department recognized Panama's "titular sovereignty" over the region, the Republic of Panama, encouraged by the Soviet Union, began to label the United States a "colonial aggressor" that was violating its sovereignty.[38] In the 1950s and 1960s, *total*—not *titular*— sovereignty became the primary catalyst of Panamanian discontent.

Flood's initial interest in Panama was cultivated by his grandfather, and it increased when he entered Congress in 1945.[39] He made regular trips to the area and witnessed the growing friction between Panamanians and the American military personnel and their families who lived in the Canal Zone, called "Zonists."[40] Native Panamanians resented the sharp contrast between their poverty-stricken country and the wealthier Canal Zone. Their bitterness was intensified by the haughtiness of the Zonists, who held themselves aloof from the Panamanians and did little to support the native economy. When the Eisenhower-Remon Treaty was signed in 1955, Flood accused the Eisenhower administration of "appeasing" the Republic of Panama, and became determined to preserve U.S. sovereignty of the Canal Zone "at all costs." According to the treaty, the United States would increase its annuity to Panama, cede waterfront and other properties (including the Panama railroad yards and terminals), and equalize pay standards for U.S. and Panamanian citizens working in the Canal Zone.[41] "I protest vehemently this treaty," Flood said, addressing the House Merchant Marine Subcommittee on the Panama Canal. "I believe the Republic of Panama will never take less than total control of the Zone and the first thing we know they'll be leasing things we now own to us."

The subcommittee was convened to consider the proposal by the Panama Canal Company, a U.S. government corporation, to abandon the Panama railroad as an outmoded operation that was losing money. Brigadier General John S. Seybold, the governor of the Canal Zone, testified that the board had decided that the railroad should be replaced by a transisthmian highway for "reasons of practicality and economy." Both the House and the Senate Appropriations committees requested that the company delay any action on the railroad until the plan could be reviewed by the proper legislative bodies.[42] Flood, given time by the subcommittee to make what he termed "a speech about the Canal situation," insisted that it was the Canal Company that should be abolished, not the railroad. He emphasized that the corporation "had become a Frankenstein" and that "the problem in the Canal Zone goes far beyond the railroad." "It is a matter of management," he added.

Infuriated by what he believed to the Panama Company's complicity in the Eisenhower-Remon Treaty, the Pennsylvania congressmen went on to attack the Defense Department's control over the corporation, stating that it has "outstayed its usefulness" in Panama. "The company, with its cavalier attitude toward Congress, behaves like a bunch of Clives of India with their ideas about colonial administration," said Flood. "As a member of the House Appropriations Committee, I can promise Governor Seybold that he won't get any of the $600,000 he wants for trucks to build his highway, and he won't get any $1 million for railroad rolling stock either."[43]

The Eisenhower-Remon Treaty was a "giveaway" in Flood's view. Afterward, he became obsessed with preserving exclusive U.S. sovereignty over the Canal Zone. He hired a retired U.S. naval captain, Miles P. DuVal, Jr., to become his legislative expert on Panama. DuVal had served in the Canal Zone in the early 1940s, overseeing the navy's marine operations on the Pacific side. He authored the Terminal Lake-Third Locks Plan, the first comprehensive proposal for the future of the canal, which was approved by president Franklin D. Roosevelt in 1945. DuVal also wrote two highly regarded books on the interoceanic passageway, *And the Mountains Will Move: The Story of the Building of the Panama Canal* and *Cadiz to Cathay: The Story of the Long Diplomatic Struggle for the Panama Canal.*[44] All legislation and correspondence on Panama that arrived at Flood's Capitol Hill office was handled by DuVal. The congressman did not issue a statement or sponsor a measure on the Canal Zone without first consulting him. Often DuVal gave his advice through buck notes, small yellow pieces of paper signed with the initial *D*, which were taped to all letters, memoranda, and legislative proposals concerning Panama. Flood would dutifully read each one before acting.[45] The correspondence became voluminous after the Egyptian seizure of the Suez Canal from the British in 1956, an incident that resulted in greater appeasement of the Panamanians by the Eisenhower administration.

Eisenhower feared that the takeover of the Suez by the Egyptians would serve as a catalyst to spark a nationalist insurrection in Panama. Newspapers around the world began to editorialize the call to place the Panama Canal under international authority. The movement gained widespread support among the American people and among several members of Congress. Accordingly, the president appeased the Panamanian people by giving technical aid and economic assistance to improve the social and living conditions in the country.

He also yielded to the longtime demand of the Panamanians to fly their own flag in the Canal Zone. "If that flag goes up," predicted Flood, it would mark "the beginning of the end of exclusive U.S. control over the Panama Canal."[46] He also suggested that the Soviet Union was behind the propaganda aimed at wresting ownership and control of the Panama Canal from the United States, and "that unfortunately many well-positioned people in the United States share Russia's feelings." "Make no mistake about it," Flood said. "We are headlong for trouble in Panama—the Reds are all over the area."[47]

By 1959 Dan Flood had become the "outstanding authority" in Congress on Panama. Hundreds of letters from constituents, as well as other Americans living in the Canal Zone or across the country, applauding his efforts can be found in the Flood Collection at King's College.[48] Naturally, the Panamanians felt differently.

When the Republic of Panama, in December 1958, passed a law giving itself control over access to the canal by water from both the Pacific and Atlantic sides—the same way the Soviet Union controlled access by land to Berlin— Flood warned Congress that the measure threatened to make the Panama Canal "another Berlin."[49] Inflamed by the remark, the Panamanian National Assembly on January 13, 1959, denounced the Pennsylvania congressman as "Public Enemy No. 1" and "a personification of the bad faith which has contributed to the ill will between the United States and Panama, countries which because of their destiny should greet each other as brothers." Afterward, the assembly rejected a U.S. request for reconsideration of its law extending Panama's territorial waters, and instead passed a resolution asking friendly nations to support the extension from the previous three-mile limit, promising free passage to their shipping. In addition, foreign minister Aquilano Boyd called on the United States to pay Panama "half of the gross revenue" from the operation of the canal, noting that the United States earned $100 million each year while paying Panama an annuity of only $1.9 million.[50]

Flood embraced his new title as "Panama's Public Enemy No. 1" like a badge of honor and ratcheted up his attack on any nation or organization that challenged U.S. control of the Canal Zone. Not even the U.S. State Department was immune from his vituperative remarks, as he made a constitutional case for exclusive U.S. sovereignty. Describing Panama as the "target of communism's fourth front," in 1960 Flood called for a modern extension of the Monroe Doctrine "not only against invading troops or fleets but against Red subversion and Communist penetration." "There ain't no such animal as 'titular' sovereignty,'" he insisted, referring to the State Department's definition of Panama's legal status. "Complete sovereignty which makes the Zone a constitutionally acquired domain of the United States was clearly specified in the Treaty of 1903, until the erosion and surrender of rights began to break the diplomatic dike in the Eisenhower-Remon Treaty of 1955." Flood accused the State Department of a policy of "let's compromise" and described some Latin American politicians as capable of "taking the gold fillings out of your teeth if you fall asleep." "Panama is not an isolated question," he insisted, "but the target of a Communist movement aimed at the destruction of the United States. Those in charge of the Communist movement in Latin America, and especially in the Caribbean area, have undoubtedly focused their conspiratorial activities on the Panama Canal with the purpose of causing destruction of amicable relations between the United States and Panama, with complete liquidation of United States control over the canal itself. The Reds have recognized the Panama Canal as the strategic center of America and that is why we must hold on to it."[51] Panama was Flood's "hot-button" issue and he would fight to retain U.S. control of the canal until the day he left office in 1980.

Panama was not the only issue, however, that gained Flood notoriety on Capitol Hill. His unwavering support for increased defense appropriations earned him the praise of congressional colleagues, who acknowledged that he was "years ahead of everyone else on Capitol Hill in seeking a build-up of conventional and atomic weapons and limited military forces."[52] Most appreciative was Rep. George H. Mahon, chair of the Defense Appropriations Subcommittee.

Mahon, a Texas Democrat, was one of the most important men in the civilian command of the U.S. military. His judgment could decide whether the air force should receive the funds to develop a new weapons system, whether the navy should have more aircraft carriers or nuclear submarines, or whether the army should have more choppers or tanks. Mahon exercised tremendous influence in the nuclear arms race as well. When the United States learned, in 1957, that the Soviets had successfully tested their first intercontinental ballistic missile—followed by the launching of the first satellite, *Sputnik*, into outer space—Mahon was the first to criticize the Defense Department for lagging behind the Soviet Union in missile development. "There is no excuse for the missile gap," said Mahon. "The United States has reached the hardware stage on the Army's Jupiter and the Air Force's Thor missiles. We are making two of these short-range missiles a month, but we should be making four or six. We should also have, in a matter of a few months, intercontinental range ballistic missiles (IRBM) rolling off the production line in large numbers. The sky should be the limit in terms of IRBM production."

Fig. 24. Rep. George H. Mahon (D-Tex.), chair of the House Defense Appropriations Subcommittee.

Flood was quick to support his chair's criticism of the missile gap. "The Eisenhower administration is just moving a few pawns around the board to give the appearance of action," he said. "The Jupiter should have been ordered into full production six months ago. It shouldn't be delayed another 10 minutes. The Thor should be put into full production, too. It ought to be done this afternoon." Flood added that the "Soviet IRBM has only an 800-mile range, compared to our 1,500-mile IRBM, but it is all they need to hit every military base in Europe."[53] The saber rattling was intended to push the administration further along in its commitment to nuclear weapons as the key to American defense. While Ike preferred "massive retaliation" over conventional forms of defense because it promised to be more effective (giving "more bang for the buck"), he was also concerned about controlling the budget and cutting taxes, and therefore bristled against the expense of unchecked missile production. During the 1960s, however, Flood and Mahon prevailed, ensuring that the United States overcame the "missile gap" and held a significant advantage over the Soviet Union.

Flood was just as adamant about increasing U.S. conventional forces. In July 1956, for example, he moved to boost the size of the air force by increasing its appropriations by $1.1 billion, a motion that had been shouted down in the House two months earlier. When another representative pointed out that even the secretary of the air force, in keeping with the Eisenhower administration's low budget estimates, opposed the increase, Flood snorted, "Secretary Quarles has long, beautiful hair and flat heels. He is an excellent scientist, but he shows no sign of being an effective administrator."[54] Similarly, throughout the 1950s and early 1960s Flood championed proposals each year to increase the size of the army and marine corps. Not until 1962 did the House approve funds for a 1 million–person army, something Flood had wanted all along. Still, he wasn't completely satisfied. Stating his understanding that the appropriation was also to include a 200,000-person marine corps, he pointed out that the increase only came to 190,000 people. "I thought I was going to get 200,000 Marines," he told the *Washington Post*, "but somewhere between the House and the foot of Capitol Hill, I lost 10,000 Marines in a half an hour. It is strange how things like that happen."[55]

Flood was so outspoken in promoting increased funding for national security that many of his colleagues on the House Appropriations Committee were flabbergasted when in 1962 he made no additions to a $47 billion Defense appropriation. "I usually have a pot full of amendments," he said, apologetically. "I have never had much success with these amendments, but I found out that all you have to do is live long enough or have the good people in your district return you often enough and you get practically everything you want. That seems to have happened to me with this bill." After the shocking admission, Flood was hit with a plethora of compliments, which he fielded in customary style.

"Will the gentleman from Pennsylvania yield?" asked Rep. Robert Sikes (D-Fla.), a brigadier general in the army reserve.

"This is a *real* general," said Flood. "If you never saw a real general this is a real general, my distinguished friend from Florida."

Sikes acknowledged his colleague's remark with a smile and began, "This might be a good time to point out one of the reasons the gentleman from Pennsylvania has nothing to be mad about is the fact that through the years he has worked so diligently and so zealously for the improvements in our Defense program which at long last are being realized. I want to commend publicly the gentleman from Pennsylvania for his great contribution to a strong defense for the United States."

"Is that not nice?" Flood replied. "I wrote that for him just ten minutes ago. He is a real fast study."

George Mahon, chair of the Defense Appropriations Subcommittee, was the next to speak. "I cannot resist saying that I know of no man in this House who more diligently pursued the cause of the defense of the United States than the gentleman from Pennsylvania. I know of no man on the committee who has been more regular or more loyal in his attendance at the sessions of the subcommittee, and they have been long and many."

"What I had better do is quit while I am ahead," interrupted Flood, much to the amusement of his colleagues.

The love feast continued with Rep. William Minshall (R-Ohio), who insisted that "there is no man on either side of the aisle, better informed on military affairs than the distinguished gentleman from Pennsylvania."

Flood savored each and every plaudit, occasionally interjecting an anecdote or reciprocating with a compliment of the speaker. Near the end of the session, he told the story of a former private who was running for the presidency against an ex-general. Speaking before a convention of veterans, the private told the audience, "I want all you fellows who are generals to vote for the general and all of you fellows who are not generals to vote for me."

Before Flood could deliver the punch line, though, Joe Evins (D-Tenn.) interrupted to ask, "How are we to address the gentleman from Pennsylvania, as general or private?"[56]

To be sure, Dan Flood was the House's greatest proponent of increasing the Defense budget at a time when the White House was extremely skeptical over a growing military-industrial complex. In fact, Rep. Gerald Ford (R-Mich.) joked that his good friend "never met a Defense appropriation he didn't like."[57] But it would be a mistake to assume that Flood favored unlimited spending simply for the sake of increasing the defense establishment. What angered him was *irresponsible* spending; as he put it, he saw "the need for smarter and more effective defense spending."[58] He rejected the usefulness of spending money to increase the quantity of conventional forces, military staff, or missiles unless the expense translated into hard, practical results. "Efficiency" was more important than "quantity." Once, for example, after listening to Brigadier General Delk Odem explain the need for additional staffing at the Pentagon, Flood responded, "I do not like to be the skunk at the lawn social or strawberry festival, but I do have a recommendation for creating a more efficient staff." He went on to suggest that several busloads of marines be dropped off at the Pentagon, permitted to enter, and "take every fourth person they run into, at random, put them on the bus and send them away." "The absence of these staffers," he said, "would probably go unnoticed, except by their immediate families." It was Flood's way of saying that the Pentagon could operate much more effectively without 25 percent of the bureaucracy it already had.[59]

Similarly, Flood, at a Defense Appropriations Subcommittee hearing, once humiliated a row of generals for their failure to accurately forecast the effectiveness of a new tank that when fired set itself ablaze.

"How the hell can you defend a piece of machinery like that?" he barked. "Whatever general made the request to fund a tank like that should be demoted to private first class!"

Pausing for effect, Flood looked directly at each of the witnesses seated before him. Then he broke the silence by pounding his fist on the desk. "In fact, the testimony before this committee for the past ten years has been a disgrace," he exploded. Turning to his colleagues on either side, he added, "The Pentagon's witnesses are incompetent. Every one of them lies through their teeth. I should bring many of those witnesses back here so we can take another shot at them."

"That's all," he said, concluding his remarks.

While it was unclear exactly what Flood meant by the "incompetence" of the Pentagon's witnesses, his rhetorical fulminations had so clearly compromised the decorum of the hearings that Rep. Gerald Ford, who was scheduled to ask questions next, was speechless. After regrouping, he asked, "How can I follow a statement like that?"[60] Ironically, Flood did not face as much resistance in promoting defense spending when John Kennedy was elected president in 1960. Although the Democrats still controlled Congress, almost all of the party's leaders in both houses were more hawkish than Kennedy. They believed he favored diplomacy over military engagement, and greater spending on foreign aide than defense.[61] Together with conservative Republicans, the Democratic leadership was expected to oppose the president and defense secretary Robert S. McNamara and insist on greater military spending. The failed Bay of Pigs invasion on April 16, 1961, less than three months after Kennedy took office, seemed to insure that fate.

Twelve hundred Cuban refugees, sponsored by the United States, stormed ashore at the Bay of Pigs in a surprise attempt to overthrow the Communist regime of Fidel Castro. Within three days, Castro crushed the invasion force, inflicting a severe blow to American prestige and the young president. Critics accused Kennedy of turning "chicken" for canceling the air and naval support that the invasion force had expected. To his credit, an embarrassed Kennedy took full responsibility for the affair. But the incident had profound implications for the relationship between the president and his national security team. Kennedy was viewed as a "dangerously weak link at the top of the chain of command" by military and intelligence officials. And the president was equally distrustful of the Central Intelligence Agency and the Joint Chiefs of Staff.[62]

Flood, as one of the few legislators privy to intelligence operations, was aware that planning for the invasion had begun within the CIA during the Eisenhower administration. He supported the invasion to topple Castro, and though he was angered by the failure of the invasion, Flood could not, in good conscience, attack Kennedy for the failure of an inherited covert scheme.

Instead, Flood endorsed the president's decision to review CIA operations and, later, to name a new director, John A. McCone, of the federal agency.

After the Bay of Pigs fiasco, a coalition of Democratic and Republican conservatives were determined to show Kennedy that they were in charge of federal spending by slashing his foreign aid program. When, in September 1961, a reduced money bill approved by the Appropriations Committee came to the House for a vote, Gerald Ford led a revolt against it. What was so unusual about the action was that Ford was the ranking Republican member of the Defense subcommittee that managed the single largest portion of the federal budget. It was rare for someone of his stature to contest a bill that emerged from Appropriations, one of the most powerful committees in Congress. Ford convinced his colleagues that Kennedy's request for additional foreign military aid was not extravagant. He proposed an amendment for $1.6 million for such assistance, insisting that it was "less than was recommended at any time by either President Eisenhower or Kennedy." "In view of the worsening world situation," he added, "the budget should not be cut further." Ford's measure survived three votes before it was finally approved.[63]

Flood had been part of the revolt from the beginning. "Dan was a very strong supporter of national defense," recalled Ford. "If I hadn't challenged that money bill, he would have done it. In fact, Dan probably fit into the same ideological categories as I did. He was a 'moderate' on domestic issues, an 'internationalist' in foreign affairs and a 'conservative' in fiscal policy. But the revolt really wasn't a question of being 'conservative' or 'liberal,' or even 'Democratic' or 'Republican.' We simply did what we believed was right."[64]

Kennedy's mettle was tested again when, in October 1962, Soviet premier Nikita Khrushchev secretly sent missiles with nuclear warheads to Cuba. The missiles were to be manned by Soviet troops and had the capacity to strike at the heart of the United States. Khrushchev was hoping not only to secure a great advantage should the cold war ever become hot, but also to gain a lever to force the West out of Berlin.

Kennedy had warned the Soviets that if there was any evidence of "significant offensive capability either in Cuban hands or under Soviet direction . . . the gravest issues would arise." After a U-2 reconnaissance aircraft brought back pictures showing missile bases in Cuba, the president ordered an air and naval blockade to prevent Soviet ships from reaching their destination in Cuba. For several days the armed forces of both countries were on high alert. War was avoided when the Soviets promised to withdraw their missiles from Cuba and the United States pledged not to invade the island.[65] While there was a marked improvement in relations between the United States and the Soviet Union following the Cuban missile crisis, the incident convinced Congress of the need for greater defense spending to insure national security.

The Soviets, determined not to be intimidated again, engaged in the largest weapons buildup in their history. Kennedy, chastened by his flirtation with nuclear disaster, called for a nuclear test ban treaty, which was eventually signed by the United States, the Soviet Union, and Great Britain in August 1963.[66] At the same time, he also increased the nation's nuclear arsenal and U.S. military commitments abroad. Kennedy favored "peace through strength" rather than "gunboat diplomacy." His preference placed him at dangerous odds against his own intelligence advisers, who were bent on a military showdown with the Communists in Cuba.[67]

Since 1959, the CIA, in its efforts to enlist the support of organized crime in assassinating Fidel Castro, shared its secret plan with some of the top Mafia bosses, including Carlos Marcello, Santo Trafficante, and Johnny Rosselli. Throughout his tenure in office, Kennedy approved and encouraged the CIA's assassination plots against the Cuban dictator, though these plans were not known to the public or to most government officials until more than a decade after the president's death.[68] Marcello, Trafficante, and Rosselli had lucrative gambling interests in Cuba prior to Castro's takeover and were eager to reclaim them; toppling the Cuban dictator would allow them to do so. The plans never materialized, however, probably because all three of the Mafia bosses were also targeted for prosecution by President Kennedy and his brother, attorney general Robert F. Kennedy.[69]

The interesting question here is how much did Flood know about the Kennedy administration's plan to employ the Mafia in assassinating Castro? Flood was no stranger to organized crime. He was certainly aware that Russell Bufalino, considered "one of the most ruthless and powerful Mafia leaders in the United States" by the U.S. Senate's McClellan Committee, had succeeded Santo Volpe as the don of northeastern Pennsylvania's Mafia.[70] Was Flood aware, however, that Bufalino had also been approached to join a CIA-Mafia plot to assassinate Castro? Like Marcello, Trafficante, and Rosselli, Bufalino had been a partial owner of a raceway and large casino in Havana, and was driven off the island during Castro's takeover in 1959.[71] While Bufalino was heavily involved in gambling, loan sharking, drug peddling, and extortion, his involvement in labor racketeering gave him tremendous clout both in the United States and abroad, and eventually made him a target of the Federal Bureau of Investigation.[72]

If Flood had any direct contact with Bufalino, it came through their mutual association with the Pittston-based Medico Industries, the largest supplier of ammunition to the U.S. government. The Pennsylvania Crime Commission identified Bufalino as a "silent partner of Medico Industries" and Philip T. Medico, Sr., its president and general manager, as a capo in the Bufalino crime family.[73] Flood, whose relationship with the company dated to the early 1960s, allegedly arranged at least sixty million dollars in government contracts for Medico Industries in return for free travel on the company's airplane between Wilkes-Barre and Washington.[74] When the congressman came under a Justice Department investigation for such influence peddling in 1978, he dismissed any notion of wrongdoing. "I see nothing unusual about helping these people," he told the *Washington Star*. "We help all kinds of contractors from A to Z. I don't know of any other way to create jobs for people in northeastern Pennsylvania other than for the business establishment in the area to obtain contracts so that people can go to work." Nor did Flood see anything "unusual" about accepting free travel to and from his congressional district if Medico Industries offered it.[75]

Tom Medico, current president and CEO of Medico Industries, rejects any notion that his father, Philip, Sr., had ties to organized crime or that Bufalino was a silent partner in his family's business. "Russell Bufalino never owned any part of Medico Industries," Medico insisted in a recent interview. "The five Medico brothers owned equal shares of the business. If Bufalino had anything to do with our business, he probably came in some time to ask for machine parts. But the Pennsylvania Crime Commission made that accusation anyway. Since then, I always thought that I had to show others that I was a good person and a hard worker. But because we're Italian and we've been successful, people want to believe that we're Mafia. It's all garbage."[76]

Medico was also adamant that his company never benefited from Flood's influence:

> Dan Flood did not get a single contract for Medico Industries, though the newspapers certainly made it seem that way. Our government contracts came from buying agents in Rock Island, Illinois. These were purchasing agents for the military. They were the ones who received the money from the Defense Appropriations Committee. As a company-owned, company-operated business, Medico Industries always had to submit bids to these purchasing agents. My father was one of Dan Flood's constituents, like anybody else in the district. As the vice chair of

the House Defense Appropriations Subcommittee, Mr. Flood certainly couldn't award us any contract. That would be collusion. All contracts were awarded to the lowest quality bid and were received from the buying agent. That was the protocol.

Now, Mr. Flood *might* have taken some credit for getting more defense industry jobs in his congressional district. But the fact of the matter is that when any contract over one million dollars is awarded, the successful bidder must notify their congressman of the award and inform him of the number of jobs that will be made available. Again, that is the protocol. But people are going to believe what they want to believe. They see that Dan Flood traveled to Washington on our family's airplane, they say that he must be getting us government contracts. Well, it is true that Medico Industries had an airplane between 1960 and 1974 and that, on occasion, we offered Mr. Flood a ride if we were flying in his direction. Did Mr. Flood use the plane on a regular, weekly basis? No. Does the offer of an occasional plane trip to Washington make Medico Industries the beneficiary of influence peddling? Absolutely not.[77]

Recently declassified FBI documents establish, however, that Flood and Philip Medico, Sr., were "close personal friends" and that Medico Industries had "been awarded numerous U.S. Department of Defense munitions contracts" in the 1960s and 1970s.[78] A Justice Department investigation, conducted in 1978, alleged that those contracts were "obtained with the assistance of Flood," who circumvented the official bidding process to favor Medico Industries. In return, Medico Industries furnished the congressman "with the use of their corporate airplane and also chartered planes for Flood's personal use."[79] If true, the arrangement violated federal laws against racketeering and bribery. At the very least, it was a conflict of interest.

One of the alleged contracts would have allowed Medico Industries to "sell franchised heavy equipment to the Bahamas and Haiti," where Flood was interested in establishing a free port for the United States as well as a "possible fallback position for U.S. troops located at Guantanamo, Cuba." According to FBI documents, Flood was negotiating these arrangements with Haitian president Jean-Claude Duvalier and prime minister Lynden Pindling of the Bahamas.[80] Although the plan never came to fruition, it certainly reflected Flood's long-standing interest Latin American affairs. By creating an ongoing military and economic relationship with Haiti and the Bahamas, the congressman could insure that communism was contained in Cuba, lest it gain a greater stronghold in the Caribbean.

During the mid to late 1970s, most of Flood's forays into U.S. foreign policy were dictated by the Latin American concern. That he even dabbled in foreign and military affairs reflected his growing seniority in Congress. The voters returned him to Capitol Hill term after term because he placed the highest priority on constituent service. As long as he satisfied their needs, they didn't care much what he did in the arena of foreign policy. Few congressmen enjoyed that kind of flexibility, and fewer still were as successful in earning it.

Fig. 25. During the 1960s, President Lyndon B. Johnson's Great Society programs allowed Flood to channel millions of health, education, and welfare dollars into his district.

6

★　　★　　★　　★　　★

PORK-BARRELING THE GREAT SOCIETY

Dan Flood was a disciple of Franklin Delano Roosevelt's New Deal. He came to Washington in 1945 with a commitment to create legislation that would offer something to everyone in the Eleventh District: jobs and a higher minimum wage for the worker, tax rebates for businesses, subsidies for farmers, vocational training for the unskilled, welfare grants for the poor, health benefits for coal miners afflicted with black lung disease, and educational assistance for the young. By the 1960s, Flood's enviable position in the seniority system, along with the ascendancy of Lyndon B. Johnson to the presidency, allowed him to fulfill the pledges that he had made to his constituents.

Flood and Johnson were kindred spirits. Both were natives of economically depressed regions, which allowed them to identify with poor people. Both had been mentored by the legendary Speaker Sam Rayburn during their early years in the House of Representatives. Extraordinarily energetic and ambitious politicians, they developed well-earned reputations for hard work, attention to detail, and great skill at reconciling varied interests.[1] While Johnson rose quickly in the Senate, becoming majority leader in 1955, Flood employed his political talents in the House, where he ascended to chair of the Labor and Health, Education, and Welfare (Labor-HEW) Appropriations Subcommittee in 1967.[2] When Johnson, as president, introduced the most expansive legislative program since the New Deal, Flood exploited the effort to benefit his congressional district. In the process, he became one of the most successful pork-barrel politicians on Capitol Hill.

Lyndon B. Johnson, early in his unexpected presidency, called on the federal government to create a "great society" in the United States. Such a society would use its economic prosperity to create an ambitious program of social reform to address the needs of the poor, the elderly, and the displaced. "The challenge of the next half century," said Johnson, shortly after becoming president, "is whether we have the wisdom to use our wealth to enrich and elevate our national life," to prevent "old values" from being "buried under unbridled growth." Johnson's "great society" would strike a perfect balance between the "demands of morality and the needs of the spirit" and "the demands of commerce and a rising Gross National Product."[3]

Initially, Johnson capitalized on many measures begun by the Kennedy administration and saw them come to fruition by evoking the need to "honor the young president's memory." He revived Kennedy's civil rights proposal, which had been sidetracked in Congress. After the House of Representatives passed the bill, the Senate became bogged down in a lengthy filibuster. Johnson responded by persuading minority leader Everett Dirksen to work for cloture—a two-thirds vote to cut off debate—and passage soon followed. It was a masterful achievement. The Civil Rights Act of 1964 was the most far-reaching civil rights legislation enacted since the end of Reconstruction. The measure outlawed racial discrimination in all public accommodations and authorized the Justice Department to act with greater authority in school and voting matters. It also included an equal opportunity provision prohibiting discriminatory hiring on the grounds of race, gender, religion, or national origin in firms with more than twenty-five employees.[4] Had Johnson achieved nothing more than the Civil Rights Act, his administration would have been notable. But the measure was only the beginning of a far greater design.

Between 1964 and 1968, Johnson, with the sometimes-willing, sometimes-unwitting support of Congress, achieved a remarkable array of legislative initiatives designed to expand the social welfare system and eliminate poverty. Following Kennedy's lead, Johnson pressed for a tax cut to stimulate the economy. To gain conservative support, he agreed to hold down spending, and the tax bill passed. With the tax cut in hand, Johnson pressed Congress for an expansive program to eliminate poverty. "This administration today, here and now, declares unconditional war on poverty in America," asserted the president in his 1964 State of the Union address. "It is a total commitment by this president with the help of Congress and this nation to pursue victory over the most ancient of mankind's enemies." Johnson believed that poverty "threatened the strength of the nation and the welfare of the people." But if poverty could be eliminated, then "Congress will have won a more secure and honorable place in the history of the nation and the enduring gratitude of generations of Americans to come."[5]

The War on Poverty was the most ambitious and controversial part of the Great Society. Its centerpiece was the Economic Opportunity Act (EOA) of 1964, which created an Office of Economic Opportunity (OEO) to oversee a variety of community-based antipoverty programs. It also challenged the traditional belief among legislators that the best way to deal with poverty was simply to raise the incomes of the poor. Instead, the OEO proposed to help the poor help themselves through education, job training, and community development. The poor would be enlisted to establish and administer the very same programs designed to help them. Among the initiatives were: the Job Corps to help disadvantaged youth develop marketable skills; Volunteers in Service to America (VISTA), a domestic version of the Peace Corps, which sent middle-class young people into poor neighborhoods to do community service projects; the Model Cities program for urban redevelopment; legal services for the poor; the Food Stamp program; and Project Head Start, which offered preschool education for poor children. Many of these programs had already been proposed by the Kennedy administration, but Johnson would package them into omnibus legislation and cleverly title it the War on Poverty.[6]

Opposition to the initiative was immediate. Even before the omnibus bill was sent to Congress, the secretaries of Labor and HEW opposed the creation of the Office of Economic Opportunity to run Head Start, the Job Corps, and VISTA. They insisted that the appropriate executive departments, such as Labor and HEW, would provide greater resources and experience. Once the legislation was sent to Capitol Hill, lawmakers in both houses balked. Some argued that the new programs were part of already-existing or -proposed legislation for economic growth and welfare, including Social Security, housing programs, health care, unemployment compensation, and area redevelopment. Others insisted that poverty as a "problem" in the United States "has been grossly exaggerated." Still others were put off by the proposed one-billion-dollar cost of the legislation.[7]

Johnson shrewdly waited until the election of 1964 gave him the mandate he needed to enact his program. With 61 percent of the popular vote and 486 electoral votes, he scored a decisive victory over Republican Barry Goldwater. Just as important, the election gave Johnson Democratic majorities of 68–32 in the Senate and 295–140 in the House, allowing him to break the conservative Republican–Southern Democratic alignment that had stalled reform programs in the past.[8]

After the election, Johnson acted swiftly and decisively. He ignored the customary function of the president, which was limited to setting priorities and offering programs for the Congress to accept, reject, or adjust.[9] Obsessed with passing bills, Johnson established task forces to study and define major issues and persuaded selected senators and congresspeople to serve on those bodies, implicating them in what was traditionally an exclusively executive function. After the task forces issued their reports, he sent his aides to Capitol Hill to confer with key senators and congresspeople to learn how to secure passage of a particular bill, first at the committee level and later in the respective house. If a particularly sensitive issue was involved, he met in person with the chair of the appropriate committee.[10] Johnson's participation in the legislative process was unprecedented. In short, he used all the legislative genius he had learned during his years on Capitol Hill to achieve a domestic program that would not only be a landmark in history, but also one that would secure an enduring legacy for his presidency.

At a time when the federal government was committed to social welfare, Dan Flood was in the right place at the right time. His seniority in the House of Representatives and his shrewd manipulation of the legislative process would be useful to the voters back home. As a ranking Democratic member of the House Appropriations Committee, Flood exerted tremendous influence on Capitol Hill.[11] Appropriations controls the operation of the entire federal bureaucracy because of its responsibility to appropriate every dollar the federal government needs to function. The programs and operations of almost every federal agency depend on the particular interests and biases of ranking committee members. As a result, those members are aggressively courted by presidents, cabinet heads, generals, and admirals, as well as by fellow legislators in the House of Representatives. While the full committee has the final word on all spending, the several subcommittees allow members to specialize in a single area of the federal bureaucracy, and the chairs of those subcommittees are granted broad latitude on spending in their area of responsibility. The departments of Labor, and Health, Education, and Welfare were at the heart of Johnson's War on Poverty as well as the other Great Society initiatives he envisioned. Flood, as the fifth-ranking Democratic member of the Labor-HEW Appropriations Subcommittee, would exercise tremendous influence over the funding of Johnson's legislative program, a fact that was not lost on the president.[12]

Johnson actively courted Flood's support during the 1964 election. On October 14, he flew to the Eleventh District, where he spoke before a crowd of ten thousand people at the Avoca Airport. In his remarks, Johnson hailed the Area Redevelopment Act, which Flood cosponsored. "Almost 10,000 new jobs have been created in Pennsylvania by 124 ARA projects," he said. "Twenty-one of those projects have been in this immediate area. That has allowed us to bring unemployment down to 6% in Wilkes-Barre." Nor did he forget to single out his "good friend, Dan Flood," urging the crowd to "get your kinfolk to vote for your congressman come election day."[13] Flood certainly was a "good friend" to Johnson in the early days of his administration. Like other ranking Democrats on the House Appropriations Committee, he was responsible for ushering the one billion dollars appropriated for the War on Poverty through the Congress, thereby securing the Economic Opportunity Act of 1964. While the measure benefited economically depressed areas across the nation, Flood also saw it as a means of expanding the social welfare programs for his own congressional district. He made sure to lay the groundwork that would enable his district to be one of the first to benefit from the legislation.

During the summer of 1964, while the economic opportunity bill was being debated in Congress, Flood was busy networking with officials back home, familiarizing them with the legislation so they would be ready to take advantage of the various antipoverty programs once it was made law. He contacted E. V. Chadwick, Luzerne County's agricultural agent, to determine how many families would benefit from the EOA's $1,500 capital grants and $2,500 loans to supplement a farm family's income.[14] Similarly, Flood wrote to the Reverend A. Ward Campbell, president of the Luzerne County Mental Health Association, and asked for advice on how the "educational programs in the bill can be utilized."[15]

Realizing that the EOA would only fund those districts with carefully organized community action programs at the local level, Flood wrote to the presidents of the chambers of commerce in all the major towns and cities in his district and demanded that they "assign a special committee to examine the bill" to "determine how our area can take advantage of it." He insisted that the committee be "set up at once" and include civic and educational leaders as well as social workers. They would be required to "survey local needs under the bill," to "identify local agencies willing to cooperate in securing federal funding," and to "check any possible funding sources from the State of Pennsylvania so as to move along if or when the bill becomes law." Flood reminded the officials that "preliminary discussions like these must get under way at once for there is always a scramble when applications for grants and loans are filed with state and federal agencies." "Good early planning and filing is half the battle," he added. "Many cities with good early plans and applications are all granted funding, others were too late—the money was gone!"[16] His efforts paid off. When Congress passed the Economic Opportunity Act in late October, Flood had thirty-five agencies in his district ready and willing to cooperate in the programs designed by the legislation. The agencies included hospitals, school districts, colleges, and labor unions, among other public bodies.[17]

Wasting no time, in early November Flood contacted the mayors in his district and demanded that they join with the Welfare Planning Council of Wilkes-Barre, the body that would coordinate the antipoverty programs, to "develop a comprehensive program for Luzerne County."[18] By December 7, 1964, Luzerne County had established the first agency in the nation responsible for "coordinating and implementing a county-wide program to reduce or eliminate poverty," and was already drafting grant applications for Head Start and work training programs.[19] Still, the Pennsylvania legislator left nothing to chance.

Flood secured funding for two Head Start programs in the first year of availability, although they only lasted for a few weeks at the end of the summer. As a result, he urged Albert Danoff, president of the Wilkes-Barre Welfare Planning Council, to apply for additional OEO money to establish a yearlong Head Start program in the county. "I am sure you know that the OEO can wave the 10% local funding for this program if we can get credit for in kind contributions," Flood reminded him. "We need a county-wide Head Start program. It is of great importance in view of the President's directive that it should be a year-round operation and not just a hit-and-run job for just a few weeks in the summer."[20] When a similar request was made to Wesley Davies, superintendent of Luzerne County Schools, Flood met with resistance. Davies informed him that the school districts in the county were "not interested in Head Start for various reasons."[21] The congressman's response was swift and sarcastic. "I was greatly disappointed to learn that the Head Start program in Luzerne County was such a dismal flop!" Flood snapped. "And yet, it is perhaps, nation-wide, the one aspect of the Poverty Program which has won almost universal plaudits! What do *you* intend to do about it?"[22] Two days later, Davies responded more positively, informing Flood that "all school administrators in the county have been alerted to prepare plans in order to take advantage of the Head Start funding for 1966."[23]

Head Start was a tremendous success in Luzerne County, largely due to Flood's persistence and legislative maneuvering. The region received a total of $2,080,651 under the Elementary and Secondary School Aid Bill of 1966, most of which went to developing a more comprehensive Head Start program. Allegheny and Philadelphia were the only Pennsylvania counties to receive more funding in this area.[24] Flood also secured more than $145,000 in federal assistance for a work training program. The funding made it possible to offer employment and training to 365 high school students for an average of 10 hours per week over a period of 28 weeks.[25] By the end of the second year of the War on Poverty, Luzerne County was the beneficiary of 124 jobs carrying a payroll of $256,690, all of which were financed by the Office of Economic Opportunity. In addition, nine Community Action Projects had been established in the county, including: five Head Start programs conducted by the Hazleton, Northwest Area, and Wilkes-Barre school districts; an after-school tutoring program run by the Wilkes-Barre YMCA; a parent education program sponsored by the Family Service Association of the Wyoming Valley; and a Medicare Alert program, which assisted the eligible aged poor to sign up for health insurance.[26]

To insure that his district would receive federal funding, Flood was in constant contact with Sargent Shriver, Johnson's special assistant and director of the federal Office of Economic Opportunity. Dozens of letters passed between the two men between 1965 and 1966 as funding for the War on Poverty increased by another two billion dollars.[27] Of course, Flood always requested more money for his district. When he learned, for example, that the OEO awarded forty-one million dollars for four projects to assist the aged poor, he complained to Shriver that Pennsylvania's anthracite region "should have been selected for that money because it is well above the national average in age."[28] Similarly, when Flood was informed that the OEO had established and funded eight comprehensive Neighborhood Health Centers in major cities across the nation, he wanted to know why Wilkes-Barre hadn't been a beneficiary of the program.[29] Shriver didn't seem to mind the constant heckling. He admired Flood's persistence and did whatever he could for a representative he considered a "firm friend of the War on Poverty."[30] No doubt, Shriver supported Flood's proposal to make Wilkes-Barre the Economic Development Administration's regional headquarters for the eastern United States, the Virgin Islands, and Puerto Rico, an action that also insured the continued flow of federal funds into the congressman's district.[31]

To be sure, Flood exploited the War on Poverty for all the federal funding he could possibly secure. Thus he emerged in the mid-1960s as one of Capitol Hill's most effective pork-barrel politicians. But according to Rep. Jim Wright of Texas, "It would be a mistake to assume that [Flood's] idea of the national welfare never extended beyond the geographical boundaries of Pennsylvania's anthracite region." "Dan was very influential in sponsoring and securing the funding for the Great Society because he had a larger commitment to the poor and working class in this country," Wright insisted. "He was very committed to getting those bills through the House and used all his dramatic flair, rhetoric, and legislative expertise for that purpose."[32] Indeed, the legislation

Fig. 26. In 1965 Flood joined forces with Sen. Robert F. Kennedy (D-N.Y.) to expand the 1961 Area Redevelopment Act into the Appalachian bill, which delivered federal funds to economically depressed counties in Pennsylvania and several other states.

Flood sponsored did have its greatest influence on the lives of the nation's poor, elderly, and working class, and he did feel strongly for the plight of those people because they most closely resembled the population of his own district. In 1965, for example, he expanded the Area Redevelopment Act that he sponsored during the Kennedy administration into the Appalachian bill, which would provide federal grants to economically depressed regions in Kentucky, West Virginia, Virginia, Maryland, Pennsylvania, and upstate New York. Flood joined forces with Senator Robert Kennedy of New York to secure passage of the bill and, as he later boasted, "lo and behold, thirteen counties on the New York–Pennsylvania border turned up in Appalachia!"[33] While Flood's district received the most funding of any county in Pennsylvania, with four million dollars to fill abandoned mines and put out mine fires, millions more went to counties in the other states.[34]

The Model Cities urban redevelopment program was a similar issue. The bill, HR 7984, was intended to provide federal funding to redevelop inner-city ghettos across the nation. When the measure encountered trouble in the House of Representatives, Flood personally took charge of the matter. Persuading Speaker John McCormack to appoint him chair of the Committee of the Whole, Flood presided over the debate of a modified bill.[35] His intention was to control the usually lax atmosphere of the House by eliminating any unnecessary disruptions and curtailing droning partisan speeches so the session would be focused and the outcome favorable to the Model Cities legislation. Even before the committee was called to order, Flood asked the sergeant at arms and the doorkeeper to "direct all employees of the House to stay off the floor while this bill is before the Committee." The only exceptions were to be one staffer on each side of the aisle to report to the congresspeople. Next, Flood refused to allow a quorum call, which might have led to a longer session and hot tempers. Over the next two days, the Pennsylvania representative handled the gavel impressively. He was a stern but fair disciplinarian who often injected levity into the debate when it was needed. When a small group of legislators clustered in the aisle, for example, Flood boomed, "As far as this Tower of Babel over here to my right is concerned, the Chair requests the Sergeant at Arms to keep this aisle clear." The group immediately dispersed amid a cascade of chuckles.

At one point the debate became especially acrimonious. Contention arose over a plan to provide rent subsidies to low-income families who were spending more than 25 percent of their budgets on housing. It proved to be the primary obstacle to the passage of the bill. Eventually a roll call vote was taken and the measure passed, 208 to 202. Flood's effort to preserve absolute decorum in the debate had prevailed. His colleagues gave him a standing ovation for his skill and humor.[36] More important, Wilkes-Barre became the first city to accept financial assistance in a program that ultimately provided $181 million to clear entire city blocks of slums and replace them with new residential and commercial buildings.[37] But that figure was only a small percentage of the total expenditure for the Model Cities program.[38]

"It's no secret that Dan admired President Johnson for his Great Society programs," said Jim Wright, a congressional colleague from Texas. "He was a good soldier to the president, among the very best in Congress."[39] "Johnson knew he could rely on Dan to support the Great Society," said William Scranton, who served in Congress with Flood before becoming governor of Pennsylvania. "Dan was a 'straight-down-the-pike Democrat' in the House. He voted for everything the president wanted. Once, when I was governor, I received a phone call from President Johnson, who was concerned about getting the necessary votes for the Appalachia bill. After I gave him several names of congressmen from Pennsylvania, I reminded him, 'You don't have to worry about Dan Flood, Mr. President. You know he's with you.' And Johnson said, 'He sure is, right down the line!'"[40]

Flood's success in securing federal funding for his district allowed him to remain above the fray of local politics. Personal animosities, power struggles, and ongoing conflict plagued the Luzerne County Democratic organization. Many members of the rank and file did not acknowledge Dr. John Dorris as the chair of the county's party machine because "there was no tally of votes at the Nanticoke election" in June 1964. Instead, the pro-Dorris faction locked out their opponents—a group called the "Democratic Minute Men"—and "simply announced that their candidate was the winner."[41] They were able to get away with the ploy because state senator Martin Murray was Dorris's strongest supporter, or "coconspirator," as the Minute Men would have it.

Murray had begun his career as the manager of a family-owned shoe store in Wilkes-Barre and climbed the ranks of the local political ladder, first as a school board director in Ashley, then as treasurer of the Luzerne County Democratic Party, before he was elected to the Pennsylvania State Senate in 1956.[42] He tried to reconcile the competing interests within the party organization by actively courting the ward leaders. "Anything I wanted, Marty gave me," said Robert Loftus, the mayor of Pittston who served as county chair of the Democratic Party late 1960s. "If I wanted to fill a post, or needed funding for a municipal project, he gave it to me. It really amazed me because when I entered politics I was a greenhorn. I had been an insurance man by trade and then a bank director. But after I became county chairman, I had Marty deferring to my judgment. After a while, politics became second nature to me. All I had to do in those days was pick up a phone and call somebody. It was a matter of networking."[43] But there were other party leaders who distrusted Murray.

Frank Slattery of Wilkes-Barre, whose candidacy for county chair had been supported by the Minute Men, considered the state senator a "deadhead." Slattery, as mayor of Wilkes-Barre in the 1960s, was a champion of political reform. During his tenure, he instituted a commission form of government to clean up the corruption that had become rampant under his predecessors. Appointing himself the head of the police department, Slattery replaced the traditional custom of police officers serving their entire careers on one beat, with a system of rotation. He also partnered with Dan Flood to create the city's Urban Renewal Authority, Redevelopment Authority, and Planning Commission, agencies that directed the demolition and removal of aged buildings in blighted neoghborhoods.[44] As mayor of the largest city in Luzerne County, Slattery's needs were great. But time and again, Murray failed to act on his funding requests for critical internal improvements. Nor did Murray or Dorris always fulfill their important obligations as campaign organizers and fund-raisers during gubernatorial or presidential election years. That point became clear to Slattery in October 1964, when President Johnson visited the Wyoming Valley. "They won't do any work for the Johnson campaign," complained the Wilkes-Barre mayor. "They've raised very little money, they have no supplies, they don't even have a store to serve as party headquarters."[45] Predictably, when Dorris attempted to welcome the president at Avoca Airport, the Democratic Minute Men and their followers lambasted him with catcalls and jeers.[46]

Flood was careful to keep his distance. He refused to play one local official against another. Nor did he concern himself with the business of local politics, which was about patronage, primary campaigns, and jobs. As a result, the local party leaders, especially Dorris, resented Flood. "By the time Dr. Dorris became county chairman in the mid-1950s, Flood was a maverick," recalled Bernard Brominski, a Luzerne County judge. "Although he ran as a regis-tered Democrat, Flood could have run as an independent because he almost always ran unopposed in the primaries. Dorris never considered him an asset to the Democratic County row offices because he rarely campaigned for any of the party's other candidates. As a matter of fact, Dorris wanted someone to run against Dan in the primary. He even asked me. I think he knew it would have to be a person of Polish or Slovak extraction in order to offer a for-midable challenge."[47]

Dorris made no secret of his disdain for Flood. Once, in May 1967, Michael Clark, who covered local politics for the *Sunday Independent* in the mid-1960s, interviewed him about his role as county chair. After boasting about the control he exercised over state officials and ward leaders, Dorris conceded that he couldn't "tell that bastard Flood anything!" "None of us can," he added.

> Marty Murray or me. I thought I got rid of him in 1964. There was a judgeship open and I told Governor [David] Lawrence to put him on the federal bench. We'll get him out of the way by making him a judge. Well, he didn't fall for it. He's still in Congress and he's still wearing those silly goddamned white suits. You know the bullshit he gets away with? The voters love that son of a bitch because he goes on with his line about how much he does for them. If I hear that line one more time, I think I'll vomit. I just don't know how he gets away with it.[48]

Flood "got away with it" because he had established such a strong power base among the voters—*both* Democrat and Republican—that his reelection was a foregone conclusion. He placed the highest priority on constituent service. In an era when members of Congress turned increasingly to television, pollsters, and computer-generated letters to keep abreast of their constituents, Flood returned to Wilkes-Barre every weekend to meet with his. Dozens of constituents thronged to his district office on the tenth floor of the Miners' Bank Building just off Public Square to seek favors or to personally thank him for his help. The mustachioed congressman referred to these meetings as "confessionals" because the voters bared their souls to him, made requests, and, of course, expected help.[49]

A heavy schedule of wedding receptions, funerals, testimonial dinners, civic organization banquets, bar mitzvahs, and church bazaars consumed the balance of his weekends, and he made it a point to attend every one.[50] Flood would only appear for five or ten minutes at each event, but as soon as he walked through the door the floor was his. "You'd have to stop the dinner for him," recalled Monsignor Andrew McGowan, who often served as Flood's toastmaster. "He was the highlight, the entertainment for the evening." Most of the time, however, the congressman was unprepared and had to "wing it," not knowing the specific organization until he arrived. "He'd simply size up the audience and then, very eloquently, sing their praises and congratulate them on all the wonders they had done," said McGowan.[51]

Once, Flood almost embarrassed himself before the Sierra Club, an international organization dedicated to environmental concerns, which was holding its annual convention in Wilkes-Barre. Shortly after he stepped to the podium, the flamboyant congressman mistakenly began to praise King's College. McGowan, who was seated next to him, almost choked on his appetizer. He quickly jotted a note and handed it to Flood, informing him that this was the Sierra convention, not the local college. Without missing a beat, the former vaudevillian made a quick but smooth transition saying, "But King's College has nothing on the Sierra Club, which has done marvelous things for our society!" For the next five minutes, Flood mustered all the eloquence and appreciation in his repertoire to praise the "many contributions of the Sierra Club." When he was finished, the audience gave him a standing ovation. After Flood took his seat at the head table, he leaned over to McGowan and whispered, "Thanks, padre. Now, what the hell is the Sierra Club?"[52]

Most of the time, however, Flood would begin his remarks by congratulating the host or praising the deceased, and then segue into his accomplishments on Capitol Hill. It was a shrewd way of justifying his legislative activities and insuring reelection. Because he attended so many local public engagements, Flood gave the impression that he never left the Wyoming Valley, even though he seldom missed a congressional roll call. Flood always understood what the voters expected from their congressman, and he delivered. It wasn't just the millions he pork-barreled from the Great Society programs either. He missed no opportunity to attach legislative riders of wider regional or national priority to benefit his district, which, for example, lacked a modern highway when he first took office. Once, while sitting on a transportation subcommittee, Flood balked at voting for the creation of Interstate 81, linking Montreal and New Orleans. "Well, that won't do me any good," he complained after looking at a map of the plans.

"Why not?" asked John Rooney, chair of the subcommittee.

"Because I'm from Wilkes-Barre, Mr. Chairman, and that damn road is too far east of my district!"

Three weeks later, Flood got his way. The highway was to be rerouted through Wilkes-Barre, and Interstate 81 was born.[53] "I think the ribbon-cutting ceremony for Interstate 81 was Dan's proudest moment," recalled Catherine Flood years later. "Before that time, we were isolated from the rest of the country with only secondary roadways. That highway gave us the possibility for greater things. Dan really believed that 81 would bring a lot of jobs and revenue into the district."[54]

Flood took a proprietary interest in I-81 after it was constructed. It was not unusual, for example, for truckers driving down the interstate to be overtaken by his speeding white Cadillac convertible. Inside were the congressman; his wife, Catherine, with the couple's dachshund, Cocoa, seated on her lap; and an aide who was driving them back to Washington after a weekend in Wilkes-Barre. A parakeet named Tony was in a cage on the floor, and a goldfish bowl rested between the congressman's legs. "The only rule Mr. Flood had was never to tip over the goldfish bowl," recalled Ed Mitchell, a former aide who frequently drove the Floods between Washington and Wilkes-Barre. "And sometimes it was very difficult to oblige him."

Mitchell remembers one occasion when he was ordered to "overtake" a tractor trailer that had cut him off. As he accelerated the Cadillac, Flood propped himself against the passenger-side car door, leaned out the window, and began shaking his fist at the trucker. "You bastard!" he screamed. "I built this highway, damn it, and you're going too goddamned fast!"

The trucker, startled by the scene, slowed down. But in the process of accelerating, Mitchell had tipped over the goldfish bowl. "The fish were laying there on the car mat and the congressman's pants legs were soaking wet," recalled Mitchell. "I'm thinking to myself, 'Oh God, this is it for me! I was given one order—don't ever dump the fish bowl—and here I've gone and done it.'"

"To my surprise," Mitchell continued, "Mr. Flood very calmly told me to pull off at the next exit. We stopped at a small restaurant where he picked up the fish off the car mat, placed them back inside the bowl, and went inside. A few minutes later, he returned with a fresh bowl of water and a dry pair of pants. Not another word of the incident was ever mentioned."[55]

Flood was also proud of his ability to reward towns and boroughs in his district with their own post office. He was especially successful in 1962 when he finagled the federal funding to build twelve such facilities, the beneficiaries being Conygham, Drums, Duryea, Exeter, Harvey's Lake, Hazleton, Hunlock's Creek, Nanticoke, Nescopeck, North Wilkes-Barre, Shavertown, and West Pittston.[56] Individual constituents fared just as well. In addition to the work training and Head Start programs that Flood secured for the youth of his district, congressional appointments to Annapolis, West Point, and the air force and merchant marine academies were awarded to the most qualified high school graduates from the district.[57] Aside from the federal area redevelopment programs Flood secured to create jobs, he addressed the need for employment in his district through Department of Defense contracts. Flood persuaded the Pentagon, for example, to convert the Tobyhanna Army Base from a shooting range into the principal East Coast base for overhauling military communications equipment. Then he insured that the region's veterans were given first propriety for employment.[58] In fact, one-third of the thousands of records in the Flood Collection at Wilkes-Barre's King's College Library are case files of individual constituents the congressman assisted in securing employment, admissions to graduate schools or service academies, Social Security, or health insurance.[59]

Flood's effectiveness at constituent service was so remarkable that the voters considered him "one of their own."[60] At a 1964 testimonial dinner, he was even feted rather dramatically as "a man who has never forgotten the needs and aspirations of the people who elected him," and who had done so while "helping to shape this nation's history in its most crucial hours."[61] Predictably, the congressman's electoral success depended more on bipartisan support than on his relationship with the local Democratic Party, though the Eleventh District changed from a Republican to a Democratic domain during his congressional tenure. By 1970 the Republicans didn't even bother to run a candidate, and Flood easily defeated a third-party challenger by capturing 97 percent of the vote.[62]

The local newspapers were another key to Flood's success. In the 1950s and 1960s there were two major daily newspapers in Wilkes-Barre—the *Wilkes-Barre Record* and the *Times Leader*. Both were operated by the Wilkes-Barre

Publishing Company, established in 1939 and owned by three families: the Smiths, Hourigans, and Johnsons. Two members of each family sat on the executive board and unanimous consent was necessary to make any change. It was an extremely conservative operation.

Because the same publishing company owned the two newspapers, there was very little competition and little critical coverage of national politics. Reporters had to travel by public transportation to cover an event because there were no company cars. Nor did either newspaper employ a Washington correspondent, making them largely dependent on the wire services and press releases from Flood's office. If the congressman phoned the newsroom, the editor or senior reporter, both of whom were on a first-name basis with Flood, always took the call. Whatever he said was quoted verbatim in the next day's newspaper. If the congressman's press secretary, Larry Casey, or his administrative assistant, Gene Hegarty, issued a press release, it appeared, virtually intact, in print the following day.[63] "We all idolized him in the press," admitted James Lee, editor of the *Times Leader* in the 1960s. "It wasn't unusual for him to phone me from Washington and tell me what he was doing for his constituents. And it was impressive given the power he exercised in Congress. Any community that wanted a post office got one. Federal buildings were being built. Anything towns needed for redevelopment, he got. How can you give bad press to someone like that?"[64]

Lee also admits that Flood knew how to play the press to his advantage. "Dan flattered us," said the former journalist. "I remember one HEW Appropriations Subcommittee meeting that I attended with my wife. He began the meeting by saying, 'Let the record show that the distinguished editor of my hometown newspaper is here with his beautiful daughter.' Then, correcting himself, he said, 'No, I'm sorry. It's his lovely wife.' Now, if that didn't win points with me and the Mrs., nothing did."[65]

Essentially, Flood controlled the local press. If a controversy was taking place and he didn't want to comment on it, he would make himself unavailable until the storm cleared. Instead, he would have his staff run interference for him. During the summer of 1968, for example, Flood, who had been weakened by an earlier battle with esophageal cancer, contracted a case of sepsis. "He was so sick that he had to be hospitalized at Georgetown," recalled Edward Mitchell, one of Flood's legislative aides:

> Even after the hospitalization, the congressman's activities were severely limited. The only thing he did that summer was go onto the House floor to vote. [Administrative assistant] Gene Hegarty ran the staff. He stayed

in contact with the various executive departments, and fended off the press and local politicians when they called the office. He would say that Mr. Flood was on the House Floor, or conducting a subcommittee hearing, or attending a committee meeting, and then handle the matter himself. Especially important messages would be conveyed to the congressman, who would later return the phone call from the hospital or his apartment. Few people in the district knew that Mr. Flood was hospitalized for most of that summer and, at one point, was near death. Hegarty made it the world's best kept secret and the fact that the press wasn't as intrusive as it is today allowed him to keep that secret.[66]

If Flood needed the press to disseminate information, on the other hand, he was quick to issue a press release. Hundreds of press releases announcing federal funding and programs for the district, as well as the congressman's sponsorship of bills, were issued during his congressional career, sometimes as many as a dozen in a month's time.[67] At other times, Flood manipulated the press to help him win reelection. In 1971, for example, William A. Schutter, who was the U.S. Department of Housing and Urban Development's director of the Wilkes-Barre Model Cities program, challenged Flood's authority on a housing project that was being built in the district, and the conflict escalated. Schutter not only questioned publicly Flood's effectiveness as a legislator, but also vowed to run against him in the next election.[68]

When Flood learned of the challenge, he phoned Schutter and offered to pay for his nominating fee for the upcoming 1972 election. He also contacted HUD and requested that it do an audit of the Wilkes-Barre Model Cities program. Paul Golias of the *Times Leader* was assigned to cover the story. "A few days before Easter weekend, we were tipped off by Flood's staff that HUD had completed the audit and that it was very critical of Schutter's management of the local Model Cities program," recalled Golias in a recent interview. "The audit was eighty-two pages long and only four copies existed. One of my sources came through on Good Friday and I got my hands on one of those audits. But I had to sit on the story because the *Times Leader* didn't publish a Sunday edition at that time. I just had to hope that the *Sunday Independent* [the most politically scrutinizing of the papers and the only one to publish once a week] wouldn't dig up another copy of the audit or that there were no leaks to the radio or TV so the story would hold until Monday."

Fortunately for Golias, the *Independent* did not obtain a copy and the story held over the weekend. On the morning of Easter Monday, he met with

Schutter to do an interview. Feigning ignorance, Golias asked him how many pages composed the audit.

"Not many," replied Schutter, "maybe fifteen at most."

"Are you sure about that, Bill?" asked the reporter. "I've heard that the audit is much longer than that."

"Yeah, why would there be more?" he retorted. "There aren't any problems up here."[69]

Golias caught Schutter in a barefaced lie. The *Times Leader* broke the story that afternoon. It was extremely critical of Schutter, alleging that he had misused funds totaling more than $119,000, failed to meet evaluation procedures, paid salary rates for in-kind services in excess of the budgeted funds, and had not kept pace with the budget process.[70] Although Schutter successfully defended himself against most of the allegations, the incident led to his resignation, and his candidacy for Flood's congressional seat never made it past the primaries.[71] The lesson was clear: Flood wielded the power and influence to destroy the career of anyone in his district who challenged his authority. He could also achieve the objective quickly and in a very public way by manipulating the press to his own advantage.

Flood's relationship with the national press was very different. Reporters from the Associated Press and the United Press International News wire services, as well as the Washington press, scrutinized public officials much more closely. They employed highly experienced staffs on Capitol Hill that were assigned by states and regions to cover the House and the Senate.

According to John Cosgrove of the Associated Press, who later became president of the National Press Club, Flood "learned the hard way" when he first came to Washington in the 1940s. "Back then, Dan and Catherine were often seen at cocktail hour and dinner at the Mayflower Hotel, one of the city's best," he recalled.

> They also made their home there. Both of them were very flamboyant. In fact, Catherine made the national gossip columns for appearing in skin-tight leotards in skits that were put on by the Congressional Wives Club, and for smoking cigarettes that came in pastel-colored wrappers. That wasn't the kind of publicity that played well back in the anthracite region. When the wire services exposed them and word of their activities reached the Eleventh District, Dan was voted out of office in the next election. The attitude was, "We didn't send Dan Flood to Congress to show off. We need help and we want results!"

To his credit, Flood learned from that experience. He realized that he had to be more careful with the national press, that it was much more scrutinizing than the local press back in his district. When he was reelected in 1948, Dan returned to Capitol Hill and lived in a more modest apartment, adjacent to the Cannon Office Building where he worked. When he wasn't at the office, he was at his apartment working for his constituents, or back in the district meeting with them. He did his homework. He knew the issues. Just as important, he knew the voters— their families, their needs, and their interests.[72]

To be sure, Dan Flood was just as much a "show horse" as he was a "work horse." He quickly learned that with the national press, the *manner* in which he delivered his message was just as important as the message itself. "If you want people to pay attention to you," Flood once admitted, "you ought to have something distinctive about you, some particular way of attracting attention and keeping it."[73] Accordingly, the mustachioed legislator conducted his press interviews in white linen suits, dark shirts, white ties, silk top hats, and dark, flowing capes. He also delivered his opinions with the overly precise clipped accent of an old-fashioned stage actor and, on occasion, the profanity-laced vocabulary of a barroom civics teacher. "Dan Flood would be a national figure if hearings of the House Appropriations Committee or its Defense subcommittee were televised," insisted James Free of the Washington press corps. "He not only has firm opinions, but he voices them in clear, colorful, often blunt, language, frequently twisting the tips of his waxed mustache as if punctuating what he has to say. Best of all, from a reporter's point of view, Flood is allergic to formality."[74] He could also be self-deprecating. Once, when asked by Seth Kantor of the Scripps Howard News Service, how he maintained his Salvador Dalí–like mustache, Flood replied, "I give it a one-minute-waxing every morning. But you should see me after my shower, when the wax has washed away. It looks like the lower half of my face is full of shredded wheat!"[75]

At the same time, the national press took him seriously. "Dan wasn't just a buffoon in a cape and top hat," said Cosgrove. "Yes, he made good copy because of his flamboyance, but after he captured their attention and was asked to comment on an issue, he was sincere and showed his genuine intelligence. The national press was intrigued by him, just as much for his keen insight into legislation and the legislative process as for his colorful manner."[76] There were those journalists, however, who sought to discredit Flood. Chief among the muckrakers were Drew Pearson and his protégé, Jack Anderson, whose nationally syndicated "Washington Merry-Go-Round" columns constituted the most scathing press the congressman received in the 1950s, 1960s, and 1970s.

Pearson, a Quaker idealist, flattered himself as a "crusader" against the hard-line cold warriors on Capitol Hill. He was extremely skeptical of the military and its congressional supporters, believing that they fostered a mentality intolerant of dissent and individual rights. Anderson, a Mormon fundamentalist, would appear to be a contrasting character. Instead, his "cut-and-slash" method of investigative journalism complemented Pearson's. Together, they formed a powerfully influential partnership to expose those high-ranking military officers and legislators who might otherwise have been considered true patriots. Sometimes their instincts were correct. Pearson and Anderson were largely responsible for destroying the political career of Senator Joseph McCarthy, whose demagoguery and unfounded accusations against alleged Communist influence in the United States destroyed the lives many unde-serving individuals. Similarly, the two muckrakers exposed General Douglas MacArthur's gross misjudgment of the Korean War, forcing Truman to dismiss the highly decorated military leader.[77] But Pearson and Anderson were not always correct in their assessment of Flood.

Pearson accused the Pennsylvania legislator of being an "imposter" who used his self-confessed patriotism as a cover for his unchecked ambition to increase his influence in military affairs.[78] He also accused Flood of "leaking classified information" for the same end.[79] Anderson was even more antagonistic, crafting an image of the anthracite congressman as a "crook" whose activities needed to be carefully scrutinized. Once he took over the "Washington Merry-Go-Round" in 1969, Anderson devoted a column to Flood almost every year. Once he alleged that Flood obtained a large defense contract for Medico Industries, which Anderson maintained had ties to organized crime.[80] Another column charged the congressman with pressuring the Department of Health, Education, and Welfare to award a five-hundred-thousand-dollar contract to an unqualified Wilkes-Barre firm.[81] All of the accusations were unfounded.

"Dan was a straight shooter," insisted Gerald Ford, one of Flood's closest allies in Congress. "He was also a very effective deal maker, both in Pennsyl-vania and in Washington. There's nothing wrong with that, though the press didn't always see it that way. As a congressman, Dan Flood had an obligation to his district to get the federal government to support economic redevelop-ment there after the mines closed. The economic needs of his district fully justified the deals he made and I'd be surprised if there were any ethical improprieties involved. Dan just had too much respect for the integrity of Congress to do something like that."[82]

Despite all the pressures of his office, Flood genuinely enjoyed being the congressman of Pennsylvania's Eleventh District. Each morning, he would wake up, shower, wax his mustache to its dagger-pointed ends, and dress in clothing with a costume effect. At precisely 9:00 A.M. Catherine would take his arm and escort him into the hallway of their apartment building. As her matinee-idol husband stepped into the elevator she bid him farewell with the vaudevillian reminder to "cut 'em deep and let 'em bleed!" A full day of committee meetings, individual appointments, and staff briefings followed, interrupted only by the necessity of casting his vote on the House floor. Flood, at work at his desk, burned the lights in his Cannon Office Building suite late into the night, sometimes four or five days a week, even delaying his trip back home to the district when absolutely necessary.[83]

Interestingly, the demanding schedule actually seemed to exhilarate Flood, especially after he had lost half his body mass to a severe bout with esophageal cancer in 1962. Once portly and round faced, he came out of the operation rail thin. While his recovery was viewed by his physicians as a near miracle, it left the congressman weak and in constant pain.[84] Through sheer will, Flood managed to represent the interests of a congressional district that by 1966 had expanded to include Carbon and Monroe counties. It was, as Flood would say, a "tough act" for an "old stage player," but he did it.[85]

Whatever aspirations Dan Flood held for higher office were dashed by his poor state of his health. He had the opportunity to run for the U.S. Senate earlier in his career, and his political platform would have been very attractive to voters in a declining industrial state like Pennsylvania. But Flood's ambitions were intimately tied to the needs and interests of his congressional district. "Dan loved being a congressman," said his wife, Catherine. "Once, he was asked to run for the Senate and he refused because he felt that he wouldn't be able to serve the needs of the people who were most important to him, the people of his district. He was also offered a federal judgeship. It was a lifetime appointment with tremendous security. But Dan turned that down too because the people of the district *always* came first for him."[86] Even within the House of Representatives, Flood never sought to become the Speaker, the most influential post in the chamber. Instead, he aspired to become the chair of the Defense Appropriations Subcommittee, a post that would allow him to control the purse strings of the military.[87] Considering his obsession with the armed forces and the temper of the cold war era, Flood, if he had secured that position, would have become the equivalent of a "civilian Joint Chief of Staff." Instead, his power and influence on Capitol Hill burgeoned when he was named the chair of the HEW Appropriations Subcommittee in 1967.

Flood was the beneficiary of a unique set of circumstances. Appointed to the HEW Appropriations Subcommittee in 1964, he immediately became the fifth-ranking Democrat on it.[88] Two years later, when three members of the Democratic majority were defeated in their bids for reelection, only Rep. John Fogerty of Rhode Island had greater seniority than Flood. Usually a member of Congress serves at least ten years on a subcommittee before advancing to the position of chair. But when Fogerty died in January 1967, Flood became the new chair of HEW Appropriations with less than three years' experience on the subcommittee.[89] With the appointment, he had become one of thirteen subcommittee chairs of the House Appropriations Committee, a group so powerful that they were known in Congress as the "College of Cardinals." The results of the 1966 congressional election had also brought Flood a step closer to his ultimate goal, as he was named vice chair of the Defense Appropriations Subcommittee. Those two positions allowed Flood to exert near veto power over the three-hundred-billion-dollar federal budget, especially on pork-barrel legislation that decides the funding for every federal project in every congressional district in the country.[90] "Defense and HEW means two-thirds of the budget goes through my hands," he boasted. "That's a big role for an old actor. Luckily, I'm a nice fellow. I can help out a lot of nice people."[91]

The HEW Appropriations Subcommittee was responsible for funding the Great Society. Its jurisdiction covered all the annual appropriations for the Department of Labor and most of the appropriations for the Department of Health, Education, and Welfare, as well as the funding for such related agencies as the Office of Economic Opportunity, the Railroad Retirement Board, the National Labor Relations Board, and the Corporation for Public Broadcasting. Considering the amounts appropriated from trust funds for Social Security, Medicare, unemployment compensation, and railroad retirement, HEW Appropriations was responsible for $31 billion when Flood first joined the subcommittee. Ten years later, in 1974, HEW Appropriations controlled $118.8 billion, or 38 percent of the total federal budget.[92] With such a considerable, fourfold increase, Flood and the members of his subcommittee were under constant pressures from lobbyists and interest groups to fund various projects. Under those circumstances, the Pennsylvania legislator established two hard and fast rules about which kinds of projects would be funded. First, "all subcommittee recommendations would be based on a review of budget documents and three months of hearings with government and public witnesses" to determine which projects were truly worthy. Second, the subcommittee would fund bills that "meet social needs but will not be subject to a veto which cannot be overridden" when they reached the House floor.[93] Of course, there was a third, "unofficial" rule, namely to ensure that Flood's own pork-barrel projects were given top consideration. And regarding that final rule, he was largely successful.

After two decades on Capitol Hill, Flood was intimately familiar with the legislative process and how to work it to his advantage. Like his mentor, Sam Rayburn, Flood was a master of the quid pro quo (an equal exchange or transaction). He worked his will through patronage, horse-trading, influence peddling, and stentorian eloquence. He saw Congress as a trading arena in which the representatives' individual interests and goals were harmonized through the time-honored techniques of bargaining, reciprocity, and payoff. The most successful players exercise the ability to initiate, monitor, and complete transactions, settle disputes, and store political credits and debts for future negotiations. Theoretically, members of Congress function on an equal footing, enjoying a certain degree of formal influence over lawmaking and over their power base in the electorate "back home." In reality, however, only those who enjoy the greatest security are able to exercise the most clout. They are true leaders who have built up a large amount of goodwill and acquired influence with congressional colleagues and constituents so that they have a reservoir of power to draw on as needed.[94] Flood was one of those few.

Rarely did another representative risk antagonizing him, realizing that Flood's goodwill as chair of HEW Appropriations was necessary to secure the money he wanted for district projects that could result in his reelection or defeat. Just as rarely was Flood challenged on the House floor. The daily demands on representatives make it difficult for them to become fully conversant with appropriations bills. Thus the collective tendency is to accept the judgment of the Appropriations Committee members, who have the responsibility of determining the merits of agency spending requests. Flood held that responsibility for all bills regarding labor, health, education, and welfare. When he defended his appropriation bills on the floor of the House—bills requiring billions of federal dollars—it was not unusual for him to secure passage without a single voiced dissent or an amendment being offered.[95]

Even the Republicans' accession to power in 1969 under the presidency of Richard Nixon failed to reverse the trend toward an expanding national government begun by the Great Society, or Flood's influence as HEW Appropriations chair. One of his greatest victories, and a fine illustration of his legislative maneuvering, was the passage in 1969 of the Coal Mine Health and Safety Act.

The act was the culmination of a decade-long battle that Flood had been fighting to halt the spread of anthracosilicosis, or black lung disease, a respiratory illness caused by the inhalation of coal dust. The medical community first identified the disease in the late nineteenth century when miners complained of shortness of breath and many began coughing up blood. But the combined failure of government, medicine, and industry to halt the spread of the disease— or even recognize it as a serious health hazard—resulted in the suffering and death of hundreds of thousands of American miners. Nor did the UMWA push for a solution. Union concern for its alliance with mine operators prompted UMWA president Tony Boyle to argue that the UMWA Welfare and Retirement Fund "took care of the miners' health care needs" and prohibited any political activity with regard to workers' compensation coverage, occupational disease prevention programs, or safety legislation related to black lung.[96] In the absence of any federal or industrial action, the Pennsylvania legislature, in 1965, amended its Occupational Disease Act to compensate anthracite and bituminous miners who had contracted black lung. On March 11, 1969, West Virginia, another major coal-producing state, signed a similar measure into law. Federal action followed swiftly in response to pressure from Flood and Rep. Ken Hechler of West Virginia.[97]

Testifying before the U.S. Senate Labor Subcommittee, Flood, on March 20, 1969, called black lung "the most important concern in [his] district for the last century."[98] Citing a 1963 study by the Public Health Service, the Pennsylvania congressman detailed the prevalence of black lung among active Appalachian coal miners being approximately 15 percent. "Severity of the disease increases among workers with twenty or more years underground," he noted, "with the high risk group being age fifty and over." Flood concluded his testimony by proposing that the federal government be "given the proper authority and funds to improve control methods for the reduction of coal dust."[99] Afterward, he put his office staff to work on a bill to promote a safe working environment for miners. Among the major reforms were:

1. To establish a permissible limit on coal dust at 3 milligrams per cubic meter of air and require that the limit be reduced to 2 milligrams within three years.

2. To improve ventilation or use water with mechanical coal-cutting machinery to reduce airborne dust and protect miners' lungs.

3. To insure that all coal operators comply with these safety standards and cooperate with the states in implementing research, development and training programs in order to prevent mine accidents and diseases acquired from coal mining.

4. To compensate victims of anthrasilicosis, or "black lung disease," with a federal benefit of $136 per month for a maximum of seven years, after which the states are required to pay the cost.[100]

Fig. 27. Rep. John H. Dent (D-Pa.), a powerful member of the House Labor Committee, cosponsored the Coal Mine Health and Safety Act of 1969.

Flood did everything in his power to insure that the bill would pass. His friend, Rep. John Dent (D-Pa.), a powerful member of the House Labor Committee, managed the bill on the floor, while Flood had himself appointed chair of the Committee of the Whole. Sensing that he didn't have a sufficient number of votes for passage, Flood held up the roll call vote until sympathetic members returned to Capitol Hill from their districts.[101]

On the day of the vote, Flood suddenly discovered that some swing votes were shifting. "Representatives from the steel and asbestos plant districts wanted to know why they shouldn't be included," he explained. "I knew I had to do something quick."[102] Taking to the floor of the House, Flood, with all the sartorial splendor he could muster, delivered what was probably the most impassioned speech of his entire congressional career.

"I may say, Mr. Chairman, that I never thought I would live to see the day when this bill would be before this House," he began, seemingly out of breath. "I am the only spokesman left in the House of Representatives who represents a hard coal district. When I came here we had 30,000 men working in the anthracite district. Now we have 3,000. However, [cough] we have 23,000 suffering from black lung. We have known about that miner hazard for a long time. Both sides of my family [cough] have worked and died in the mines from anthracosilicosis and members of my wife's family on both sides have worked under these conditions for a hundred years." Another pause. Flood was wheezing now, like an afflicted coal miner.

"If one were to review the history of workmen's compensation for occupational diseases in this country, one would find that these laws, for the most part, [cough] have been inadequate and so inflexible that they have not been able to deal with new disease problems."

Flood went on to detail the history of occupational diseases and the discovery of black lung by the Public Health Service, frequently interrupting his speech to cough or wheeze like a victim of black lung. Being careful to identify both bituminous (soft coal) and anthracite (hard coal) miners in Pennsylvania as well as West Virginia, Flood noted that "statistical studies indicate that the death rate for coal miners is about twice that of the general working male population." Again, the mustachioed legislator paused to catch his breath.

"One of the great injustices today under the compensation laws of the States is the inability of the States to give aid to miners suffering from black lung who are not receiving compensation [cough] either because their claims for benefits have been denied, or because their claims have expired."

"You have to be born and raised in the coal fields [cough] to fully understand the dangers of the work," he continued, struggling to catch his breath. "There is a hopeless, endless suffering of the man . . . "

"Excuse me," he said. "As I was saying, [cough] the endless suffering of the man struggling with 'miner's asthma' or 'black lung' . . . "

Again, Flood interrupted his speech with a guttural noise followed by an intense bout of coughing.

"There is an endless desperation of the widows and dependents of these afflicted miners, who watch helplessly [cough] as the years of progressively worse illness unfold, ending in a painful death." Flood paused, doubled over, gagging and wheezing in a desperate effort to catch his breath.

"Afterwards, the widow and her dependents try to live on a pension that is far below the poverty level." Once again, the vaudevillian congressman was seized with a coughing jag.

The speech went on for another twenty minutes, interrupted by simulated wheezing and coughing bouts. Flood explained the benefits of the bill for the afflicted miners and the advantages of federal reimbursement to progressive states with comprehensive workers' compensation laws.

"So, I come here today as an old friend and an old neighbor representing the hard coal miners," he concluded. "I never worked in the mines myself. I worked outside, but I lived over them. I thank God for this House of Representatives and for the efforts of this committee and especially those of the gentleman from Pennsylvania, Mr. Dent."[103]

Flood had given his colleagues a firsthand account of what it was like to suffer from black lung disease. "You can't get away with that kind of performance very often," he admitted afterward. "I went pretty far—a very stylized performance in full costume. I pulled out all the stops."[104]

"It was an extremely poignant speech," recalled Rep. Joseph McDade of Lackawanna County. "Floody made these sounds that were so painful that many of the members were literally cringing. By the time he was through, everyone in the House understood just how important the issue was. I don't think he received more than a few nay votes."[105]

The bill passed the House almost unanimously. "Ordinarily, speeches don't change votes," said Speaker of the House Thomas "Tip" O'Neill, "but this one did. It was one of the two or three most impressive speeches I've ever heard. Most of us hadn't ever heard of black lung before that day. But that speech completely killed the opposition. Flood received a standing ovation for it." Rep. Robert Casey of Texas agreed. "You won't find a similar piece of legislation on the books, not for the steel workers or the asbestos workers or the textile workers," Casey said. "Flood convinced the rest of us that he had more afflicted miners in his district than anywhere else. I can assure you that you won't find any black lung in Texas, yet the whole delegation voted for it."[106] According to Rep. Fred Rooney, who represented Pennsylvania's Lehigh Valley, Flood was able to persuade members from states as diverse as Texas and Oklahoma to vote for the measure "because the members who represented those areas of the United State had such a fine regard for him and his diligent pleading for help for the problems in the anthracite region." "Dan was able to register his points intellectually as well as emotionally and I think that that had a lot to do with his success as a legislator in general," he added.[107]

When the measure passed the Senate by a vote of seventy-three to twenty-seven, it appeared that Flood had prevailed. Then, in December, President Nixon, who had previously supported the legislation, threatened to veto it strictly on the basis of the black lung provision. He was concerned about the inflationary impact that the $136 monthly payments to each victim would have on the federal budget, totaling as much as $385 million. Nixon felt that the payments should be the responsibility of the state, not the federal government.[108]

Congressional Democrats launched a protest, insisting that the maximum cost would be closer to $60 million. Congressman John H. Dent, who cosponsored the bill, convened a joint meeting of the House and Senate Appropriations Committees to resolve the issue. At that meeting, Flood proposed that an additional $10 million be added to the bill to cover the cost of the black lung payments.[109] The motion passed unanimously and the legislation was signed into law by the president on December 30, 1969.[110]

Flood hailed the Federal Coal Mine Health and Safety Act of 1969 (Public Law 91-173) the "best mine health and safety bill in the world."[111] Nearly twenty-five thousand affected coal miners in his district began receiving $165 a month in the first year of the law's enactment, and the federal expenditure totaled more than $300 million.[112] But the celebration was premature. "In 1970, after the passage of the act, our office actually hired staffers just to handle black lung cases," recalled Michael Clark, a former Flood aide. "The traffic of business was unreal. As it turned out, too many miners were being rejected for compensation because they hadn't been down in the mines long enough, or because the medical community couldn't find any trace of the disease through X-rays. There was a problem with the way the law was written."[113]

According to the new law, black lung payments were to be offset against Pennsylvania state benefits, including workers' compensation, unemployment compensation, or any other state disability payments requiring an employer's contribution.[114] In addition, some miners and widows were denied benefits because the law required proof of disability or death due to black lung arising from employment in the coal mines. Such "proof" was determined primarily through chest X-rays. If a chest X-ray revealed that a miner had "complicated pneumoconiosis," the law deemed him "disabled." But if the disease had not advanced to the complicated stage, he was deemed not "disabled" and still able to work.[115]

In March 1971 the Anthracosilicosis League of Pennsylvania, a women's auxiliary composed mostly of widows of coal miners, sent Flood a petition to consider them for benefits. The petition had more than one thousand signatures and requested that a statute of limitations of ten years or more of working in the mines be established for black lung benefits.[116] Flood immediately took up their cause, promising to "do all that is possible to amend the act and urge Social Security to pay some of the claims that have been denied."[117] He challenged the law's "proof" of black lung as being determined solely through X-rays by requesting a study from researchers at the National Institute of Environmental Health Sciences in North Carolina. That study revealed that black lung may not be detected by X-rays.[118] With that evidence in hand, Flood composed a series of amendments to Title IV of the 1969 coal mine law. The first amendment removed the provision that X-ray evidence or the lack of it was the only determining factor in the denial of black lung pension requests. A second amendment eliminated black lung as one of the disabilities classified under the Social Security Act, thereby guaranteeing victims and their families that they would not be deprived of other federal benefits. A third amendment extended the law to December 1975 to give states sufficient time to establish the administrative framework to run the black lung program. A fourth amendment removed the word "underground" from the 1969 law so that strip miners could also receive black lung benefits. Finally, a fifth amendment assured that "double orphans"—those children whose fathers died of black lung and whose mothers were also deceased—would be eligible for payments. These amendments were packaged together in the Black Lung Benefits Act of 1972, which passed both houses of Congress by mid-April and was signed into law by President Nixon on May 19, 1972.[119]

The act was a blessing to afflicted miners like Bill Barnes, who fought a daily battle against black lung. Forced to spend the rest of his life attached to an oxygen inhaler, Barnes was the most recent victim in a family of miners that had died of black lung. "I'm just waiting my time," he admits. "There's no work I could do, and you can't collect Social Security until you're sixty-two, and then it's only $165 a month. How ya goin' to live on that? It's only because of Dan Flood that I have a chance of living a little longer."[120]

Flood publicly admitted that his focus on a specific need like black lung had "cast [him] as a villain among the new wave of reformers on Capitol Hill who favor more generic approach to health care." It was pork-barrel politics at its finest. But he was quick to point out that he had also supported more generic programs for the aged, like Medicare, as well as "integrated or allied services" with a greater national impact. It wasn't an "either-or" proposition for Flood. "We are all striving for the same thing—better human services for all Americans," he insisted. To that end, Flood suggested that it will take a "blend of specific and generic approaches to deal with the human needs of our time."[121] That is, as long as the generic approaches didn't compromise the specific needs of his congressional district.

When Frank Carlucci, the new director of the Office of Economic Opportunity, informed Flood in 1970 that some of the OEO programs in his district would have to be cut back in keeping with nationwide reductions, the HEW Appropriations chair simply reminded him that "there comes a time when every man must learn to rise above principle." Carlucci, who was born and raised in northeastern Pennsylvania, duly adjusted the funding in the entire state just to keep the program intact in Flood's district.[122]

"There aren't many programs originating from Washington that we haven't participated in," noted Edgar Lashford, director of the Wilkes-Barre Chamber of Commerce in the early 1970s. "Flood finds them and he's on the phone telling you to get a committee together to apply for them. From the time he first calls, you better believe you'll get a couple of letters a week asking what you've done and telephone calls at all hours of the night. He'll either have us go to Washington to meet with a representative of the given funding agency, or they'll come up here. They'll even fill in the applications for you if you need the help. I shudder to think of the frustration we'd encounter if Flood wasn't in Washington."[123]

In the end, the War on Poverty, and the Great Society of which it was part, left the nation with a mixed legacy. While the programs permanently expanded the American welfare and social insurance system, mounting political opposition to the community action programs, as well as budgetary pressures caused by the expansion of the Vietnam conflict, brought the War on Poverty to a premature end after 1967. Similarly, the largest Great Society programs—Medicare and Medicaid—proved to be two of the most costly programs in the federal budget and fueled later conservative arguments that the federal government is not an appropriate vehicle for solving social problems.[124] But for Dan Flood and the Eleventh District, the War on Poverty and the Great Society were godsends.

Flood seized the opportunity presented by the Great Society to become the consummate pork-barrel politician on Capitol Hill in the 1960s. In the process, he channeled millions of federal health, education, and welfare dollars into his congressional district. Despite the criticism of colleagues and all the negative press he received, Flood never saw a conflict of interest between the national interest and the welfare of his constituents. He had matured politically during the Great Depression and came to Washington as New Deal Democrat. Both of those experiences influenced his approach to politics in a profound way. When he had the opportunity to sponsor and pass measures that would assist the working class and the poor, especially in his district, he used all his legislative clout to make it happen. Lyndon Johnson understood that and probably admired it because he was cut in the same mold.

When Johnson died in 1973, Flood offered a moving tribute to him on the House floor. "I am proud to say that Lyndon Johnson was a friend of mine," he began. "We served together when he was a member of the House, we worked together on legislation when he was a majority leader in the United States Senate; and we joined together when he was President to create new programs in the fields of labor, health education and welfare." "Lyndon Johnson made the dreams of the poor and the sick and the aged and the minorities a reality, too," Flood continued. "Medicare, Federal Aid to Education, better housing, Head

Start, the Job Corps, Model Cities, Appalachia, and Civil Rights are among the programs that exist today because he was a master legislative technician, the best I ever knew. He seemed to be able to make the impossible—possible."

"Lyndon Johnson was a man who never forgot the need for a good education," Flood said as he concluded his tribute. "He was a man who never forgot that the government is to do for the people that which they cannot do for themselves. Above all, history will surely remember him for that."[125]

It was an epitaph that might have easily been Flood's own.

7

RECONSIDERING VIETNAM

The Great Society not only allowed Dan Flood to channel millions of federal dollars into his congressional district, but also gave him tremendous national influence. At a time when the federal government was committed to social reform, Flood's positions as chair of the House Appropriations Subcommittee for Labor and Health, Education, and Welfare, and vice chair of the Defense Appropriations Subcommittee gave him near veto power over the three-hundred-billion-dollar national budget. But over the course of the late 1960s and early 1970s, the two roles would come into serious conflict with each other.

As U.S. involvement in the Vietnam War escalated, Flood realized that the federal revenue earmarked for that conflict was being siphoned off the Great Society programs he so enthusiastically embraced. Beginning in 1964, the U.S. government would spend over $140 billion on the war, enough money to fund urban renewal projects in every major American city. Flood found it difficult to reconcile his hawkish views with the necessity of limiting defense spending to save the War on Poverty at home. Publicly, the Pennsylvania congressman would be a strong supporter of American involvement in Vietnam throughout the war, but in subcommittee hearings on defense spending he expressed his growing concern about the cost of the conflict.

The original reasons for U.S. involvement in Vietnam seemed to be logical and compelling for the leaders of the national security and military establishments, though our current understanding reveals their naiveté. The cold war ideology that dominated U.S. foreign policy after World War II held that the principal threat to national security and world peace was a monolithic communism that emanated from the Soviet Union. Thus communism anywhere in the world was, by definition, an enemy to American interests and had to be contained by the United States and its allies. Vietnam, a narrow, thousand-mile-long stretch of land along the Asian rim, had by the early 1960s become one of the trouble spots.[1]

Before World War II, Vietnam was part of the French colonial territory of Indochina. Seized by Japan during the war, the French had considerable difficulty in reestablishing control there. The French faced the opposition of the Viet Minh, a pro-Communist and strongly nationalist organization led by Ho Chi Minh, who had declared Vietnam an independent republic in 1945. Based in the north, the Viet Minh was supported by the Soviet Union and later Communist China. For almost ten years, France fought a costly battle against the powerful guerrilla forces of the Viet Minh. Finally, despite increased aid from the Truman administration, the French decided that the costs of the empire in Asia were too high in soldiers and money.

In 1954 France accepted the independence of Vietnam as well as Laos, Cambodia, and other parts of Indochina. Vietnam was partitioned between Communist and non-Communist forces along the seventeenth parallel until free elections could be held to provide a single government for the entire country. The elections, scheduled for 1956, were never held. As a result, North and South Vietnam went their own ways, each aligning itself with one of the world's great power blocs: the Soviet Union for the North and the United States for the South.[2]

Eisenhower, a firm believer in the "domino theory," threw his support behind South Vietnam's autocratic president, Ngo Dinh Diem, fearing that if the Communists succeeded in controlling Vietnam they would eventually control all Southeast Asia.[3] Despite over one billion dollars of U.S. aid between 1955 and 1961, the South Vietnamese economy continued to fail and internal security deteriorated. Capitalizing on grievances among the peasants, Communist agitators in South Vietnam revolted against Diem's government in Saigon, the nation's capital. In 1960 the Communists established the South Vietnamese Liberation Front, a political organization to support the South Vietnamese guerrilla terrorists known as the Viet Cong, whose stated purpose was "to seize control of their country."[4]

Strongly aided by Ho Chi Minh's government in Hanoi, the Viet Cong's success in South Vietnam convinced new president John F. Kennedy to follow Eisenhower's lead and increase American aid to South Vietnam. Kennedy shared Ike's concern over the domino effect in Southeast Asia and the necessity of preserving U.S. credibility around the world by supporting anti-Communist regimes. But he did not agree with Eisenhower's belief in the military doctrine of "massive retaliation"—that is, to maintain a credible deterrent against Communist aggression, the United States needed to give top priority in the defense budget to the air force and nuclear weaponry. Such a doctrine allowed Eisenhower to balance the budget by cutting defense spending and keeping the United States out of another protracted, limited conflict in a distant land (something he believed the American people would not support after Korea). Instead, Kennedy, secretary of defense Robert McNamara, and the chair of the Joint Chiefs of Staff, General Maxwell Taylor, believed in a military doctrine of "flexible response," which stressed multiple alternatives ranging from subversive insurgency, to conventional warfare, to a limited nuclear war, and finally to unlimited nuclear war.

Kennedy was not opposed to expanding the U.S. nuclear arsenal. But he viewed any nuclear advantage as part of the flexible response strategy, one that would further a policy of "peace through strength" that recognized "diplomacy" and "political engagement" rather than war as the means of settlement. To achieve that objective, the Kennedy administration continued to enhance the nation's nuclear arsenal while simultaneously strengthening its ability to fight conventional wars by expanding and reinforcing ground forces overseas and creating a strategic reserve of ground and air forces at home.[5] "Flexible response," in other words, allowed Kennedy to keep "one foot in the Cold War, and another foot in a new world" where the means and objectives of warfare would be very different.[6]

The new paradigm was at distinct odds with the U.S. military establishment, however, which saw itself as being marginalized by the Kennedy administration. The Joint Chiefs of Staff and other military officers in the Pentagon chaffed at the doctrine of "flexible response." They viewed Vietnam strictly in military terms, just as they did World War II and Korea. They believed that any military action short of large-scale deployment and the possible use of nuclear weaponry would result in defeat and weaken U.S. credibility abroad. Such a limited view ignored political considerations, as well as the fact that the conflict was an *internal revolution*—not an international Communist conspiracy—that involved many aspects of Vietnamese society.[7]

Disagreement also focused on McNamara's management style. Unlike former defense secretaries who mediated the partisan disputes between the various service branches, McNamara was autocratic. Shortly after his appointment, he embarked on a comprehensive program to eliminate waste and inefficiency in the Pentagon and quickly lost patience with the Chiefs' constant squabbling and unresponsiveness to his demands. When Kennedy gave him carte blanche to centralize authority in the Department of Defense, McNamara, the former CEO of the Ford Motor Company, hired his own staff of bright young civilian analysts. These "Whiz Kids" had worked for think tanks and research corporations and shared McNamara's experience with analytical methods and statistics. Eager to apply quantitative analysis to the problems of the Defense establishment, they ignored the proposals of the Chiefs and other officers in the Pentagon, which were based solely on "military experience." The Pentagon, on the other hand, distrusted statistical analysis and insisted that McNamara and his Whiz Kids lacked the actual operational experience to employ such analysis in a meaningful and sophisticated way. Taylor, the JCS chair, was used to run interference for the administration by misleading the Chiefs, the press, and the National Security Council whenever expedient.[8]

This model of decision making, and the doctrine of "flexible response" that informed it, exerted civilian control over what had once been almost exclusively the purview of the Pentagon. It also resulted in greater U.S. military and financial assistance to the Diem government. Kennedy increased American expenditures in South Vietnam to three billion dollars and the number of military advisers from fewer than seven hundred in 1961 to more than sixteen thousand by the time of his assassination on November 22, 1963.[9] Despite the assistance, however, Diem's regime still failed to show economic or political progress. Buddhist priests, the spiritual leaders for the majority of Vietnamese, staged dramatic protests against Diem's dictatorial rule, including acts of self-immolation. Diem, a Catholic, and his brother, Ngo Dinh Nhu, responded to the protest by crushing Buddhist resistance. Kennedy, frustrated by the internal rebellion and the growing Communist insurgency, conceded that the war could not be won as long as Diem was in power. He deferred to Henry Cabot Lodge, the U.S. ambassador to Saigon, who encouraged the removal of Diem. Three weeks before Kennedy's death, on November 1, 1963, South Vietnamese military officers conducted a coup that ended with the murders of Diem and Nhu.[10]

Several historians have shown that Kennedy intended to withdraw all U.S. military personnel from Vietnam, beginning in December 1963 and finishing in 1965 after his presumed reelection gave him the political capital to take such a controversial action. But Kennedy kept his plans hidden from the military establishment while cleverly deflecting their demands for escalation. This elusiveness allowed his successor, Lyndon Johnson, and his national security advisers to present continued U.S. involvement in Vietnam as the direct result of JFK's policies.[11] Ironically, Robert McNamara, who in October 1963 encouraged Kennedy to withdraw the first one thousand military advisers by the end of the year, abruptly shifted his position during the Johnson administration. McNamara not only encouraged the new president to escalate the war and hide its cost from the American people, but also became the prime architect of the failed U.S. effort in Vietnam.[12] Years later, the former defense secretary admitted that the decision to escalate was a mistake and explained that, at the time, he failed to consider "crucial military questions" that dealt with the "human and financial cost of success" in Southeast Asia. While he strongly disagreed with the Joint Chiefs' assessment that nuclear weapons would have to be used, McNamara felt that a conventional war was winnable. He also admitted to an "impulsive" and "ill-considered public statement" he made at an April 24, 1964, Pentagon news conference in which he defended the "President's policy on Vietnam." "I don't object to its being called 'McNamara's War' and I am pleased to be identified with it and do whatever I can to win it," he added.[13]

Dan Flood would also reconsider his thinking about U.S. involvement in Vietnam as the war escalated. One of Capitol Hill's most prominent hawks, Flood would begin to question the financial cost of the war in Defense Appropriations Subcommittee hearings by 1965. Flood's initial support for U.S. military and financial aid to South Vietnam is well documented. Like other hawks on Capitol Hill in the 1950s, he firmly believed that communism was monolithic and that U.S. credibility depended on containing the Communist threat wherever it emerged in the world. He stated this position repeatedly throughout the 1950s, insisting that "all possible aid within the strength of our budget should be given in aid to Southeast Asia to help them in opposing the encroachment of atheistic communism."[14] In 1955, after the Viet Minh's bloody persecution of North Vietnamese Catholics in violation of the Geneva agreement, Flood took to the House floor and urged Congress to "do everything possible to free these [non-Communist] souls from the heel of implacable and unconscionable tyrants, the Communist government."[15] He firmly believed that the nation's foreign policy must be exercised from a base of strength, as is expected of a world leader, and should not capitulate to less powerful third-world nations. Nor was he hesitant in suggesting the use of nuclear weapons to achieve that objective. "If the Communists try to take over, I say use nuclear weapons," said Flood, echoing the sentiments of the JCS. "If you're going to be a leader, then lead. If not, then take two laps around the field and go to the shower. We're a two-hundred-year-old democracy. We should know something about that form of government. We must also be strong militarily in order to preserve freedom around the world."[16]

To be sure, Flood was an old-fashioned, flag-waving jingoist. Michael Clark, a former aide, described him as the "northern version of a southern, right-wing

Democrat, much like Representatives Ed Herbert of Louisiana and Bob Sikes of Florida." "Naturally, Mr. Flood strongly supported the Vietnam War in the beginning," he added.[17] In that respect, Flood was like all of the hawks on Capitol Hill. They actively promoted post–World War II beliefs in the superiority of American values, the dangers of appeasement, and the necessity of the United States to meet the responsibility of global leadership by taking on the challenge of godless communism wherever it surfaced. "I viewed Dan as pro-defense and his support for the Vietnam conflict was similar to my own," said former congressman Jim Wright of Texas:

> I felt, in those days, that if we hadn't learned anything else from World War II it was that we cannot tolerate the expansion by military aggression of any one country over another. Both Dan and I viewed the Vietnam situation as one in which one part of the nation separated from the other and that under the rule of law and the terms of the international treaties, each country had been granted its own independence. Then, when North Vietnam, which was a socialist country, invaded the south, a democratic country, it became an aggressor.
>
> Those beliefs were not uncommon among Democratic members. We had been brought up on certain principles, like the "domino theory." We'd also seen that kind of aggression at work during the Second World War when Hitler invaded the Sudetenland and then Poland in order to expand his Third Reich. So we saw aggression as an undisputed truth. We didn't understand that the Vietnamese never should have been divided in the first place and that they had a responsibility to unite again. We were prone to think of Ho Chi Minh as a puppet of Communist China and a marauder who wanted control of South Vietnam at the expense of others.[18]

In other words, Congress, like the U.S. State Department, the Department of Defense, and the Pentagon, failed to make important ideological distinctions between those nations that embraced communism. The domino theory and the naïve assumption that all Southeast Asia would collapse if the Communists took over Vietnam ignored the complex nationalistic diversity of that region. Laos and Cambodia, the two countries that neighbored Vietnam to the west, had either been controlled or invaded by Vietnam for centuries, creating a historical animosity. Both countries became Communist after the war, but not because of Ho Chi Minh's ambitions. Communist regimes in Laos and Cambodia, originally organized by the Viet Minh, asserted their own autonomy during the 1970s and developed their own doctrines that addressed their unique historical circumstances.[19] Similarly, Ho was not "a puppet of Communist China" as U.S. leaders had assumed. Centuries of distrust existed between Vietnam and China. Ho resented chairman Mao Tse-tung's pressure to fight a protracted war against the United States. He understood Mao's duplicitous nature and his desire to use the Vietnamese as proxies in China's struggle against the United States. For Mao, a protracted war contained within Vietnam's boundaries would gradually weaken the Vietnamese, making them vulnerable to an invasion by China, and slowly drain American resources without jeopardizing China's own security.[20] Finally, U.S. leaders failed to make the critical distinction between the communism espoused by Mao, which promoted "perpetual revolution" to unite all Asian countries under Chinese rule, and Soviet communism, which advocated "worldwide revolution" that transcended nationalist sentiments.[21] Ultimately, this important difference prevented the Soviet Union and China from joining forces against the United States and its allies.

Ironically, the first time Flood locked horns with McNamara was in June 1961 when the new secretary of defense, in a cost-cutting measure, proposed to reduce the number of army troops in western Europe in favor of deploying a greater number of nuclear missiles. Flood, using McNamara's own doctrine of "flexible response" against him, demanded that both nuclear weapons and conventional forces be maintained there. "I have voted for every appropriation for missiles from the very first one," he reminded the secretary of defense, but "ground forces" are more important for "fighting limited wars":

> Now, Mr. McNamara came to my [Defense Appropriations] subcommittee and made this proposal to reduce the ground forces in Western Europe. But the position of the Army is that they need those 925,000 troops and that position has never changed. Another thing: The Army, the Army Ordnance people, and the Army Command say, and have been saying this for four years, that they need $2.5 billion a year for five years to modernize our Army. But in the budget [proposed by McNamara], we have $2 billion for Army hardware. Of that $2 billion, $1.5 billion is merely to replace what wears out every year; nothing new; no additions. So only $500 million is in this bill to modernize the Army.
>
> Now somebody, beginning with the Secretary of Defense, down through the Joint Chiefs of Staff, has substituted their opinion for the Army's opinion, and the answer is that we do not have the money. We

are told that we need a "balanced defense." Well, I am not for a balanced defense. I want a *better* defense than the Russians.

Do you know the size of the Russian ground forces? Five times what we have. Do you know what condition they are in? There is not a better-trained and equipped army on the face of the earth. The Russian army has been modernized from top to bottom. From top to bottom, every phase, every department, every bureau, every piece of hardware, every command of supply in Russia from top to bottom has been modernized, done over, completely new, with the latest things conceivable, not once but one and a half times since 1942. How do you like that? What about our Army?[22]

Flood's remarks were classic: condescending, self-righteous, and direct. He viewed the world in black and white, and exaggerated the preparedness of the Soviet Army to make his case. He was convinced, in 1961, that the Soviets were winning the cold war and that the United States needed to make national security its top priority. In Flood's estimation, the United States could not spend enough money to insure its defense, especially when it came to building up its nuclear arsenal or modernizing its ground forces. This is not to say, however, that Flood promoted irresponsible spending.

That same year, when he discovered that several air force officers were drawing flight pay to visit Boy Scout centers as "advisers," Flood, during a Defense Appropriation Subcommittee hearing, vented his anger at Major General Elvin S. Lignon, Jr., the Pentagon's director of personnel planning. "General," began the congressman, "you have already made a great to-do about what will happen to the Air Force if these fly boys do not get proficiency pay . . . "

"Flying pay?" corrected Lignon.

Flood, angered by the interruption, continued: "You call it 'flying pay'!? What sacred cows are you fly boys that you should have it but not the Army and Navy? What is it about the blue uniform that gives you that privilege?"

Embarrassed by the question, Lignon sheepishly asked, "Do you want this in the record?"

"Why are you any different!?" Flood thundered, noticeably agitated by the general's response.

There was silence. When it was clear that no answer was forthcoming, Flood continued his condescending lecture: "General, I've heard of twenty instances where Air Force Officers were drawing flight pay for going out to Boy Scout Centers. Now, I am for the Boy Scouts, but why a rated officer of the United States Air Force with my scout troops? I don't mind a young fellow being motivated for God, country and Yale, but this is a motivated, rated flier!"

"Congressman Flood, there are very few instances of experienced fighter pilots . . . " began Lignon, attempting to minimize the number of cases. But Flood cut him off.

"General," he continued, producing a sheet of paper. "I have statistical data here from the General Accounting Office showing that there were 27,000 Air Force Officers drawing up to $2,938 a year fly pay for doing nothing. In the first place, why give a bonus for flying? A jungle fighter, is he different from your fly boys?"

There was no response from the general, who by now had resigned himself to suffering through the tongue-lashing.

"That is a tough man, that jungle fighter," Flood raved on. "That is tough warfare with a knife in a jungle, fighting against Vietnamese guerrillas. Can your fly boys top that? If you cannot answer the question, will you get a hold of somebody in the Office of the Secretary of Defense who can?"[23]

Flood would continue throughout his tenure in Congress to berate any officer who tried to defend such indefensible spending. In the process, he earned a reputation among witnesses for hard, critical cross-examination, a condescending manner, and fiscal accountability.

By 1964 there was a huge leadership vacuum in South Vietnam. The Viet Minh had gained control over much of the countryside. Despite American economic and military aid, a succession of governments in South Vietnam proved unable to destroy the Viet Cong or to prevent the spread of terrorism in Saigon itself. Faced with this dire situation and an upcoming presidential election, president Lyndon Johnson admitted to an adviser, "I don't think Vietnam is worth fighting for and I don't think we can get out. But I am not going to be the president who saw Southeast Asia go the way China went." As a result, Johnson, also a prisoner of the "domino theory," increased U.S. military aid to South Vietnam. But instead of committing American ground forces, he emphasized strategic planning, increased covert raids against North Vietnam, and began a massive public awareness campaign to generate support for a larger American role in defending South Vietnam by stressing the Communist threat to that country.[24]

Flood was agitated by the failure of the administration to take a more proactive role in Vietnam and voiced his displeasure in hearings on the defense budget. He didn't understand, for example, why U.S. officers did not take at least joint command of the South Vietnamese troops, rather than being limited to an advisory capacity. Nor did he understand why U.S. ground forces hadn't been committed to Southeast Asia. When McNamara and Taylor testified before the Defense Appropriations Subcommittee on February 17, 1964, they

Fig. 28. Despite Flood's close scrutiny of the Defense budget, he often enjoyed test rides in the air force's most up-to-date aircraft.

explained that Major General Nguyen Khanh, the South Vietnamese commander, would have to agree to such an arrangement. If he consented, then Lieutenant General William Westmoreland would assume overall command of the war. But if Khanh balked at the idea, McNamara would tell him that President Johnson has no alternative but to "review" the U.S. commitment to South Vietnam, a clear warning that the United States would consider a *political* rather than military solution to the conflict.

McNamara also identified the principal difficulty in prosecuting the war as South Vietnam's reluctance to take the offensive against the Communists. He added that no decision had yet been made on carrying the war to North Vietnam by guerrilla raids and by aerial attacks on depots, supply lines, and other targets. Disappointed by the news and hoping to achieve a better understanding of the risks involved in a greater U.S. commitment, Flood asked Taylor, "Do you believe the Chinese Communists would intervene either openly or with so-called 'volunteers' if we should blockade North Vietnam and send guerrillas there?"

"No, I do not," replied the Joint Chiefs' chair. Taylor added that he also opposed the use of American troops as "the direct means of suppressing guerrillas in South Vietnam under all circumstances I can think of."[25]

Two months later, McNamara and Taylor came before the Defense Appropriations Subcommittee again and still the question of U.S. command and ground troops had not been resolved. "You have come to the Rubicon in South Vietnam," Flood told them with bitter consternation. "You are at the end of the line. You have to command or you are not going to command. If you are not going to command you are a dead duck, you cannot win."

Flood, regardless of whether he realized it, was articulating the very same sentiments of the Joint Chiefs of Staff and the Pentagon, who were pressuring the Johnson administration to "Americanize" the war. When Flood stated his belief that the U.S. "commands and controls *nothing* in South Vietnam," Taylor was quick to object.

"Tell me then, general," Flood shot back, "what do you command there!?"

"Nothing," admitted Taylor.

"What do you control there?"

Before Taylor could answer, McNamara interceded. He explained that Congress had hurt the military assistance program to South Vietnam by cutting it from $1.4 billion to just $1 billion in the last fiscal year, and that the additional $1 billion requested for fiscal year 1965 would not be enough to achieve the kind of control Flood desired.

Rep. Gerald Ford cut Flood off before he could respond. "It would be easy to blame the last Congressional appropriation for the lack of control in Vietnam," said Ford. "But it seems to me that there is a reluctance on the part of administration officials to commit U.S. forces to combat for a South Vietnamese victory and I don't think this is a proper or prudent attitude."

"If we want victory, or if we want to prevent a Communist victory," added Ford, "I think we have to be prepared to make commitments."

"We will make whatever hard choices have to be made," replied McNamara. "But the kind of war now going on in Vietnam can only be won by the Vietnamese people themselves."[26]

Johnson officials were forced to make the "hard choice" in the summer of 1964. In July, Taylor was replaced as chair of the JCS by General Earle G. Wheeler, a skilled staff officer who was more familiar with the political machinations of the Pentagon, Congress, and the White House. He was viewed as an individual who could mend the breach that had formerly existed in the Defense establishment between the civilian and military decision makers.

Johnson continued to rely on Taylor's expertise by appointing him ambassador to South Vietnam.[27]

The real turning point, however, came in August, after North Vietnamese torpedo boats skirmished with the American destroyer *Maddox* in the Gulf of Tonkin. The president immediately ordered retaliatory air strikes on North Vietnam and asked Congress for—and received—a resolution allowing the United States "to take all necessary measures to repel attacks against American forces" and "to prevent further aggression." The House passed the measure by a vote of 414 to 0, and the Senate, 88 to 2. Johnson signed the resolution on August 10. In fact, the attack on the *Maddox* was overblown and used by the administration to justify U.S. entry into the war. The Gulf of Tonkin Resolution gave Johnson the freedom to take whatever measures he wanted in Vietnam. He decided on a two-pronged strategy: (1) to commit more U.S. advisers; and (2) to pursue an extensive bombing campaign of North Vietnam. While these actions helped Johnson to win the 1964 election, they did not discourage the Viet Cong from pressuring the Saigon government. By the beginning of 1965, Johnson began committing U.S. combat forces to Vietnam. On July 28, 1965, the president increased U.S. ground forces from 75,000 to 125,000 troops. Three years later, the number exceeded 500,000. The military establishment had succeeded in "Americanizing" the war.[28]

While Flood strongly supported escalation, he began to realize that McNamara was intentionally providing Congress with lower budget estimates for Vietnam. That fact became clear on March 24, 1965, during the first of many supplemental Defense Appropriations hearings. After listening to the testimony of Lieutenant General Duward L. Crow, the air force budget director, Flood observed, "There has been a noticeable step-up in the Vietnam problem since [the] budget [for fiscal year 1966] was prepared." Then he asked Crow, "Has that been reflected in any of the figures given to us?"

Crow: In 1965 we budgeted something on the order of $17 million for activities in Southeast Asia. At the present time, it appears that our 1965 requirements will be in the order of $—— to $—— million. As far as 1966 is concerned, we budgeted 1966 on the basis of the previously planned activity, and the budget may not reflect the current level, or certainly any significant increase to it. Any additional monies required would depend on the course of events.

Flood: And would be reflected by supplementals?

Crow: Yes, sir.

Flood: You went from $—— to $—— million in 1965.

Crow: We came in 1966 with a total of $—— million, sir.

Flood: That is where you wound up in 1965?

Crow: No. I'm afraid we are going to wind up in 1965 at a higher level.

Flood: You will come in in 1966 with what?

Crow: A lower figure.

Flood: Why?

Crow: Many of the costs could be characterized as one-time costs. In the preparation of the 1966 budget, we did not forecast a higher level activity in Southeast Asia.

Flood: You had nothing to indicate it would be lower?

Crow: We did not.

Flood: You had a reasonable cause to believe that it would most probably be increased.

Crow: Let me say, Mr. Flood, we responded to uniform guidelines in the preparation of this budget.

Flood: What did you ask the Defense people for for this particular question? What did you ask for Southeast Asia?

Crow: We responded to the guidelines.

Flood: Never mind the guidelines. What did you ask for in terms of dollars?

Crow: We asked for the $——million.

Flood: If there is anything wrong, it is your fault.

Crow: I do not believe you could really put us in a position of unilaterally pursuing a higher level of activity in Southeast Asia.

Flood: I will put you where I want. You came in in 1966 and you asked for $—— million. Would you not say that you have reasonable cause to believe the tempo would be increased rather than lowered? Would that be a fair assumption from reading the newspapers?

Crow: I would say so.

Flood: Then why did you not ask for more money? Is this a phony budget figure to keep the budget down?

Crow: No, sir. In the preparation of the Department of Defense budget it is necessary for someone in the overall spectrum to lay down certain ground rules and assumptions, and one of the assumptions laid down was that the activity in Southeast Asia would not increase.

Flood: And acting on those ground rules, assumptions, or whatever, the Air Force came in for operations in Southeast Asia where it left off in 1965. In other words, you took a hint from the Department of Defense and left it alone; is that it?

Crow: That is it, sir.[29]

It was clear to Flood that the "someone in the overall spectrum of the Defense Department," the individual Crow "took a hint from," was the secretary of defense.

McNamara was handcuffed by Johnson's refusal to call for a tax increase to fund the war. The president rightly feared that a tax bill would detract from his Great Society programs. At the same time, Johnson wanted to downplay the escalation of the war on Capitol Hill and to the American public. Instead of the $12.7 billion that the JCS wanted for additional deployments, he insisted that the administration limit additional funding to the $1 billion already requested in the 1966 Defense Appropriations Bill. He was also intent on delaying any additional funding until January 1966, at which time the need would be understated by half.[30]

Johnson's decision forced McNamara to find a way to hide the cost of the war from Congress. When the Joint Chiefs of Staff submitted their service estimates to him, McNamara handed them over to his own civilian analysts. After scrutinizing the estimates, the Whiz Kids would make recommendations as to which expenditures he should retain and which ones he should cut from each proposal. In every case, the recommendations conformed to the defense secretary's policy of streamlining the budget. As a result, McNamara consciously presented understated budgets to Congress each year. When he needed more money, he would submit a supplemental budget request and propose the diversion of funds from other areas, such as U.S. funding of the North Atlantic Treaty Organization, or revenue that was earmarked for other agencies.[31] Initially, the strategy worked. In March 1966, for example, the House supported a supplemental funding bill for military spending by a roll call vote of 389 to 3. Most of those funds were intended to fight the war in Vietnam.[32]

Flood was in a quandary. He firmly believed in the necessity of U.S. military involvement in Vietnam as essential to the cold war commitment to contain communism. As a Democrat, he realized the partisan responsibility of being a loyal supporter of the Johnson administration's policy in Southeast Asia. At the same time, he became increasingly concerned about the deceitful budget estimates that were presented by McNamara at the Defense Appropriations Subcommittee hearings. Though he never voiced the concern in public, Flood, like other congressmen whose constituencies benefited from the Great Society, most certainly made the connection between the increase in defense spending and the decline in funding of Johnson's domestic programs. "I think we all realized that the money being invested in Vietnam would have some adverse impact on the reforms we were pursuing at home," said Rep. Fred Rooney of Pennsylvania in a recent interview. "That's a sad reality in a time of war. But Dan scrutinized every nickel that was due to labor, health, education, and welfare. At the same time, he realized the necessity of standing by the president on all our international involvements, whether it be in terms of the military hardware or the presence of conventional forces. His support was unqualified."[33]

To avoid any personal disloyalty to the administration, Flood tended to be critical of *specific* expenditures during defense budget hearings rather than on the cost of the Vietnam War as a whole. For example, he berated Major General Ralph Haines, deputy assistant chief of staff for force development, for the army's "gross negligence in delaying the reprogramming of 20-millimeter cannon" and then having "the audacity to ask for more funding for new, more expensive ordnance."[34] On another occasion, he reprimanded Admiral Semmes, the navy's budget director, for his failure to account for the discrepancies in ordnance estimates between the navy and the marine corps that had existed for four years. When Semmes finally admitted that "the Secretary of Defense is to propose legislation to the Congress that will remedy the situation," Flood exploded. "Will you get a hold of somebody in of the Office of the Secretary of Defense who is doing this job and tell them Flood wants to know why it has taken four years to come up with this?" he thundered. "I thought those whiz kids in McNamara's office could move faster than that. Tell them to get out a slide rule and cut it out. Why four years?!"[35] More often, Flood would simply vent his frustration over the "lack of honesty" he was hearing in the presentation of procurement estimates from "the Defense Department and all the branches of service."[36]

As the war dragged on, the Pennsylvania legislator became critical of the military's tactical failures, considering the increasing expenditures for the training of combat troops and communications equipment. On March 8, 1967, for example, Flood questioned JCS chair General Earle Wheeler about "lack of communication" that resulted in the "strafing of an American patrol boat by our own aircraft." When Wheeler told him that he had been misinformed and that there was "excellent land-air communication," Flood replied that "there had better be, considering what we're paying for communications equipment."[37] Nor did Flood spare the secretary of defense. When McNamara, in a budget-cutting measure, ordered 751 reserve units dissolved and tried to merge other reserve units into the National Guard without congressional approval, the Pennsylvania congressman threatened to "take the matter up with the Supreme Court."[38]

On another occasion Flood lectured McNamara over the "urgent need to develop significant improvements to our rescue-recovery operations in Vietnam," given the "increasing rate of downed air crewmen lost to the enemy."

When the secretary of defense insisted that the "present search-and-rescue aircraft have been accomplishing a remarkable job of recovering downed pilots," Flood responded that "this committee, which funded those birds," didn't believe the efforts were "remarkable enough."[39]

"McNamara never leveled with us about the actual cost of the war," recalled Rep. Melvin Laird of Wisconsin, who served on the Defense Appropriations Subcommittee and would later become secretary of defense:

> He would come before us three or four times a year, always with an optimistic report on Vietnam. However, George Mahon, the chair of the subcommittee, Dan, myself, and Gerry Ford questioned his optimism as well as the budget estimates he and the Joint Chiefs were presenting. Dan was especially critical. He always asked some good tough questions.
>
> It turned out that McNamara had misused money from other appropriations. He had robbed money from our NATO commitment that was targeted for aircraft, military supplies and other material. He also stole money from the Operations and Maintenance Account and other appropriations accounts to pay for that war. I think Dan knew that long before we did, but he wrestled with his responsibility to support the troops and the president. Having said that, I don't think Dan was wholeheartedly behind Vietnam. I think his support of the war came because of his admiration for President Johnson and because he simply didn't know how to stop it.[40]

By August 1967, tens of thousands of antiwar protesters marched on Washington. Vietnam was costing two billion dollars a month as inflation soared. Still, Johnson, despite the urging of the nation's top economists, had repeatedly refused to call for a general tax increase. To close the financial gap, Republicans set out to reduce the spending on the Great Society. Realizing that his legislative legacy was at stake, Johnson finally pressed Congress for a tax increase. But Ways and Means chair Wilbur Mills gave him an ultimatum: "Choose between guns and butter, war and domestic spending." Johnson relented, cutting six billion dollars from domestic spending in return for the tax cut. In so doing, he all but destroyed his beloved Great Society.[41]

The president was also losing his defense secretary's support for the war. McNamara's growing belief that escalation had been a mistake led him to encourage Johnson to initiate a settlement to the war. Johnson felt betrayed and thereafter limited the secretary's access to him. Then, in November 1967, the president suddenly announced that McNamara was leaving the Defense Department to become director of the World Bank. He would later explain that "the pressures of the war had become so great" on McNamara that he feared the defense secretary "might have a nervous break down."[42]

McNamara's final appearance before the Defense Appropriations Subcommittee came in mid-February 1968. This time Melvin Laird—not Flood—grilled the outgoing secretary of defense. Laird, a Republican, had no reservations about reprimanding McNamara for what he now considered to be "deceitful" budget estimates to hide the cost of the war. When the secretary of defense insisted that he gave "no misleading estimates, other than those discovered, in hindsight, to be mistaken and then, only within the limits of human infallibility," Laird pointed out that the budget estimates McNamara presented Defense Appropriations had been "off over $10 billion each of the previous two years" and that his most recent budget was "off by almost $5 billion."

Incensed by the charge of deceitfulness, McNamara shot back:

> I can prove that the incremental costs of the Vietnam war—which I think is the most meaningful figure—is nowhere near $29 billion. The incremental cost is on the order of $17 to $20 billion. You cannot get the defense budget much below $50 billion between Fiscal Year 1962–63, plus the $10 to $12 billion of inflation since that time. And that is $60 billion versus $77 to $78 billion. The difference of $17 to $18 billion is the incremental cost. Therefore, I completely disagree with your charge that we have been guilty of misleading the American people as to the cost of the war over the past 36 months. There is no basis for it whatsoever.[43]

In fact, McNamara had been exposed. His defensiveness only served to reinforce his guilt in the eyes of the subcommittee members. Worse, the Johnson administration itself, which had already lost significant credibility with the American public, would soon lose the trust of Congress.

Before McNamara left the hearings, Flood, possibly feeling guilty over his own castigation of the defense secretary, commended him for his service. "I have had the honor and privilege of sitting in the front row since you first came on stage," he said. "I have seen you subjected to slings and arrows of outrageous fortune, and I have shot a few of the arrows myself. As has been said in another great play, you are a man worthy of our steel. This is one for your valedictory. It is from the fourth act of *Julius Caesar,* scene three, toward the end:

> There is a tide in the affairs of men
> Which, taken at the flood, leads on to fortune;
> Omitted, all the voyage of their life.
> Is bound in shallows and in miseries.

"So I say, from where I sit," concluded Flood, "hail and farewell."[44]

Shortly after he left Congress in 1980, Flood was asked if he felt deceived by President Johnson's decision to escalate the Vietnam War. "No, I did not," he insisted, still maintaining his loyalty to a president who had died nearly a decade earlier:

> The administration was developing a national policy that the Congress seemed to think was in the nation's best interests for many reasons and they pursued that policy. As the war dragged on, some congressmen disavowed that policy. But I've found that very seldom is there a policy that somebody in Congress does not disavow and I see nothing improper about that either.
>
> It was very difficult to approve appropriations for the Vietnam War, not only with the military establishment, but with the American people. There were certain elements who were opposed to the war. Thank God, in those days, the nation as a whole, was united heart and soul behind the war until the last troops were taken out.[45]

Flood's assessment of a nation "united heart and soul" behind Vietnam was wishful thinking.

When Richard Nixon assumed the presidency in 1969, the nation was deeply divided by the war. The new president gave top priority to extricating U.S. forces from Vietnam while still trying to find a way to win the war. In mid-1969 he announced the "Nixon Doctrine," which asserted that the United States would give aid to friends and allies but would not accept the full burden of troop defense. This doctrine marked the "Vietnamization" of the war, which entailed removing American forces and replacing them with Vietnamese ones. At the same time, Nixon, exploiting the War Powers Resolution, launched a series of ferocious air attacks on North Vietnam, which only served to increase public discontent.[46]

Nixon's decision to invade Vietnamese sanctuaries in Laos and Cambodia, in April 1970, brought renewed demonstrations on college campuses, some with tragic results. At Kent State University in Ohio, the National Guard fired on student protestors, killing four and wounding nine others. A year later, the *New York Times* published classified Pentagon documents outlining the history of American involvement in Vietnam and the role of presidents and military leaders in deceiving the American people and Congress. Outraged by the revelations, more than thirty thousand war protesters descended on Washington to demand a peace settlement. Nixon understood that he had to end the conflict, and promised "peace with honor," a slogan he used to secure his reelection in 1972.[47]

Historically, northeastern Pennsylvanians firmly supported U.S. military involvement in wartime, viewing themselves as "true patriots" who defended the nation's policies, "right or wrong." But now Flood's office was receiving a growing number of letters demanding U.S. withdrawal from Vietnam. In every case, the congressman's staff prepared a response stating his disagreement with the constituent's opinion and Flood's insistence that the president of the United States has "more information than you do to justify American involvement in the war."[48] In fact, Flood's support of the war was so strong that, in 1971, he voted for 89 percent of the legislation backed by the pro-military American Security Council and favored just three of the twelve bills endorsed by the dovish Friends Committee on National Legislation.[49] His public support for Vietnam was due, in part, to the economic benefits the war was bringing to his district.

Flood's genius during these tumultuous years was his ability to discover alternative ways to channel federal funding and jobs into his congressional district. When he realized that the increasing cost of Vietnam was detracting from the Great Society, he sought to benefit his constituents through defense contracts. In 1972 alone, the Eleventh District's share of federal funding was $378 million, and it was largely spent for military-industrial purposes. Among the beneficiaries were: Kennedy Van Saun Inc., manufacturers of projectiles; Philco and Ford Industries, telecommunications equipment; Medico Industries, defense equipment; Kanarr Corporation, grenade launchers; and the Benton Air Force Station.[50] According to Tom Medico, the current CEO and president of Medico Industries, his family's business "was extremely prosperous during the Vietnam War." "We made the metal bodies for the 2.75 rocket used in helicopter warfare," he explained. "Defense budgets were very high at that time and our bids were always very competitive with other companies. We were operating at full capacity with 375 workers and we worked three shifts, around the clock."[51] One estimate maintains that Medico Industries received as much as sixty million dollars in defense contracts from 1965 to 1978 for rocket warheads, tank parts, and other military equipment.[52]

When asked about his assistance in helping constituent companies secure millions of dollars in contracts, Flood admitted that "my big concern is getting jobs for the people in my area." "Jobs, jobs, jobs," he insisted. "That's what those contracts are all about. I don't know of any other way to create jobs for people in northeastern Pennsylvania other than for the business establishment in the area to obtain contracts so that people can go to work."[53]

Perhaps Flood's greatest coup was preventing the Pentagon from closing the Tobyhanna Army Base. Originally established as an artillery training site during World War I, Tobyhanna, at Flood's insistence, was converted into the principle East Coast base for overhauling military communications equipment in the 1950s. By 1970 the facility was the largest single employer in northeastern Pennsylvania with more than three thousand employees.[54] "Dan protected Tobyhanna like a mother bear," said former Rep. Joseph McDade of Lackawanna County. "Although the facility was located outside of his district, Floody's constituents represented about 40 percent of the employees there. Another 30 percent came from my district, and the remaining 30 percent came from Fred Rooney's district in the Lehigh Valley. So, whenever Tobyhanna would come up for discussion, Dan would put the military brass in their place. One of the more memorable confrontations came in 1970."[55]

That year, the Pentagon planned to reduce its budget by transferring some of Tobyhanna's operations to the Letterkenny Depot 130 miles away. The possible relocation would result in the elimination of five hundred jobs at Tobyhanna, which would create considerable economic distress in the Eleventh District. When Flood heard the rumors, he phoned Senate minority leader Hugh Scott, a fellow Pennsylvanian. "Scottie, do you know what those bastards at the Pentagon are trying to do to us?" he barked over the receiver. Scott, a Republican running for a third term in a Democratic state, listened attentively as Flood assaulted every possible suspect in the Pentagon's "conspiracy." Once he secured Scott's support, Flood went on the attack. Demanding an explanation, he scheduled a meeting with the army on Capitol Hill. Secretary of the Army Stanley Resor, a longtime Flood confidant, was scheduled to represent the defense agencies. But the military brass quickly canceled his appearance, assigning an army assistant secretary to take his place. Almost as soon as he had been named, the designee discovered he had a "conflict" and bowed out to the army comptroller. Soon, he too asked to be relieved from the meeting. It was clear that none of the senior officers relished the possibility of confronting Flood face-to-face over Tobyhanna. The unenviable responsibility eventually fell to an army official by the name of Crooker, who served as a cost accountant.

The showdown occurred on a snowy Wednesday afternoon, March 13, 1970, at the Russell Senate Office Building. Flood, dressed in a Russian fur hat, raccoon coat, and leather gloves, stormed into the conference room with aide Michael Clark in tow. Although the meeting was held at the Russell Building for Scott's convenience, the Senate minority leader decided at the last minute not to attend. It wouldn't be wise for the Pennsylvania senator to support Tobyhanna over Letterkenny in an election year. Crooker, the army accountant, and a group of junior Pentagon staffers had already arrived. Also waiting were congressmen Fred Rooney and Joe McDade. They relished the opportunity to watch Flood preside over the meeting, and he would not disappoint them.

"Floody marched right to the front of the conference room, sat down at the head table, opened the *Washington Post* and began reading," recalled McDade. "Crooker didn't know what to say, so he just sat there in silence waiting for Dan to begin the meeting. Finally, Flood put down the paper, looked him square in the eyes, and said, 'Go ahead, you're here to talk. Go ahead and talk!'"

As Crooker began his presentation, Flood resumed reading his newspaper. After forty minutes, the army accountant concluded his talk and the flamboyant congressman put the newspaper aside.

Flood: Are you finished?

Crooker: Yes, sir.

Flood: Good. Now, what exactly is your job over there at the Pentagon?

Crooker: I'm a senior cost accountant, sir.

Flood: So, you're a cost accountant. Is that all?

Crooker: Yes, sir. That's basically it.

Flood: You mean the goddamn Army sent a cost accountant to see me? Do you know who I am? Do you know I am the vice chairman of Defense Appropriations?

Crooker: Yes, sir.

Flood: Do you know why you're here today?

Crooker: I'm here because the Secretary of the Army could not be here.

Flood: No you're not! You're here today because the people above you are scared shitless of me! Let me tell you something, I'm the Army's best friend in the House. Secretary Resor knows that. They all know that over there, and the bastards have the unmitigated gall to make cutbacks at the most efficient Army Depot in the United States. Our workforce is the best. It's two, three times more efficient at Tobyhanna than at most other depots. But you clowns want to cut it back. I suppose if I let you get away with it, you would close it all together. Well, you're not going to, mister.

You go back to the Pentagon and tell those folks above you that Flood is the greatest goddamn friend the Army has in Congress. You tell them that Flood remembers the many times that Resor slipped in my back door and asked for my support for programs that the Budget Bureau didn't want and the Army got their money. And you tell them that Flood is insulted, pissed off, outraged, and that I'm not going to tolerate this. Will you do that for me?

Crooker: Oh, yes, sir.

Flood: And there's one more message, I'd like you to deliver.

Crooker: Yes, sir. What is that, sir?

Flood: You tell them to keep their fucking hands off Tobyhanna. Will you do that?

Crooker: Yes, sir.

Satisfied with the response, Flood turned to McDade and asked, "Anything else Congressman?"

McDade, trying to control his laughter, shook his head no.

"Anything else, Rooney?

"No, Dan," said Rooney, who had been laughing so hard that tears were rolling down his cheeks.

"Okay then," said Flood. "I guess that's all."[56] Within a month's time, the army announced that the national reorganization would not involve any job cuts at Tobyhanna after all. What's more, by year's end more than six hundred new jobs were created at Tobyhanna because of transfers from other army depots. Once again, Flood delivered.[57]

As public disaffection with the war continued, criticism in Congress became more vocal. Increasing demands that U.S. troops be withdrawn and that a specific timetable be devised to end the war resulted in extended negotiations with North Vietnam. Finally, on January 27, 1973, the Nixon administration reached a peace settlement. National security adviser Henry Kissinger and Le Duc Tho of North Vietnam agreed to a mutual withdrawal of troops, a return of prisoners of war, and free elections in South Vietnam to be conducted under international supervision. Initial enthusiasm over the settlement proved to be premature. The Viet Cong continued their guerrilla attacks and the United States stepped up its bombing of Communist strongholds in Laos and Cambodia, where peace had not been proclaimed. Without American military support, however, the fragile and corrupt regime in South Vietnam could not survive, and in April 1975 the capital, Saigon, fell. Vietnam was once again united—under the Communist rule of the north—and the United States had squandered nearly fifty thousand young lives and billions of dollars in a lost cause.[58]

"Vietnam was a good show by the troops, but a bad performance by the defense establishment," Flood concluded after the war had ended.[59] But he refused to brood about the outcome. Instead, he turned his attention to the domestic front and the needs of his constituents. "I know well about the cost of war," he boasted in a speech to the Wilkes-Barre Lions Club:

> By a strange anomaly, I am vice chairman of the Appropriations Committee of the Department of Defense. Now how do you like that one?
>
> I've been on that committee since it was created just after World War II. I know what wars cost, oh-ho! Does Gimbels tell Macy? I know. I also know what that money can do for us here at home if there is no war.
>
> I propose today, that as our involvement in Indo-China becomes lesser, and these fantastic costs of military operations become smaller, that our president and the Congress redirect appropriations to education, health care and jobs.[60]

In the end, Flood didn't view Vietnam as a matter of "containing communism," or "preserving U.S. credibility abroad," or even "spreading the benefits of democracy to a third-world nation." He saw the war, at various times, as an obstacle to and vehicle for securing the federal money and jobs that were so vital to the welfare of his congressional district. His greatest challenge was yet to come.

8

ELKO'S PAYOFF

Dan Flood was at the height of his power as the 1970s began. His seniority on the House Appropriations Committee made him the envy of congressional colleagues who were at his beck and call. Already chair of the Labor and Health, Education, and Welfare Appropriations Subcommittee, the mustachioed legislator became vice chair of Defense Appropriations in 1972, only a step away from his dream of chairing that key subcommittee. Nor did he ever fail to capitalize on the opportunity to remind others of his influence on Capitol Hill. "Chairman, HEW Appropriations" and "Vice chairman, Defense Appropriations" were titles that rolled off his tongue thousands of times. The more he used them, the more he liked them, and anyone in earshot knew it too. In other words, Flood was as powerful as he'd have you believe, and his influence stemmed from the near veto control he exercised over the three-hundred-billion-dollar federal budget.[1]

Flood used his growing influence on Capitol Hill to promote his peculiar brand of politics, which endorsed an expanding welfare system and internal improvements at home and insuring U.S. military superiority abroad. In key votes in the early 1970s, Flood supported prayer in public schools, public television funding, a stiffer crime bill, consumer protection, family assistance, a clean-water appropriations bill, jets for Taiwan, and the Safeguard antiballistic missile system. He opposed breaking up the highway trust, ending the House Internal Security Committee, an amendment to limit presidential authority to conduct Cambodian military operations, and successive measures to amend the Panama Canal treaty that would lessen U.S. control over the waterway.[2]

Fig. 29. Stephen B. Elko, Flood's administrative assistant from 1970 to 1976, traded on the congressman's name for personal financial gain.

Flood was also a workaholic. His personal and political lives were inextricable. Constituent service was the priority, whether on Capitol Hill or back in the district on weekends. "Dan didn't know what it was to have a personal life," said Michael Clark, who joined the congressman's Washington staff in 1967:

> His life was the Congress, morning, noon, and night. He was the type of person who'd make you feel guilty if you didn't invest the same attention—in some cases, devotion—to whatever task you were working on. Things had to get done and get done the "right" way. Naturally, there were three golden rules in his office and he made sure that all of us were accountable to them. First, you *always* returned phone calls. Dan had a list of phone numbers both at home in Wilkes-Barre and in the Washington office that was a mile long. He also had a special phone number that was easy to remember because it reminded him of his favorite president and the year he was elected to office—"LINCOLN 1860" or "546 265 1860." Second, he dictated nearly every letter that went out to a constituent. If you didn't receive a response from him, God love you, because the office would catch hell. Finally, if you were a

constituent and you wanted an appointment with him, you got it. It didn't matter if you were a Democrat or Republican, rich or poor, male or female—Dan saw you, listened to your concern and acted on it. Never were we to turn anyone away.[3]

But Flood's breakneck pace was beginning to catch up with him. The esophageal cancer he suffered in 1962 left him emaciated and weak. He struggled with a plethora of physical ailments, including chronic gastric ulcers, hypoglycemia, chronic inflammation of the larynx, recurrent intestinal problems, cataracts, and arthritis in the lower back and knees. To cope with these maladies, he relied on a combination of sedatives, opiates, and alcohol. Over time, the congressman's dependence on medication increased. So did his forgetfulness. He'd always had difficulty remembering names and, as a result, referred to others with the generic name "Murph." But as the 1970s unfolded, Flood experienced increasing difficulty remembering past events, appointments, and conversations.[4]

Despite his poor health, Flood was still able to be an effective legislator because of a remarkably dedicated and experienced staff headed by Gene Hegarty. The former marine was not only Flood's confidant and protector, but he ran an efficient office where the staff knew their roles and carried out their responsibilities with a diligence that surpassed many of the other congressional staffs on Capitol Hill.[5] Helen Tomascik, who joined Flood in 1955, was executive secretary and second to Hegarty in command. Tomascik, once a minor league baseball administrator in Wilkes-Barre, seemed to know everyone from the district. She was also extremely protective of the congressman and enjoyed his complete trust. Tomascik not only paid all of Flood's bills out of his sergeant at arms account in the House of Representatives, but also managed his calendar, correspondence, all long-distance phone calls from constituents, took dictation, and typed his speeches. After sitting down with him to review the various letters, she would determine which staffer should act on it, affixing a small yellow "buck note" with the congressman's instructions. Tomascik's loyalty to Flood was surpassed only by her personal honesty. When she made suggestions, he listened carefully and usually respected them.[6]

Sarah Sheerin, Catherine Voytko, and Leona Yurishin were the other secretaries. Sheerin had worked on Capitol Hill since 1959 and joined Flood's staff in 1967, shortly after his appointment as chairman of HEW Appropriations. Her previous experience with Rep. Francis "Tad" Walters, a ranking Pennsylvania congressman who chaired several committees, quickly proved beneficial to Flood in his new leadership role. Yurishin handled all constituent mail and filing with the assistance of Voytko.[7] Male staff members handled all legislative research, the media, and constituent cases. Robert Hanover, who joined Flood's staff in the late 1950s, was the caseworker, serving as a liaison between the congressman and his constituents on all matters pertaining to veterans issues, employment, and Social Security. Larry Casey, who had been with Flood since 1947, was the press secretary. Michael Clark, who joined the staff in 1968, assisted Casey initially, but his talent for speechwriting and public relations quickly elevated him to the congressman's special assistant. Ed Mitchell and Richard Altman served as legislative assistants, sometimes with assistance from local law students. Miles DuVal, a retired navy captain, volunteered his services. He worked exclusively on all issues pertaining to Latin America and, in particular, the Panama Canal, which had, over the years, become Flood's special foreign policy concern.[8] Though Flood rarely confided in anyone, Tomascik, Hegarty, Clark, and DuVal came the closest to composing the congressman's inner circle.

"Mr. Flood was an Irish male chauvinist," laughed Sarah Sheerin, recalling her former boss in a recent interview:

> He really had little to do with the women in the office. That is, with the exception of Helen. It was strictly a "Boys' Club." But the secretaries understood that. Dan Flood was a "man's man" and he simply preferred male company. At the same time, our office was like a family in the 1960s and early 1970s. Most of the Pennsylvania representatives were on the same hallway of the Cannon Office Building, so our staffs knew each other pretty well. I think there was a special affection for each other that developed among the staff members in Mr. Flood's office, though. We all came from the same congressional district. It's not like today when congressional staffs come from all over the country. We were also very careful to look out for the younger people who came on board, whether they were pages, volunteers, interns or law students.[9]

Tom Makowski was one of the "younger people" on Flood's staff. A native of the Wyoming Valley, Makowski attended Georgetown Law School and volunteered in the office before he became a paid legislative assistant in 1976. "I revered Congressman Flood," he said. "He and Mrs. Flood treated us all like family. Since they didn't have any children, the young people on staff became their children. Mr. Flood also gave us our first taste of politics. It didn't matter that we weren't as experienced as some of the veteran staffers, he trusted each one of us to do the appropriate thing when he gave us an issue to handle."[10]

Unfortunately, the unconditional trust Flood invested in one staff member would eventually destroy his political career. He was Stephen B. Elko, a forty-year-old businessman who became administrative assistant in September 1970. Elko, a native of Wilkes-Barre, was a shadowy figure. The absence of details about his life was by design. What is known is that Elko was a graduate of Wyoming Seminary, a college preparatory school in Kingston. His yearbook describes him as "the class playboy," one who liked "fast music, fast cars, and fast women." Though he boasted that he was admitted to both Harvard and Yale, Elko attended Wilkes College briefly before gaining employment as a local beer distributor.[11] During the mid-1960s, Elko, working as a business loan specialist for the Economic Development Administration at the Department of Commerce, ingratiated himself with Flood by volunteering in the congressman's Washington office. Though Intech Inc., a computer software and consulting firm in Wilkes-Barre, employed him in 1970, Elko returned to the congressman's staff after Gene Hegarty died in August of that year.[12] According to court records, Elko claimed that Flood approached him after Hegarty's death, "pleading" with him "to take command" of his Washington staff and refused to take "no" for an answer.[13] But other staff members believe that Elko was blackmailing Flood, threatening to expose the congressman's alcohol abuse and addiction to painkilling medications.[14]

Whatever the case, on September 2 Flood executed the appropriate documents and personnel changes necessary to make Elko his administrative assistant. He was now responsible for supervising a staff of at least twelve individuals. Among his specific duties were serving as a liaison for constituents with various federal agencies, making the congressman's travel arrangements and paying travel expenses, and communicating with all the federal agencies, specifically the departments of Labor and Health, Education, and Welfare. Elko was also responsible for managing Flood's campaign business, which gave him access to all campaign funds and contributions. In these various capacities, he had the authority to sign Flood's name on letters that were sent from the congressman's office and to sign checks from his congressional bank account.[15]

Over the next few months, Elko learned everything he could about the operation of the office and how he could exploit his position for personal financial gain. He also kept a low profile on Capitol Hill. Elko not only refused to provide a biography for the Congressional Staff Directory, but he shunned colleagues on other congressional staffs, considering them "overeducated" and "prissily professional." In a city where connections are essential for success, Elko had no one in Washington he could call a friend. Instead, he cultivated relationships with lobbyists and others who could benefit him financially.[16]

According to court testimony, he insisted that Flood encouraged him to do so. "Stephen, you want to use your discretion in dealing with the people who will be looking for my assistance," the congressman allegedly told him. "Keep in mind, this is a business. If you have any problems, just come to me and let me know. But, if you handle this the way I know you can, the rewards will be there for both of us."[17]

Elko interpreted Flood's statement as permission to accumulate as much of the easy money as he could, whether it came in the form of simple gifts, special privileges, or outright cash—but that he should exercise "discretion" in doing so. Most easy money came in the form of campaign contributions from special interests.[18] Flood knew that. Over the twenty-five years he served in Congress, the federal government increasingly responded to the demands of all major organized interests and their lobbyists by crafting programs beneficial to them. Through a process of accommodation, government agencies and the legislators themselves became captives of special interests.[19]

There were even loopholes in the existing federal laws that allowed special interests and their lobbyists to operate without much regulation at all.[20] As a result, lobbyists not only influenced legislation, but also circumvented already existing laws to secure priorities and preferences for their clients who had no legal rights to them. To do that, the lobbyist secured the cooperation of one or more members of Congress to write a letter or make a telephone call to the government agency handling the matter. The more influential the congressperson, the better the chance of success. What made the system work were the "campaign donations"—or bribes—provided to the member of Congress by the special interest through the lobbyist.[21]

Flood understood how the system worked and, like every member of Congress, he operated within it. Over the course of his congressional career, lobbyists weren't the only people who approached him for favors. He was also pressured by other legislators, executive departments, the White House, state and local politicians, and organized crime. Initially, Flood may have resisted the pressure, but after three electoral defeats, he soon realized that he would have to yield to the requests if he wanted to survive politically. The longer he survived, the lower his resistance became. Even if he wanted to, Flood couldn't extricate himself from the special interest groups and easy money that influenced the departments he worked most closely with: Health, Education, and Welfare; Labor; and Defense. But he did differ from many members of Congress in that he did not keep the money for himself, but rather funneled it back into his own district. Elko, on the other hand, exploited Flood's authority and then pocketed the cash.

The administrative assistant was abusing his authority by the spring of 1971, when he demanded a one-thousand-dollar campaign contribution from the Northeastern Training Institute (NTI) of Fleetville, Pennsylvania, to obtain Flood's support for manpower training grants with the Department of Labor. Elko was successful in securing an eight-hundred-thousand-dollar grant for NTI and continued to assist them in securing federal grants through 1976, in return for several "campaign contributions" of between two hundred and seven hundred dollars.[22] But there was bigger money to be made, and he went after it.

Between April 1971 and August 1974, Elko collected forty-eight thousand dollars in bribes from Dr. Murdock Head, a George Washington University physician and director of the Airlie Foundation, a multimillion-dollar think tank based in Warrenton, Virginia. In return for the cash payments, Elko used Flood's influence to secure more than fifteen million dollars in federal grants and contracts from the Agency for International Development and the Department of Health, Education, and Welfare.[23]

Airlie's work involved educational projects dealing with environmental issues, family planning, cancer, and other social problems. It also had a subsidiary company, Raven's Hollow Ltd., that produced award-winning film documentaries on such controversial subjects as drug and alcohol abuse, birth control, and abortion. Elko soon became a regular visitor at the foundation.

Located fifty miles west of Washington on 1,700 acres of gently sloping farmland in the foothills of the Blue Ridge Mountains, the tax-exempt foundation offered various groups and federal agencies a bucolic setting for seminars, training programs, and conferences away from the distractions of the nation's capital. There they could enjoy a glistening, blue lake, waterfalls, a swimming pool, airstrip, and game preserve.[24] Head, the Texas-born founder of the Airlie Foundation, was adept at navigating the bureaucracy on Capitol Hill, which enabling him to secure millions in federal grant money for his programs.[25] He was also paranoiac about being investigated by the Justice Department. As a result, Head was obsessive about privacy in his dealings with Elko. In fact, his methods can be best described as the "cloak-and-dagger" activity popularized by spy novels.

In April 1971 Head invited Elko to "do a little fishing" with him at the Airlie estate. Once he arrived, the two men met in the physician's private office in the International House. Head asked that he "be acknowledged" by Flood or Elko "if anybody from the federal agencies contacted them" about Airlie. Near the end of the conversation, Head placed a facial tissue in his hand, opened a desk drawer, and took out an envelope containing five thousand dollars in one-hundred-dollar bills. Handing the envelope to Elko, the Airlie director requested that he "give this to Congressman Flood."[26] Five months later, in September 1971, Elko was invited back to the Warrenton estate. Once again, he met privately with Head, who expressed his hope that Flood would be attending the annual Statesman in Medicine Awards Dinner that was sponsored by the Airlie Foundation. After Elko assured him that both he and the congressman would attend the dinner, Head, with facial tissue in hand, picked up an envelope containing one thousand dollars, handed it to his guest, and said, "This is taxi fare to make sure Mr. Flood is at the dinner."[27]

The very next day, Head summoned Elko to Airlie to discuss two projects involving the physically handicapped for which he needed funding. One was a large conference to be held at Airlie, and the other was a documentary film. Suggesting that the funding could be secured through the Department of Education's Bureau of the Handicapped, Head requested that Flood contact Ted Martin, the associate commissioner of the bureau, on his behalf. Elko agreed to the request, but made the phone call to Martin himself, telling the associate commissioner, "I just want you to know, Ed, that Congressman Flood is very interested in this project."[28]

As the requests for federal grant money became greater, so did the cash payments to Elko and the remarkable nature of the meetings. In April 1972, for example, Head asked for help in securing federal grant money amounting to one million dollars annually for five years from the Agency for International Development (AID). The money was to fund a research study in population planning in twelve to fourteen Latin American countries. Elko was given five thousand dollars in return for securing the support of Rep. Otto Passman, chair of Foreign Aid Appropriations, which had jurisdiction over AID. During this meeting, Head not only continued to use facial tissue to avoid leaving fingerprints on the bribery money, but also referred to Flood and Passman by code names. Flood was called "the mustache" and Passman, "the priest." Airlie was eventually awarded a $1.6 million grant by AID.[29]

By December 1973 Head had become extremely concerned about "electronic surveillance" and took additional measures to insure the secrecy of their meetings. That month, he called Elko into a screening room at the Raven Hollow film studio and suggested, in code, that they should suspend their dealings temporarily. "The long knives are out," Head wrote on a newsprint easel. "I'm going fishing for about a year. I think you better duck. The cannon balls are flying." Then the two men bargained over the amount of Elko's payoff, compromising on eight thousand dollars.[30]

Murdock Head and Stephen Elko were consummate schemers, using each other for their own personal gain. Head realized that Flood's assistance, as chair of HEW Appropriations, was critical to his operation if he hoped to secure federal grant money. Once he determined that he could purchase the congressman's influence through an unsavory administrative assistant, Head courted Elko, appealing to his inflated sense of self-importance. At the same time, Elko was impressed by Head's luxurious lifestyle and his ability to attract high-ranking government officials to his conferences and projects. He knew that there was considerable easy money to be made as a liaison between the Arlie director and Flood. He also understood that the federal laws governing campaign financing at the time limited individual contributions to one thousand dollars and corporate pack contributions to five thousand dollars.[31] As a result, he was always careful to demand cash payments of those specific amounts. If more money was paid, it meant an additional profit for him. Elko also requested that the contributions be paid in smaller bills, which were easier for him to pocket and spend. Head obliged, and, in the process, financed a fairly luxurious lifestyle for the administrative assistant.

Elko would later insist that of the forty-eight thousand dollars in bribes he collected from the Airlie director, Flood was given twenty-eight thousand dollars and Passman, twelve thousand dollars, while he admitted to pocketing just eight thousand.[32] Even if Elko divided the profits as he claimed, a significant portion of the bribe money still found its way into his pocket. What's more, the administrative assistant had developed a deceitful tendency to speak for Flood without his permission.

Elko's abuse of the congressman's authority did not go unnoticed by other staff members. Few, if any, trusted him, describing Elko as a "political muscleman" who fancied himself a "tough guy from the coal region." "Mr. Flood started getting in trouble once Steve came on board," recalled Sarah Sheerin, one of the secretaries. "Steve never did any of the [constituent] case work, it was Helen [Tomascik] or someone else who did that. He sat at his desk and phoned the executive departments to pressure them, using veiled threats in Mr. Flood's name. He was a very high-strung person, and if he didn't get his way, he'd become pretty belligerent in those phone conversations."

"Steve would throw his weight around the office, too," said Sheerin. "He knew he could get away with it because Mr. Flood wasn't well and he counted on him to run the office. Something I really didn't like about Steve was that he referred to Mr. Flood as the 'old man' all the time. It was *very* disrespectful. Steve was just a miserable individual and I made sure to keep my distance from him as much as possible."[33]

Ed Mitchell, a legislative aide, described Elko as "very greedy and power-hungry." "Steve liked to speak on behalf of Mr. Flood, who was very vulnerable because of his illness," he said. "The congressman needed to have someone like [former administrative assistant] Gene Hagerty to reign Elko in. Hagerty had had several dealings with Steve and was extremely wary of him. Gene was also very protective of Mr. Flood and he had much better political judgment than Elko. The congressman would have never gotten into the legal troubles that Elko created for him if Gene was around. All the problems began when Steve Elko took over the operation."[34]

Nor did Elko's own secretary have much respect for him. When asked about her opinion of the administrative assistant, Leona Yurishin told FBI agents that he was a "braggart" who was "unduly secretive about his activities." She also admitted that the congressman "placed too much trust in Elko," who was "not a very good administrator." As a result, Mr. Flood was "not generally concerned with the affairs of the office." She, too, insisted that Elko created "all of Mr. Flood's problems."[35]

Visitors to Flood's Capitol Hill office also gained the impression that Elko wasn't to be trusted. "I remember talking to Helen Tomascik, Dan's executive secretary, about Steve Elko," said Dr. Francis Michelini, former president of Wilkes College, in a recent interview. "There were times she was literally in tears about what he was doing. Dan didn't pay as much attention to office activities as he should have and Steve just abused his trust. Helen knew what was going on and couldn't do anything about it. Most of the people on the inside knew what games he was playing. I've always felt that Elko made Dan the scapegoat for his own illegal activities."[36]

Instead of monitoring Elko, Flood invested almost all of his energies on the House floor and committee matters. He relished the task of presiding over the House of Representatives in the Speaker's absence and was often asked to do so. When the opportunity arose, Flood acted like a schoolmaster, demanding absolute silence from members who usually gathered around the back rail of the chamber to gossip. Once, Flood went so far as to order Speaker John McCormack off the floor for talking out of turn. McCormack (D-Mass.) was, at the time, trying to secure enough votes for a crucial piece of legislation, which was his reason for turning the gavel over to Flood. But Flood didn't care. Instead, he reprimanded McCormack. "Our chief trouble is over in this right aisle," said Flood, pointing to a cluster of representatives who had gathered around the Massachusetts congressman. McCormack took the hint and retreated from the chamber with his cronies.[37]

Flood took special pride in his chairing of HEW Appropriations, which operated differently from most of the other subcommittees of Congress. When he first became chair in 1967, Flood called for a vote and lost, eight to

Fig. 30. Helen Tomascik joined Flood's Washington staff in 1955 as executive secretary. Devoted to the congressman, she paid all of his bills and managed his personal calendar, correspondence, and phone calls.

one. Thereafter, no more votes were taken. Instead, he insisted that the sub-committee reach a tacit consensus on all budget matters that came before it. Naturally, the resulting consensus tended to reflect Flood's own agenda. After-ward, he'd take the proposed HEW budget before the full Appropriations Committee, where it was, in theory, subjected to review and changes. But rarely were changes made. On July 22, 1971, for example, Flood, in top form, went before the full Appropriations Committee to present the HEW budget. He started his remarks with a controversial appropriation to combat alcoholism, a personal concern.

"I had an uncle that used to go up San Juan Hill every day years before Teddy Roosevelt ever heard of the place," he began in a humorous effort to disarm the critics.

Flood then paused to acknowledge the chuckles of appreciation.

"He was a drunk, an alcoholic," he continued. "Now I've seen these things, and there's enough money in this bill to do something about it."

Working from typewritten notes, Flood turned to the issue of funding for venereal disease. When he noticed the attention of the committee mem-bers was waning, he declared, "Gonorrhea is absolutely rampant! Rampant, I say, rampant!"

Again there were chuckles from the representatives.

"Now you better be careful," he warned, as laughter now rippled through the room.

"Okay," Flood said. "But you'll be laughing out the other side of your mouth after another seven days."

"Don't tinker with these numbers," he added, more seriously.

Next, Flood addressed President Nixon's sudden decision to spend one hundred million dollars on cancer research. "I have spies," he admitted. "How else do you think I know what's going on over there in the White House? And my spies tell me that the first draft of the President's speech didn't contain a word about cancer!"

Flood continued to hold court as only he could, cajoling, exhorting, warning, and pleading. When it came time for him to conclude, he emphasized the fantastic scope of his subcommittee's portion of the federal budget.

"The total for this bill," he said, "is $20,364,746,000."

"Do you hear that Casey?" asked Flood, turning to Rep. Robert Casey, a Democrat from Texas.

Repeating the figure, the flamboyant congressman asked, "Do you think we're moth-eaten, hunched-back chiselers? We're up two and a half billion since last year?"

Silence filled the room as the congressmen anticipated the punch line.

"You want to add another $500 billion?" snapped Flood. "We have another thirty minutes here. Why not add a billion?"

Waiting for someone to challenge him, the Pennsylvania legislator took a sip of water as the enormity of the figure sank in. There were no questions, no comments, no challenges.

"There are no magic numbers," he admitted. "Houdini couldn't do it, couldn't pick the right numbers. So the Lord asked Flood to do it!"

Before anyone could object, Flood snuck in additional expenditures for Social Security, railroad retirement, and other pension benefits.

"Eighty-three billion in the bill," he concluded. "It's bigger than Defense. Do you hear that? HEW is bigger than Defense."

As usual, House Appropriations approved Flood's budget and proceeded to review other proposals.[38]

Flood continued to be just as strong willed about constituent services as well. If anyone in the Eleventh District needed assistance, he simply refused to take "no" for an answer from the federal bureaucracy. "If you were a bureaucrat, you didn't want to get a call from Dan Flood," said Ed Mitchell, a former legislative aide:

> He would get on the phone and berate people to get what he wanted for his constituents. If a constituent sent him a letter complaining that

they weren't receiving their black lung payments, or their Social Security check was lost, he would pick up the phone and call the appropriate department and read them the riot act. You'd listen to the yelling coming out of the congressman's office and you knew the person on the receiving end couldn't be happy that he was talking to him. He was that way with local political figures, too. The bottom line was: "You don't mess with Flood."[39]

Tom Makowski, another aide, discovered that "other than God and country, Mr. Flood's greatest concern was for the folks back in the district." "I remember one occasion when an official in Columbia County called us in Washington," said Makowski.

They were concerned about an underground mine fire and how far it had spread. They phoned Congressman Flood and asked if we could somehow get them aerial photographs of the town that would show how far the fire had gone. We didn't know if we could do that or if the equipment even existed to do that.

Well, the congressman promised to deliver. He told me to get the Pentagon on the phone and see what they could do for us. The one advantage we had working for Mr. Flood is that his requests were always taken seriously. In fact, when I phoned the Pentagon and mentioned his name, the general on the other end of the line dropped the phone he was so shaken up. After he got himself together, he promised that he would act on the request immediately. That call took place late on a Friday afternoon.

On Monday morning, when the congressman returned to his office, he had a series of aerial photographs of Centralia on his desk, compliments of the Pentagon. The general had ordered a FR91 fighter jet with special photography equipment to fly over the town and take those photos. In other words, when Flood wanted something, it was taken care of immediately.[40]

Not all constituents felt comfortable approaching the congressman, though. Many of these were professional people who realized that Flood could be impetuous if not downright rude at times, especially if the individual was uninformed on the matter in question. "Dan was so ubiquitous, a consummate politician," recalled Francis Michelini, former Wilkes College president. "When he'd walk into a social gathering he'd treat you like you were his long-lost buddy. But we did not have a personal relationship. Dan was subject to different moods. You learned to keep a certain distance, unless you wanted to run the risk of being berated for not being properly educated on the issue you were addressing with him. So I didn't approach Dan unless I had a good reason. I dealt with him on various college-related issues and I always made sure that I was extremely well informed about the issue."[41]

Unfortunately for Flood, he was not as scrutinizing of Elko, who continued to exploit the congressman's authority for his own financial gain. One of the biggest scandals began in the spring of 1972 and involved a group of five Los Angeles educational institutions. Known as the West Coast Trade Schools, the centers offered courses in mechanics, welding, and drafting as well as secretarial skills. While they were accredited by the state of California, the trade schools were not accredited by the federal government, which was necessary for participation in the federally insured student loan program.[42] William Fred Peters, who became executive vice president of the West Coast Trade Schools in October 1971, was under tremendous pressure to secure federal accreditation by October 1972 or close the schools.[43] Peters decided to use a two-pronged strategy to achieve his goal. He would not only pursue accreditation through the appropriate legal channels by working with the National Association for Trade and Technical Schools (NATTS), the federal accrediting agency, but also employ a lobbyist on Capitol Hill in the hope of purchasing congressional influence to expedite the process.[44]

Peters retained the services of Deryl Fleming, a lobbyist employed by Kellogg, the cereal corporation of Battle Creek, Michigan. Fleming maintained an office at the Congressional Hotel, which also served as the National Democratic Social Club. He had worked on Capitol Hill since the early 1960s and had become acquainted with many congressmen, including Flood, who also kept an apartment at the Congressional Hotel.[45]

On February 11, 1972, Peters and Fleming met with William Goddard, NATTS executive secretary and the official in charge of the accreditation process. Goddard told them that it would take two years for accreditation and that Peters would stand a better chance if he submitted just two of the schools for review instead of all five. Peters insisted that all five schools be considered by the accreditation board in July, the earliest possible date to meet his October deadline. After considerable argument, Goddard agreed to accept the required three-thousand-dollar fee to initiate the review process, but cautioned Peters that "it was unlikely that he could get anything done in just under a year."[46]

Shortly thereafter, Fleming suggested that Peters "start spreading some money around if he wanted to get the schools on the agenda for accreditation," and that if he wanted "political intervention" he should "talk to Steve Elko."[47] In March, Peters met with Elko and gave him the paperwork he needed to investigate the accreditation matter. The administrative assistant allegedly informed Flood of the conversation and convinced him of Peters's credibility because of their mutual friendship with lobbyist Deryl Fleming.[48]

On April 12 the NATTS survey team visited the five West Coast Trade Schools to complete their review.[49] The following week, Peters phoned Elko from Los Angeles for an update. He also mentioned that he would be flying in to Washington to meet with him and he wanted to get the accreditation on the NATTS agenda as soon as possible. Elko asked Peters if he "had his long underwear ready" and the trade school executive said that he did. "That's good," replied Elko, suggesting that he bring five pairs. "It is still a little chilly in Pennsylvania, and the Congressman needs long underwear to keep warm." Both men understood that "a pair of long underwear" referred to a thousand-dollar cash payment.[50]

A few days later, Peters flew to Washington and met with Elko and Fleming at the Congressional Hotel. Gathering in Elko's apartment, Peters gave five thousand dollars to Elko, who pocketed the money, saying that it would "come in handy now because it was right before Pennsylvania's primary election." That afternoon, Elko drove up to Wilkes-Barre and allegedly split the bribe with Flood, giving him three thousand dollars and keeping two thousand dollars to pay miscellaneous bills he had run up at restaurants and a liquor store on Capitol Hill.[51] Elko and Peters continued to phone each other over the next month, discussing the accreditation process and how the congressman might be able to assist in the matter.

In early May, Peters flew to Washington again. Fleming and Elko met him at National Airport and drove him the Cannon Office Building to meet Flood. During the car ride, Peters handed Fleming an envelope with five thousand dollars in it. When Elko saw the envelope he asked, "Is that for me?" At first, Fleming dismissed the question, but eventually turned the envelope over to Elko, who placed it in his pocket.[52]

When the three men arrived at the Cannon Building, Elko ushered Peters into the congressman's office. "This is Mr. Peters from the West Coast Trade Schools," said the administrative assistant, introducing him to Flood. Peters began to explain the difficulty he was having getting accreditation. "I know all about that," Flood allegedly said. "That is a very complex business. You just work with Stephen and you will get it all straightened out. I will help in whatever way I have to."[53]

On May 12 Elko, using Flood's congressional stationery, wrote a letter to Sidney Marland, commissioner in the Office of Education, requesting his assistance in securing accreditation for the West Coast Trade Schools. Elko signed Flood's name at the end of the letter and mailed it.[54] He had now incriminated the congressman in a bribery scandal.

Having already extracted ten thousand dollars from Fred Peters, Elko began to explore other ways to exploit the relationship. Intech, the Wilkes-Barre consulting and computer software company that formerly employed him, was in severe financial trouble. Patricia Brislin, the owner of the company, was also Elko's girlfriend. Hoping to milk more money from Peters, Elko contacted him in early June demanding more compensation for Congressman Flood's involvement in the accreditation process.

On June 16 Peters flew to Washington and met with Elko and Fleming at the administrative assistant's Congressional Hotel apartment. After giving Elko five thousand dollars and Fleming two thousand dollars for their services, Peters was informed of Intech's situation. Elko said that Flood had a "special interest" in the company and suggested that Peters might want to contribute fifteen thousand dollars to save Flood from "great embarrassment" if it had to declare bankruptcy.[55] In other words, Elko was now making Flood's assistance for accreditation contingent on Peters's help in bailing out Intech.

On June 23, Education Commissioner Marland informed Congressman Flood's office that NATTS was going to place the accreditation of the West Coast Trade Schools on its July agenda for review.[56] When Peters heard the news, he was hard-pressed to reject Elko's demand. Only one thing prevented him from fulfilling it sooner—a hurricane named Agnes.

9

ONE FLOOD AGAINST ANOTHER

Flood may have invested unwarranted trust and authority in Stephen Elko, but he still yearned to be the center of attention. His swan song came in the summer of 1972, when he took on the challenge of a ferocious hurricane that pelted the eastern seaboard.

Known as Agnes, the hurricane proved to be the nation's most destructive natural disaster up to that time, with total losses estimated at $3.5 billion. Pennsylvania suffered more than any other state, with damages valued at more than one billion dollars. Hundreds of industrial plants were closed, putting more than fifty thousand people out of work. Thousands were homeless. Nowhere was the devastation more severe than in the Wyoming Valley, where torrential rains sent the Susquehanna River over its dike-lined banks and chased thousands of residents to higher ground.

Agnes was unforgiving. It transformed the valley into a muddy ghost town. More than 20,000 homes, 159 factories, and 2,728 business establishments were destroyed. Debris hung from telephone wires. The newborn and the elderly crowded into makeshift hospitals while families tried to find lost members. The final estimation of damage was over one billion dollars.[1] Initially, Flood admitted that "for the first time in my life, I didn't know what to say." But he quickly regrouped and left no stone unturned to secure all the federal, state, and local assistance his influence could muster. Rising to the seemingly insurmountable challenge, Flood prepared himself for the recovery effort, proclaiming, "This is going to be one flood against another!"[2]

Hurricane Agnes was not the first flood to ravage the Wyoming Valley. In March 1936 severe rainstorms caused the Susquehanna to crest more than thirty-five feet above the watermark, flooding over a forty-five-square-mile area that included Wilkes-Barre, Kingston, Exeter, Forty-Fort, Plymouth, Nanticoke, West Pittston, Wyoming, and several other smaller towns. The Flood of 1936 created losses valued at more than ten million dollars. As a result, the Army Corps of Engineers spent twenty-seven million dollars to build a levee system of dikes and interlocking piles to prevent another similar disaster.[3] But over the years, the dikes eroded because of ongoing mining under the levee system and the resulting subsidence.[4]

By the 1960s, the corps of engineers recommended that the sagging flood walls be repaired. The most vulnerable sections of the levee system were the dike at Wilkes-Barre's Horton Street pumping station, which had settled sixty inches, and the dike at Kingston's Church Street station, which had settled forty-two inches. Other subsided sections in Wilkes-Barre ran about 5,800 feet, and in Hanover Township approximately 6,300 feet. In the summer of 1959, Dan Flood secured $305,000 to repair these sections with sheet steel piling, but these were only stopgap measures. Flood continued his efforts for emergency funding to repair the dikes, eventually restoring them to their original height.[5] But the highest of the levees was 37 feet, still lower than the 40.6-foot crest later reached by Agnes.[6] Thus the Wyoming Valley was woefully unprepared for what would become the worst natural disaster in its history.

The storm began as a "tropical depression," or area of low barometric pressure, over Mexico's Yucatán Peninsula on Thursday, June 15, 1972. Dubbed Agnes by the meteorologists, who name the first storm of the hurricane season after the letter A, the gale quickly developed into a tropical storm the following day, and then, on June 17, a Category 1 hurricane. Though the Category 1 is the weakest of the five possible classifications, the hurricane can still be tremendously destructive. Agnes reached Florida on June 19 with full gale-force winds. Traveling up the East Coast about 150 miles inland, the hurricane traversed across Georgia, South Carolina, North Carolina, and Virginia. When Agnes reached New Jersey it appeared to be heading out to sea. Instead, the hurricane shifted abruptly inland from the Atlantic coast toward Pennsylvania on June 22. For three days, torrential rains poured down on the Commonwealth, first pelting the eastern part of the state then circling over central Pennsylvania before moving northwest across New York State and into western Ontario. Finally, Agnes dissipated off the coast of Nova Scotia on Tuesday, June 27.[7]

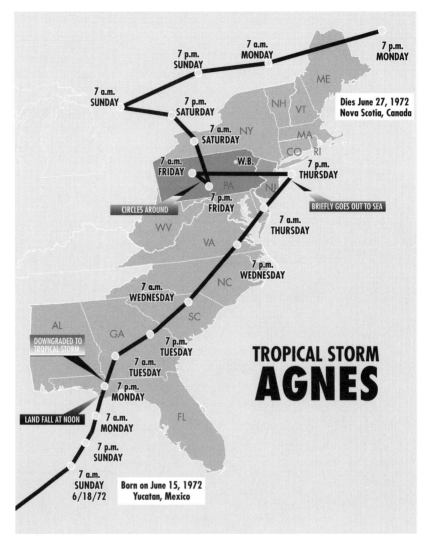

Fig. 31. Map of Hurricane Agnes's path, June 15–27, 1972.

On Thursday, June 22, Congressman Flood was preparing for the annual markup of his Labor-HEW Appropriations bill and entertaining the various generals who were making their pilgrimage to obtain his support for defense appropriations. That night Flood received a series of phone calls indicating the trouble that lay ahead. Nicholas Souchik of the Civil Defense Office at the Luzerne County Courthouse informed the congressman that the underground water table had become saturated, forcing the rainwater to run off immediately into the Susquehanna, and that the river was rising fast and running swiftly.

Joe Collis of the *Wilkes-Barre Record* indicated that extremely severe flooding was anticipated by morning, and that General Frank Townend, head of the local civil defense, had already urged the evacuation of patients from hospitals in the flood plain and the removal of vital equipment and records from government installations. Doug Thomas, Flood's Wilkes-Barre driver, confirmed the reports, adding that residents of low-lying areas unprotected by the levees were also urged to evacuate, and that a call had gone out for volunteers to sandbag the levee system.[8] It was time to act.

Flood phoned his aide Michael Clark and instructed him to "line up a special plane, maybe a chopper, we're going to have to go up in the morning."

There was no sleep. The early morning news that the river had spilled over the dikes and volunteers were desperately filling sandbags prompted the congressman to phone secretary of defense Melvin Laird, a former colleague on House Appropriations.[9]

"Dan, it's one thirty in the morning," Laird said, trying to awaken from a deep sleep. "What on earth do you want at this hour?"

"Melvin," said Flood, "you can get your sleep some other time. Right now, I need your help. I've got a natural disaster in my district. The rains from Agnes have left people homeless."

"What do you need?" asked Laird.

"I need a fleet of helicopters with good pilots so I can deliver supplies and rescue people who are stranded and all the military assistance you can get me," replied Flood.

"How soon do you need 'em?" asked the secretary of defense.

"By tomorrow morning."

"Anything else?"

"Yes," replied Flood. "I need a command center up there."

"Okay," said Laird. "Give me an hour, I'll see what I can do."

By dawn, Flood had secured a fleet of military choppers as well as the secretary of defense's personal helicopter to travel to Wilkes-Barre. Laird also arranged to have a large trailer delivered to the congressman to use as a mobile command post and issued general alerts to the army reserve, navy reserve, and the National Guard that "Congressman Flood would need help—expect his call, and take care of it."[10]

On Friday morning, June 23, a state of chaos existed at 108 Cannon Building, where Flood's Capitol Hill office suite was located. Ringing phones, unconfirmed reports, and rumors constantly interrupted his staff as they attempted to conduct a comprehensive review of the situation. "I had a hard time trying to digest what we were hearing about the level of suffering," recalled Jim

Dyer, legislative director for congressman Joseph McDade, who ordered his staff to assist Flood. "We were hearing about coffins being washed up from cemeteries and floating down river and whole communities being under water. We wondered whether the rural communities along the tributaries of the Susquehanna could even continue to exist."[11]

Special assistant Michael Clark, legislative aide Richard Altmann, and assistant Tom Jones were told that they would be accompanying the congressman on the flight back to the flood-ravaged district. Steve Elko, the administrative assistant, insisted that he should also go. When Clark asked Flood where they would land, he said that they would go to the new Naval Reserve Center at Avoca. "We'll go with the military," added the congressman. "Always go with the military in emergencies like this, you're going to need them." It was a logical choice since it was located near the airport and far from the river, where the telephone lines had not been washed away.[12]

Just before 1:00 P.M., Flood and his staffers rushed to a waiting car and sped to the Pentagon, where they boarded Laird's helicopter. Within minutes they were airborne, bound for Wilkes-Barre. Flood, usually loquacious, remained silent for most of the ride. He was shocked by the devastation he observed below. Flying over Harrisburg, the new governor's mansion was hardly visible. Houses were immersed in ugly brown floodwaters. Another helicopter was lifting residents off rooftops in a rescue mission. The closer they came to the Wyoming Valley, the more surreal it all seemed. Forty Fort Borough was under water. Nothing but rooftops could be seen over Kingston. Wilkes-Barre looked like a war zone. The dikes were invisible and largely destroyed. Motor- and rowboats were buzzing across Public Square. Army, navy, coast guard, and National Guard troops were barricading impassable roads and bridges. Choppers resembling giant dragonflies flew across the sky, plucking refugees off rooftops and ferrying them to the local airport. When Flood finally landed at Avoca, there was no one to drive him to the Naval Reserve Center. Instead, Clark hailed a pickup truck and the small party rushed off.[13]

By the time Flood's party arrived at the makeshift command center, General Townend had given the order to abandon the sandbagging effort as the rampaging river had already broken through the levee at two points—on the west side, at Forty Fort, and on the east side along Riverside Drive—and was spilling over the levee in several other areas.

Howard Glad, a thirty-year-old navy lieutenant, had assumed command at the Avoca Naval Reserve Center just a few days earlier. Glad was hardly prepared for Flood's arrival when the congressman swept in, commandeered his office, and made him his "Navy lieutenant two-striper operations officer."

Fig. 32. Aerial view of Public Square in Wilkes-Barre at the height of the flooding, June 1972.

Throughout the summer of 1972, Glad would supervise nine thousand military personnel who provided twenty-four-hour guard over the Wyoming Valley, restored electrical service, arrested looters, and enforced an 8:00 P.M. curfew during the cleanup.[14] "He had no authority to do this," Glad later explained. But the young lieutenant certainly wasn't going to challenge a congressman who had just arrived in the secretary of defense's personal helicopter.

"What do you need here?" Flood asked.

"More helicopters," Glad replied, and then explained the difficulty in getting the authorization to have them sent in.

Flood got on the phone to an out-of-state military installation. When he met with resistance, the congressman made it clear that he was a senior member of the Defense Appropriations Committee. "If your boss is a four striper with stars in his eyes," Flood added, "tell him to get moving or he'll never see those stars." Forty additional choppers arrived that afternoon.[15]

During the next few days, the helicopters were making around 1,600 sorties a day, airlifting patients to hospitals on higher ground, evacuating stranded victims, or dropping relief supplies. "We were yanking people off of rooftops and porches, hilltops and trucks," recalled Glad. "There were eighteen cardiac arrests, two Caesarean sections, two appendectomies, and two tracheotomies following helicopter evacuations. Without Mr. Flood we wouldn't have had any helicopter support in those critical first days. Without the helicopters, at least 1,000 people might have died. As it was there were only four deaths."[16]

Flood also contacted several hospitals that were unaffected by the flood-waters to ascertain their patient capacity and coordinated the evacuation of patients from hospitals in the afflicted areas, including the Mercy, Nesbitt, and Wilkes-Barre General.[17] "Congressman Flood just took over," recalled John McKeown, former personnel officer at the Veterans Hospital. "General Townend had begun the evacuation of patients the night before, but with Flood it became more organized. Everyone knew he was running the show. At the VA, we took in patients from the Mercy, Nesbitt, and the Leader nursing home. We even created a heliport behind the hospital to receive emergency patients from Misericordia's nursing home. Since we had access to our supply depot at Summerville, New Jersey, we were able to accommodate the congressman's need for medical supplies at the makeshift clinics that were set up at the airport, Pocono Downs Raceway, and GAR High School."[18]

Meanwhile a conflict was brewing with General Townend, who resented federal intervention in a crisis that he believed could have been handled locally. Flood and Townend were friends, but they had strikingly different views about the role of government and the use of the military during natural disasters. Matters came to a head when Flood discovered that a local contingent of the Pennsylvania National Guard was heading out of the district for military exercises in Virginia. "What the hell are they going to Virginia for," he barked over the phone to Governor Milton Shapp. "We have a *real* war right here damn it! I want them to stay here!" Shapp informed the congressman that such action could not occur until Civil Defense had requested a declaration of disaster. The order had to come from Pennsylvania's civil defense director, Lieutenant Governor Ernest Kline, and that such an order could only come after General Townend, as director of the Luzerne County Civil Defense, requested a declaration of disaster.

Flood spent the next twelve hours waging a battle of wills with Townend. The general had established his command post at the old Wilkes-Barre School District Administrative Building on South Main Street. Since the city's phone lines were down, Flood ordered the state police to drive his assistant, Richard Altmann, into Wilkes-Barre, where he would be taken by motorboat across Public Square for a personal meeting with Townend. When Altmann returned to Avoca a few hours later, he had in hand a list of the general's objections of why the National Guard should not be redeployed to Wilkes-Barre. Townend believed that since ten thousand volunteers had already manned the sandbag operation on the dikes that morning, there was plenty of civilian help available. Flood, referring to the dike rupture on South River Street, barked, "Go back and tell him it didn't work!"

Again, the state police drove Altmann to the brink of the floodwaters at Wilkes-Barre, where he boated across Public Square to the general's command post on South Main Street. And once again, he returned to Flood with another list of objections. Determined to have his way, Flood circumvented Townend's authority by placing a series of phone calls to army generals, Lieutenant Governor Kline, and his close friend Secretary of Defense Laird. By noon the following day, the congressman had achieved his goal. The local National Guard contingent did an about face en route to Virginia and returned to the Wyoming Valley.[19]

On Saturday, June 24, at 4:00 P.M., Flood met with his closest congressional colleague, Joseph McDade of neighboring Lackawanna County, and Secretary of Housing and Urban Development (HUD) George Romney. Their primary concern was how to provide housing for the thousands of people left homeless by the natural disaster. The conversation would lead to the greatest federal disaster response to that date, the Agnes Recovery Act. Tens of thousands of displaced homeowners would receive 1 percent Small Business Administration disaster loans, with the first five thousand dollars completely forgiven. The measure also provided for federally backed business loans in the millions at preferred rates, emergency grants for hospitals and medical centers, federal funds for local colleges, the rebuilding of bridges, and a master plan for higher dikes.[20]

The same night, a fire started in Wilkes-Barre and threatened to spread throughout the downtown. Because the burning office buildings were surrounded by floodwaters, it was impossible for fire trucks to get to the scene. Flood, likening the situation to a fire at sea, contacted the coast guard and secured a fireboat. Then he placed a call to an air force general who found him a C-130 transport to fly the boat to Wilkes-Barre. When the plane touched down at Avoca, two flatbed trucks from the Tobyhanna Army Depot rushed the boat to the city, where it motored off to put out the fire.[21]

On Sunday afternoon, June 25, Flood, wearing army fatigues and standing on a hill with a sea of muddy waters in the background, appeared on television and announced, "Today I have ordered the Army Corps of Engineers not to allow the Susquehanna River to rise one more inch."[22] It never did. By 8:00 P.M. the water had fallen below dike level, and by the following day the river was below the twenty-two-foot flood stage.

Dan Flood seemed to be everywhere during the first week of the recovery effort. At age sixty-eight, he was putting in twenty-hour days, a fact that concerned one of his physicians, Dr. Edward Janjigan, president of the Luzerne County Medical Society. "During the Agnes Disaster it was necessary for me to make frequent trips to the Navy Reserve Center at Avoca," recalled Janjigan. "Often I saw Mr. Flood there, working at his desk, phoning here, there and everywhere, interviewing homeless residents. When not at his command post, he was riding in helicopters, surveying the damage in the valley, or visiting the various evacuation centers. Too often, he would brunch on a stale ham sandwich, washing it down with a soda. There were times I noticed that he was exhausted, even dizzy, and I would encourage him to rest. But he refused saying, 'My people need me, Murph.'"[23] Flood somehow managed to persevere as the demands on him grew. He directed, firsthand, the rescue operation of stranded flood victims, mustering military equipment and personnel to carry out a massive food and medical supply airlift for more than seventy thousand refugees. For three weeks, the congressman made nightly reports from WNEP-TV's studio on the federal government's ongoing role in victims' assistance. He read messages from loved ones in an effort to reunite them with their families, reported on road conditions, and identified telephone numbers for emergency relief. And he fulfilled requests from every local state representative and constituent who came to see him at his Avoca command post.[24]

"Dan Flood ran the show," recalled Raphael Musto, then a newly elected state representative from Pittston who would later succeed Flood on Capitol Hill.

> Whatever had to be done, he did. Whatever the state representatives requested he got for us. All we had to do was go to Avoca and ask. I remember making several requests for my constituents and Dan fulfilled every one. Lombardo's Bakery in Exeter, for example, met a critical need for the region for supplying bread and other baked goods during that time. Their operation was not damaged by the floodwaters so they were still up and running. But they couldn't get flour. So I went up to Avoca and asked Dan for help. Within twenty-four hours, he got his hands on more flour than you can ever imagine. Lombardo's was making and distributing bread for many of the towns on that side of the river.[25]

Through it all, Flood made sure he was the center of attention, going so far as to hire a photographer to document his activities.

"During the Agnes recovery, I'd go up in the army helicopters with the congressman," recalled James Kozemchak, who became Flood's personal photographer in June 1972:

> I'd photograph him at different places, documenting his role in leading the recovery. Mr. Flood was easy to shoot because he had two outstanding features that defined him—his mustache and his wardrobe. The waxed mustache was his signature mark and the flamboyant clothing added to his dramatic presence, especially that cream-colored Edwardian suit he'd wear when making an announcement.
>
> When it came to being photographed, there was only one thing he insisted on. He'd always tell me, "Jim, remember, I want to be in the middle of the photograph. I don't want to be cut out of it." I had heard that the *Wilkes-Barre Record* had done that to him sometime in the late forties when he was fighting for reelection and it cost him his congressional seat. He certainly remembered the incident and refused to let it happen again.
>
> Of course, after I went on a shoot with the congressman, I'd send the proofs to his special assistant Michael Clark and he would decide which ones to send out to the press. That summer, the congressman's photo was in the newspaper almost on a daily basis. We didn't miss a single photo opportunity. Shooting Dan Flood was without a doubt, the most exciting experience I ever had as a photographer.[26]

The photographs weren't just for show; they served a practical purpose. Flood was extremely sensitive about his responsibility for constituent service. He wanted the voters of his district to know that he was there for them in their greatest moment of need. Flood realized that newspaper coverage was instrumental in delivering that message on a daily basis. News stories were good, but photos were even better. What made him so special during the recovery effort was his ability to change roles from "show horse" to "work horse" in such a fluid manner that the transition went largely unnoticed. To lobby for disaster relief assistance, Flood invited several of his congressional colleagues to the Wyoming Valley that summer.[27] He also summoned bureaucrats from an assortment of federal agencies to his command post at the Naval Reserve Center. It was clear to all of them that the congressman wanted results, not excuses. Two HUD officials arrived to determine temporary housing needs. Three days later, they returned, covered with mud and in a state of shock. After they gave a detailed account of the damage, Flood remarked, sarcastically, "Why you must have crystal balls. Those are the very questions I was going to ask you to look into." When one of the officials began making excuses for the agency's inability to meet the demanding housing needs in a timely manner, Flood cut him off. "Okay, that's enough," he said. "Pull down the curtain!"[28] On another occasion, an official from the General Services Administration made a mistake in fulfilling one of Flood's requests and offered alternative supplies to make up for it. Visibly angered by the gaffe, the congressman barked, "I'm getting food flown in here. I'm getting medicine and personnel. Now I want germicides from you. I want soap and I want it tonight!" The official mumbled his assent as Flood waved him away, saying, "That's it, enough for one show."[29]

"Anything Dan Flood wanted that summer, Washington was prepared to give him," recalled Melvin Laird, then secretary of defense. "I know that I certainly did. In fact, my wife, who was the head of the volunteers for national disasters, went up to Wilkes-Barre to help him out at his command center. It was that way with the military, too. You have to remember that Dan was a major part of the Defense Appropriations Subcommittee. That meant that when he told those staff officers to 'jump,' they asked, 'How high?' If they didn't, there'd be consequences."[30]

Realizing that he would also need assistance from the local community, on Monday, June 26, Flood called a meeting of prominent business and civic leaders at the Naval Reserve Center. Their charge was to address the pressing issues of emergency shelter, food, and medical care. "Most of the members at that meeting were bankers, because they understood how important economic recovery was going to be," recalled Harold Rosenn, an attorney who was among the twenty citizens at the gathering. "Dan explained to us how the federal loans he was bringing in were to be used. In turn, we were asked to educate the community. He expected us to work long, hard hours, and no one was going to be paid. It was a civic responsibility."[31] Another attendee was Rosenn's older brother, Max, a longtime civic leader and federal judge who had been appointed to the U.S. Third Circuit Court of Appeals by president Richard Nixon two years earlier. It was apparent to those who met with Flood that the judge was the most obvious choice to lead a local task force because of his tremendous influence in the community as well as in Washington. Accordingly, the group championed a movement among the valley's businessmen, bankers, lawyers, social workers, and community activists to recruit Judge Rosenn as the leader of the Flood Recovery Task Force.[32]

The nonprofit, grassroots organization was formally established on July 4 at a meeting held in Rosenn's judicial chambers in the old Wilkes-Barre Post Office, now the Wilkes-Barre Federal Building. Comprising more than one hundred people and led by an executive committee of about twenty-five, the task force, whose five-hundred-thousand-dollar budget was paid for by the federal government, "coordinated emergency recovery measures with long range area urban development." Their initial task was to attack the issues of transportation, construction, flood control, financial aid, and social service and educational needs.[33]

"The community was paralyzed," recalled Rosenn. "It would take a herculean effort by some organized movement to bring the Valley back to life. One of the first things we did was to ask the presidents of each lending institution to suspend payments on mortgages and loans for ninety days. Without a murmur, they did. The next thing we did was to establish contact with key people in the federal government."[34] Rosenn solicited help from Senators Richard Schweiker and Hugh Scott, then the Republican minority leader of the Senate. When Scott toured the Wyoming Valley in early July, he described the scene as "the greatest natural catastrophe in the history of this country."[35] When President Nixon heard Scott's account, he instantly pledged unprecedented federal aid, though he stopped short of any specifics.[36] Scott, on the other hand, drafted a five-point plan to rebuild flood-ravaged Wilkes-Barre and the surrounding area.

Scott's plan would transform all of Wilkes-Barre into a "Model City" eligible for additional millions of dollars in funding from the U.S. Department of Housing and Urban Development.[37] The plan also proposed new legislation to increase federal grants to homeowners from $2,500 to $4,500, and included recommendations that more federal money be made available through the Economic Development Administration, the U.S. Department of Transportation, and a revision of Disaster and Relief Act of 1970. Scott estimated that the cost of recovery for the entire Commonwealth of Pennsylvania would be two billion dollars, and that half of that total would go to the Wyoming Valley.[38]

In the private sector, Thomas H. Kiley, chair of the board of the First National Bank of Eastern Pennsylvania, and Harold J. Rose, Jr., president and CEO of the Wyoming National Bank, went to work on an equity proposal that was based on the idea of coinsurance. Under the plan, the federal government would reimburse home owners for 70 percent of their losses up to thirty thousand dollars, state government would cover 20 percent, and the individual, 10 percent. Kiley and Rose, along with other leaders from the private sector, traveled to Washington to present the plan to Nixon administration officials, who appeared to be intrigued by it.[39]

Administration officials gave serious consideration to both the private sector's proposal and various elements of Senator Scott's legislation. John Ehrlichman, Nixon's chief domestic policy adviser, urged the president to take a very generous and humanistic approach toward the Agnes victims. By doing so, Nixon, a Republican, would improve his standing in a heavily Democratic state in his bid for reelection. It would be a clever way to "out-McGovern" Senator George McGovern, his liberal Democratic challenger from South Dakota. Nixon seized the moment and offered an extremely liberal recovery package. "Confronted with so massive a disaster emergency, our response as a nation must also be massive," he reasoned. "Conscience commands it; humanity impels it."

On July 14, vice president Spiro Agnew revealed the administration's proposal before a gathering of five hundred in the East Room of the White House. Known as the Agnes Recovery Act of 1972, the package proposed an unprecedented request for $1.6 billion in aid, including: up to $60 million in emergency transportation relief; up to $40 million in long-term loans for damaged railroad facilities; low-interest loans through the Farmer's Home Administration; and a significant expansion of the federal flood insurance program. Although the private sector's plan for coinsurance was not part of the proposal, the legislation revised the Disaster Relief Act of 1970 in two important ways. First, Small Business Administration (SBA) loans would be granted at the remarkable rate of 1 percent interest for up to thirty years, with the first $5,000 forgiven or granted to the recipient. The provisions of this measure were applicable to home owners as well as renters, businesspeople, and bankers. Another crucial change in the 1970 law made recovery funds available to private, nonprofit educational institutions.[40]

Agnew was followed by Frank Carlucci, deputy director of the Office of Management and Budget, who drafted the administration's proposal. Carlucci, a native of Beer Creek and a graduate of Wyoming Seminary, expressed the need for dynamic local leadership if the recovery effort was to be successful. "We will do all we can to see that the federal government implements these measures rapidly and effectively," he promised. "But we will need rapid local decisions to do this." "We must create a psychology in our communities that looks not backward to tragedy, but forward into the future with enthusiasm," he added.[41]

The administration sent the proposal to Capitol Hill on July 17. The measure was introduced in the Senate by Scott and Schweiker, and in the House by Flood, who began his presentation with the tongue-in-cheek remark: "My name is Flood, and I am from Wilkes-Barre." Superbly timed, the comment was received by his colleagues with laughter and applause, which quickly became a standing ovation. It was a moving gesture of the respect and affection the representatives had for Flood, as well as an emotional response to the stories of devastation they had heard about his ravaged district.[42] But passage was not immediate or assured.

Five weeks of intense debate ensued. Initially, the administration caused confusion by sending two different Agnes bills to Capitol Hill within the span of twenty-four hours, the second (HR 15935) being more liberal than the first (HR 15890). After the matter was resolved and the second bill was debated, its extremely liberal provisions caused some consternation among conservatives. "In the space of five months we have seen a complete reversal of the Administration's position," complained Rep. Wright Patman of Mississippi, chair of the House Banking Committee. Patman was referring to the president's Office of Emergency Preparedness, which had sent an earlier bill to Congress eliminating the $2,500 SBA loan forgiveness and set loan interest rates in the 2 percent range.

Complicating matters was the fact that on June 29, 1972, two weeks before the administration submitted its bill, the House of Representatives passed HR 15692, which already reformed the Disaster Relief Act of 1970 by approving 1 percent SBA disaster loan interest rates. At the time, there was significant opposition to lowering rates, not only within the administration and the SBA, but also in the House, where Republicans argued that the existing $2,500 forgiveness and 3 percent rates were "more than adequate." When HR 15692 came to a vote, the 1 percent rate was rejected but the main bill passed.

The Flood Recovery Task Force followed the congressional deliberations carefully. An amended version of HR 15692 was approved in the Senate Banking Committee before it went to the floor. The amended version included SBA loans at the 1 percent interest rate and five-thousand-dollar forgiveness. The debate was intense. Task force members traveled to Washington to urge passage of the bill. Senator Richard Schweiker's passionate floor speech appeared to save the day. "Since the end of World War II, we have given away $210 billion in foreign aid and Marshall plan aid," he reminded his colleagues. "When at the drop of the hat, we will decide to spend $100 billion to rebuild Europe and rebuild the industries of Japan, I think it is about time we paid attention to our own people when they get hit with the greatest natural disaster in the history of the United States of America."

The Senate passed the amended bill on August 4, but because of the differences between it and the House version, a Joint Conference Committee comprising members of both houses met to craft a compromise. During their deliberations, tremendous political pressure was being applied in all

Fig. 33. Flood directs a bipartisan effort to pass legislation for the Agnes Recovery with Pennsylvania senators
Hugh Scott and Richard Schweiker.

corridors of power. Task force members met with presidential assistant John
Ehrlichman and OMB deputy chief Frank Carlucci to make sure that the
White House was doing everything it could to influence passage. They also
met with various representatives trying to persuade them to vote for the most
liberal measure of the bill. Flood was busy in the House calling in his IOUs to
make loan forgiveness easier for victims and insure tax relief for the stricken
communities and private educational institutions in his congressional district.
Scott and Schweiker were doing the same in the Senate. All their efforts paid off
when the committee agreed on the 1 percent interest rates and five-thousand-
dollar forgiveness.

On August 11 the final bill passed the Senate. Three days later, Flood and
Rep. Joseph McDade introduced the final bill in the House, where it passed
by a unanimous 392–0 vote. Finally, on August 16, President Nixon signed
the main bill and the supplemental appropriations bill into law, insuring a
federal disaster relief package totaling $1.6 billion. The major portion of that
funding was made available through liberalized SBA grants and loans to
restore homes, businesses, and farms.[43]

The Agnes Recovery Act of 1972 provided a level of assistance for disaster
victims unprecedented in the history of the nation. Prior to that time, federal
disaster loans were at 6 percent of the going rate of interest. Reducing the rate
to 1 percent had never been done before. What's more, the reduced rate applied
to home owners as well as renters, businesspeople, and bankers. The Agnes
measure also marked the first time that private educational institutions were

included in federal disaster legislation. "It was a very liberal piece of legislation for the Nixon administration," admitted Carlucci. "The president realized
that the present program needed to be liberalized if we were to help the Agnes
victims recover from the disaster and he gave me carte blanche to draft that legislation. To the administration's credit, the measure provided a level of assistance
for disaster victims that no United States government had ever provided."[44]

"Dan saved our ass," admitted Dr. Francis Michelini, then president of
Wilkes College.

> We had a total of fifty-eight buildings on our campus all of which were
> affected by the floodwaters, some more severely than others. The total
> estimate of damages was ten million dollars. There was no way that we
> could have repaired that level of damage with our own limited financial
> resources, and at that time private colleges were not envisioned as the fed-
> eral government's responsibility in any way. But Dan had three private
> educational institutions in his district that were in serious need of disaster
> relief assistance: Wilkes, King's [College], and Wyoming Seminary. So he
> looked into the legislative history and found an earlier precedent for the
> federal government's funding of a private Catholic hospital in Alaska that
> had been severely damaged by an earthquake a few years earlier. Dan used
> that case as the precedent to push for federal relief for the private educa-
> tional institutions in his district. Thank goodness he did because Wilkes
> received almost eleven million dollars in disaster relief funds. Without that
> assistance it's doubtful that we would have been able to recover.[45]

To be sure, the Agnes Recovery Act saved the Wyoming Valley. "It was a
godsend for everybody up here," insisted Harold Rosenn, a member of the
Flood Recovery Task Force. "It saved local lending institutions from almost
certain disaster and a lot of homeowners and small businessmen as well. It
revitalized industry, got our homes built, and allowed us to return to a normal
way of living in about a year's time. And you really had to thank Dan Flood
for that. In his own inimitable way, Dan got the measure passed in the House.
I see that legislation as one of his greatest achievements."[46]

Meanwhile, frustrations were running high in the Wyoming Valley. Although
work crews had removed 75 percent of the flood debris by mid-July, temporary
housing in the form of trailers provided by the U.S. Department of Housing
and Urban Development was difficult to secure. Angry residents blamed the
HUD bureaucracy for their troubles. To ease the tension, President Nixon sent
HUD secretary George Romney to northeastern Pennsylvania. He arrived on

Fig. 34. President Nixon and special assistant Frank Carlucci (*center*) present a check for four million dollars to Wilkes College president Francis Michelini (*right*) to assist the college in its recovery. The Agnes disaster marked the first time that private educational institutions were included in federal disaster legislation.

August 7 and spent the next three days touring disaster sites, reassuring victims, and conferring with local officials. Tempers flared on the final day of Romney's visit when he was confronted by a group of twenty-five angry protesters at the Dan Flood Elementary School in Wilkes-Barre, where the HUD secretary had attended a meeting with local, county, and state officials.

Angry over being turned away from the meeting, the protesters met Romney at a postmeeting press conference at the front of the school. Governor Shapp's opening comments, criticizing the federal government for not releasing funds in a timely manner, didn't help matters. When Romney, a conservative Republican, took the microphone he not only lectured Shapp, a liberal Democrat, for his "unrealistic and demagogic rhetoric," but also chastised the demonstrators. Min Matheson, the prominent leader of the local garment workers union, had heard enough. She charged Romney, shoving a photograph of her daughter's flood-ravaged home in his face. "You don't give a damn if we live or die," she shouted. "Why did you come and meet with the officials? They haven't done anything! They ran away and haven't even seen the flood area. Why not meet with the people?"

Amid a shower of jeers, Romney responded by insisting that the principal recovery effort must come from individuals with help from volunteers and the private sector. But Matheson and Shapp held their ground, declaring that only the federal government had the resources to solve the problem. Shapp reinforced the point by criticizing Nixon's refusal to release a surplus of twelve billion dollars left over from various federal programs for use by Agnes victims. The confrontation made front-page headlines across the nation the next day, prompting Romney to tender his resignation.[47]

Nixon could ill afford the negative publicity in an election year, especially in a critical state like Pennsylvania. On August 12 the president appointed Frank Carlucci as his special representative to the flood-ravaged Wyoming Valley. "After the Romney visit, the president asked me to review the management of the recovery," recalled Carlucci in a recent interview.

> I made several recommendations to him, one of which was *not* to send a czar. Instead, I suggested that the Federal Regional Council assume responsibility in Wilkes-Barre with one of its members receiving a special presidential appointment as chairman. This was in keeping with my belief that the federal government can help in the recovery but local leadership would have to assume the primary responsibility for it. I also wanted to strengthen the Federal Regional Councils and I thought a czar would set an undesirable precedent. Of course, the president felt differently.
>
> That weekend, the president asked me to meet with him at Camp David. When we met he told me that we had a mess in Wilkes-Barre and he wanted me to straighten it out. He was making me the federal officer in charge of the recovery. President Nixon was also clear that I would get all the assistance I needed. I was, at the time, the deputy director of the Office of Management and Budget and knew where all the federal resources were. I was also born in Scranton and raised in the Wilkes-Barre/Kingston area, so I was very familiar with the area. So "flood czar" was a natural position.[48]

From mid-August through December 1972, Carlucci directed the recovery effort. To avoid any confusion, he immediately met with Flood and insisted that he respect his authority. The two men had known each other for many years and Carlucci was familiar with Flood's strong-willed nature. "When I first got to Wilkes-Barre, I assured Dan that he was a shoe-in for reelection," recalled the former OMB administrator. "So reelection should not be a concern for him. At the same time, I emphasized that there had to be one point person and the president gave me that responsibility, not him." When Carlucci insisted that he would announce all federal grants, Flood grumbled his displeasure but eventually agreed to the arrangement. Having secured the congressman's support, Carlucci proceeded to direct the recovery and announce all federal grants.[49] He was extremely successful too.

Residents were in a state of shock and many considered relocating elsewhere. But Carlucci, with the assistance of Flood, Max Rosenn, and the recovery task force, was instrumental in securing the federal resources necessary to address the community's needs. In 1972 alone, the region received a staggering $379 million in federal funds, most of which went to the rescue and recovery efforts after the devastation of Agnes. That achievement convinced many people that they could rebuild their lives in the Wyoming Valley. In fact, Wilkes-Barre city officials even decided to rebuild the downtown commercial center in exactly the same area that was ravaged by the flood.[50]

Yet, more than thirty years later, Carlucci dismisses the vital role he played in the recovery effort. "I was simply following the president's orders," he said in a recent interview. "Mr. Nixon told me to go up there and solve the problem, and I'd get whatever resources I'd need. Since I was one of the top officials in the Office of Management and Budget, I knew where the resources were. So all I really needed to do was make sure that the local and federal officials would cooperate with each other."[51]

In early October, the postmaster general visited the Wyoming Valley to present a check for a new post office. Within five minutes of Carlucci's announcement, Flood, who had always taken great pride in securing the funding for local post offices, was on the phone to him.

"What the hell are you doing?" thundered the disgruntled congressman.

"Remember Dan, I told you that I was going to make all announcements concerning federal grants," replied Carlucci.

"Yeah," said Flood, pulling in his horns. "But Jesus Christ, did you have to announce a new post office?"[52]

Flood generally cooperated with Carlucci. He limited his involvements to the Agnes legislation, serving as a tour guide for President Nixon when he visited Wilkes-Barre in early September, and hosting congressional colleagues and luminaries, such as entertainer Bob Hope, who lent their fund-raising skills and moral support to the recovery effort. It was really all he had the energy to do.

By the beginning of August, Flood was suffering from severe exhaustion. Dr. Edward Janjigan was extremely concerned about the congressman's condition.

Fig. 35. Comedian Bob Hope embraces Flood during the Agnes recovery. Hope visited Wilkes-Barre to offer his moral support and to raise money for victims of the devastating flood.

"I could see the complete fatigue, his stooped posture, and the short shuffling gait he had when he walked," recalled the Kingston physician. "He was suffering from abdominal pains, insomnia, dizziness, and forgetfulness, among other ailments. I'd often receive phone calls from him when he returned to the district on weekends from Washington. He would usually ask for advice regarding the various medications he was taking. Sometimes he'd confide his suspicions about members of his staff who he felt were 'pulling the wool over [his] eyes.' But he always ended the conversation with a firm resolve not to give up."[53]

Chief among those who attempted to "pull the wool over Flood's eyes" was Steve Elko, who continued to exploit the congressman's authority. He even tried to impose his will on flood czar Frank Carlucci. "Elko was constantly bullying my staff," Carlucci recalled. "He pushed his own friends ahead of the line when it came to distributing resources and there were several occasions when he tried to undermine my authority. Finally, I had had enough. I called Dan Flood and told him that I wouldn't deal with Elko anymore, and he agreed to get him off my back."[54] As a result, Elko found other ways to exploit the recovery effort.

On June 28, 1972, Fred Peters, the naïve but desperate executive of the West Coast Trade Schools, flew to Washington to give Elko the fifteen thousand dollars he requested to bail out Intech. He met the administrative assistant at his Capitol Hill apartment, where they concocted a plan to sell prefabricated housing units to the Pennsylvania government using Flood's influence. Peters had a financial interest in a company called Sterling-Homex, which made prefabricated modular housing, and stood to profit handsomely if he could somehow arrange a deal with flood-ravaged Luzerne County. Elko encouraged Peters to meet with Flood on the matter, saying that the "old man" could "talk HUD or HEW into buying the Sterling-Homex housing if he could beat out Senator Eastland of Mississippi and Senator Tower of Delaware who also had some interest in mobile homes."[55]

Shortly thereafter, Peters flew to Wilkes-Barre and met with Flood at his Avoca command center. The congressman expressed an interest in Sterling-Homex, but said that there were "other heavyweights who [were] also interested in selling temporary housing to the [Pennsylvania] government" for the victims. Peters then handed the congressman an envelope with five thousand dollars in it. Flood allegedly took the envelope, placed it in his pocket, and said good-bye to the trade school executive.[56] Five days later, Peters met with Elko, Fleming, and John Willingham, the owner of Sterling-Homex, at Elko's Capitol Hill apartment. There, Peters agreed to be the company's Wilkes-Barre agent for the sale of modular housing to Pennsylvania officials. His commission would amount to 2 percent of the gross sales. Peters also agreed to split his commission with Elko and Fleming.[57] Within days, Peters purchased more than fifty thousand dollars worth of stock in Sterling-Homex. But unfortunately for him—and Elko—the company declared bankruptcy in late July and their deal to house Agnes victims never materialized.[58]

The setback, however, didn't affect their arrangement for the accreditation of the West Coast Trade Schools. On August 1, 1972, Elko, with Fleming's assistance, prepared another letter to education commissioner Sidney Marland on Flood's congressional stationery. The letter complained about the inaction of NATTS on the accreditation of the schools and the fact that the matter should have been resolved in July. Elko, taking liberties with Flood's vocabulary, wrote that "this is a shocking case of misfeasance, nonfeasance and possibly malfeasance, which is simply beyond my understanding."[59] Again, Elko signed Flood's name to the letter without acknowledgment of his authorship.

Marland responded in an August 14 letter, stating that "further information" was needed from the schools, and that "further review of the schools' claim was necessary for continuing eligibility" in the federally insured student loan program.[60] Once again, Elko and Fleming drafted a response on Flood's congressional stationery. The first five paragraphs of the letter take extreme liberties with the congressman's vocabulary and written expression:

> Dear Mr. Commissioner:
>
> Thank you for your letter of August 14 concerning the West Coast Trade Schools, and your acknowledgement of the egg crate full of backup material handcarried by my staff with my accompanying letter of August 1.
>
> Your voluminous tome of August 14 is simply beyond my understanding.
>
> On page 2, paragraph 3, section (1), where you refer to further steps in behalf of the schools, item (1) suggests securing further information from the schools is appalling. I personally examined all of the documents provided by the West Coast Trade Schools and I'll be damned if there isn't sufficient documentation to accredit <u>every trade school in the 50 states of the Union</u>.
>
> In addition, referring to item 2, where you suggest conducting a further review of the schools' claim to continuing eligibility, I hereby furnish copies of their allocations under the College Work Study program and/or National Direct Student Loan program, which I had previously referred to in my letter of August 1 on page 3, paragraph 4—ugh!
>
> <u>Somebody is nuts.</u>[61]

The letter went on to demand that Marland take action to help the West Coast Trade Schools obtain accreditation, which would make them eligible for federal student loan guarantees. The letter concludes with the threat, "Let's knock off the waffle job now—unless somebody wants a war." While the sarcastic style of the letter and such colloquial phrases as "I'll be damned if there isn't sufficient documentation to accredit <u>every trade school in the 50 states of the Union</u>," "<u>Somebody is nuts</u>," and "Let's knock off the waffle job now," are reflective of the colorful *oral* expression Flood used in personal conversation with high-ranking military officials, he would never use that kind of vocabulary or tone in a letter with a civilian government official. What's more, he had too much respect for the federal government to register such sentiments in a written document that gave permanence to his views. But Elko, who could not make that distinction, signed the congressman's name without any acknowledgment of his own authorship.[62]

A week later, Fleming went to Elko's apartment at the Congressional Hotel, where he met Flood. The congressman, who was suffering from exhaustion, was heavily medicated and asleep in his own apartment on the eighth floor when he arrived. Elko phoned him to come over to his apartment to meet with Fleming. When Flood arrived he was dressed in a bathrobe and slippers and seemingly dazed. When Elko left the apartment, the congressman took a seat on a sofa. Fleming then handed him an envelope containing one thousand dollars, a bribe for the use of his influence in the effort to obtain accreditation for the trade schools. There was no discussion. Flood simply took the money in his right hand, placed it in his bathrobe pocket, and excused himself, indicating that he was tired and was going back to bed.[63]

When Flood testified at Elko's trial in October 1977, he not only insisted that "knew nothing about any payments" from Peters to him or to Elko, but that he would never have allowed such letters to be sent out over his signature.[64] Despite all his efforts, Fred Peters never did succeed in obtaining accreditation from NATTS, and the West Coast Trade Schools were forced to close in May 1973.[65]

Dan Flood would later remember the Agnes recovery as his "finest moment" because of the "cooperation of the entire community." "Luzerne County never saw anything like the way the Wyoming Valley and adjacent areas worked together," he said. "Man and woman. Boy and girl. Day and night. People would get in touch with me and I would get in touch with committees, and it all worked because of the deep heartfelt feelings and understanding that existed. To see this terrible disaster and how the community came together to overcome it was a personal highlight for me."[66]

Unfortunately, Flood's "finest moment" was tarnished by scandal, thanks to an untrustworthy aide who would eventually destroy a legendary political career.

10

PANAMA'S PUBLIC ENEMY NO. 1

Dan Flood's impressive performance during the Agnes recovery made national headlines and established him as the prototype of a pork-barrel politician. But he would become better known for his controversial stand on the Panama Canal, the interoceanic passageway that gave the United States commercial and military dominance during the first half of the twentieth century.

Flood's ties to the canal were deep-rooted. His grandfather, Daniel J. McCarthy, educated him on the historical significance of the canal when he was a youngster during their winter sojourns to Florida.[1] Throughout his congressional career, Flood was a fierce proponent of preserving exclusive U.S. sovereignty over the Canal Zone, which was located in an area that had come under Communist influence during the cold war. "Panama is our jugular vein," he told *60 Minutes* in a 1974 interview. "If you have good kidneys, you can piss from there to Cuba. The Caribbean is our mare nostrum. We can't afford to lose it to the Communists."[2] Some of Flood's efforts were so appalling to the Panamanian government that it dubbed the jingoistic congressman "Public Enemy No. 1."[3] Of course, he wore the label with enormous pride.

But by the late 1970s, Flood's cold war rhetoric was out of step with the Democratic liberals, who were receptive to détente. His repeated attempts to thwart president Jimmy Carter's effort to amend the Canal Treaty caused consternation within the executive cabinet and on Capitol Hill at a time when the Pennsylvania legislator was politically vulnerable. Panama would be Flood's last great fight.

The idea of building a canal to link the Atlantic and Pacific oceans had existed since the early sixteenth century, but none of the various plans came to fruition until 1903, when the United States and Panama signed the Hay-Bunau-Varilla Treaty. According to the treaty, the United States was granted "sovereign right" to the ten-mile-wide Canal Zone for ninety-nine years, as well as the right to build and operate a canal. In return, president Theodore Roosevelt agreed to obtain the Canal Zone from Panama for $10 million and make an annual payment of $250,000 for assuming ownership of the Panama railroad.[4]

Roosevelt viewed Panama as the cornerstone of U.S. foreign policy in the Western Hemisphere. Since the introduction of the Monroe Doctrine in 1823, the United States operated on the understanding that any attempt by the European powers to gain territorial possessions in the Americas would be treated as a threat to U.S. national security. At the same time, all nations had equal commercial rights to conduct trade in the Western Hemisphere. But as American investments poured into Central America and the Caribbean islands, that policy changed to one of the primary right of the United States to dominate influence in the Caribbean basin.

Roosevelt, an activist president, believed that military preparedness was the true sign of national greatness. Best known for his advice to "speak softly and carry a big stick," he insisted that "to be prepared militarily is the most effectual means to promote peace." Accordingly, TR asserted the right of the United States to act as an "international policeman" and intervene in the affairs of Latin American nations to prevent European powers from using military force to collect debts in the Western Hemisphere, as Germany and Great Britain attempted to do in Venezuela in 1902. This so-called Roosevelt Corollary to the Monroe Doctrine resulted in unprecedented U.S. intervention in the Caribbean in the early part of the twentieth century.[5]

During the Roosevelt administration, the United States intervened in the affairs of Venezuela, Haiti, the Dominican Republic, Nicaragua, and Cuba, brandishing the "big stick" against Europeans and Latin Americans.[6] The key to insular imperialism, however, was the building of the Panama Canal, which enabled the United States to move its naval and trading vessels more rapidly between the Atlantic and Pacific than ever before. Roosevelt used his executive power to engineer the separation of Panama from Colombia. In effect, he gave military and financial support to Panamanian revolutionaries intent on breaking away from Colombia, and then recognized Panama as an independent country. Of course, TR's ulterior motive was to secure U.S. control over the Isthmus of Panama so that he could build a canal there. His plan worked brilliantly and construction of the canal began in 1904. Afterward, Roosevelt would dismiss charges of imperialism in dealing with Panama by saying, "I took the Canal Zone and let Congress debate."[7]

Realizing the military and economic significance of the Panama Canal, Roosevelt's successors sought to protect U.S. control over the interoceanic passageway.[8] After World War II, U.S. sovereignty of the Canal Zone was challenged. Although the U.S. State Department recognized Panama's "titular sovereignty" over the region, the Republic of Panama began to label the United States a "colonial aggressor" violating its sovereignty.[9] In the 1950s, Panamanians demanded total—not titular—sovereignty. When the Eisenhower administration in 1955 attempted to ease tensions by agreeing to increase annuity payments to Panama, cede waterfront and other properties, and equalize pay standards for U.S. and Panamanian citizens working in the Canal Zone, Flood was furious.[10] "I protest vehemently the [Eisenhower-Remon] treaty," he snapped. "I believe the Republic of Panama will never take less than total control of the Zone and the first thing we know they'll be leasing things we now own to us."[11] Declaring his intention to preserve total U.S. sovereignty of the Canal Zone "at all costs," Flood hired a retired U.S. naval captain, Miles P. DuVal, Jr., to become his legislative expert on Panama.

DuVal had served in the Canal Zone in the early 1940s in charge of the navy's marine operations on the Pacific side. Like Flood, the retired captain was determined to protect exclusive U.S. sovereignty of the canal. It had been a longtime obsession. Graduating from Annapolis in 1918, DuVal was assigned to the U.S. First Fleet in World War I. After the war, he served as staff commander of aircraft squadrons on the USS *Wright* and an instructor at the Naval War College at Newport, Rhode Island. He would go on to serve as a naval intelligence officer until March 5, 1941, when he was appointed captain of the Port of the Pacific Terminal at the Panama Canal. The following year, DuVal planned and coordinated the enlargement of the Pacific Terminal to accommodate U.S. carriers for World War II. He also authored the first comprehensive proposal for the future of the canal, which was approved by president Franklin D. Roosevelt in 1945. After the war, DuVal was designated by secretary of the navy James Forrestal as the navy's Panama liaison officer. He served in that capacity until August 1949, when he voluntarily retired from the navy. A lifelong bachelor, DuVal embarked on a writing career that focused on the history of and U.S. policy making on the Panama Canal. Among the works were two highly regarded books on the interoceanic passageway, *And the*

Mountains Will Move: The Story of the Building of the Panama Canal and *Cadiz to Cathay: The Story of the Long Diplomatic Struggle for the Panama Canal.*[12]

Impressed by DuVal's writing, Flood asked the fifty-one-year-old DuVal to join his congressional staff. Afterward, all legislation and correspondence on Panama that arrived at Flood's Capitol Hill office was handled by DuVal. The congressman almost always followed his counsel on the Canal Zone.[13]

With DuVal's assistance, Flood soon became the "outstanding authority" in Congress on Panama. Hundreds of letters from constituents as well as other Americans living in the Canal Zone attest to his reputation.[14] But Panamanians felt differently. When the Republic of Panama, in December 1958, passed a law giving itself control over access to the canal by water from both the Pacific and Atlantic sides, Flood warned Congress that the measure threatened to make the Panama Canal "another Berlin."[15] As noted earlier, on January 13, 1959, the Panamanian National Assembly declared the Pennsylvania congressman "Public Enemy No. 1" and "a personification of the bad faith which has contributed to the ill will between the United States and Panama, countries which because of their destiny should greet each other as brothers." Aquilano Boyd later asserted that the United States should pay Panama "half of the gross revenue" from the canal's operation, which brought in $100 million to the United States each year.[16]

For his part, Flood intensified his defense of U.S. control of the Canal Zone. He saw Panama as the "target of communism's fourth front," and in 1960, he argued for an extension of the Monroe Doctrine—"not only against invading troops or fleets but against Red subversion and Communist penetration." Flood refused to see Panama as "an isolated question." Rather, he insisted that the Canal Zone was key to preserving the interests of the United States: "The Reds have recognized the Panama Canal as the strategic center of America and that is why we must hold on to it."[17]

During the 1960s, the political controversy and international tensions involved with the Panama Canal increased. Flood's repeated warnings about a Communist takeover of the Latin American country were reinforced in April 1959 when Cuban dictator Fidel Castro sent eighty armed socialist revolutionaries on an aborted invasion of Panama.[18] Seizing the occasion to press for tighter control over the canal, Flood sarcastically told a House Subcommittee on Internal American Affairs that when his "bewhiskered friend, Mr. Castro, took over in Cuba it was only a matter of time before he struck at the canal." In light of the recent invasion, Flood said that it was "simply nauseating" to "listen to the State Department's views on respecting Panama's titular sovereignty."

Instead, the jingoistic congressman urged the drafting of a proclamation stating that the Canal Zone is "constitutionally acquired territory by the United States," and that a special service squadron of the U.S. Navy be activated "for continuous display of the U.S. flag in the Caribbean."[19] The later suggestion was a direct reference to the ongoing controversy on whether the Panamanian government had a right to fly their flag alongside the Stars and Stripes in the Canal Zone. When Eisenhower granted that concession in the late 1950s, Flood was one of several congressmen who objected and led the fight to pass an amendment in the House revoking that action in 1960.[20] "If that [Panamanian] flag goes up," he insisted, "you are a dead pigeon. . . . The day it is formally hoisted marks the beginning of the end of exclusive U.S. control over the Panama Canal."[21] Eisenhower, acting on the advice of the State Department, ignored the opposition and directed that the Panamanian flag be flown together with the U.S. flag at a single location in the Canal Zone. Congress continued to debate the issue but no formal action was taken.[22]

When John Kennedy became president, he revised the Eisenhower amendment by adding more sites in the Canal Zone where the U.S. and Panamanian flags could be jointly flown.[23] Once again, Flood went on the attack. On April 16, 1963, he took the House floor and gave an impassioned two-hour speech about on how the "rights of the United States are gradually being diluted by our government." He continued his remarks for another two hours the following day. By the time he relinquished the floor at 5:30 P.M., there were only four representatives in the chamber and Flood was forced to place the rest of his diatribe in the *Congressional Record.*[24]

On January 2, 1964, Robert Fleming, the Canal Zone governor, announced that the Eisenhower-Kennedy amendment would be put into effect. All American flags were ordered down until dual flagstaffs could be fastened to the poles. Many Zonists (i.e., U.S. residents of the Canal Zone) were outraged. One of the Zonists sent Flood a miniature Panamanian flag, requesting that he give it to "Corporal Eisenhower, who started this mess." "If I were not a gentleman," he added, "I would tell him what to do with the damned thing!"[25]

On January 8 a peaceful demonstration of American students was held at the Canal Zone's Balboa High School. One student climbed the flagpole and fastened an American flag. An all-night vigil followed to prevent officials from taking down the pole. Students recited the Pledge of Allegiance, sang the national anthem, and signed a petition to president Lyndon Johnson demanding that they be allowed to fly the U.S. flag at the Canal Zone's schools.[26] The following day, the American students tried to prevent Panamanian students from lowering the U.S. flag and hoisting Panama's banner. Violence erupted when the Panamanian flag was trampled on and defiled. Crowds of Panamanians came storming into the Canal Zone. Rioting broke out on the border of the Canal Zone and Panama City, and continued for three days before U.S. Army troops could put a stop to it. When the dust settled, 24 persons were killed and another 450 were injured.[27]

Panamanian president Roberto Chiari responded to the incident by suspending diplomatic relations with Washington. He also called on the United Nations and the Organization of American States to investigate Panama's claim to the Canal Zone, though his efforts were in vain.[28] President Johnson could have taken a hard-line stance against the small Caribbean nation; instead, he agreed to Panama's demand to appoint a special ambassador with "powers to seek the prompt elimination of conflict between the two countries."[29] Flood's response was more vituperative. "The raising of the Panamanian flag in the Canal Zone would be like giving back the Louisiana Purchase to France, Alaska to Russia, or Florida to Spain," he said in a congressional address on March 9. "It would be just as logical to contend that these great regions, as now developed, should be returned to their original sovereigns as gifts." While Flood's fatalistic comparison of flying the Panamanian flag in the Canal Zone to the return of the Louisiana Purchase, Alaska, and Florida amounted to little more than inflated rhetoric, he concluded his remarks with a valid point. "Where there is responsibility, there must be authority," he said. "Indeed the Panama Canal cannot serve two masters." He should have ended there. But Flood couldn't resist the temptation to vent his trademark sarcasm, adding, "The very idea of giving such vital property of the United States to a country that cannot even collect its own garbage is unthinkable!"[30]

To be sure, Flood's reference to the inability of Panama to "collect its own garbage" was an extremely sensitive issue for Panamanians. Like any third-world nation, Panama struggled with poverty and a meager quality of life. The marked contrast between the well-manicured Canal Zone and the slum-infested neighborhoods of Panama City only served to intensify the animosity between the Panamanians and the Zonists, who held themselves aloof from the native population. The inflammatory rhetoric certainly didn't improve the tenuous relationship between the two countries. If anything, Flood's sarcasm might have nudged Panama even closer to a relationship with neighboring Cuba. Such a scenario concerned the congressman just as much—if not more—than losing U.S. control of the Canal Zone. He believed that the "fate of the entire world in this tragic era of communist revolutionary activity and conquest depended upon the continued operation and protection of the canal by [the U.S.] government." Flood also believed that the Panama's demand for control of the canal was "aided, abetted and measurably formulated by Panamanian Castroites, who want it under communist control."[31] And he enjoyed significant support for his position too.

On Capitol Hill the fight to retain U.S. control over the canal was a bipartisan effort led not only by Flood, a Democrat, but also by such prominent politicians as: Rep. Clarence Canon (D-Miss.), the chair of the House Appropriations Committee; Senator Strom Thurmond (R-S.C.); and Senator John Tower (R-Tex.). Just as important, a majority of the American public supported the cause. A February 12, 1964, Gallup poll revealed that among the 64 percent of the respondents who had followed the dispute, the vote ran six to one against making concessions to Panama. The response indicated that there would be considerable opposition to a revised treaty in the U.S. Senate.[32] Finally, influential journalists like Robert Novak and Rowland Evans of the *Washington Post* made sure to keep U.S. control over the canal in the national news.[33]

Despite public and congressional pressure, in December 1964 Johnson announced that he would renegotiate the 1903 treaty and build a new sea-level canal to replace the existing one, which was too congested, too vulnerable to sabotage, and too small for larger American vessels.[34] Flood, in a lengthy address before the House, criticized the Johnson administration for "ignoring a previous study he commissioned by the U.S. Army Corps of Engineers for a new interoceanic canal" and for "proposing a renegotiated treaty that will recognize the sovereignty of Panama." He went on to accuse the administration of "covering up" key issues concerning U.S. policy on the Panama Canal, and called for an official "rigorous inquiry" to "set straight the record in order to determine this nation's course in the Canal Zone."[35]

Choosing diplomacy, Johnson agreed to three new treaties with the Republic of Panama on June 26, 1967. The first treaty would terminate the original 1903 pact and give Panama greater control over the Zone and the canal. The second would provide for joint defense of the area, and the third would allow for the rebuilding of the canal at sea level.[36] After the announcement of the treaties, Flood admitted, "I am so mad that I could spit." Careful not to further alienate a president of his own party, the Pennsylvania congressman insisted that Johnson had been "grossly misled by his advisers" and that he would be better served if "he considered congressional counsel and expertise on the canal issue."[37] Flood proceeded to lobby the Senate against ratification, writing personal letters to those who shared his sentiments, asking them to register their opposition in the *Congressional Record*.[38] He also joined forces with Rep. Leonor Sullivan, chair of the subcommittee dealing with the Panama Canal, to mobilize House colleagues for a nonbinding resolution registering their displeasure with the treaties. Finally, Flood encouraged his colleagues to attend the Senate hearings on the treaties and make a formal statement against them.[39] Flood ultimately prevailed, but not because of his own efforts.

Unwilling to be second-class citizens in their own country, Panamanians demanded exclusive control over the canal. Following a year of political turmoil in which the three treaties were abandoned, Panama's National Guard seized control of the country on October 11, 1968. General Omar Torrijos Herrera became chief executive and de facto dictator of Panama's 1.6 million people. Shortly thereafter, he committed the new populist government to securing a canal agreement that would be more favorable to Panama but not alienate the U.S. residents of the Canal Zone.[40] Unfortunately for Flood, Torrijos's presidency marked the beginning of the end of U.S. sovereignty in the region.

During the late 1960s and early 1970s, the global desire to prevent Vietnam and other third-world trouble spots like Panama from escalating into another world war stimulated efforts to reduce the cold war tensions between the United States and the Soviet Union. President Richard Nixon paved the way for détente with increased diplomatic, economic, and cultural exchanges between the two superpowers. In 1972 Nixon visited the Soviet Union, where he and Soviet premier Leonid Brezhnev agreed to limit nuclear stockpiles, work together in space, and ease the long-standing restrictions on trade. Nixon also visited Communist China the same year, thereby relaxing U.S. tensions significantly with that country. Predictably, the administration's position on Panama was strongly influenced by the desire for détente, much to the chagrin of Dan Flood and other hard-liners.

In October 1971, at Washington's prestigious Cosmos Club, Flood convened a luncheon meeting of the leading defenders of a U.S.-controlled canal. The objective was to condemn their opponents who were demanding both that a second canal be constructed because of the obsolescence of the existing one, and that the original passageway be turned over to Panama. Flood and his point man on Latin American affairs, Captain Miles DuVal, regarded the opposition as "lefties and unethical business moguls," and insisted that U.S. international trade would suffer were a second canal to be opened. They insisted that the "international liberals" were hatching a "conspiracy" to return the original canal to Panama, "a nation typical of the many unstable, Marxist-infiltrated governments in Central and South America."

It was an oppressively hot Saturday afternoon, but the poor air conditioning at the Cosmos Club did little to deplete the enthusiasm of the participants, who were firmly wedded to the security of the canal. DuVal introduced one anxious speaker after another. Flood spoke for nearly an hour, wearing the audience down. Next was Senator Strom Thurmond of South Carolina, chair of the Senate Armed Services Committee. Thurmond and Flood were joined at the hip by zealously pro-American positions and the unshakable belief that it was impossible to spend too much in federal funding for the defense of the nation. The senator made the case that surrender of the canal was central to both Hanoi's and Moscow's vision of "taking over the western world," and that President Nixon was "duty bound to land U.S. forces in Panama should there be an insurrection." But the best was yet to come.

A leading environmentalist rose to assert that a second canal would threaten the tourist economies of Florida and surrounding states as well as the safety of swimmers on two continents. He based his argument on the existence of "sea snakes" that would cross Caribbean waters from their Pacific habitation and infiltrate the shores of Mexico, Texas, Mississippi, Louisiana, and Florida if a new ocean passage was built. As the audience roared their approval, DuVal jumped from his chair, producing two large transparent containers of sea snakes, which appeared to be crashing through the glass. Women screamed while Flood and Thurmond rose to the podium in Hollywood poses of outrage. DuVal egged them on. Once again, the audience roared, this time in protest.

The theatrics continued with various speakers until about 5:00 P.M., when the "noon luncheon" finally ended. Driving back to the Congressional Hotel, Flood asked his special assistant Michael Clark what they might do for a "relaxing Sunday." Clark remembered that he had been given complimentary tickets to the World Series, which was being played in Baltimore, and he suggested that they attend the game. Flood declined, telling Clark that he could not imagine a "more boring afternoon" than "sitting in an oppressively hot ballpark." "You go," he said. "A World Series game would only pale in comparison to the excitement we just enjoyed this afternoon."[41]

Despite Flood's best efforts, Nixon and secretary of state Henry Kissinger pursued a new treaty that would give Panama greater control over the canal. They had a high regard for Panamanian president General Omar Torrijos and believed he could guarantee the terms of such a new treaty. While Torrijos maintained law and order by controlling the media and squelching all political opposition, he also understood that his political future depended on the outcome of a new treaty with the United States. Both Nixon and Torrijos agreed that Panama should have a greater voice in canal operations and defense, and that its sovereignty in the zone should be recognized. Accordingly, Kissinger articulated eight principles that he intended to constitute the basis of a new treaty. Essentially, the forthcoming treaty would end after a fixed number of years, after which time the United States would no longer retain its exercise of sovereign rights and jurisdiction in the Canal Zone. In the meantime, the United States would share with Panama the responsibility for the operation and defense of the canal, while Panama would guarantee to the United States the rights, facilities, and lands necessary to continue operating and defending the canal. In addition, the two nations would provide for any future expansion of the canal as needed, and Panama would receive a larger share in the tolls and revenue accruing from the canal and the Canal Zone. Kissinger pledged these principles to Panama's foreign minister, Juan Antonio Tack, in February 1974 with the intention of concluding a new treaty later that year.[42] But Nixon's resignation from the presidency in August, coupled with the fact that a large segment of the American public was unwilling to surrender the canal, postponed the signing of such a pact.

Once again, Flood seized the moment. Manipulating public opinion, the savvy congressman torpedoed the Kissinger-Tack treaty. When the treaty was first announced in January 1974, Flood insisted that the pact would "not be authorized by the Congress" and that it constituted "one of the most disgraceful diplomatic episodes in the history of the United States." Calling on "all citizens to take up this vital matter with your Senators and Representatives," he swore to lead the battle in Congress against such "trickery, chicanery and skullduggery."[43] Flood furthered his case on July 7, 1974, when he went before a national television audience on *60 Minutes* to denounce the proposed treaty. "To concede control of such a vital waterway to a small country, which is ill-equipped to administer or defend it, I think, would be a manifest and appalling act of irresponsibility by a great world power," he declared. Flood also cited the need for the United States to contain the internal political turmoil in Panama because of its vulnerability to a Communist takeover. Insisting that the region was "the key to American defense," the jingoistic congressman compared the canal to the United States' "jugular vein." He also referred to Panama's proximity to Cuba, playing on the fears of the American people, who still considered the Panama Canal a cherished possession and symbol of U.S. national security.

Flood concluded the interview with a sobering warning: "The Soviets now control every interoceanic connection in the world—dominate it, or are in a position to control it—the Kiel, the Dardanelles, the Suez, and the Straits of

Belukha. The only thing left is Panama. And now, with the domination of Cuba by the Soviets, you can stand in the main street of Havana and take a bottle of Bacardi and, with a good arm, you can hit the canal. We cannot turn the region into a Soviet Lake!"[44]

The *60 Minutes* interview made Flood appear like a melodramatic hawk, and CBS was soundly criticized for biased reporting. But the program also resonated with an American public that feared the spread of communism. Flood's Washington office was overwhelmed with letters from across the nation supporting his position.[45] Suddenly the Pennsylvania legislator had become the national face of the fight to retain control over the Panama Canal and to contain communism in the Caribbean.

Flood had been engaged in efforts to secure U.S. economic assistance for third-world countries in the Caribbean for many years. Naturally, his objective was to purchase their loyalty to the United States, thus preventing any economic dependency on Cuba or the Soviet Union. Flood's most recent effort was in Haiti, where he was encouraging president Jean-Claude Duvalier to request U.S. assistance to develop that country's infrastructure. On November 28, 1973, the Pennsylvania congressman sent his administrative assistant, Stephen Elko, to meet with Duvalier and encourage the request. Elko met with the Haitian president and his special assistant, Lucien Rigaud, and informed them of Flood's interest.[46] According to Justice Department documents, Flood indicated that the governments of Haiti and the Bahamas should be "beefed up with U.S. economic assistance in order to effect a ring around Cuba." He was also interested in the possibility of using the island of Gonâve, near the Haitian mainland, as "a possible fallback position for U.S. troops located at Guantánamo, Cuba."[47] In return, Elko stated that Flood would secure full U.S. economic assistance to Haiti. He reminded them that their country had received only limited U.S. aid since 1963, when Duvalier's father, François, seized power with five bloody years of terror. Finally, Elko suggested that full economic assistance would be restored only if Duvalier made a request for such help. Shortly thereafter, the Haitian president wrote a letter to Flood requesting U.S. aid for developing his country's farming, health care, and roads. The letter was hand delivered to Flood by Rigaud and Major Roger Cazeau of the Haitian Air Force on December 4, 1973.[48]

With the request in hand, Flood began to wield his clout on Capitol Hill. He contacted the Department of Agriculture and secured an estimate of staffing requirements for assessing the potential agricultural development of Haiti. He also requested and received from the State Department a five-year summary of Haitian political and economic development, as well as an analysis of the island nation's current situation. At the same time, Flood began a letter-writing campaign to mobilize support for his effort with other members of Congress who had influence over foreign affairs legislation, as well as to State Department officials like Daniel Parker, chief administrator of the Agency for International Development.[49]

Before the year was out, Congress, bending to Flood's will, voted for a twenty-six-million-dollar foreign assistance appropriation for Haiti, and Nixon signed the measure into law. In 1974 the U.S. Agency for International Development reopened its Haitian offices and approved its first substantial loan to Haiti in fifteen years—three million dollars for road construction, with an annual grant of five hundred thousand dollars for maintenance once the roads were completed. Agricultural loans followed. Construction began on hospitals and low-cost housing projects. There were also plans to build a cable car facility.[50] In each instance, Flood's office, specifically Elko, would "designate the companies who would receive the contracts." Chief among the firms was Medico Industries, the Plains Township military and heavy equipment company with which Flood had been connected for many years.[51] But Elko was less interested in reinforcing his boss's loyalty to a longtime—and questionable—constituent than he was in padding his own profits. Once again, he acted in Flood's name, this time to arrange federal funding for U.S. businesspeople seeking to build for-profit hospitals and even hotel casinos on the island nation.[52]

Meanwhile, Flood's uncompromising defense of U.S. sovereignty in the Canal Zone was beginning to create tensions between himself and the new president, Gerald Ford, once a House colleague and close friend. The initial conflict came in December 1974 and concerned Ford's selection of Nelson A. Rockefeller as his vice president. Rockefeller, the former New York governor and a longtime Republican presidential aspirant, had recently funded a U.S.–Latin American study that recommended returning the canal to Panama as well as opening up relations with Cuba. When Flood learned of the study, he insisted that if Rockefeller agreed with the findings he would not vote for his confirmation as vice president. But Rockefeller was too seasoned a politician to fall for the trap.

During the confirmation hearings, he refused to answer any questions about foreign policy, saying they were "too complex" to be discussed in such a short period of time. Frustrated, Flood turned to his own Panamanian expert, Captain Miles DuVal, who did extensive research on the vice presidential nominee's background. DuVal discovered some potential conflicts of interest regarding donations Rockefeller gave to various Latin American officials in countries where he had financial relationships. There were also some questions about Rockefeller's connections to William D. Rogers, former head of the Commission on United States–Latin American Relations and then assistant secretary of state for inter-American affairs. Flood submitted these findings to the House Judiciary Committee, which quickly dismissed them.[53]

On the day the House was to vote on the Rockefeller nomination, Michael Clark, one of Flood's chief aides, who was traveling outside the country, received a phone call from another staffer. The panic-stricken caller reported that the congressman intended to vote against Rockefeller's nomination. "I couldn't believe it," recalled Clark in a recent interview. "I just couldn't understand why Dan would do something like that. He had been a good friend to Nelson Rockefeller since the 1940s and the confirmation was a 'sure thing.' If Dan had voted against him, he would have been the only one in the entire House of Representatives to do so. I immediately phoned the congressman and told him that he was 'off his rocker' if he voted against the nomination. His response was typical—'You talk to Captain DuVal and change his mind!'"[54] Fortunately, the vote was postponed for a few days, giving Clark enough time to return to Washington and convince Flood, face to face, that voting against Rockefeller was not in his best interests.[55] But the incident illustrated how unreasonable the Pennsylvania legislator could be on any issue that threatened his position on the Panama Canal. As it turned out, Flood needn't have worried.

By the summer of 1975, the Ford administration was coming under increasing attack on Capitol Hill for pursuing the Kissinger-Tack treaty. Congressional opposition centered on the damage to American credibility around the world that would follow if the U.S. surrendered its sovereignty of the Canal Zone. This was an especially strong concern after the fall of Saigon that April, which brought a humiliating end to the Vietnam War for the United States. Some members of Congress warned that a pullout from Panama, measured against the American setback in Vietnam, would "encourage penny-dictators and minor aggressions everywhere."[56] Of course, Flood was most critical, going so far as to demand that President Ford, a close friend, "publicly disavow" the Kissinger plan. "Secretary Kissinger cannot deceive either Congress or the American people with his calculated ambiguities and sophistries on the Canal issue," declared Flood, a ranking Democrat on the Defense Appropriations Subcommittee. "They are well informed and see through his rhetoric. Further, I can think of no better way for the Administration to precipitate a serious confrontation with Congress than by persisting in its highly dangerous course of giving away U.S. sovereignty over the U.S.-owned

Canal Zone and Canal. If the Administration is looking for grievous trouble, it will get far more than it can handle on this issue."[57] It wasn't an idle threat either.

In June, the House of Representatives attached an amendment to the State Department's appropriations bill that would prohibit the use of U.S. currency in negotiating the surrender of any U.S. rights in the Panama Canal Zone.[58] The following month, Flood, now widely regarded as the House's leading critic on the administration's Panama policy, ratcheted up his attack against the Ford administration in a speech before the Institute on Comparative Political and Economic Systems in Washington. After an extensive survey of the history of the U.S. role in the Panama Canal Zone, Flood argued that the financial benefits to Latin America were far greater than those realized by the United States as long as it had been recognized as canal's "lawful owner with full sovereign rights, power and authority over it." Flood suggested that if Latin America hoped to continue realizing these economic benefits, the canal would have to be modernized. Of course, that would not happen unless U.S. sovereignty was retained "because history shows that the American people and Congress will never approve the expenditure of huge sums on a major canal project in an area not under the sovereign control of the United States." He then criticized the Ford administration for "diplomatic trickery" that "constitutes a program of abject surrender of U.S. Treaty-based sovereign rights," and suggested that the State Department was engaged in a conspiracy with the mass media to "give away the Canal." Flood believed that such an insidious design would have dire consequences for the Western Hemisphere, and he exploited the rhetoric of a cold war showdown to reinforce his point.

"U.S. sovereignty of the Canal Zone is in the best interests of Latin American countries," he added. "The present threat to the Canal Zone is not a meaningless gesture but part of the Soviet Empire's global drive for securing control over narrow waterways and strategic islands. In meeting the current drive for world power, a line has to be drawn somewhere and there is no better place to draw it than at the U.S. Canal Zone. Unless this is done, there will be untold consequences for evil in the entire Western Hemisphere." Defying the State Department to challenge the "constitutional authority" of Congress's treaty-making power, Flood called on "all Americans to join in a national crusade to expose all mass media deceptions and to preserve our full and undiluted sovereign control over the Isthmian Canal and its protective frame not only for inter-oceanic commerce but also for the security of the United States and the entire Free World."[59]

Flood's reference to Congress's authority in treaty-making appears, at first glance, to be a misinterpretation of the U.S. Constitution, which specifically

Fig. 36. Flood with longtime House colleague and friend President Gerald Ford.

assigns the ratification of treaties to the Senate, not the House of Representatives. In the case of Panama, however, Flood was correct. The House would have to play a key role on any new treaty because relinquishing U.S. control over the Panama Canal would involve the transfer of U.S. property, something that would require House approval. In addition, during the fall of 1975 a Senate resolution was introduced that opposed any new treaty and expressed strong opposition to any termination of U.S. sovereignty over the Canal Zone. Thirty-eight senators, four more than the one-third necessary to prevent the ratification of a treaty, sponsored the resolution.[60]

President Ford did not take Flood's criticism personally. "There's no question that Dan could be rough on me when it came to Panama," admitted Ford near the end of his life.

> He had a keen insight into that issue and it allowed him to ask the difficult questions. I can remember when we sat on Defense Appropriations together in the 1960s. He would ask some pretty probing questions of the admirals whenever the Navy presented their budgets, especially when it had anything to do with the Canal Zone. I even began referring to him as "Admiral" and he reciprocated by calling me "General" because I was just as tough on the army. We continued to call each other by those names during my presidency. They were terms of endearment. I think Dan's admiration for my work in Congress continued during my years in the Oval Office. True, by the late 1970s, we differed philosophically on Panama, but those differences did not jeopardize our friendship. If anything, our relationship became stronger.[61]

To be sure, Ford was forced to reconsider his position on Panama during the Republican primaries in the spring of 1976. Many members of the GOP viewed his foreign policy as too moderate and courted Ronald Reagan, former California governor and champion of the party's conservative wing. When Reagan challenged Ford for the GOP nomination, he pointed to Panama as evidence of the president's insufficiently hard-line point of view. "Our government has maintained a mouse-like silence as criticisms of the giveaway have increased," Reagan charged. "I don't understand how the State Department can suggest we pay blackmail to this dictator Torrijos, for blackmail is what it is. When it comes to the Canal, we built it, we paid for it, it's ours and we should tell Torrijos and Company that we are going to keep it."[62] Interestingly, Flood and Reagan were in strong agreement on the canal, something that further distanced the Pennsylvania congressman from the national Democratic Party, which was much less defense-oriented in the late 1970s. Ford reacted to the criticism by proclaiming, "I can say emphatically that the United States will never give up its defense rights to the Panama Canal and will never give up its operational rights as far as the Panama is concerned."[63] At the same time, however, the president directed ambassador Ellsworth Bunker, his special representative on Panama, to negotiate a treaty that would "give up the Canal Zone after a period of time" and the canal after a "longer period of time."[64]

Ford was in a precarious position. While Secretary of State Kissinger was pushing ahead with détente, there was growing opposition in the administration to that policy. Secretary of defense James Schlesinger, fearful of a Soviet military buildup, publicly criticized Kissinger for participating in the thirty-five-nation Conference on Security and Cooperation in Europe convened at Helsinki the previous summer. The Helsinki Accords accepted the legitimacy of Communist regimes in Eastern Europe by acknowledging the boundaries established in the aftermath of World War II and opposing any change to those boundaries by force. While Kissinger defended the Accords by insisting that the inviolability of Eastern European borders would allow the Soviets to be forthcoming on arms control, Schlesinger resented such an endorsement, viewing it as an acknowledgment of permanent Communist control over Eastern Europe. Together with other conservative Republicans, the secretary of defense accused Kissinger of abandoning the national aspirations of the peoples of Communist-controlled Europe.[65]

Kissinger's feud with Schlesinger, along with Ford's concern for his own authority, prompted the president to make significant changes in his cabinet. He replaced Schlesinger with White House chief of staff Donald Rumsfeld, a more trustworthy and moderate voice. The president also made Rumsfeld's deputy, air force lieutenant general Brent Scowcroft, national security adviser, stripping Kissinger of that role (though he retained his position of secretary of state). Finally, Ford stopped using the word "détente" in any of his speeches and official correspondence on foreign policy.[66] Throughout the 1976 presidential campaign, U.S. ambassador Ellsworth Bunker and Panama's foreign minister Aquilino Boyd continued their deliberations on a canal treaty. Kissinger was determined to conclude the pact by the end of the year, regardless of the election's outcome. He believed that there existed sufficient bipartisan support on the Senate Foreign Relations Committee to win approval for a treaty that extensively modified U.S. sovereignty over the waterway.[67] But Kissinger was wrong. The new treaty was never ratified during the Ford administration and the volatile issue was handed off to the new president, Jimmy Carter, the former governor of Georgia.

Carter, a Democrat and strong proponent of détente, paid more attention to human rights and third-world problems than did either of his Republican predecessors. Although he insisted during his campaign that he would "not relinquish practical control of the Panama Canal anytime in the foreseeable future," Carter feared that a refusal to give the Republic of Panama total sovereignty of the Canal Zone would push that Latin American country further into the Communist sphere.[68] Once he took office, however, Carter became convinced of the necessity of a new treaty that would "phase out absolute U.S. control of the Canal and acknowledge Panamanian sovereignty." He viewed such a treaty as "absolutely necessary" to "correct the injustice" of the gunboat diplomacy that had originally secured U.S. control over the canal, as well as the U.S. "failure to take action after years of promises to Panama under five previous Presidents." Carter also believed that the United States should take a more humanitarian approach to third-world countries like Panama, which were increasingly outvoting the Western superpower in the United Nations.[69]

Shortly after his inauguration, Carter received a letter from Dan Flood expressing the concern that the new president would "push ahead on the projected give away treaty for the U.S. Canal Zone." Flood warned Carter that such a course "could well be your 'Bay of Pigs' and prevent your re-nomination or re-election." He concluded the letter by stating that his belief reflected the "predominant view in Congress."[70] And Flood was correct in his assertion that his opposition to a "give away treaty" was the prevailing view on Capitol Hill, especially in the House of Representatives.

Despite significant opposition from Congress and the public, Carter pursued a new treaty in the hope that he could secure ratification before the 1978 congressional elections. On March 13, 1977, Panamanian foreign minister Aquilino Boyd met with in Washington with U.S. Secretary of State Cyrus Vance, chief negotiator Ellsworth Bunker, and Sol Linowitz, an expert on Latin American relations and former ambassador to the Organization of American States. The United States proposed two treaties. One treaty outlined arrangements for the joint operation of the canal for the remainder of the century, at the end of which Panama would assume total control. The other treaty guaranteed the permanent neutrality of the canal and the right of the United States to defend it. Although the Panamanians eventually agreed to the treaties in principle, they demanded a one-million-dollar payoff and three hundred million dollars annually until the year 2000. When the Carter administration refused the extraordinary demand, negotiations stalled for four months.[71] Finally, Carter told Torrijos that the proposed treaties were his administration's final offer and that the only payments to Panama would come from revenues from the canal itself. Torrijos, after consulting with other Latin American leaders, agreed on the condition that the U.S. right of defending the canal would apply to *external* threats only, and that Panama would protect the waterway from any internal threats. On September 7, 1977, Carter and Torrijos signed the treaties.[72]

Flood was furious. On October 13 he, along with like-minded senators Jesse Helms, James McClure, Strom Thurmond, and Orrin Hatch, filed a suit with the Supreme Court against the Carter administration, challenging the right of the president to dispose of the Canal Zone.[73] Flood's particular suit was "to preserve the voting rights of all members of the House of Representatives," and specifically to protect the House's constitutional right to determine the transfer of property involved in any treaty by the federal government.[74] There was nothing new about his position. Flood had been threatening to take such an action since the 1950s, when he adopted the Panama Canal his chief foreign policy issue. Since that time, Flood had been a stringent opponent of a "giveaway," stressing such arguments as the continued economic and strategic value of the canal to the United States, a concern that the Communist-oriented government of Panama would join with Castro to close the waterway to U.S. shipping, and that surrendering the canal would be a further sign of appeasement to the Communists.[75] Flood followed up his suit in December by sponsoring a concurrent House resolution with other like-minded representatives stating that the "Congress has not authorized the President or any other representative of the United States to enter into or to conclude a treaty or other negotiations which may result in the disposition of Canal Zone territory."[76]

Carter spent the next several months mobilizing support while the Senate conducted hearings. The president lobbied key senators, addressed their concerns, and encouraged them to visit Panama to speak with the Panamanians themselves. He also enlisted the efforts of former president Gerald Ford, who lobbied undecided Republican senators for ratification.[77] Carter also seized the initiative to silence Flood. Highly placed sources within the federal government indicate that the White House was leaking information about a Justice Department investigation of the Pennsylvania congressman. Flood's name had been linked to a bribery scandal involving West Coast Trade Schools and a questionable relationship to Medico Industries, the manufacturer of military equipment with alleged ties to the Mafia.[78] Finally, on February 1, 1978, Carter took his case to the American people. In a nationally televised speech, the president said that the Senate should approve the Panama Canal treaties because they will "not only protect U.S. interests, but will demonstrate the kind of great power we wish to be." The speech came at a time of increasing signs that public opinion was changing; a recent Gallup poll showed 43 percent of the public in favor of treaties and 42 percent opposed. It was a significant shift from a year earlier, when a similar poll showed 78 percent against the treaties.[79]

Carter's strategy worked. In the spring of 1978 the Senate ratified the treaties. The second treaty, guaranteeing perpetual neutrality of the canal, was voted on first because the Carter administration viewed it as more palatable. It squeaked through the Senate on March 16 by a bipartisan vote of 68 to 32, narrowly gaining the necessary two-thirds majority. A month later, after heated debate, the first treaty, which identified the stipulations for gradually turning over the canal to Panama by the year 2000, was approved by exactly the same one-vote margin as the earlier one.[80] Carter received more good news in June when the Supreme Court ruled against Flood and the treaty opponents in the Senate.[81]

The canal treaties were now law, so Flood and his supporters in the House shifted their attention to preventing their implementation, which was scheduled to begin on October 1, 1979. They lined up votes to oppose the necessary legislation to cover retirement benefits to employees of the Canal Zone, the relocation of military forces, and the establishment of procedures for the orderly transfer of property to the Panamanians. All these measures would have to be approved by both houses of Congress. Treaty opponents ratcheted up their efforts beginning in late fall 1978. For sixteen weeks, Flood and the antitreaty forces held up the necessary implementation legislation through a series of deceptive maneuvers. First, they moved to prohibit any transfers in the canal military forces. Next, they issued punitive votes against Panama

Fig. 37. Flood stands behind President Jimmy Carter at a 1979 bill signing. Carter's decision to relinquish U.S. control of the Panama Canal created a bitter rivalry with Flood, Congress's most outspoken critic of the new treaties.

that altered previous agreements involving U.S. economic aide for job training, schools, and the improvement of medical facilities. Finally, efforts were made to alter specific provisions in the treaty to force Panama to pay the full costs of the canal, and to implement an exorbitant increase of canal toll fees. Throughout the process, House members were told by the treaty opponents that their vote could prevent the surrender of the canal; that the federal government would be forced to pay Panama billions of dollars from U.S. tax revenues; that Torrijos was a puppet of the Communist Party; and that U.S. military leaders were forced by the Carter administration to support the treaties against their will.[82]

The Carter administration countered by sending State and Defense officials on rounds of representatives' offices to correct the inaccuracies. Appealing to the House leadership, Carter secured the support of Speaker Tip O'Neill and majority leader Jim Wright of Texas. On September 26, 1979, O'Neill and Wright gave floor speeches appealing to members' sense of responsibility to pass the legislation necessary to implement the Panama Canal treaties. Afterward, the House voted by a margin of 224 to 202 to pass the implementation legislation.[83] "I think that Jimmy Carter's championing of the Panama Canal treaties was probably one of the most courageous things that a president could have done," said Wright in a recent interview. "He faced tremendous opposition by [congressional] hawks, but he held his ground. Dan Flood was one of those hawks, and I disagreed with him on Panama." "You have to put yourselves in the position of the Panamanians," continued Wright. "They saw us as 'occupiers.' We didn't want to buy any of their products. Instead we imposed our goods on them. Imagine, if you can, that the United States is not a superpower and that another, more powerful country had gotten control of the Mississippi River. If you wanted to pass from one part of our country to the other, you had to go through there. We'd be at the mercy of this other country. I certainly wouldn't like that position, nor did the Republic of Panama."[84] Even Rep. Joe McDade, Flood's closest friend in the House, voted for the legislation. "I think Dan was off the reservation on Panama," he said. "Dan's belief that the United States had an international responsibility to remain a supreme power or there wouldn't be any peace in the world wouldn't allow him to see the realities of the situation in Latin America. We were losing support down there and the best way for us to maintain a good relationship with Panama—to keep her from joining the Communist countries—was to give her the canal."[85]

While the Panama Canal treaties may have prevented a Communist takeover in the Latin American country, they also weakened Jimmy Carter's relationship with the House of Representatives and cost many senators who voted in favor of ratification their political careers.[86] The treaties also damaged Carter's own

Fig. 38. Rep. James Wright (D-Tex.), like Flood, was a cold warrior and committed to U.S. military involvement in Vietnam.

chances for reelection and—along with the fall of the shah and the seizure of American hostages in Iran, and the chill in U.S.-Soviet relations following the Soviet invasion of Afghanistan—seriously weakened the international status of the United States.[87] But by the time those events played out, Dan Flood had been forced out of Congress by a Justice Department investigation into allegations of bribery, influence peddling, and conspiracy.[88]

11

FEDERAL INVESTIGATION

Flood's problems were mounting by 1975. He was fighting a losing battle against addiction to painkillers and alcohol. Steve Elko, his untrustworthy administrative assistant, was shamelessly exploiting the congressman's authority to secure government contracts for any organization that would pay him. And syndicated Washington columnist Jack Anderson, known for his muckraking, was determined to expose Flood for improprieties in arranging those federal contracts. All these events emerged in the aftermath of the Watergate scandal during a period of public skepticism over the trustworthiness of elected officials. Dan Flood would become a victim of the political reform that occurred on Capitol Hill to win back the trust of the American people.

Watergate represented a crossroads in American political culture. President Richard Nixon's attempt to cover up the break-in of the Democratic National Committee headquarters by his campaign staff resulted not only in his resignation from office in 1974, but also revelations of an "imperial presidency" independent of constitutional restraints. Congress tried to fill the leadership void by asserting legislative supremacy, only to fall victim to scandals by its own members.[1] The House of Representatives was especially rife with sex, corruption, and conflicts of interest.

Shortly after the Nixon impeachment hearings, Wilbur Mills (D-Ark.) was forced to resign as chair of the powerful Ways and Means Committee for his affair with a thirty-eight-year-old stripper named "Fanne Fox."[2] More scandals followed in 1976: Andrew Hinshaw (R-Calif.) was convicted of bribery, misappropriations of public funds, and petty theft; Robert Sikes (D-Fla.) was censured by the House for financial misconduct; James Hastings (R-N.Y.) was convicted on twenty-eight counts involving kickbacks from staff members; Wendell Wyatt (R-Ore.) pleaded guilty to violating federal campaign spending laws; Allan Howe (D-Utah) was arrested in Salt Lake City after soliciting two under-cover policewomen who were posing as prostitutes; and Wayne Hays (D-Ohio), the sixty-five-year-old chair of the House Administration Committee, resigned after it was discovered that he kept his thirty-three-year-old mistress, Elizabeth Ray, on the federal payroll for nearly two years, despite her own admission that she "didn't know how to type, file, or answer the phone."[3] Another scandal, known as "Koreagate," followed in 1977 and 1978 when eleven House members were accused of taking payoffs from a South Korean businessman, Tongsun Park. While several of the accused representatives were indicted on charges of conspiracy, bribery, mail fraud, and acceptance of illegal gratuities, only one—Richard Hanna (D-Calif.)—went to jail. The House Ethics Committee recommended nothing more than censure for the others, and even that was reduced to reprimand when the accused denied any intentional wrongdoing.[4]

The scandals created a rift between a younger, more idealistic generation of congresspeople and their senior colleagues. Many of the young members refused to play by the old rules of the House, which emphasized "going along to get along," deference to seniority, and utter discretion. One of the young Turks, David Obey (D-Wis.), who had the good fortune to be appointed to House Appropriations, had the audacity to tell a senior colleague to "kiss [his] ass" after being reprimanded for questioning the committee's policy of banning the general public from public hearings. "I thought senior members like Dan Flood, Otto Passman and Bob Sikes were going to go into cardiac arrest," recalled Obey in a recent autobiography. "They were clearly shocked that one so new as I should utter a word of anything but the most profound respect for the sainted senior members."[5] The internal challenges and embarrassing scandals resulted both in a loss of public confidence in elected officials as well as in the ability of Congress to enforce its own ethics code.

Under these circumstances, it was inevitable that Flood, one of the most powerful senior legislators on Capitol Hill, would come under greater scrutiny. Beginning in 1970, Jack Anderson crafted an image of the elderly congressman as a "crook" in his controversial "Washington Merry-Go-Round" columns. The muckraking journalist charged that Flood obtained large defense contracts for Medico Industries, which Anderson maintained had ties to organized crime. In return for his influence, the Pennsylvania congressman "frequently caught rides in Medico's private plane."[6] Another column charged the congressman with pressuring the Department of Health, Education, and Welfare to award a five-hundred-thousand-dollar contract to an unqualified Wilkes-Barre firm.[7] Though Flood did not deny assisting either firm in securing federal contracts, he flatly rejected any knowledge of Medico's ties to the Mafia.[8]

To be sure, allegations of Flood's relationship to organized crime were nothing new. As early as 1958, the Senate Rackets hearings exposed Medico's alleged ties to the Mafia in several pages of testimony.[9] Further, in 1964 Senator John McClellan (D-Ark.) revealed that William Medico was a close associate of Russell Bufalino, one of the most ruthless Mafia bosses and a native of Luzerne County.[10] Despite the revelations, Flood assisted Medico Industries in securing defense contracts between 1967 and 1974.[11] He should have exercised better judgment. In the atmosphere of cynicism that surrounded elective politics, Flood's continued association with Medico Industries could only fuel suspicions of his ties to organized crime. When Donald Rothberg, an Associated Press writer, in 1969 suggested a direct link between the congressman and the Mafia, the *Wyoming Observer*, a biweekly Luzerne County newspaper, ran an exposé on alleged underworld figures who lived in the county and Flood's association with at least one of them, William Medico.[12] The story not only stirred a long-dormant suspicion that Flood had ties to the Mafia, but also laid the foundation for Anderson's accusation a year later.

At the same time, the various congressional scandals involving kickbacks and illegal campaign contributions brought Flood under a cloud of suspicion. The flamboyant congressman had always had a mixed voting record on the sensitive issue of campaign financing. When he ran for reelection in 1976 and in 1978, Flood publicly supported the idea of underwriting congressional campaigns with public money. But his Republican opponents rejected the idea and made the issue a cornerstone of their campaigns, questioning Flood's fund-raising methods.[13] The attacks motivated the U.S. Justice Department to launch its own investigation into allegations that Flood had long accepted illegal campaign contributions and violated election laws by paying off his Republican opponents.[14]

Then there was Steve Elko, whose shady activities became cause for growing concern among Flood's congressional colleagues. Between 1974 and 1976, Elko tried to milk one hundred thousand dollars in bribes from housing developer Robert Gennaro. In exchange, Elko promised to use Flood's influence with officials of the U.S. Department of Housing and Urban Development and the Farmers Home Administration of the U.S. Department of Agriculture to provide financial assistance to the Gateway Housing Corporation, which hoped to build the Crestwood Hills Development in Mountaintop, Pennsylvania.[15] During the same period, Elko accepted at least five thousand dollars from Lieb Pinter, a Brooklyn rabbi, in exchange for Flood's assistance in securing federal funds for social service programs run by the B'nai Torah Institute.[16] But the incident that triggered a House Ethics investigation of Flood was the congressman's complicity with Elko in securing a $14.5 million appropriation for Philadelphia's Hahnemann Hospital.

Flood's involvement with Hahnemann dated to 1971, when he helped to establish an innovative medical school partnership between the Philadelphia hospital and Wilkes College. Flood envisioned the joint, six-year medical program between Hahnemann Medical College and Wilkes as "a vital part" of both a proposed series of rural health care clinics known as the Northeast Regional Medical Complex, as well as "long-range plans for medical and health care needs" of the area. At a time when northeastern Pennsylvania suffered from a severe physician shortage, which numbered one hundred doctors for every one hundred thousand residents, the partnership was expected to produce twenty-five additional family medicine graduates each year. Flood assured his full commitment in seeking successful passage of authorizing legislation and appropriation of funds.[17]

The program, which began in September 1972, provided students with a streamlined curriculum at both the undergraduate and medical school levels to obtain a bachelor's and medical degree in a total of six year's time. Students who enrolled in the program were encouraged to return to the area to practice in exchange for a three-year remission of their tuition after they graduated.[18] "The concept of a streamlined curriculum that could turn out specialists in family practice made a lot of sense," insists Dr. Francis Michelini, then president of Wilkes College.

> Prior to World War II, you could enter medical school after three years of college. The four-year baccalaureate degree as a prerequisite to medical school came after the war when there were so many returning GIs who wanted to go to medical school. The four-year requirement was a way to slow down the entry pool to the pipeline and to create the bottleneck at the postbaccalaureate level rather than at the junior year level. But during the 1950s and early '60s there were still three-year entries into most medical and dental schools. It was reasonable to say that if you could collapse the baccalaureate degree to three years and the medical degree by compressing some of the specialty training you'd undergo in medical school, then why couldn't we have a medical program that would be based on three years of undergrad and three years of medical training.[19]

Dr. Ralph Rozelle, the graduate division chair at Wilkes, coordinated the partnership with Dr. Wilbur Oaks, a professor of Internal Medicine at Hahnemann Medical College. Together, they articulated the curriculum, wrote grants for financial support from private foundations and government agencies, and counseled students enrolled in the innovative program. Just as important, they worked closely with the local medical community to secure residencies for the students in their final year of the program. "We had fairly strong support from many of the family physicians in the region," recalled Rozelle. "Of those physicians, David Kistler and Charlie Meyers were most responsible for the concept of a undergraduate-medical school partnership and supported the program wholeheartedly. There were others who felt threatened by the competition of young physicians coming back into the region to practice and begrudgingly agreed to supervise residencies. However, the physicians at the Wilkes-Barre General, Nesbitt, the Veterans hospitals strongly supported us."[20]

Rozelle and Oaks also secured the support of General Electric, which linked the two schools through a closed-circuit television network. Students at Wilkes were able to attend lectures and symposia that were taking place at the medical college in Philadelphia. In addition, all the cooperating hospitals in northeastern Pennsylvania were linked to Hahnemann so they could access educational conferences for professional credit.[21] "Congressman Flood was instrumental in securing the funding for the whole program," said Rozelle. "He knew a good idea when he saw it and was largely responsible for securing the money through the Institute of General Medical Sciences, a federally funded program. It meant more than one million dollars coming into Hahnemann each year, and about three hundred thousand dollars a year for Wilkes."[22]

According to Michael Clark, Flood's special assistant, Hahnemann's president, E. Wharton Shober, used the partnership to "exploit the Congressman's position as chairman of HEW Appropriations." "Hahnemann bought into the partnership for only one reason—Shober needed Dan Flood much more than he needed him," insists Clark. "Hahnemann was planning to build a multimillion-dollar wing to its hospital and Shober needed political clout to secure the federal funding for it. Only Dan Flood could provide that kind of clout."[23] There's much validity to Clark's assertion.

In the 1960s and early 1970s, Hahnemann Medical College and Hospital were in chronic financial straits. At a time when hospitals were forced to operate in the national and international marketplace, Hahnemann was a regional institution that relied on local fund-raising, alumni contributions, and the philanthropy of its trustees to sustain itself. The only way to expand its operation was to secure considerably more funding from the state and federal government, and that required political patronage. In 1971 E. Wharton Shober was hired as president by the Hahnemann trustees to streamline the operation, increase fund-raising, and generate greater visibility to rival Philadelphia's more prominent medical colleges and hospitals, Temple, Jefferson, and the University of Pennsylvania. Thus Shober's appointment signaled a move away from the institution's traditional emphasis on academic research and toward a vision of corporate medicine.[24]

Shober did not have a medical or doctoral degree, which was at the time unusual for the CEO of a hospital. Instead, his background was in the military and in business. He attended Princeton before serving in the Office of Strategic Services during World War II. After the war, Shober founded the ATEK Corporation, which sold printing machinery and provided financial services to anti-Communist publishers in Latin and Central America.[25] Some believe that Shober's fortune was amassed not through ATEK but through his work for the Central Intelligence Agency, specifically as the codirector of a Philadelphia-based operation that assisted anti-Batista professionals to flee Cuba.[26]

Shober also had an impressive social background. He was a nephew of former Pennsylvania governor George H. Earle and a member of Philadelphia's elite First City Troop. Residing on Philadelphia's Main Line, Shober vacationed in the Swiss Alps, flew his own private airplane, and played polo at the exclusive Merion Cricket Club.[27] Duly impressed, Hahnemann's board of trustees appointed him president in 1971. Apparently, Shober's special flair for business and high-society background made up for his lack of academic experience and qualifications.

"Shober was a pretty cagey figure," recalled Wilkes president Francis Michelini. "He had a business background—not medical or academic—and when you move into the administration of a medical college without any knowledge or experience in those two areas, you're always suspect. He also dabbled in international politics, which didn't go over too well at Hahnemann. Shober was very tight with Anastasio Somoza, the Nicaraguan dictator, and arranged for him to receive an honorary degree over the strong objections of the medical school faculty and students. So Shober moved the entire commencement off campus to a private estate and billed the affair to Hahnemann."[28]

Shortly after his appointment as president, Shober ingratiated himself with local and state politicians to secure the patronage he needed for funding. Among those he courted were Philadelphia mayor Frank Rizzo, congressman Joshua Eilberg, and, of course, Flood.[29] Eilberg, a member of the House Judiciary Committee, was a seasoned Philadelphia politician. After earning an economics degree from the University of Pennsylvania's prestigious Wharton School of Finance and a law degree from Temple University, he served as an assistant district attorney for two years and then in the state legislature for over a decade, becoming majority leader of the Pennsylvania House of Representatives. Together with Rizzo and Peter J. Camiel, Philadelphia's Democratic Party boss, Eilberg was central to the leadership of the city's Democratic machine. Like Flood, Eilberg had the power and influence to tap into significant government funding at both the federal and state levels. Unlike Flood, he distanced himself from the spotlight, preferring to work behind the scenes.[30]

Shober also expanded the initiatives of his predecessor, Charles Cameron, by courting greater racial and ethnic diversity (something the federal government insisted on as a prerequisite to financial assistance). Accordingly, Shober pursued other partnerships like the Wilkes-Hahnemann program with such undergraduate institutions like Cheyney University, a historically African American college.[31] Having laid the foundations for greater federal funding, in February 1974 Shober sought financing for the construction of an addition to the medical college. "It was difficult to get any federal funding in the 1970s," recalled Dr. William Kashatus, former dean of admissions for Hahnemann and a native of Luzerne County. "We needed three million dollars to build a School of Allied and Health Sciences. Shober knew that I was one of Dan Flood's constituents and asked me if I'd approach him for assistance. I knew the congressman had an ego, so I asked him to be the commencement speaker for the class of 1974. Of course, he accepted the invitation and, a few months later, Hahnemann received the three million dollars for the new school."[32]

Having achieved success, Shober decided to move ahead with plans for a new $65 million wing for the hospital, an initiative known as the "Tower Project." In April 1974 he met with congressman Joshua Eilberg to "discuss the political help" that his law firm could provide Hahnemann "in getting money for the new wing." Shortly thereafter, Shober fired Hahnemann's legal counsel and hired Eilberg's law firm at a cost of more than $500,000 to convince the Philadelphia Hospital Authority to approve a $39.5 million tax-exempt bond issue. To avoid the appearance of impropriety, Eilberg's law partners established a separate group to handle the Hahnemann account.[33]

In June, Shober contacted Flood's Washington office and spoke with Steve Elko, who helped him file a grant application for $14.5 million. Elko also suggested that Shober gather together "a $10,000 campaign contribution to Flood to insure his assistance." Shober delivered about $8,500 to Elko, and Flood did some legislative jostling on behalf of Hahnemann. When the Department of Health, Education, and Welfare and many members of the HEW Appropriations Subcommittee opposed the expenditure, Flood pushed the $14.5 million through the House at the last minute in the form of a grant from the Community Services Administration.[34] But Elko's interest in the Hahnemann project was inspired by more than the $10,000 "campaign contribution" he received.

Elko viewed Hahnemann as a continuous source of soft money and patronage for himself, his family, and his friends. He often tried to manipulate the Wilkes-Hahnemann program to gain admission as well as financial aid for the sons and daughters of relatives and cronies. Dr. Ralph Rozelle, one of the coordinators of the program, contends that he was pressured by Flood's administrative assistant to admit candidates. "Dan Flood never asked me for anything in the way of admitting a particular applicant," recalled Rozelle.

> He respected my position and never tried to compromise me. But Elko was a different story. He pushed for his [relative] to be admitted into the program when he was a freshman at Wilkes. The kid was a marginal admit, but we accepted him. Shober approached me shortly after and said, "I assume it won't cost [the relative] anything to go to school up there. When he gets to Hahnemann, we will pick up the entire tab." It was clear to me then and there that Steve Elko had Shober in his pocket.
>
> Well, the [relative] entered the Wilkes-Hahnemann program and he did not do well, so he lost his scholarship. Elko came into my office and told me to get a financial commitment from the Pennsylvania Higher Education Assistance Agency to pay his [relative's] way. I said that I couldn't do it, that it was unethical. I was no good to Steve Elko after that. He went down to Hahnemann and bad-mouthed me.[35]

Kashatus, Hahnemann's dean of admissions, had a similar experience with Flood's administrative assistant.

> I had to be real careful. Before I became dean in 1972, Shober had compromised the Admissions Department by forcing the board to accept unqualified applicants. I was hired because I was a graduate of the medical college and I taught there, but I also took my salary from the Upjohn Corporation, so I couldn't be compromised. That didn't stop Steve Elko, though.
>
> Once he phoned me and insisted that Congressman Flood wanted to know why a certain candidate from Bethlehem wasn't admitted. I explained that the candidate didn't have the test scores to warrant

admission. I also said that I thought it was strange that the congressman would have an interest in a candidate who wasn't from his district. Elko snapped at me: "Look, the old man [Flood] wants this kid in, so do it." Then he hung up on me. Later that week, I ran into Dan at a testimonial dinner for a mutual friend. I asked him why he was supporting an unqualified med-school applicant who wasn't even from his congressional district. Flood said he didn't know what I was talking about. Turned out that Elko was putting words in the congressman's mouth. The applicant was the son of Elko's friend. Needless to say, I didn't take any more phone calls from Steve Elko after that.[36]

Securing admission to Hahnemann Medical College for family and friends was only part of Elko's design. He also wanted to share in the profits generated by the construction of the new hospital wing. In July 1974, one month after Hahnemann submitted its grant application, Elko contacted Shober and said that the congressman was "very interested in" the Environmental Design Center Inc. (EDCI), an architectural and engineering firm run by Jack and Ed Dixon of Frackville, Pennsylvania, and "would appreciate [his] assistance in giving them work for the hospital's [constriction project]."[37] Later that month, Elko met with the Dixon brothers and told them that Flood could arrange for EDCI's involvement in the Hahnemann project, but he "wanted to know what they could do for [him] and the Congressman." The Dixons and Elko agreed to split the engineering fees, with 4 percent of the proceeds received by EDCI going to the brothers and another 4 percent to Elko.[38] Shortly thereafter, Jack Dixon and his associate Richard Spang, EDCI's primary stockholder, met with Shober and submitted a proposal for a contract fee in excess if one million dollars.[39]

In August 1974 Elko met with the Dixon brothers to discuss EDCI's contract fee and was told that Hahnemann wanted to reduce the fee and that the firm could not do the job for less money. Elko, finagling to salvage the arrangement, told the brothers that the initial contract was only to get EDCI's "foot in the door," and that additional money could be earned from change orders or supplemental contracts in the future. When Jack Dixon informed Spang of this possibility, Spang, acting as EDCI's representative, submitted another proposal to Hahnemann, in September, for a contract fee of five hundred thousand dollars. Hahnemann never agreed to the offer and by year's end it looked as if the arrangement with EDCI had fallen through.[40]

In March 1975 Spang contacted George Guerra, the owner of Capital Investment Development Corporation (CIDC), to discuss the possibility of his firm assuming EDCI's negotiations with Hahnemann. Spang informed Guerra of his relationship to the Dixon brothers, as well as the Dixons' arrangements with Steve Elko. Guerra agreed to have Spang run CIDC while still maintaining his ownership interest in the inactive EDCI. Guerra also agreed to certain payments from the proceeds of the contract, with 5 percent going to the Dixon brothers and another 3 percent to Elko. After Elko agreed to the terms, he telephoned Shober and said that "friends of Congressman Flood from CIDC would be contacting him for an interview."[41]

On April 23, 1975, Spang and Guerra met with Shober to explain EDCI's working relationship with CIDC. Guerra also submitted a CIDC proposal for the Hahnemann construction project. Over the next six months, as Hahnemann and CIDC carried out negotiations, Jack Dixon repeatedly placed pressure on Elko to "put the hammer on Shober."[42] During the negotiations, on November 15, 1975, the Community Services Administration, the federal agency controlled by Flood's HEW Appropriations Subcommittee, approved the release of $2.5 million of the $14.5 million grant program to Hahnemann. Shortly thereafter, Elko received $1,500—the first of eight payments—from the Dixons for his assistance.[43] On December 8, 1975, the Hahnemann board of trustees approved the hiring of CIDC as project monitor on the Tower Project for a fee of $835,000.[44]

By this time, many of Flood's colleagues had become wary of Stephen Elko. Some, like Rep. Robert Michel, who also served on the House Appropriations Committee, advised the congressman to "distance himself" from the administrative assistant. "I think Dan put too much trust in Elko," Michel said in a recent interview. "What I knew of him, I didn't trust and there were other members on the House Appropriations Committee who didn't trust him either. Many of us on the HEW Subcommittee were surprised that Dan got a $14.5 million appropriation for Hahnemann. That was a pretty big earmark for one hospital. That appropriation raised a lot of red flags and I just knew that Elko was behind it."[45] Rep. Fred Rooney agreed. "When you're in a position like Dan Flood and you're relying on your staff, occasionally there's somebody who's going to disappoint you," he said. "In Dan's case, it was Steve Elko. He was untrustworthy and he brought discredit upon the congressman. It's too bad that Dan didn't dismiss him earlier."[46]

In fact, Flood never did dismiss Elko. The House Standards of Official Conduct Committee, better known as the House Ethics Committee, forced the untrustworthy aide's resignation in June 1976. For two years prior, committee chair Rep. John Flynt purposely avoided an investigation, despite mounting evidence he received of Flood's involvement in questionable activities. But in April 1976, the Senate Permanent Investigations Subcommittee sent Flynt confidential evidence of Flood's complicity in the West Coast Trade Schools scandal. The Senate subcommittee also referred its findings to the U.S. Department of Justice. Never before had a complaint against a House member come from the Senate. It was a delicate situation for Flynt, a courtly southerner, who also sat on the House Appropriations Committee with Flood. Not only was he being barraged with similar cases involving conflicts of interest, but he had also been a close friend of Flood's.[47] Instead of pursuing an investigation, Flynt, through committee staffers, quietly encouraged Elko to resign. According to one congressional source, "Elko was a bad apple and the House Ethics Committee was up to its ears in other investigations in 1976." "Elko was told that if he resigned, the Committee would no longer have any jurisdiction over the matter because most of the evidence pointed to Elko's improprieties and not Flood's," he said. "The whole matter was handled at the staff level and the Ethics Committee was spared the embarrassment of investigating one of the House's most powerful members."[48] More accurately, the "embarrassment" of an investigation would be postponed.

Elko initially resisted the pressure to resign. Infuriated, he confided to a close friend that "for years [he'd] been doing all the dirty work and the old man [Flood] [had] been getting all the gravy." Elko insisted that he was "not going to be forced out of a job" that earned him one hundred thousand dollars a year.[49] But the administrative assistant eventually relented. Before leaving the staff, however, Elko rifled through Flood's files. He burned some of the records and held onto others in case he needed documentation for a legal defense in the future.[50]

Meanwhile, the Justice Department, acting on the information from the Senate Permanent Investigations Subcommittee, undertook an investigation of West Coast Trade Schools. In February 1977 a federal grand jury in Los Angeles indicted five men with bribery, conspiracy, and securities fraud. The charges were in connection with seeking to obtain accreditation for five of the six schools so they could continue to participate in various federal financial assistance programs. All five subjects either pled guilty or were convicted, including lobbyist Deryl Fleming and William Fred Peters, former executive officer of the schools. Both of them identified Steve Elko and Dan Flood as accomplices.[51]

On June 9, 1977, Elko and his girlfriend, Patricia Brislin, were indicted on charges of conspiring to obtain bribes to gain accreditation for the schools. According to attorney general Griffin Bell, the indictment, returned in U.S.

District Court in Los Angeles, also charged that Elko issued letters purport-edly signed by Flood to be sent to former commissioner of education Sidney Marland. The letters demanded that the schools be accredited and threatened "war" if accreditation was not granted. The indictment also alleged that during the Los Angeles federal grand jury investigation, Elko and Brislin conspired to obstruct justice and committed perjury to conceal their illegal activities.[52]

During the trial, Elko was hired for consulting jobs by Roy Morgan, the president of the Wilkes-Barre Industrial Fund, a branch of the Greater Wilkes-Barre Chamber of Commerce, and American Klean Air, a company reportedly operated by Phillip Medico's son, Charles. His pay from both companies amounted to twenty-five thousand dollars—fifteen thousand dollars from the Industrial Fund and ten thousand dollars from Klean Air. In addition, James Tedesco, a regional coal operator, reportedly contributed fifteen thou-sand for Elko's legal fees. Since Morgan, Medico, and Tedesco were longtime friends of Flood's, federal investigators alleged that the money was paid to buy Elko's silence.[53]

While the Elko case unfolded, Flood was subpoenaed to the federal grand jury in Los Angeles. Advised of his Miranda rights, the Pennsylvania legis-lator denied receiving payoffs from anyone.[54] His legal difficulties were just beginning though. The Justice Department began to investigate Flood's and Eilberg's involvement in the Hahnemann construction project. In July 1977 David Marston, U.S. attorney for the Eastern District of Pennsylvania, began looking into allegations that the two congressmen had accepted kickbacks from both Hahnemann and CIDC in return for securing government funding for the construction project. Marston, one of the most effective prosecutors of political corruption in Pennsylvania, was relentless in pursuing leads and securing testimony from potential witnesses.[55] On November 2, 1977, FBI agents in Philadelphia visited Eilberg's law firm and asked questions that made it clear an investigation involving Hahnemann was underway. Two days later, Eilberg, fearing the worst, contacted president Jimmy Carter to discuss "political problems with the U.S. Attorney in Philadelphia." Eilberg also requested Marston's removal and urged the president to "expedite" the process. On that same day, Justice Department prosecutors obtained permis-sion to grant Steve Elko immunity from further prosecution in return for information about other possible crimes involving Flood.[56]

In October, Elko, along with Patricia Brislin, were convicted of bribery, perjury, obstruction of justice, and conspiracy for accepting bribes of between four thousand dollars and fifteen thousand dollars for their role in the West Coast Trade School accreditation scandal. U.S. District Court judge Albert

Lee Stephens would later sentence Elko to three years imprisonment and Brislin to one, far less than the maximum penalty. The reduced sentences were given in return for a grant of immunity and their cooperation in the Justice Department's investigation of Flood.[57]

For nearly thirty days, members of a special organized crime task force headed by John Dowd, a Washington-based federal prosecutor, questioned Elko. During that time, the former administrative assistant charged Flood with a wide range of improprieties, including:

- manipulation of federal aid in connection with the construction project at Hahnemann and conspiring to have Eilberg's law firm handle the contract negotiations;
- accepting one hundred thousand dollars in cash and bank stock from the West Coast Trade Schools and other organizations that obtained federal financing with his assistance;
- paying more than ninety thousand dollars to Elko and Brislin for legal fees during their October 1977 trial as well as for their "silence about Flood's transactions on Capitol Hill";
- obtaining congressional approval, in 1973, of ten million dollars for a livestock development project in the Bahamas and then attempting to place a friend, Bahamian lawyer F. Nigel Bowe, in charge of the project;
- exercising veto power over which companies would be hired to set up aid programs in Haiti (for which Flood obtained financial assistance through his position as chair of HEW Appropriations);
- accepting a payment of ten thousand dollars from Rabbi Lieb Pinter of Brooklyn, New York, in exchange for Flood's intervention with the Labor Department for a training program for Soviet Jewish immigrants.[58]

On January 12, 1978, when U.S. attorney general Griffin Bell, acting on President Carter's directive, removed David Marston from his post as U.S. attorney for the Eastern District of Pennsylvania, the Flood investigation made front-page headlines across the nation. Eilberg, who requested Marston's removal, insisted that he did not know he and Flood were under investigation at the time. He also stated that his motive for urging the U.S. attorney's removal was strictly political—that he wanted Marston, a Republican, replaced by a Democrat.[59] Whether Eilberg was attempting to sidetrack an investigation and whether Carter and Bell knew that an investigation was in progress were never determined. Further complicating matters was the fact that Carter administration officials made so many public statements about the Marston affair that later had to be modified, qualified, or retracted entirely.[60] As a result of the contradictions, Marston's defenders were able to turn the affair into a credibility problem for the Carter administration. Dan Flood would be used as a pawn in a highly charged partisan battle.

In early February 1978, the House Republican leadership called on the Ethics Committee to investigate Flood and Eilberg.[61] Only GOP House whip Robert Michel of Illinois abstained from making the request. Though Michel had been critical of Flood's role in pushing the $14.5 million federal grant to Hahnemann through the House in 1975, he was a member of Flood's HEW Appropriations Subcommittee and a close friend. His abstention was a matter of personal loyalty, something that was quickly becoming rare on Capitol Hill.[62] Flood's own party was even beginning to desert him as thirty-two junior Democratic House members also sent a letter requesting a thorough investigation of his alleged improprieties.[63]

Initially, Rep. John Flynt, the chair of the Ethics Committee, stalled for time. Like Michel, Flynt belonged to the old school on Capitol Hill. He refused to desert Flood, a close friend, in his greatest hour of need. Flynt still hoped that the Justice Department's investigation would preempt the necessity for a congressional inquiry.[64] But increasing pressure from the GOP and the negative publicity generated by his reluctance eventually forced him to comply.[65] On May 25 Flynt sent Ethics Committee staff director John Swanner to interview Steve Elko at Lompoc, the federal minimum security prison in Southern California where he had begun serving his three-year sentence.[66] Swanner concluded that there was, indeed, enough evidence to launch a House investigation. Accordingly, on June 1 Flynt appointed Washington attorney Elliot Goldstein as special counsel to study reports of wrongdoing by Flood.[67]

By the summertime, the Justice Department had expanded its investigation of Flood based on his alleged violations of the Racketeer Influenced and Corrupt Organizations Act (RICO).[68] The Hahnemann and California Trade Schools scandals were only the most publicized of the improprieties. Other investigations focused on Flood's involvement in obtaining government grants for the Airlie Foundation of Warrenton, Virginia; B'nai Torah Institute of Brooklyn, New York; Crestwood Hills Housing Development of Mountaintop, Pennsylvania; Anthra-Penn Inc. of Frackville, Pennsylvania; and the government of Haiti.[69] Justice Department offices in Washington, Los Angeles, and Philadelphia were engaged in a joint effort to prosecute Flood on a comprehensive RICO indictment in the District of Columbia. U.S. attorney John M. Dowd of the Washington office coordinated the investigation.[70]

On September 5, 1978, Flood was indicted by a federal grand jury in Los Angeles on three counts of perjury. The indictment charged that Flood lied at Elko's trial a year earlier when he denied knowing that his former administrative assistant received five thousand dollars from William F. Peters, former director of West Coast Trade Schools, in spring 1972. A second count accused Flood of testifying falsely to a federal grand jury on June 2, 1977, when he denied receiving one thousand dollars in cash from former lobbyist Deryl Fleming, a friend of Peters and Elko. The third count alleged that Flood lied when he told the grand jury that he did not receive five thousand dollars in cash from Peters at Flood's command post after Hurricane Agnes hit Wilkes-Barre in 1972. If convicted on all three counts, the flamboyant congressman would face up to five years in prison and a ten-thousand-dollar fine.[71] Flood insisted that he was innocent. "For thirty years, I have served the people who elected me in the best manner I know how," declared the elderly congressman to a gathering of media outside his Wilkes-Barre home. "Time after time they have demonstrated their confidence by returning me to office for fourteen additional terms. I have never done anything to destroy that confidence. I do not intend for one minute to falter in my endeavor as I seek my sixteenth term in the United States House of Representatives."[72]

As Flood turned his attention to reelection, the Dowd investigation completed its work. On October 12 a federal grand jury in Washington, D.C., indicted the embattled congressman on ten counts of conspiracy and bribery. The first count charged Flood with conspiring with Stephen Elko for accepting $65,000 and one hundred shares of stock in First Valley Bank of Bethlehem, Pennsylvania, in return for the congressman's influence with various federal agencies. The remaining nine counts charged that Flood took $16,500 in bribes and asked for another $100,000 from a variety of sources in return for arranging federal aid.[73] After learning of the most recent indictment, Flood, once again, declared his innocence:

> I have been informed of the indictment made by the Grand Jury here in Washington. I deny all of these allegations, totally and unequivocally. I am confident that I will be proven innocent in a court of law.
>
> The timing of this indictment is, of course, controlled by the Department of Justice. And that Department is well aware that in a matter of days, the voters in my Congressional District will be going to the polls.
>
> As far as I am aware, no indictment has ever been issued at the request of the Department of Justice against a candidate for Congressional office

Fig. 39. Flood meets with the press outside of his Wilkes-Barre home on September 5, 1978, after being indicted by a federal grand jury in Los Angeles on three counts of perjury. Insisting that he was innocent, the flamboyant legislator announced his intention to seek reelection to a sixteenth term in Congress.

in such proximity to an election date. But, nonetheless, in spite of such timing, I am certain that the outstanding record of my thirty years of service in the Congress will serve as the ultimate basis on which my constituents will decide to return me to this House by another overwhelming margin.

Neither adversity nor the demands of pursuing the proof of my innocence will deter me in my duties of serving the people of my Congressional District. Neither absurd charges nor their attendant innuendos will prevent my constituents from expressing once more their belief and trust in my integrity.

Nothing will stand in the way as I continue to serve the people who elected me in the best way I know how, as I continue to trust that in the courts the charges leveled against me will be revealed for what they are—baseless charges made by desperate men under pressure.

I will have no further comment whatsoever on these matters until they are disposed of in the court of law, where I will be proved innocent.[74]

On October 19 Flood appeared in the U.S. District Court in Washington before Judge Louis F. Oberdorfer for arraignment. Axel Kleiboemer, a Washington attorney who had been retained as legal representation, accompanied him. Flood entered a plea of not guilty and was released on his own recognizance.[75]

Nineteen days later, on November 7, the voters of the embattled congressman's district reelected him by a landslide to a sixteenth term in the House of Representatives. "We don't care what outsiders say," cried one constituent. "They're just trying to hurt a member of the family. Dan Flood is the next closest thing to God."[76]

12

TRIAL AND TRIBULATION

The ordeal of a Justice Department investigation, as well as an impending probe by the House Ethics Committee, took its toll on Flood. Since undergoing cancer surgery in 1962, the congressman's health had always been precarious at best. But the stress of his legal problems now left him psychologically depressed and constantly fatigued. Flood lay in bed sleepless at night, worrying about the federal investigation and unable to decide on how to proceed with a defense. Most of the time he was entirely lucid and clear. On other occasions, however, he spoke slowly, sometimes slurring his words, and his memory failed him. As a result, conversations would deteriorate into long, rambling expositions dominated by inconsequential details.[1]

Flood rarely, if ever, displayed the dramatic outbursts that had once characterized his speeches on the House floor. The daily business of being a congressman—presenting legislation, cutting deals with his colleagues, conducting subcommittee hearings—no longer energized him as they once did. He even began to give his closest friends difficulty in channeling their pork-barrel projects through Appropriations. On one occasion, Speaker Tip O'Neill, wanting to secure an appropriation out of Flood's HEW Subcommittee, phoned his friend. O'Neill, who was pretty colorful and irreverent in his own right, tried to cheer him up by singing into the receiver:

"Oh Danny Boy, the pipes, the pipes are calling . . . "

"What is it, Tip?" replied Flood, apathetically.

" . . . from glen to glen, and down the mountainside," O'Neill continued to sing.

"It's about the Appropriations bill, isn't it?"

" . . . the summer's gone and all the roses are dying . . . "

"What has the White House put you up to?"

" . . . 'tis you, 'tis you, must go and I must bide . . . "

"All right, Tip. All right."

" . . . but come ye back, when summer's in the meadow . . . "

"You got your bill," said Flood flatly, ending the conversation.[2]

Part of Flood's difficulty was due to drug addiction, though he saw himself as practicing "preventative medicine." He admitted to taking the following medications on an almost daily basis: stress caps (which Flood considered a "vitamin supplement"); feosol spansules, for "iron"; yeast, a "nutrient"; Periactin, for "itching of the skin"; Arlidin, "for blood pressure"; Betelin complex, "one ounce a day for indigestion"; tuonal, "a sleeping pill [he'd] taken every night for five years"; Librium, "for anxiety"; Inderol, "for blood pressure"; senegran expectorant, a "cough syrup"; and Lomotil. Flood had become so dependent on these drugs that occasionally he tried to refill prescriptions without medical authorization. The frequent use and interaction between the various drugs could easily produce lethargy, anxiety, depression, dizzy spells, blackouts, confusion, or memory loss, especially given Flood's history of alcohol abuse. Naturally, he complained about the disabling effects to those closest to him.[3]

According to Axel Kleiboemer, Flood's legal counsel, the congressman's staff had become impatient with him. "Some staff members will lecture him as if he was a child," observed Kleiboemer. "Their tone of voice becomes sharp and I have seen him unable to resist the demands made upon him. He has never corrected the implicit impertinence of his subordinates, but rather admitted to me that he finds himself totally unable to ever refuse any demands from the senior members of his staff." Flood also confided to his lawyer that he felt as if "he doesn't have a single friend in this world."[4]

Under the circumstances, Kleiboemer decided to have the congressman hospitalized in the spring of 1978 to "prepare a defense" and to "initiate medical treatment." He made arrangements with Flood's physician, Dr. Marvin Small, for his client to "undergo a complete physical and psychiatric evaluation" at George Washington University Hospital and requested that he be "furnished with an appropriate report of the findings."[5]

In addition to Flood's health concerns, he was also facing severe financial pressures. Contrary to media reports that the pork-barreling congressman had accumulated a personal fortune during his years on Capitol Hill, Flood's total estate amounted to just $83,827.66.[6] Of that figure, Flood owned $712.50 in government savings bonds; $32,904.90 in stocks; $22,932.09 in savings accounts; $10,244.00 in banking shares; and $17,034.17 in life insurance policies.[7] The home in which he and his wife lived in Wilkes-Barre, and a small parcel of land the couple owned in Bear Creek, outside the city's boundaries, might have increased the value of the estate to over $100,000. But Edward Jones, the executor, insisted, "The value of these parcels are at best a guess and do not represent any substantial value."[8] Flood's legal fees would easily consume whatever savings he had. In fact, he was forced to liquidate $52,000 of assets and take out a loan from United Penn Bank for another $50,000 to pay legal expenses prior to his trial.[9] Realizing his dire financial straits, the congressman's constituents came to his aide. On December 7, 1978, some three hundred people attended a fund-raiser at Wilkes-Barre's Treadway Inn. William Reishstein, a retired obstetrician and shopping mall developer who hoped to raise $500,000 for the legal fund, organized the event. Though the proceeds fell far short of the goal, Flood was deeply touched by the gesture.[10]

Flood's constituents proved to be his only salvation during these trying times. In a show of defiance toward his accusers, the citizens of Wilkes-Barre honored the congressman as "Citizen of the Year" in 1978.[11] While the national media excoriated Flood both in print and cartoon, the daily newspapers in northeastern Pennsylvania simply ran the Associated Press's articles on the congressman's alleged improprieties, refusing to do any investigative reporting to determine the validity of the charges. Most letters to the editor regarding Flood were supportive, if not protective of him.[12] Some of the editorials were even written by members of Luzerne County's GOP, reflecting the bipartisan support that existed for the Democratic congressman. "Let's remember that no one is guilty until proven to be," editorialized Roy Morgan, a Republican who owned WILK, a local radio station. "Let's also remember the many services that Congressman Flood has rendered to this area. His assistance has touched the lives of most of us at one time or another."[13] Other constituents insisted that Flood was being used as a "scapegoat" by the Carter administration because the congressman "opposes giving up the Panama Canal," or by the "all powerful abortion lobby" that couldn't get their bills passed by Flood's HEW Appropriations Subcommittee.[14]

Throughout the ordeal, the embattled legislator continued to return to his district each weekend to meet with constituents and listen to their concerns. "Mr. Flood was like a modern-day Christ in the Wyoming Valley," said Mariclare Wysocki-Hahn, a secretary at the congressman's district office. "He just had an incredible presence. You knew he was a man to be reckoned with if you challenged the needs of his constituents. Even during his final years in office, he put the concerns of the people he represented up here before his own problems. On Saturday mornings, they'd stream into the office for 'confessional,' and Mr. Flood would set behind his cherry desk and listen patiently to each and every one."[15]

Dan Flood's case went to trial before judge Oliver Gasch of the U.S. Circuit Court in Washington, D.C., on January 15, 1979. As a courtesy to the congressman, the federal court in Los Angeles agreed to have Flood's perjury case reassigned to the District of Columbia. The day before, the Pennsylvania representative, wearing a navy blue gabardine suit and matching suede shoes, was excused from jury selection at noon so he could attend the swearing-in ceremonies for his sixteenth term at the Capitol. After he returned, the selection process was completed and twelve jurors were chosen along with six alternates. The jury would be sequestered for the duration of the trial.[16]

In his opening statement, David Hinden, the Justice Department's prosecuting attorney, painted Flood as a "corrupt" politician whose "influence was for sale." He stated he would prove that the congressman accepted thousands of dollars in cash, stock, and thinly disguised campaign contributions in exchange for wielding his considerable influence in the House of Representatives to aid others in procuring government grants, approval of bank mergers, contracts, government loan guarantees, and favorable government rulings. In his opening rebuttal, Axel Kleiboemer, Flood's lawyer, denied that his client took any bribes. He also attacked the credibility of Stephen Elko, the prosecution's lead witness, stating that Elko had abused his position and kept money that he said he delivered to the congressman. During the opening statements, Flood sat almost impassively, except for the continual tapping of his feet and the twitching of his right eye.[17]

Elko was called as the prosecution's first witness and recounted his and Flood's association with Dr. Murdock Head and the Airlie Foundation Conference Center. Crafting a story of code names, fingerprint protection, and fears of eavesdropping, the slightly nervous former administrative assistant said that he was required to identify himself as "Dr. Malik" when he phoned Head at a "super unlisted" number. He maintained that Flood was referred to as "The Mandrake" or "The Mustache," and former Louisiana representative Otto Passman, whom Elko also implicated, was "The Parish Priest." Elko testified that Head always used facial tissue in handling the envelopes of cash meant for Flood. The money, according to Elko, was "sometimes as much as $5,000 in $100 bills." Elko maintained that of all the transactions over a three-year period he kept only "$9,000 and gave $28,000 to Flood and about $11,000 to Passman." He also stated that the payments to Flood and Passman (former chair of the Foreign Aid Appropriations Subcommittee) were in return for directing appropriations to the Agency for International Development (AID), which financed some of Head's projects, and for using their influence with officials of the agency to give favorable treatment to the Airlie Foundation. Letters between the two congressmen and AID, as well as a letter from Passman to Flood assuring his continued support for Airlie, were introduced as evidence to support the government's case.[18]

Despite the defense's effort to portray Elko as a liar, he stood firm in his story that he delivered thousands of dollars in payoffs to Flood. Elko testified that he was the go-between for Flood and several individuals who wanted federal contract, grants, and loan guarantees, accepting payments for the congressman in increments of one-thousand-, two-thousand-, and five-thousand-dollar bribes as well as one hundred shares of bank stock. At one point in the cross-examination, an exasperated Kleiboemer asked, "Isn't it true that you kept all the money for yourself?" "No sir," Elko replied. "Get all you can while you can get it," he quoted the Congressman as saying in 1975 after accepting a two-thousand-dollar payment from Rabbi Lieb Pinter of Brooklyn.[19]

Kleiboemer forced the issue. Contending that Elko kept all the payoff money, he produced several bank deposit forms, all for cash and totaling the same amount of the bribes. He proceeded to show that all the money had been placed in the former administrative assistant's bank account during the period the bribes were being paid. But Elko said that the bank deposits came from legitimate business payments he received from Intech, a company that employed him prior to joining Flood's staff, and the payments represented vacation pay, service pay, and salary as part of his termination agreement. He explained further that Intech paid him with checks made out to cash, and that he and the company's comptroller usually went to a bank together to cash the checks. He would then deposit that cash into his own account. Hinden, the prosecutor, proved Elko's claim by producing nine specific checks from Intech made out to cash. In each case, the company's comptroller endorsed the checks for the exact amounts written on the corresponding deposit slip, and the dates and deposit slips matched almost exactly.[20]

Kleiboemer also called T. Newell Wood, a former Pennsylvania state senator and banker, to disprove Elko's claim that Flood accepted one hundred shares of stock worth about four thousand dollars as a kickback for his role in expediting a merger between two Pennsylvania banks. Wood, who had known Flood for more than fifteen years, was the controlling stockholder in one of the banks. He stated that after the Federal Deposit Insurance Corporation had approved the merger, he approached Flood to make a contribution to his 1972 reelection campaign. When the congressman refused to accept the contribution, Wood offered bank stock "in appreciation for [Flood's] friendship to the bank." Shortly after Flood accepted the gift, Elko approached Wood saying that he had done most of the work to expedite the merger and that "if anybody receives a political contribution, it should be me." Insulted, Wood phoned Flood to complain about the aide's behavior and stated that he "didn't want to have any more to do with [Elko], directly or indirectly."[21]

Finally, the defense lawyer attacked Elko's credibility by asking him if he stole files from Flood's office, implying that he tried to frame the congressman. But Elko diffused the charge. After admitting that he rifled through Flood's files, burned some of the records, and later gave others to federal investigators, he insisted that he had permission from the congressman to do so and that the documents he took dealt only with his—and not Flood's—activities.[22]

For three days, the defense challenged Elko's memory in direct and cross-examination. But Flood's former administrative assistant only seemed to restore his credibility. As the week unfolded, the prosecution's other witnesses—William Fred Peters, former executive officer of West Coast Trade Schools, and lobbyist Deryl Fleming—corroborated Elko's testimony.[23] Fleming testified that in August 1972 he met with Flood at Elko's apartment in the Congressional Hotel, down the hall from the representative's own suite. According to Fleming, Flood accepted an envelope filled with one thousand dollars in cash, stuffed it in the pocket of his bathrobe without looking inside, complained that he was tired, and then went off to bed.[24] Similarly, Peters testified that on June 27, 1972, he traveled to Wilkes-Barre during the Agnes recovery and met with Flood at his command post. He claimed to have been escorted into the congressman's office by special assistant Michael Clark. Peters spoke with Flood about the availability of Sterling-Homex modular housing for homeless Agnes victims, and the congressman said he thought "something could be done about it." Peters then gave Flood an envelope stuffed with five thousand dollars in cash, which he "put in his pocket."[25]

Since Fleming and Peters, like Elko, were testifying under a grant of immunity, Kleiboemer painted the government witnesses as "dregs" whose testimonies could not be considered "credible," and he called several witnesses to discredit their testimonies.[26] Michael Clark, for example, contradicted Fleming's assertion that he met with Flood on June 27 because he and the congressman flew back to Washington the day before and remained there through June 30 because of an important House session on that particular day.[27] John Jenkins, the tally clerk of the House of Representatives, who records all votes cast by the members, verified Clark's statement, reporting that Flood was present in the House for all votes between June 27 and June 30.[28] Similarly, Kleiboemer tried to discredit Fleming's claim that he had first met with Flood at his Washington apartment sometime during the weekend of April 21–22, 1972, by producing three witnesses who insisted that the congressman was attending various events in Wilkes-Barre and a mock convention at Bloomsburg University that weekend.[29]

Flood never took the stand during the three-week trial, and the only announcement he made during that period regarded his resignation as chair of the HEW Appropriations Committee.[30] When the twelve jurors retired to consider the verdict, eleven of them voted to convict Flood on at least four counts of bribery and three counts of perjury. But one of the jurors—a retired sixty-three-year-old navy cook by the name of William Cash—held out for Flood's acquittal. Initially, he refused to explain his decision, but he eventually told the others that he had learned from "confidential sources" that three of the prosecution's witnesses, including Elko, had "stolen" $176,000 from Flood. Under the circumstances, Cash believed that the three witnesses were "guiltier than Flood" and that they had "taken advantage of the Congressman." When Daniel Robinson, the jury foreman, proposed a guilty verdict on just one of the eleven counts, Cash refused, saying that he couldn't bring himself to convict Flood because of his advanced age. After Judge Gasch learned of Cash's alleged "confidential information" and questioned him about it, the obstinate juror shrugged and said it was a "joke." Gasch sent the jury back to deliberate, instructing them to consider only evidence presented in court. Once again, the jury deadlocked. They had deliberated for more than twelve hours and still could not reach a verdict. Having exhausted virtually every power at his command, Gasch was forced to declare a mistrial.[31]

Flood smiled when he learned of the outcome, then walked gingerly from the courtroom. Later, before a gathering of television cameras and newspaper reporters, he read a brief statement: "I regret that the jury was unable to reach a unanimous verdict of acquittal. I maintain my innocence of any wrongdoing in the charges against me."[32]

A second trial was scheduled to begin on June 4, but the retrial was postponed indefinitely on May 30 after Flood was admitted to Georgetown University Hospital for various ailments, including cataract, gall bladder, and intestinal problems, as well as to undergo a psychiatric evaluation. In September 1979 Flood was diagnosed as "suffering from depressive neurosis and senility." His physicians maintained that the congressman's "loss of recall and impaired comprehension will result in profound disability in regard to communicating with and assisting his counsel in preparing his own defense." In addition,

Fig. 40. Flood smiles as he leaves the federal courthouse in Washington after his case was dismissed on February 3, 1979. He is accompanied by aide Robert Kulick (*left*) and attorney Axel Kleiboemer (*right*).

the physicians insisted that Flood remain in the hospital for another month to be weaned from "all the sedative-hypnotic and tranquilizing drugs" he had been taking for "severe episodic anxiety and depression" as well as his "multiple physical disorders."[33] As a result of the hospitalization, Gasch would be forced to postpone a second trial on four separate occasions.

Meanwhile, the House Ethics Committee, which held its investigation in abeyance pending the outcome of the trial, adopted on June 7 a "Statement of Alleged Violations" against Flood. The statement charged that the Pennsylvania legislator, during the period 1971 to 1976, "discredited the House of Representatives" by "receiving payments, either directly or through an assistant, from individuals in exchange for his attempt to influence government agencies." The statement also charged that Flood "willfully and contrary to his oath, made statements which he did not believe to be true in testimony [at the trial of Stephen Elko] in October 1977 in a United States District Court trial at Los Angeles."[34] Confronted with a congressional hearing as well as the possibility of a second federal trial, Flood's attorneys began to consider a plea bargain.

The Justice Department demanded that any arrangement must include Flood's resignation from the House of Representatives. Initially, Kleiboemer offered a deal that would have included the congressman pleading no contest to one count of bribery, receiving a six-month suspended sentence, and payment of a one-thousand-dollar fine. But Flood refused to resign from Congress—a nonnegotiable for the Justice Department—and the deal was rejected.[35] By the

Fig. 41. Rep. Thomas P. "Tip" O'Neill (D-Mass.) was one of the few members of the House who remained loyal to Flood after he announced his resignation from Congress on November 7, 1979.

late autumn, however, he realized that a seat in the House of Representatives was a luxury he could no longer afford.

Broke and in extremely poor health, on November 7 Flood resigned from Congress, effective January 31, 1980. In duplicate letters to Pennsylvania governor Richard Thornburgh and House Speaker Tip O'Neill, Jr., the embattled congressman wrote that the "state of my health no longer permits me to discharge fully my responsibilities in Congress."[36] Flood's resignation did not deter Rep. Charles Bennett (D-Fla.), who replaced Flynt as the chair of House Ethics, from insisting that his committee continue its investigation. Bennett wrote to House Speaker Tip O'Neill, stating that the Ethics Committee "has a responsibility to continue the proceedings," in spite of the congressman's resignation. "The country will expect us to proceed," wrote the chair, "otherwise the public view of Congress may be improperly damaged."[37] But O'Neill saw no reason to prolong the investigation in light of Flood's resignation since it would "serve no practical purpose," and the case was dropped.[38] There was, however, probably more to the Speaker's decision than he revealed.

O'Neill empathized with Flood, a close friend and colleague for more than twenty years. In addition, the FBI was also investigating his own financial affairs and he couldn't quite divorce his own circumstances from those of his former colleague. "I have never had the thirst for money," O'Neill replied when asked about his investigation.

Have I done things in the course of my career you would not possibly do today? No question about it. I've done a million favors. And in that million favors I helped the poor, the needy, and the indigent and the underprivileged and I had to twist the law a little bit sometimes to be able to do it.

Today you wouldn't be able to do things like that: to save a family man from disgrace or ruination by talking to a judge. You thought nothing of it in those days. Thirty-five years ago it was a legitimate thing to do. But when you go over that history in the light of today you ask, "What the hell kind of scoundrel was he? A typical Irish politician?"

I lived my times as the times were. Always in mind that the day I leave that I hold up my head and say, hey, I left a good family name, and never betrayed my God or my country.[39]

Flood could have just as easily responded the same way. He, too, had acted like a "political Robin Hood," using his power and influence to distribute money and services to those people who were truly in need of them. Sometimes he accepted a plane ride between Wilkes-Barre and Washington, or, at least on one occasion, one hundred shares of bank stock as a gift of appreciation. Prior to Watergate, these things did not represent "conflicts of interest," but rather "perks" of elective office. Yet Flood was painted as a "crook" who traded his congressional influence for personal gain. If so, where did he hide his profits? Certainly not in the modest white frame house in which he lived, located in one of Wilkes-Barre's blue-collar neighborhoods. If Flood was more concerned with accumulating personal wealth than serving the public good, he certainly could have done much better than a total estate of $83,827.66. At the very least, he should have been able to pay his considerable legal bills without going broke. When these facts are considered, Flood emerges not as a "corrupt politician" or a "crook," but rather a victim of the post-Watergate era in American politics.

On January 15, 1980, the beleaguered congressman went before Judge Gasch to determine whether he was competent to stand trial. "Do you know where you are today?" asked his attorney, Axel Kleiboemer. After a prolonged pause, the seventy-six-year-old congressman whispered, "Washington, D.C."

For the next thirty minutes, Flood, dressed in a light blue suit, sat ramrod straight and fumbled questions from his attorney, leaving some spectators to wonder whether the former vaudevillian actor was playing the greatest role of his life.

"What year is this?" asked Kleiboemer.

"Nineteen, I think, oh yes, 1990," Flood said in a faltering voice.

Flood also wrongly indicated that Calvin Coolidge was president when he was first elected to Congress in 1944. When Kleiboemer continued his simple line of questioning, the bewildered legislator interrupted him. "Why do you keep asking me these kinds of questions?" he asked. "You never said you were going to do this to me." When asked about his first trial, however, Flood perked up. Not only did he recall specific details of the case, but he flatly denied that he ever took any bribes.[40]

The following day, Dr. Mary Reidy, the clinical psychologist who evaluated Flood at Georgetown University Hospital, testified. She said that after listening to the congressman's befuddled testimony she was convinced that his "intelligence is impaired" and that he is "not faking memory loss." Reidy also expressed serious doubts that he could follow the testimony of witnesses at a trial. The prosecution countered by calling Flood's personal physician, Dr. Melvin Small, to the stand. When asked whether drugs fogged the congressman's memory, Small disclosed that less than two months ago Flood was being given Cimetidine, a drug that can cause confusion in some elderly people. But he defended the decision to administer the drug while Flood was withdrawing from his addiction from the various medications he had been given for anxiety and his physical ailments.[41] It was clear to the prosecution and to Judge Gasch that the congressman was incapable of withstanding the mental stress of another trial.

On February 26 the once-flamboyant legislator went before Gasch for the final time. Shuffling to the judge's bench, Flood, speaking in a barely audible voice, said, "I do not think I have the physical or intellectual resources to defend myself adequately." He then pleaded guilty to a single count of conspiracy to violate the federal campaign laws in accepting payoffs. The specific instances cited in the conspiracy charge were that Flood: (1) solicited and received one hundred shares of stock in the First Valley Bank of Bethlehem, Pennsylvania, in return for using his influence for a bank merger; (2) solicited, and Elko received on his behalf, $3,000 from Robert Gennaro, who was seeking government contracts; (3) solicited and received $2,000 from Rabbi Lieb Pinter of Brooklyn in return for his efforts to obtain favorable government aid for the rabbi's social service programs at the B'nai Torah Institute; and (4) solicited and received, along with Elko, $2,500 from Dr. Murdock Head, founder and director of the Airlie Foundation.[42]

The single count of conspiracy was a misdemeanor, punishable by a fine of up to $25,000 and a prison sentence of up to one year. But the prosecuting attorneys said they felt that imprisonment would be "inappropriate in this

case." Kleiboemer agreed, describing his client as "an old man whose dignity
has already been stripped away." He also asked that no fine be imposed since
Flood's income, from his congressional pension and Social Security, totaled
$3,700 a month, and most of that would be consumed by taxes and interest
on loans he had taken out to pay legal expenses. "Mr. Flood has had to taste
the bitter dregs from the cup of humiliation," said the defense attorney.
"Whatever he once had, he has lost. Let him go in peace."[43]

Gasch sentenced Flood to one year of probation, calling a prison sentence
"inappropriate" because of his advanced age. Government prosecutors dropped
the other more serious charges of bribery and perjury and promised not to
lodge any further charges, such as criminal tax violations.[44] In addition, the
Justice Department was forced to abandon their investigations into Flood's
involvement with Hahnemann, Haiti, and Medico Industries because of lack
of sufficient evidence.[45]

Dan Flood spent his final days on Capitol Hill in his apartment at the Congressional Hotel, telephoning instructions to aides who were preparing for
his return to Wilkes-Barre. Although Congress normally recognizes a veteran
member's career with a plethora of celebratory speeches, there were none for
Flood.[46] While many of his colleagues distanced themselves from him, there
were others who demonstrated great sympathy. "Dan was an honest and dedicated member of the United States Congress and anything that happened
to bring discredit upon him was a disgrace," insisted Rep. Fred Rooney of
Allentown. "Dan was not responsible for any wrongdoing and the press, if
they were honest, would have recognized that fact."[47] Another former House
colleague, William Scranton of northeastern Pennsylvania, viewed Flood as a
victim of the public cynicism that emerged in the post-Watergate era. "Dan
took very seriously his responsibility to work hard for the people he represented," said Scranton in a recent interview. "Despite his flamboyance, I don't
think Dan ever thought about how the office could advance his career or
make him wealthy or prestigious. I have a great deal of difficulty believing,
for example, that he was accepting bribes. Unfortunately, most people believe
that politicians are corrupt and that they wouldn't be holding office if they
weren't. That's truly a shame. Men like Dan Flood realized that politics is a
public service and that to be elected to office is among the highest of trusts
the public can bestow."[48]

Rep. Jim Wright, who would later become the subject of a House Ethics
investigation himself, added that the jealousy of some colleagues also led to
Flood's downfall. "There were members of the House who didn't like the fact
that whenever an omnibus bill passed, Dan's district would get more than its

fair share of the federal money," recalled Wright. "They became extremely envious of him. So when Dan was indicted, there were those who relished his misfortune. They should have realized that as congressmen we all have a responsibility to look out for our little part of America and see that it gets its fair share. Dan did that so well that he became one of the most effective legislators on Capitol Hill. I never believed that Dan Flood was a thief. He loved and respected the Congress so much that he wouldn't have knowingly done anything to discredit the institution."[49]

Still others believed that president Jimmy Carter initiated the Justice Department investigation of Flood to silence his opposition to his Panama policy. "Many of Dan's colleagues in the House and the skeptics in the press as well as multitudes back in the district, believed that the Carter administration brought the hammer down on the congressman," said Flood aide Michael Clark "I think most of us in Flood's inner circle dismissed that notion, except for Captain DuVal."

"Some years after the Congressman's resignation," Clark continued, "I ran into DuVal, who was then working as an adviser to North Carolina Senator Jesse Helms. We exchanged pleasantries and then, shortly before parting ways, he pointed a finger in my direction and said: 'Remember, young man, it was Jimmy Carter and his misguided fellow travelers who are responsible for Mr. Flood being back in Wilkes-Bare today.'"[50]

Those who knew Flood more intimately, however, felt that the congressman paved the way for his own misfortune by investing unconditional trust in his former administrative assistant Stephen Elko. "If Mr. Flood had a fault, it was that he trusted his staff implicitly," said Tom Makowski, a legislative aide. "All of us were given his complete authority to act in his name. So if someone screwed up, the congressman paid the price for it. It wasn't in his character to take a bribe. To do a favor for somebody? Absolutely. To take money for that favor? No. I never saw any indication of impropriety on his part. But it certainly would be easy for Mr. Flood to take the fall for someone else's misuse of his authority."[51] Attorney Harold Rosenn, a longtime friend, agreed. "I think Dan's downfall had a lot to do with the fact that when it came to money, he was somewhat aloof," said Rosenn. "He trusted his staff completely and let them take care of the financial issues. Because of his position, Dan could have accumulated all the wealth he desired, but money didn't mean much to him. He got along on very little. If Dan was responsible for his demise, it was because he trusted an untrustworthy aide."[52]

Dan Flood returned to Wilkes-Barre in February 1980 with no regrets. "If there's one thing I've been proud of during my political career," he said at a testimonial dinner in his honor, "it's that I've been able to work for the government of my nation, my district, and my people. And I will continue to work for my nation, my district and my people."[53]

His Washington staff carried out the work of Pennsylvania's Eleventh Congressional District (with the exclusion of voting on the House floor) until April 9, when Raphael Musto, a member of the Pennsylvania House of Representatives, won a special election to fill the vacant seat.[54] Flood was pleased with the voters' choice. Musto, like his father, James, who had also served in the state legislature, had an impeccable record for constituent service and labor issues, much like Flood himself.[55] Although Musto also won the April 22 primary as the Democratic Party's endorsed candidate, he lost in the general election to Republican candidate James Nelligan, who was carried into office by the Reagan landslide.[56] In 1982 the voters of the Eleventh District returned a Democrat to Congress, electing Frank Harrison to the House of Representatives.[57]

Flood "steadfastly maintain[ed] that [he] [was] innocent of any wrong-doing," and few constituents held him accountable for the charges that brought an end to his congressional career. Instead, most people felt that the amount of alleged bribe money involved was negligible and was far outweighed by the good Flood did for his district.[58] Over the years, a grateful constituency rewarded their congressman by naming an elementary school, health care center, industrial park, and senior center after him.[59] Naturally, they would remain loyal to him during his retirement. "I think the congressman's best years came after he left Washington," said Monsignor Andrew McGowan, a close friend. "He was wounded badly and came home on a shield. To survive the ordeal was miraculous. It was a real test of who he was as an individual. Afterwards, I think he was able to enjoy his life because he was so totally embraced by the people of the Wyoming Valley."[60]

Flood lived the remainder of his life as Luzerne County's biggest celebrity. He continued to appear at the head of parades—usually in his 1951 white convertible Cadillac—and attended as many social and civic functions as his health permitted.[61] But rarely did Flood campaign for other candidates. One of the very few was Raphael Musto, who succeeded him in the House of Representatives. "Dan continued to support me in every election, going so far as to post a campaign sign up on his house," recalled Raphael Musto, now a Pennsylvania state senator:

> He also spoke with others on my behalf. He didn't do that for anyone else. Something I found rather sad though, was that in 1984, when Walter Mondale was running as the Democratic nominee for the presidency,

Fig. 42. Catherine and Dan Flood continued to serve as Luzerne County's "First Couple" after he left Congress in 1980.

he came to the Wyoming Valley to campaign. Every Democratic presidential candidate who came through here since Harry Truman actively
sought Dan Flood's support. But not Walter Mondale. He purposely
avoided Flood. That campaign wanted nothing to do with him. I felt
badly about that because Dan Flood deserved better. He deserved to be
recognized by the party at all levels because he made life better for so
many people, not just here in the Eleventh District, but across the nation.
That is why I've always viewed Dan Flood as an exceptional example of
complete service to people.[62]

Frugal by nature, Flood and his wife, Catherine, continued to live in their
modest, two-story, white-frame house on North Pennsylvania Avenue, where
they found enjoyment and comfort in each other's company. "I think there
was a total metamorphosis in their relationship after Dan left Congress,"
observed Bill Breslin, a nephew. "He cared for Catherine like a child all of her
life up to that point. The roles were reversed when they came home in 1980.
She cared for him like a child from that point on. Of course, he did have
nurses because of his fragile health, and they took very good care of him
physically. But emotionally, Catherine took care of him like a child, who
needed constant attention and affection."[63]

Flood also found comfort in his religious faith. He had never been an
especially devout Catholic during his lifetime. Though he regularly attended
St. John's Church in Wilkes-Barre, his Catholicism was driven more by political
considerations and family tradition than spirituality. But in his last years,
Flood often spoke with his priest and the deacon of his church, Joseph DeVizia,
who occasionally visited the former congressman to administer Holy Commu-
nion. "Mr. Flood's health was failing and he was confined to his bed," recalled
DeVizia. "He knew that he was close to dying and, like many people near the
end of their lives, he tended to reflect on the past and his faith. It was very
humbling for me to see a man who was once so powerful trying to come to
terms with those things. Through it all, you could see that he had a deep faith."[64]

Dan Flood died at the age of ninety on Saturday, May 28, 1994, at Wilkes-
Barre's Mercy Hospital, where he had been hospitalized three days earlier after
suffering a stroke.[65] Two days later, his flag-draped coffin lay inside the Luzerne
County Court House as hundreds of grieving mourners solemnly filed past to
bid a final farewell. Catherine, his widow, sat near the casket, greeting each
well-wisher with a hug, a handshake, and a few words of gratitude.[66]

On a sun-drenched, windy Tuesday, May 31, Dan Flood was laid to rest.
Three hundred people packed St. John the Evangelist Church for a two-hour

funeral service that ended with a rousing standing ovation, a heartfelt gesture of appreciation for all the contributions the sixteen-term congressman made to his beloved Eleventh District. Pennsylvania governor Robert P. Casey headed a long list of dignitaries who delivered personal, often amusing, eulogies. The flag-draped coffin was then removed to St. Mary's Catholic Cemetery in Wilkes-Barre, where members of the National Guard with M16 rifles fired a three-round volley. Afterward, a constituent sang, "Danny boy, oh Danny boy, we love you so," a finale tribute to a folk hero considered one of the greatest congressmen in Pennsylvania's history.[67]

CONCLUSION

Dan Flood was among the last of the movers and shakers of the old school on Capitol Hill. As chair of the Health, Education, and Welfare Appropriations Committee and vice chair of the Defense Appropriations Committee, he wielded near veto power over the three-hundred-billion-dollar federal budget and was instrumental in funding the cold war as well as the Great Society social reforms of the 1960s.

Just as important, Flood was accountable to his own congressional district. He worked hard to understand what the voters wanted, and he used that knowledge to channel billions of dollars for health, education, and welfare programs into northeastern Pennsylvania. In so doing, he became the consummate pork-barrel politician. As a result, this flamboyant, well-educated scion of the middle class was accepted by his blue-collar constituents as "one of their own" and elected to the U.S. House of Representatives for sixteen terms.

Today it's difficult to find any member of Congress with Flood's dedication or political clout not only because of a popular distrust of politics, but also because the legislative process itself has been reduced to imagery rather than substantive change. Effective legislative leadership is directed by the understanding that the House chamber typically operates as a trading arena in which members' individual interests and goals are harmonized through age-old techniques of bargaining, reciprocity, and payoff. The most successful players exercise the ability to initiate, monitor, and complete transactions, settle disputes, and store up political credits and debts for future needs.

Theoretically, the members of Congress function on an equal plane, enjoying a certain degree of formal influence over lawmaking and over their power base in the electorate "back home." In reality, only those who enjoy the greatest security exercise the most clout. They are the ones who have built up goodwill and influence with congressional colleagues and constituents so that they have a reservoir of power to draw on as needed. But these legislators are the exception. The majority of congresspeople operate on the instinct of sheer political survival in the hope of being reelected.

As a group, today's representatives are much less effective legislators and much less dedicated to their constituencies than was Dan Flood. But it is not entirely their fault. The post-Watergate era has left voters with a highly cynical view of public service. Few people trust that their representative will act in their best interests rather than her own. Representatives are also handcuffed by an

Fig. 43. U.S. congressman Daniel J. Flood, 1978.

unrelenting press, which scrutinizes their political activities and personal lives. Most congresspeople try to play it safe to avoid the kind of legislative risks that can affect positive change for their constituents. Instead, their first term or two in Congress is spent learning the legislative process and planning for reelection. To wield any significant influence, a representative must be continually reelected. Even then, few will ever enjoy the seniority of a Dan Flood simply because their constituencies demand more from them than they are capable of delivering. Predictably, image has become more important than substance.

Although most representatives might have gone to Washington to make laws, they try to remain in office by producing quotes that will capture a headline in the *Washington Post* or the *New York Times*. The more ambitious representatives clamor for airtime: a televised committee hearing, a floor speech carried by C-SPAN, a one-on-one interview with national media, and, if they're lucky, a spot on one of the major nightly news programs. They are much less productive on the House floor, where one-third of all the bills proposed each year are legally meaningless commemorative resolutions designed merely to make constituents feel good without addressing their more substantive needs. Almost all the rest of the bills have little chance of passage because they lack bipartisan support. When the more controversial bills are proposed, many representatives exercise the "junk vote," an avoidance tactic that allows them to take a stand on both sides of a major issue. Depending on the audience, they can later tell the voters that they voted for the bill or against it.

Even the speeches delivered on the House floor are routinely rewritten by staff before being published in the *Congressional Record*. The time that passes between the delivery of their address and its publication is used for troubleshooting, to steer clear of possible conflict back in the district or among congressional colleagues who were absent during the presentation. It's yet another way to avoid any political cost.

Unfortunately, our congresspeople have become almost totally preoccupied with achieving high visibility, but they refuse to take the risks or invest the energy that warrants such positive exposure. None, for example, would ever challenge the legal authority of a state or local government to take control of a disaster relief mission as Flood did in 1972 during Hurricane Agnes. They would prefer to remain in seclusion on Capitol Hill. Essentially, most representatives want to be "show horses," but few are willing to become "work horses." Flood wore both labels with pride and did so in an effort to improve the welfare of the working people.

After his resignation from Congress in 1980, the political scientists and the national media dismissed Flood as a pugnacious wheeler-dealer whose vision of the national interest never seemed to extend beyond the borders of his own congressional district, and a jingoist whose hawkish attitude and defense of a U.S.-controlled Panama Canal was out of step with détente. Historians will hopefully be more objective.

Dan Flood was a product of his time. He acted on what he genuinely believed to be the best interests of both his congressional district and the nation. For most of his congressional tenure there was nothing illegal about creating slush funds, taking costly junkets abroad, accepting expensive gifts and lucrative honoraria, and using hefty campaign contributions for personal use. These were common practices among congressional legislators until 1977–78, when the House abolished or limited them. If there was any impropriety in obtaining the federal funding Flood amassed for his constituents, it was so artfully interwoven into the accepted relations on Capitol Hill among politics, business, and government regulation that it was either concealed or, technically, legal. In other words, Flood was no more "corrupt" than any of the other high-profile and effective congresspeople or senators of the post–World War II era. And like many of them, he too became a victim of the new morality and rules of behavior that emerged in Washington after Watergate.

Whatever the case may be, one thing is certain: sometimes Congress and the voters don't fully appreciate what they have until its gone. In Dan Flood, they both had something pretty special.

NOTES

PREFACE

1. Sandy Grady, "The Flood They Can't Dam," *Philadelphia Bulletin Magazine*, August 31, 1975, 7–8; George Crile, "The Best Congressman," *Harper's Magazine*, January 1975, 61–63; Michael Clark, "Agnes Stories," *Citizens' Voice* (Wilkes-Barre, Pa.), June 23, 2002; Robert P. Wolensky, *Better Than Ever! The Flood Recovery Task Force and the 1972 Agnes Disaster* (Stevens Point: University of Wisconsin–Stevens Point Foundation Press, 1993), 4–9; and interview of Michael Clark, Wilkes-Barre, Pa., July 5, 2007.

2. U.S. Congress, *Who's Who in American Politics, 1977–78* (Washington, D.C.: Government Printing Office, 1978), 134; and Marjorie Hunter, "Two Pennsylvania Politicians: One Behind the Scenes and the Other at Center Stage, Daniel John Flood," *New York Times*, January 31, 1978.

3. See Harry G. Frankfurt, *On Bullshit* (Princeton: Princeton University Press, 2005), 54, 62–63. Flood, in more colloquial terms, can more accurately be described as a "bullshitter." Frankfurt, an emeritus professor of philosophy at Princeton University, offers a sound definition of a "bullshitter" as one who "does not intend to deceive his audience, either about the facts or about what he takes the facts to be." Instead, a bullshitter "really doesn't know which statements are true and which ones aren't," so he simply "makes assertions that purport to be the truth." Unlike a "liar," who intentionally deceives his audience by "misrepresenting the truth," a bullshitter only "misrepresents himself."

4. U.S. Congress, *Who's Who in American Politics, 1977–78*, 134.

5. David Boldt, "Flood, the Flamboyant," *Philadelphia Inquirer Magazine*, July 7, 1974, 21.

6. The only other book-length treatment of Flood's congressional career is Sheldon Spear, *Daniel J. Flood: The Congressional Career of an Economic Savior and Cold War Nationalist* (Bethlehem: Lehigh University Press, 2008). Other notable accounts are: Boldt, "Flood, the Flamboyant," 20–25; Crile, "Best Congressman," 60–66; Grady, "Flood They Can't Dam," 6–8; Hunter, "Two Pennsylvania Politicians"; Lance Evans, "Dan Flood Wins a Battle But War's Still in Doubt," *Scranton (Pa.) Times*, November 8, 1978; Tom Mooney, "'Best Congressman' Is Dead at Age of 90," *Times Leader* (Wilkes-Barre, Pa.), May 29, 1994; Paul Golias, "Dan Flood Succumbs at Age 90; He Was Legend in His Own Time," *Citizens' Voice*, May 29, 1994; and William C. Kashatus, "'Dapper Dan' Flood, Pennsylvania's Legendary Congressman," *Pennsylvania Heritage* 21 (Summer 1995): 4–11.

7. See Nicholas M. Horrock, "Former Aide Charges Rep. Flood Sold His Influence for $100,000," *New York Times*, January 28, 1978; Edward T. Pound, "Ethics Panel Probing Flood," *Washington Star*, February 9, 1978; "Dapper Dan's Toughest Scene," *Time*, February 20, 1978, 22; Charles R. Babcock, "Rep. Flood Indicted on Perjury Charges," *Washington Post*, September 6, 1978; Garry Trudeau, "Doonesbury" (political cartoon), *Washington Post*, December 15, 1978; Wendell Rawls, Jr., "Ex-aide Testifies He Delivered Money to Rep. Flood as Payoffs," *New York Times*, January 17, 1979; Wendell Rawls, Jr., "Flood Aide Says He Was Told to 'Get All You Can Get,'" *New York Times*, January 18, 1979; and Wendell Rawls, Jr., "Banker Says He Told Rep. Flood in 1972 of Top Aide's Solicitation," *New York Times*, January 23, 1979.

CHAPTER I

1. U.S. Bureau of the Census, *Historical Statistics of the United States: Colonial Times to 1957* (Washington, D.C.: Government Printing Office, 1960), 355.

2. Donald L. Miller and Richard E. Sharpless, *The Kingdom of Coal: Work, Enterprise, and Ethnic Communities in the Mine Fields* (Philadelphia: University of Pennsylvania Press, 1985), 6–10.

3. Commonwealth of Pennsylvania, *Report of the Department of Mines of Pennsylvania* (Harrisburg: Commonwealth of Pennsylvania, 1924), 18 (hereafter cited as *Mine Reports*). The most accurate records of total production, numbers of workforce, and fatalities for Pennsylvania's anthracite coalfields are provided in these reports beginning in 1870.

4. Victor Greene, *The Slavic Community on Strike: Immigrant Labor in Pennsylvania Anthracite* (South Bend: Notre Dame University Press, 1968), 2–3; see also Michael Barendse, *Social Expectations and Perception: The Case of the Slavic Anthracite Workers* (University Park: Penn State University Press, 1981), 226.

5. Greene, *Slavic Community on Strike*, 3.

6. Interview of Robert Janosov, professor of history at Luzerne County Community College, Nanticoke, Pa., November 19, 1991; and *Mine Reports* (1923), 12–13.

7. Oscar Handlin, in his Pulitzer Prize–winning work *The Uprooted: The Epic Story of the Great Migrations That Made the American People* (New York: Grosset and Dunlap, 1951), was the first historian to concentrate on eastern European assimilation into American life. He emphasized the importance of ethnic consciousness as an important first step in the assimilation process, particularly in urban areas where the members of the same ethnic group congregated to help one another translate their new American culture. A decade later, John Higham offered a more compelling argument by attributing nativism as the primary motivation for immigrants to assimilate. Nativist attitudes demanded that immigrants conform to traditional Protestant-American values (see Higham, *Strangers in the Land: Patterns of American Nativism, 1860–1925* [New York: Atheneum, 1967]). Michael Barendse, in *Social Expectations and Perception*, and Victor Greene, in *For God and Country: The Rise of Polish and Lithuanian Ethnic Consciousness in America, 1860–1910* (Madison: Historical Society of Wisconsin, 1975), both agree with Higham's argument and apply it to the Polish and Lithuanian immigrants of northeastern Pennsylvania. Kevin Kenny, in *Making Sense of the Molly Maguires* (New York: Oxford University Press, 1988), and Terry Golway, in *The Irish in America* (New York: Hyperion Press, 1997), make the same argument for the Irish. These historians also claim that a split labor market divided along ethnic lines interrupted the assimilation process for these three ethnic groups. This divided market resulted in severe social animosities among the Irish, the eastern Europeans, and the members of the more established northern European immigrants, most notably the English and Welsh.

8. Miller and Sharpless, *Kingdom of Coal*, 121–25.

9. *Mine Reports* (1905), xi; see also Robert Janosov, "The Auchincloss Mine Disaster of 1904" (unpublished paper, Luzerne County Community College, Nanticoke, Pa., 1989), 2.

10. Twenty Irish coal workers, allegedly members of a secret society called the Molly Maguires, were executed in Schuylkill County in the 1870s for the murders of sixteen men, most of them mine officials. Since that time, there has been tremendous disagreement over who the Molly Maguires were, what they did, and why they did it. The most recent study is Kevin Kenny, *Making Sense of the Molly Maguires* (New York: Oxford University Press, 1998).

11. Barendse, *Social Expectations*, 15–17.

12. On September 10, 1897, about three hundred nonunion Polish and Hungarian mine workers near Hazleton tried to encourage mine employees at the Lattimer Colliery to join their walkout over reduced wages. Anticipating trouble, the operators called on more than one hundred Coal and Iron Police to protect their property. When Luzerne County sheriff James Martin drew his pistol and fired it into the air to stop the march, the police officers opened fire on the marchers. At least nineteen unarmed miners were shot, many in the back. The so-called Lattimer massacre provided the United Mine Workers with the incentive to unite ethnic and Anglo-Saxon mine workers around a common identity based on their occupation. See Greg Matkosky and Thomas M. Curra, *Stories From the Mines* (Scranton: Lackawanna Heritage Valley and University of Scranton Press, 2002), 47, 50.

13. Craig Phelan, *Divided Loyalties: The Public and Private Life of Labor Leader John Mitchell* (Albany: State University of New York Press, 1994), 48–115; and Thomas Dublin and Walter

Licht, *The Face of Decline: The Pennsylvania Anthracite Region in the Twentieth Century* (Ithaca: Cornell University Press, 2005), 35–43.

14. See letter of Charles B. Lenahan to Frank J. McDonnell, March 30, 1934, Wilkes-Barre, Pa., Daniel J. Flood Collection, Luzerne County Historical Society, Wilkes-Barre, Pa. (hereafter cited as LCHS); "Dan Flood Takes Oath as Margiotti Aide," *Wilkes-Barre (Pa.) Record*, May 5, 1938; and Boldt, "Flood, the Flamboyant," 23. Other members of the special commission appointed by President Roosevelt included the nationally renowned attorneys Clarence Darrow and James Shea, and prominent Wilkes-Barre attorneys John T. and James Lenahan.

15. See "Daniel J. McCarthy," Arrival Date: August 21, 1866, *Passenger and Lists of Vessels Arriving at New York, 1820–1897* (National Archives Microfilm Publication M237–270, Line: 50; List Number: 962), Records of the U.S. Customs Service, Record Group 36, National Archives, Washington, D.C.

16. Kay Dangerfield, "Palette: Vignettes of the Wyoming Valley," *Times Leader*, February 19, 1945.

17. Boldt, "Flood, the Flamboyant," 23.

18. United States Census, 1880, Wilkes-Barre, Luzerne County, Pennsylvania, roll T9–1149, page 568.4000, enumeration district 114, image 0461.

19. See "Flood," the National History Research Center; and Drew Pearson, "Flood in Dublin Where Uncle Slain 50 Years Ago," *Washington Post*, April 9, 1966. Flood visited Ireland on the fiftieth anniversary of the 1916 Easter Rebellion to dedicate a statue of Robert Emmet, the famed Irish rebel who planned and led an earlier uprising against British rule in 1803. Eamon de Valera, the eighty-three-year-old president of the Irish Republic and one of the last surviving leaders of the crushed 1916 rebellion, was on hand to welcome Flood.

20. United States Census, 1900, Hazleton, Luzerne County, Pennsylvania, roll T9–1149, page 568.4000, enumeration district 114, image 0461.

21. United States Census, 1910, Wilkes-Barre, Luzerne County, Pennsylvania, roll T624–1370, page 3-A, enumeration district, 131, image 666; and United States Census, 1920, Wilkes-Barre, Luzerne County, Pennsylvania, roll T625–1598, page 5-A, enumeration district 266, image 236.

22. See United States Census, 1920, Wilkes-Barre, Luzerne County, Pennsylvania, roll T625–1598, page 5-A, enumeration district 266, image 236.

23. Dan Flood quoted in Grady, "Flood They Can't Dam," 8.

24. Several biographical accounts mention that Flood spent his elementary school years at the Florida Military Academy, the most official being his congressional biography. See U.S. Congress, *Who's Who in American Politics, 1977–78*; and "Biographical Data, Congressman Daniel J. Flood," LCHS.

25. For a history of the Kentucky Military Institute, see Cindy Gnegy, "History of KMI" (unpublished paper, Venice Archives and Area Historical Collection, Venice, Fla., 2001); and James D. Stevens, *Reflections: A Portrait of the Kentucky Military Institute, 1845–1971* (privately published, 1991). Captain Robert T. P. Allen, commander of a Texas Infantry Regiment during the Civil War, established the Kentucky Military Institute in 1845 just south of Frankfort. The school quickly developed a fine reputation for excellent instructors, strict discipline, and demanding academics. In 1894 Colonel Charles Fowler obtained the KMI charter after the school's original site was sold through bankruptcy; he eventually relocated it to a historic plantation house in Lyndon, Kentucky. Fowler, in 1906, also established a winter quarters in Eau Gallie, Florida, believing that outdoor recreation in the winter months would be a great benefit to the cadets.

26. Interview of William A. Breslin, executor of Flood estate, Wilkes-Barre, Pa., December 30, 2006.

27. "Statistical and Descriptive Data," Wilkes-Barre High School, 1912, James M. Coughlin High School Archives.

28. "A Tribute to Mr. Breidinger," *1926 Coughlin High School Yearbook* (Wilkes-Barre, Pa.: James M. Coughlin High School, 1926), 103.

29. Flood quoted in Dangerfield, "Palette."

30. Transcript, "Daniel J. Flood, 20," Wilkes-Barre City High School, James M. Coughlin High School, Wilkes-Barre, Pa.

31. Dangerfield, "Palette."

32. Daniel J. Flood, "School Spirit," *The Journal* (Wilkes-Barre High School, Wilkes-Barre, Pa.), October–November 1919, 6, 32.

33. See "Athletics," *The Journal* (Wilkes-Barre High School, Wilkes-Barre, Pa.), October–November 1919, 12–13.

34. Daniel J. Flood, "Preston's Hero," *The Journal*, December 1919, 5–6, 28.

35. See "Our Soldiers," *The Journal*, May–June 1918, 17.

36. See "Editorials," *The Journal*, May–June 1918, 13, 20.

37. "Our New Teachers," *The Journal*, October–November 1919, 10.

38. "Senior Play," *The Journal*, May–June 1920, 14, 27.

39. "Junior Records—Daniel J. Flood," *The Onondagan, 1924* (Syracuse, N.Y.: Junior Class of Syracuse University, 1924), 101 (hereafter cited as *Onondagan*).

40. For the statement that Flood graduated with bachelor's and master's degrees in history from Syracuse University, see "Biographical Data—Congressman Daniel J. Flood," Daniel J. Flood Collection, Kings College Library, Wilkes-Barre, Pa. (hereafter cited as KCL); for evidence of Flood's bachelor's degree in business administration, see "Senior Records," *Onondagan* (1925), 51. Syracuse University refused to allow access to Flood's transcript, even when presented with a letter of permission from the executor of his estate. The registrar insisted that it was a matter of the deceased congressman's privacy.

41. Paula S. Fass, *The Damned and the Beautiful: American Youth in the 1920s* (New York: Oxford University Press, 1977), 7–8.

42. "Janus Oratorical Contest—March 28, 1922," *Onondagan* (1924), 383.

43. "Janus," *Onondagan* (1925), 315.

44. "Senior Records," *Onondagan* (1925), 51.

45. "Debating, 1923–24," *Onondagan* (1925), 426–27.

46. Flood quoted in Bolt, "Flood, the Flamboyant," 24.

47. For references to Flood's involvement in boxing at Syracuse, see ibid.; Dangerfield, "Palette"; Charles Moritz, ed., "Daniel J. Flood," in *Current Biography, 1978* (New York: H. H. Wilson, 1979), 132; and Mooney, "'Best Congressman.'" Flood's participation on the Syracuse track team is cited in "Junior Records," *Onondagan* (1924), 101. His participation in the cross-country team is cited in "Senior Records," *Onondagan* (1925), 51.

48. Transcript, "Daniel J. Flood, 27," Office of the Registrar, Harvard Law School, Cambridge, Mass. The law school used a numerical grading system prior to 1969, when it adopted letter grades. Flood's courses and grades (both numerical and the letter equivalent) were: Civil Procedure (62/C); Contracts (55/D); Property Law (62/C); and Torts (60/D).

49. Interview of Catherine Flood, Wilkes-Barre, Pa., August 12, 2003.

50. "Reporter Untwists Knotty Secret from Dan Flood on That Mustache," *Sunday Independent* (Wilkes-Barre, Pa.), May 2, 1965.

51. Catherine Flood interview; Grady, "Flood They Can't Dam," 6; and Bolt, "Flood, the Flamboyant," 24.

52. Transcript, "Daniel J. Flood, L.L.D., 1929," Office of the Registrar, Dickinson School of Law, Pennsylvania State University, Carlisle, Pa.

53. Petition, "Admission of Daniel J. F. Flood as Attorney at Law," to the Honorable E. Foster Heller, judge of the Orphan's Court of Luzerne County, September 4, 1931, LCHS.

54. Letter, Charles B. Lenahan to Frank J. McDonnell, Wilkes-Barre, Pa., March 30, 1934, KCL. Lenahan mistakenly credited Flood with *three* precedent-setting cases, including the "Exploding Bottle case," in which Flood successfully sued a bottler on behalf of a pregnant woman who was injured after a bottle of soda blew up in her hand, causing shards of glass to rip into her hand and leg. Flood bypassed the standard practice that would have required the woman to first sue the store before going after the bottler. See "Couple Files $15,000 Suit; Damages Claimed After Pop Bottle Explodes," *Times Leader*, December 20, 1946. While this may have been the first case of its kind in Pennsylvania, it was not the first in the nation. That distinction goes to a 1944 case involving the Coca-Cola Bottling Company of Fresno, California, which established the strict liability doctrine known as "res ipsa loquitur." See Edwin Duval,

"Strict Liability: Responsibility of Manufacturers for Injuries from Defective Products," *California Law Review* 33 (December 1945): 637–42.

55. Bolt, "Flood, the Flamboyant," 24–25.

56. "Bartelson Suit Heard by Farrell," *Times Leader*, October 6, 1946.

57. "Flood Makes Accusations in U.S. Court," *Wilkes-Barre Record*, October 15, 1947; and Bolt, "Flood, the Flamboyant," 24.

58. Interview of Harold Rosenn, Wilkes-Barre, Pa., May 13, 2005.

59. Interview of Joseph B. Farrell, Mountaintop, Pa., December 5, 2007.

60. Interview of Bernard C. Brominski, Wilkes-Barre, Pa., March 13, 1996.

61. Frances Jacques, "Mrs. Flood 'Feels at Home' on Stage or in Classroom," *Patriot News* (Harrisburg, Pa.), August 25, 1957.

62. Catherine Flood interview.

63. "Obituary of Catherine Flood," *Citizens' Voice*, August 16, 2005; and United States Census, 1900, Wilkes-Barre, Luzerne County, Pennsylvania, roll T623–1435, page 12-B, enumeration district 151.

64. Catherine Flood interview.

65. Jacques, "Mrs. Flood 'Feels at Home'"; "Little Theater Had Humble Start," *Wilkes-Barre Record*, June 23, 1946; and Little Theater of Wilkes-Barre, "Our History," http://www.ltwb.org/about/Default.htm.

66. Catherine Flood interview; and *The Swan*, by Ferenc Molnar, Little Theater Company, Wilkes-Barre, Pa., playbill, June 6 and 7, 1933.

67. Catherine Flood interview.

68. Roy Morgan quoted in Christina Binkley, "Flood Was Everyman's Champion," *Times Leader*, April 25, 1992, special report, 42.

69. See letter of Charles B. Lenahan to Frank J. McDonnell, Wilkes-Barre, Pa., March 30, 1934, Flood Estate.

70. "Daniel Flood Takes Oath as Margiotti Aide," *Wilkes-Barre Record*, January 25, 1935.

71. Ibid.

72. Louis Feldman quoted in *Dan Flood: A Retrospective*, WBRE-TV, Scranton/Wilkes-Barre, Pa., June 15, 1980.

73. "State-County Launch Liquor Law Campaign," *Times Leader*, September 15, 1937; and "Political Chatter," *Scrantonian* (Scranton, Pa.), October 3, 1937.

74. Interview of John "Dada" Kashatus, Glen Lyon, Pa., July 10, 1984.

75. Ibid.; and Flood quoted in "Liquor Dealers Urged to Act," *Times Leader*, April 21, 1943.

76. "Flood and Bryan Named by State Treasurer," *Sunday Independent*, April 13, 1941; and "Flood, Bryan Are Appointed," *Times Leader*, April 14, 1941.

CHAPTER 2

1. For a detailed list of Luzerne County's legislative districts, wards, and precincts, see "Election Proclamation," *Times Leader*, October 26, 1946.

2. Kenneth C. Martis, *The Historical Atlas of the United States Congressional Districts, 1789–1983* (New York: Macmillan, 1982), 265; and Robert Mittrick, "John S. Fine: The Rise and Fall of a Political Boss" (unpublished paper delivered at Northeast Pennsylvania History Conference, Nanticoke, Pa., October 13, 1995). The Eleventh district was one of four congressional districts in northeastern Pennsylvania in the 1930s. The others were the Twelfth, Fifteenth, and Twenty-first. All four of these districts were overwhelmingly Republican in the 1920s and early 1930s.

3. Mittrick, "John S. Fine."

4. Sheldon Spear, *Wyoming Valley Revisited* (Shavertown, Pa.: Jemags, 1994), 122. Casey had also won three earlier elections to the House of Representatives in 1912, 1914, and 1916. Together with his three electoral victories in the 1920s, Casey enjoyed a ten-year career on Capitol Hill. It was the longest tenure for a congressperson from the Eleventh district until Dan Flood's.

5. Ibid., 121–22.

6. Congressional Quarterly, *Guide to United States Elections* (Washington, D.C.: Congressional Quarterly, 1985), 930.

7. *Times Leader*, May 7–9; June 3, 7, 1935; and Dublin and Licht, *Face of Decline*, 72–73.

8. John Bodnar, *Anthracite People: Families, Unions, and Work, 1900–1940* (Harrisburg: Pennsylvania Historical and Museum Commission, 1983), 96–98; and Dublin and Licht, *Face of Decline*, 74.

9. Robert P. Wolensky, Kenneth C. Wolensky, and Nicole H. Wolensky, *The Knox Mine Disaster: The Final Years of the Northern Anthracite Industry and the Effort to Rebuild a Regional Economy* (Harrisburg: Pennsylvania Historical and Museum Commission, 1999), 4, 105–6.

10. Ibid., 107; and Commonwealth of Pennsylvania, *Pennsylvania Crime Commission Report* (St. David's: Commonwealth of Pennsylvania, 1980), 50. According to William Hastie, a Pittston historian who has researched organized crime in northeastern Pennsylvania, Steve LaTorre was the first Mafia boss of the region. He also immigrated from Montedoro, Sicily, in the late nineteenth century. Santo Volpe succeeded LaTorre, who was married to Volpe's sister, Rose. See interview of William Hastie, West Pittston, Pa., March 20, 2007.

11. Wolensky, *Knox Mine Disaster*, 107–8; and Hastie interview. See also Jerry Capeci, *Gang Land: Fifteen Years of Covering the Mafia* (New York: Alpha Books, 2003); and Stephen Fox, *Blood and Power: Organized Crime in the Twentieth Century* (New York: William Morrow, 1989). Both Capeci and Fox provide comprehensive accounts of organized crime's role in northeastern Pennsylvania's anthracite industry during the 1930s, 1940s, and 1950s.

12. Sheldon Spear, "The Wyoming Valley During the Great Depression" (unpublished paper delivered at Northeastern Pennsylvania History Conference, Nanticoke, Pa., October 27, 1989); and William F. Gustafson, "Bootleg Coal Mining, 1925–1953" (unpublished paper delivered at Northeastern Pennsylvania History Conference, Nanticoke, Pa., October 10, 1997).

13. David R. Contosta, "Reforming the Commonwealth, 1900–1950," in *Pennsylvania: A History of the Commonwealth*, ed. Randall M. Miller and William Pencak (University Park: Penn State University Press and the Pennsylvania Historical and Museum Commission, 2002), 295.

14. Spear, "Wyoming Valley During Great Depression."

15. Ibid.

16. Contosta, "Reforming the Commonwealth," 296.

17. See Philip Grant, "Northeastern Pennsylvania Congressmen and the New Deal, 1933–1940" (unpublished paper presented at the Northeastern Pennsylvania History Conference, Nanticoke, Pa., October 11, 1991). J. Harold Flannery was born in Pittston, Pennsylvania, on April 19, 1898. He graduated from Wyoming Seminary in Kingston, after which he entered the army during World War I. After the war, he earned his law degree at Dickinson Law School in Carlisle, Pennsylvania, and was admitted to the bar in March 1921. Before his election to Congress, Flannery served as solicitor of the City of Pittston (1926–30) and an assistant district attorney of Luzerne County (1932–36). Elected to the U.S. House of Representatives in 1936, Flannery succeeded Republican C. Murray Turpin of Kingston. Flannery served in Congress for three straight terms (1937–45) before he became judge of Luzerne County Court of Common Pleas. At the time of his death in 1961, at age sixty-three, he was the president judge of that court. See "Judge J. Harold Flannery Is Claimed by Death," *Sunday Independent*, June 4, 1961; and "Judge Flannery Rites Wednesday at 9:30 A.M.," *Times Leader*, June 5, 1961.

18. Grant, "Northeastern Pennsylvania Congressmen"; and "Flannery Claimed by Death."

19. Contosta, "Reforming the Commonwealth," 296.

20. See "Dr. Leo C. Mundy, State Senator and Democrat Leader, Dies in Hospital," *Wilkes-Barre Record*, June 12, 1944; and "Democratic Leader and State Senator Leo Mundy Dies," *Times Leader*, June 12, 1944.

21. See Bolt, "Flood, the Flamboyant," 25; and "Judge Flannery's Rites Will Be Held Wednesday Morning," *Wilkes-Barre Record*, June 5, 1961.

22. See "Democrats Pick Flood for Congress," *Times Leader*, January 19, 1942.

23. Ibid.; and Bolt, "Flood, the Flamboyant," 25.

24. Bolt, "Flood, the Flamboyant," 25.

25. Interview of J. Lawrence Brown, Forty Fort, Pa., January 22, 2008.

26. Farrell interview.

27. Brown interview.

28. Farrell interview.

29. "Political Comment," *Sunday Independent*, February 1, 1942.

30. See "Flood, Margie Are Elected Lawmakers," *Times Leader*, November 8, 1944.

31. "Miller Defeats Flood for Congressional Seat," *Wilkes-Barre Record*, November 8, 1944.

32. Letter of Senator Leo Mundy to Daniel J. Flood, Harrisburg, Pa., December 17, 1942, LCHS.

33. "Margin of Victory for Democrats Is Increased," *Times Leader*, November 12, 1944.

34. "Women Voters Hear Issues," *Wilkes-Barre Record*, May 12, 1944.

35. Thomas B. Miller quoted in "Soldier Training Weakened by Furloughs and Gifts, Miller Tells War Mothers," *Times Leader*, December 30, 1942.

36. "Flood Ahead of Miller for Congress Seat," *Wilkes-Barre Record*, November 8, 1944.

37. "Navy Promotes Gerald Flood to Rank of Lieutenant Commander," *Sunday Independent*, August 21, 1945.

38. Interview of John C. McKeown, Wilkes-Barre, Pa., May 11, 2005.

39. "Soldier Vote Boosts FDR's Margin Here," *Times Leader*, November 27, 1944. Flood gained 1,427 more military votes than his Republican opponent, Thomas B. Miller.

40. "President Roosevelt Carries County by a Margin of 4,112," *Times Leader*, November 8, 1944.

41. "Our New Congressman," *Times Leader*, November 8, 1944.

42. Spear, *Wyoming Valley Revisited*, 224–25.

43. Flood quoted in Grady, "Flood They Can't Dam," 7.

44. Boldt, "Flood, the Flamboyant," 22.

45. Alfred T. Zubrov, *Speakers of the U.S. House of Representatives, 1789–2002* (New York: Novinka Books, 2002), 51.

46. Paul F. Boller, Jr., *Congressional Anecdotes* (New York: Oxford University Press, 1991), 255–56.

47. William F. Arbogast, "The Rayburn Saga: The Story of a Dream Come True," *Washington Post*, October 10, 1961.

48. See "Flood Is Placed on Appropriations; Neely Also Named," *Times Leader*, March 1, 1945; and "Dan Flood Is Happy Man over Appropriations Post: Precedent Is Set Aside," *Times Leader*, March 3, 1945. Flood had a slightly different version of his appointment to the House Appropriations Committee. He claimed that he would agree to the appointment only if he could "be on the subcommittee dealing with the State Department." He admitted that "foreign affairs was [his] métier" and that he wanted to "have [his] cake and eat it too." See interview of Dan Flood by Richard Fenno, Jr., Washington, D.C., May 29, 1959, Center for Legislative Archives, National Archives and Records Administration, Washington, D.C.

49. Interview of Rep. Jim Wright, Fort Worth, Tex., January 9, 2007.

50. Flood quoted in U.S. Congress, *Memorial Services Held in the House of Representatives for Sam Rayburn, Late a Representative from Texas* (Washington, D.C.: Government Printing Office, 1962), 142–43.

51. Flood quoted in Norman Walker, "Flood Wants Help for Area," *Philadelphia Inquirer*, January 12, 1945.

52. Flood quoted in "Flood Fights Area Division," *Times Leader*, January 13, 1945; and "City's Name Added to Labor Area," *Times Leader*, January 25, 1945.

53. "Army Engineers Making Survey of Industrial Sites in the Area," *Times Leader*, March 7, 1945.

54. "Flood Reminding Capitol of Wilkes-Barre's Needs," *Sunday Independent*, March 10, 1945.

55. See "Flood Helps Get Local Contract," *Times Leader*, March 9, 1945; and "West Side Armory Leased to Sylvania Corporation," *Wilkes-Barre Record*, February 26, 1945.

56. "Flood Shows He's Awake at Washington," *Pittston (Pa.) Bulletin*, February 23, 1945.

57. Flood quoted in *Congressional Record*, February 12, 1945.

58. "Flood Tax Exemption Bill Not Intended for Rich GIs But for Needy Servicemen," *Times Leader*, April 19, 1945; "Flood Asks for GI Tax Relief," *Wilkes-Barre Record*, April 20, 1945; "Flood Feels Avoca Airport Uncertainty Has Ended," *Sunday Independent*, April 14, 1945; and "Truman Approves Site for $2,650,000 Veterans Hospital," *Times Leader*, September 19, 1945.

59. "Vet Hospital for Valley Is Urged by Flood," *Times Leader*, November 12, 1944.

60. "Flood Shows New Interest in Veterans Hospital," *Philadelphia Bulletin*, April 29, 1945.

61. "Truman Approves Site for $2,650,000 Veterans Hospital."

62. "Murphy Named to U.S. Bench by President," *Times Leader*, May 8, 1945. Johnson, age seventy-two, was being investigated by a grand jury, though he claimed to resign because of his advancing years. Shortly after his resignation, Flood was considered a leading candidate for the post (see "Many Seeking Johnson Post, Flood Reported to be Leading Candidate," *Wilkes-Barre Record*, January 7, 1945). According to John C. McKeown, a former personnel officer at the VA hospital, Flood "agreed to back Murphy for the judgeship if Murphy backed [him] to build the VA hospital in Wilkes-Barre" (see McKeown interview). According to Michael Clark, a former Flood aide, Murphy was named to the bench by Truman to stifle any discussion of Murphy's role on the Pearl Harbor Commission, which was established to investigate the controversial circumstances surrounding the Japanese attack on December 7, 1941. Clark claims that Flood called Murphy a "very self-serving man" who would "gladly take the federal judgeship over the Veterans hospital because it would benefit him" (see Clark interview, July 5, 2007).

63. "Truman Approves Site for $2,650,000 Veterans Hospital"; and "Civic Groups Clear Way for Start of Hospital," *Times Leader*, September 20, 1945.

64. See U.S. Congress, *Congressional Directory, 79th Congress, 1st Session* (Washington, D.C.: Government Printing Office, 1945), 203; and "Flood May Have a Voice in Making of the Peace," *Sunday Independent*, January 21, 1945.

65. "Flood Heads Peace Plan," *Wilkes-Barre Record*, January 27, 1945.

66. "Congressman Flood Is Strong Advocate of Lend-Lease Act," *Philadelphia Bulletin*, March 30, 1945.

67. "Dan Flood Recalls Meeting with Britain's Churchill," *Times Leader*, January 29, 1965.

68. Flood quoted in *Congressional Record*, April 20, 1945; and "Flood Wants Probe of Atrocities," *Times Leader*, April 21, 1945.

69. Flood quoted in *Congressional Record*, May 17, 1945; and "Flood Is Vexed on Treatment Given Goering," *Philadelphia Bulletin*, May 18, 1945.

70. Flood quoted in "Flood Can Relax Now; His List of Nazis Face Trial," *Scranton (Pa.) Times*, September 4, 1945; and "Flood's Favorite Nazi War Villains Rank High on List," *Times Leader*, September 7, 1945.

71. *Congressional Record*, January 4, 1945. Formerly known as the "Dies Committee," after its chair, Martin Dies (D-Tex.), the Un-American Activities Committee spent the war years as a temporary body charged with investigating national security concerns. When the House made the committee part of its permanent structure, it paved the way for the McCarthy scare of the 1950s.

72. Flood quoted in "Flood Given Assignment by House," *Times Leader*, March 20, 1945.

73. Maury Maverick, "The Case for the Congressman," *Washington Post*, February 25, 1945.

74. Kay Dangerfield, "Palette: Vignettes of the Wyoming Valley," *Times Leader*, January 6, 1945; and Daniel J. Flood, "The Mayflower Hotel," *Congressional Record*, February 11, 1960.

75. Initially, Dorothy Kennedy served as Flood's administrative assistant. Within three month's time, however, she resigned due to illness, and Joseph Gillespie, an army veteran and native of Wilkes-Barre, assumed the position. See "Gillespie Named Flood's Secretary," *Times Leader*, March 20, 1945.

76. Crile, "Best Congressman," 61.

77. John "Dada" Kashatus interview.

78. "Main Idea of Voters Seems to Be to Elect New People to Office," *Sunday Independent*, September 1, 1946.

79. "Dan Flood Won by Large Majority," *Times Leader*, May 8, 1946.

80. "Flood Backs Strike Control," *Times Leader*, May 27, 1946.

81. Letter from Local 2444, United Mine Workers of America, to congressman Daniel J. Flood, Loomis, Pennsylvania, May 27, 1946, KCL.

82. "Flood Urges Truman Veto of Case Bill," *Times Leader*, June 7, 1946.

83. Mitchell Jenkins quoted in Boldt, "Flood, the Flamboyant," 25.

84. *Congressional Record*, July 15, 1946. The agricultural measures Flood voted against would have: transferred food control from the Office of Price Adjustment to the Agriculture Department; given the secretary of agriculture a veto on OPA food regulations; and made OPA penalties reviewable in federal courts.

85. "Jenkins Wins Race for Congress," *Wilkes-Barre Record*, November 6, 1946. Attorney Mitchell Jenkins narrowly defeated Flood, 58,347 to 56,498.

86. Robert V. Remini, *The House: The History of the House of Representatives* (Washington, D.C.: Smithsonian Books, 2007), 348.

CHAPTER 3

1. Dan Flood quoted in Paul B. Beers, *Pennsylvania Politics Today and Yesterday: The Tolerable Accommodation* (University Park: Penn State University Press, 1980), 178.

2. Interview of John S. Fine by Edward Tracey, Wilkes-Barre, Pa., May 10, 1971, LCHS.

3. See "John S. Fine," *Pennsylvania Biographical Dictionary* (Wilmington, Del.: American Historical Publications, 1989), 128–29; and "John S. Fine, State's 36th Governor, Dies," *Times Leader*, May 22, 1978.

4. Governor Gifford Pinchot deviated from traditional Republican Party politics in his advocacy for natural resource conservation, labor rights, public service reform, and women's suffrage. In fact, Pinchot's wife, Cornelia, ran unsuccessfully for Congress twice to represent Pike, Wayne, and Monroe counties. Therefore, Pinchot's support for Fine, whose politics embodied conservative Republicanism, was highly unusual. See Kenneth C. Wolensky, "He, On the Whole, Stood First: Gifford Pinchot," *Pennsylvania Heritage* (Winter 2004): 20–27.

5. Robert Mittrick, "John S. Fine: The Rise and Fall of a Political Boss" (unpublished paper delivered at Northeast Pennsylvania History Conference, Nanticoke, Pa., October 13, 1995), 48, LCHS.

6. Fine quoted in "President Maker," *Time*, June 30, 1952, 18.

7. See "Flood Admitted to U.S. Supreme Court," *Times Leader*, March 8, 1946. Some accounts suggest that Flood, after his defeat in the 1948 election, accepted a post as special ambassador to Peru offered to him by President Truman. Although he may have been offered such a diplomatic position, there is no evidence that he accepted it (see "Flood Gets Diplomatic Post," *Times Leader*, December 15, 1945; and Boldt, "Flood, the Flamboyant," 22). According to Michael Clark, Flood's longtime special assistant, the congressman was asked by Truman to attend the funeral of Peruvian president Óscar Raymundo Benavides Larrea during his first term in the House. Flood would later exaggerate that role, referring to himself as a "special ambassador to Peru" (see Clark interview, June 27, 2008).

8. "Long-Dreamed Major Airdrome Becomes Reality," *Wilkes-Barre Record*, June 2, 1947; and "More Federal Money Is Coming for Avoca Airport," *Sunday Independent*, June 16, 1946.

9. "Dinner Tonight Climaxes Work on VA Building," *Times Leader*, June 26, 1947.

10. "Ground Is Broken for $11,000,000 Veterans' Hospital," *Times Leader*, April 2, 1948.

11. "Mrs. Roosevelt Participates in Sugar Notch Program at Unveiling of Memorial," *Times Leader*, July 31, 1948.

12. See Robert J. Donovan, *Conflict and Crisis: The Presidency of Harry S. Truman, 1945–1948* (New York: Norton, 1977), 388–94; Alonzo L. Hamby, *Beyond the New Deal: Harry S. Truman and American Liberalism* (New York: Columbia University Press, 1973), 241–66; and David Lawrence, "Democrats' Future Dim," *Times Leader*, July 15, 1948.

13. "Duff Carrying the Ball," *Newsweek*, October 23, 1950, 30.

14. "County Democrats Are Worrying State Leaders," *Sunday Independent*, June 19, 1948.

15. "Flood Unopposed Among Democrats," *Times Leader*, April 28, 1948.

16. Flood quoted in Boldt, "Flood, the Flamboyant, 25.

17. "Republican Leader Jibes Flood on Fraud Charges," *Times Leader*, August 30, 1948.

18. "Flood Answers Watro with Suggestion That Court Be Asked to Purge Vote Lists," *Times Leader*, September 1, 1948.

19. "Flood Is Giving Jobs," *Pittston Bulletin*, March 11, 1949.

20. "Two Candidates Tell Why They Should Be Elected," *Times Leader*, October 8, 1948.

21. "Being a Good Fireman Not Enough for Kashatus," *Sunday Independent*, August 8, 1948.

22. John "Dada" Kashatus interview.

23. "Triumph for Mr. Flood," *Times Leader*, November 3, 1948. Flood picked up endorsements from the United Mine Workers of America, the Brotherhood of Railroad Trainmen, and the Brotherhood of Maintenance Employees.

24. "Flood Regains House Seat," *Times Leader*, November 4, 1948.

25. "Flood Shows All That's Needed to Beat County Political Machine," *Sunday Independent*, November 7, 1948.

26. "Flood Regains House Seat."

27. "Flood Is Giving Jobs."

28. Interview of Robert Loftus, Pittston, Pa., February 14, 2005.

29. John Riley quoted in "Flood Is Giving Jobs."

30. Ibid.

31. Letter from John B. Kelly to Dan Flood, Philadelphia, Pa., February 11, 1949, KCL.

32. "Forty Fort Man Named Congressman Flood's Secretary," *Times Leader*, January 21, 1949; and "Eugene D. Hegarty Appointed Federal Housing Expediter for Luzerne, Lackawanna Counties," *Times Leader*, August 13, 1946.

33. Interview of Ed Mitchell, Wilkes-Barre, Pa., January 30, 2007.

34. Interviews of Catherine Flood; president Gerald R. Ford, Rancho Mirage, Calif., October 28, 2003; Rep. Jim Wright; John Cosgrove, Washington, D.C., May 26, 2005; and Michael Clark, Washington, D.C., April 2, 2005.

35. The pressure placed on John F. Kennedy by his father, Joseph P. Kennedy, Sr., to become president of the United States is commonly known and has been detailed in several works, including: David E. Koskoff, *Joseph P. Kennedy: A Life and Times* (Englewood Cliffs, N.J.: Prentice Hall, 1974), 405, 434–35; Herbert S. Parmet, *Jack: The Struggles of John F. Kennedy* (New York: Dial Press, 1980), 56, 137; John H. Davis, *The Kennedys: Dynasty and Disaster, 1848–1983* (New York: McGraw-Hill, 1984), 50–51, 72–73; and Laurence Leamer, *The Kennedy Men, 1901–1963* (New York: William Morrow, 2001), 305. Some historians insist, however, that after 1948 Kennedy's "political ambition—and his life—began to become his own" (Lance Morrow, *The Best Year of Their Lives: Kennedy, Johnson, and Nixon in 1948* [New York: Basic Books, 2005], xviii).

36. "Flood Slated for Top Post," *Times Leader*, November 10, 1948. The two Pennsylvania Republicans assigned to the House Appropriations Committee were Ivor Fenton of Mahanoy City and Harvey Tibbott of Ebensburg.

37. See "$5,000,000 RFC Loan Is Sought by Flood to Bring New Industry to County," *White Haven (Pa.) Record*, June 23, 1950; "Vulcan Gets Contract for Mine Supplies," *Times Leader*, September 8, 1950; "Government to Build $800,000 Mine Bureau Building Here," *Times Leader*, November 30, 1949; "Nurse Applications for VA Hospital Jobs Heavy," *Times Leader*, March 8, 1950; "Flood Gates Are Approved," *Times Leader*, April 27, 1950; and "Shipping Pool to Boost U.S. Coal Exports Proposed to Government by UMWA Operators," *United Mine Workers Journal*, January 1, 1950, 10.

38. *Congressional Record*, May 22, 1950.

39. Ibid.

40. "Catherine Helene Swank Becomes Bride of Congressman," *Times Leader*, September 24, 1949.

41. Interview of William A. Breslin, Wilkes-Barre, Pa., September 3, 2005.

42. "To Wed Congressman Daniel Flood," *Pittston (Pa.) Dispatch*, September 4, 1949.

43. Catherine Flood interview.

44. Breslin interview, September 3, 2005.

45. Catherine Flood and Breslin interviews.

46. Breslin interview.

47. Catherine Flood and Ford interviews.

48. Cosgrove interview.

49. Gwen Gibson, "Congressman's Wife Dons Fig Leaf at D.C. Fashion Show," *New York Daily News*, March 7, 1959.

50. Catherine Flood interview.

51. Breslin interview.

52. Frances Jaques, "Mrs. Flood 'Feels at Home' on Stage or in Classroom," *Patriot News*, August 25, 1957.

53. Catherine Flood interview.

54. Breslin interview.

55. "Honeymoon Picture 'Backfires' on GOP," *Times Leader*, February 19, 1951; and Catherine Flood interview.

56. John C. O'Brien, "Pennsylvania Key Spot in Congress Fight," *Philadelphia Inquirer*, March 19, 1950. Of Pennsylvania's thirteen "battleground" districts, six were in Philadelphia: the First, held by William A. Barrett (Democrat); Second, William T. Granahan (D); Third, Hardis Scott (D); Fourth, Earl Chudoff (D); Fifth, William J. Green (D); and Sixth, Hugh Scott (R). Other Pennsylvania "battleground" districts included: the Tenth, Harry P. O'Neil (D), and the Thirteenth, George M. Rhodes (D).

57. Ernest Lindley, "Pennsylvania's Elections: Duff Carrying the Ball," *Newsweek*, October 23, 1950, 30–31.

58. John Kunkel quoted in Robert Bendiner, "Anything Goes in Pennsylvania," *The Nation*, October 28, 1950, 387.

59. Mittrick, "John S. Fine," 31.

60. Ibid., 32; and "Split in Pennsylvania," *Time*, July 30, 1951, 13.

61. "Fine Bid for Governor Expected to Bring Out Record GOP Vote Today," *Times Leader*, May 16, 1950.

62. See "Riley Refuses to Call Convention for New Democrat Chairman," *Sunday Independent*, June 10, 1950; and "Democrats Elect Farris New Chairman," *Times Leader*, July 22, 1950.

63. "How Low Can the Fine Machine Get?" *Times Leader*, November 3, 1950; and "Open Letter to Judge John S. Fine, Republican Candidate for Governor," *Times Leader*, November 4, 1950.

64. "UMW Endorses Flood for Congress," *Times Leader*, November 2, 1950.

65. See Letter of John W. McCormack to Dan Flood, Washington. D.C., October 31, 1950, LCHS. McCormack asked that the $250 campaign contribution be kept confidential. "This is between you, Sam and myself," he wrote, "purely on a personal basis and to be construed by you as evidence of our friendship and support, in the nature of a gift." Rayburn had also expressed his "desire to help" Flood on Capitol Hill during the 1948 campaign. See Letter of Sam Rayburn to Dan Flood, Washington, D.C., October 13, 1947, LCHS.

66. "Democrats Promise to Keep Annoying GOP," *Sunday Independent*, November 26, 1950.

67. See Paul Golias, "Flood, Winner 15 Times, Knows How Losers Feel," *Times Leader*, November 4, 1976; Mittrick, "John S. Fine," 31–32; and "County Republicans Have Strong Ties to Harrisburg," *Sunday Independent*, February 18, 1951. Fine defeated Dilworth in Luzerne County, 76,661 to 65,837. The statewide totals were closer, with Fine narrowly defeating Dilworth 1,796,119 to 1,710,355.

68. "Flood Reveals Senate Hopes," *Wilkes-Barre Record*, October 4, 1951. Local Democratic Party leaders also encouraged Flood to make a run for the U.S. Senate. See Letter of John L. Dorris, MD, to Dan Flood, Wilkes-Barre, Pa., November 8, 1950, KCL.

69. Catherine Flood interview.

70. Ruth Montgomery, "Pennsylvania Congressman Took 'Free Rides' on Colonial Airlines," *New York Daily News*, December 14, 1951.

71. Flood quoted in "Flood Recorded as Accepting 'Free' Rides on Colonial Planes," *Wilkes-Barre Record*, December 15, 1951.

72. U.S. House of Representatives, *Appropriations Subcommittee Hearings* (Washington, D.C.: Government Printing Office, 1951), 1857–77.

73. Montgomery, "Pennsylvania Congressman Took 'Free Rides.'"

74. Ruth Montgomery, "Congressman Flood's Wife Enjoys a 'Free Ride' of Her Own," *New York Daily News*, December 18, 1951.

75. Flood quoted in "Mrs. Flood's Activities Come Under Spotlight," *Times Leader*, December 19, 1951.

76. Ibid.

77. "Mayor Bonin GOP Candidate for Congress," *Hazleton (Pa.) Standard Sentinel*, February 19, 1952.

78. Platforms of Dan Flood and Edward Bonin quoted in "Luzerne County Voter's Guide," *Wilkes-Barre Record*, October 31, 1952.

79. See endorsement, "Flood for Congress," *Hazleton Standard Sentinel*, October 30, 1952; and Flood quoted in "Flood Ready for a Fight," *Hazleton Standard Sentinel*, February 18, 1952.

80. "Our Next Congressman," *Wilkes-Barre Record*, October 29, 1952.

81. "A Pitiful Record, Mr. Flood!" *Wilkes-Barre Record*, October 27, 1952; "Bonin Flays Flood Tours," *Wilkes-Barre Record*, October 17, 1952; "Bonin Raps Flood on Proposed Plant, " *Hazleton Standard Sentinel*, October 18, 1952; "Bonin Promises He Will Seek Industries for His Area," *Hazleton Standard Sentinel*, October 21, 1952; and "Bonin Attacks Flood Record," *Wilkes-Barre Record*, October 29, 1952.

82. "Flood Backs Stand on Overseas Trips," *Hazleton Standard Sentinel*, October 22, 1952; Flood's claim that his trips overseas were part of his congressional duties is validated by a August 1, 1952, letter from George Mahon, chair of the Defense Appropriations Committee. According to the letter, Mahon requested that Flood "spend as much time as possible between August 1952 and January 1953 visiting and inspecting installations of the Army, Navy and Air Force, industrial facilities and any other facilities which relate to the defense program and for which our committee handles appropriations" (see letter of George Mahon to Dan Flood, Washington, D.C., August 1, 1952, LCHS).

83. "Flood 'Great Congressman,' Says UMW Leader," *Anthracite Tri-District News* (Hazleton, Pa.), October 31, 1952; and Min Lurye Matheson, "Do You Want an Effective Congressman?" *Wilkes-Barre Record*, October 30, 1952.

84. See "Bonin Unofficial Victor Over Flood," *Hazleton Standard Sentinel*, November 5, 1952; "Flood Not Ready to Concede Defeat," *Times Leader*, November 5, 1952; "Flood Wants Count from Voting Machines," *Times Leader*, November 8, 1952; and "Supreme Court Aids Flood's Recanvass Move," *Sunday Independent*, November 23, 1952.

85. Flood quoted in Grady, "Flood They Can't Dam," 8; and Boldt, "Flood, the Flamboyant," 25.

86. Catherine Flood interview.

87. Farrell interview.

88. "Ike Wins Presidency in Landslide Victory," *Times Leader*, November 5, 1952.

89. Newell Wood quoted in "Wood May Continue Contest," *Sunday Independent*, June 6, 1954.

90. "Some Republicans Will Vote for Flood," *Sunday Independent*, June 18, 1954.

91. "Politics," *Sunday Independent*, July 4, 1954.

92. "Dr. John Dorris Renamed County Democratic Leader," *Valley News*, July 8, 1954.

93. Flood quoted in "Politics," *Sunday Independent*, July 4, 1954.

94. "Another Election Case Faces County Officials," *Sunday Independent*, July 25, 1954.

95. Dan Flood, "TV Speech," WILK-TV, Scranton/Wilkes-Barre, Pa., November 1, 1954, LCHS.

96. Golias, "Flood, Winner 15 Times, Knows How Losers Feel."

97. See Philip Jenkins, "The Postindustrial Age: 1950–2000," in Miller and Pencak, *Pennsylvania*, 329. George H. Earle, elected in 1934, was the last Democratic governor before Leader.

98. "Bonin Says Fine Machine Gave Him 'Double Cross,'" *Sunday Independent*, November 21, 1954.

CHAPTER 4

1. Miller and Sharpless, *Kingdom of Coal*, 325–26. In 1941, anthracite production exceeded fifty-six million tons and miners worked in average more than 200 days. Coal production peaked at sixty-four million tons in 1944, when the mines operated on average 292 days. See Dublin and Licht, *Face of Decline*, 85.

2. Dublin and Licht, *Face of Decline*, 92–94. In 1966 the Glen Alden Coal Company got out of the anthracite business altogether when it sold its coal lands to the Blue Coal Corporation.

3. "Governor Fine to Send Upheaval Probers Today," *Wilkes-Barre Record*, February 25, 1954; "Port Griffith Cave in Report Given Flood," *Times Leader*, July 26, 1955; and "Mining Is Blamed for Subsidence," *Times Leader*, February 19, 1957.

4. Miller and Sharpless, *Kingdom of Coal*, 323–24.

5. Richard Bolling, *Power in the House: A History of the Leadership of the House of Representatives* (New York: Dutton, 1968), 18–19.

6. Cosgrove interview.

7. Bolling, *Power in the House*, 161–63.

8. Tom Mooney, "Dan Flood: The Man for All Seasons," *Times Leader*, April 27, 1991, special report, 102.

9. Bolling, *Power in the House*, 189; and Remini, *House*, 360–61.

10. Stephen E. Ambrose, *Eisenhower: Soldier and President* (1983; repr, New York: Simon and Schuster, 1990), 347.

11. Flood quoted in *Congressional Record*, May 2, 1955.

12. Flood quoted in *Congressional Record*, January 10, 1955.

13. Flood quoted in *Congressional Record*, May 22, 1950; and "Flood Urges Coal Stockpiling," *Times Leader*, August 30, 1950.

14. "Flood Proposed Stockpile Bill Fails Again," *Scranton (Pa.) Tribune*, January 23, 1951.

15. Noting the shortage of coke used for the smelting of iron ore, Flood urged the U.S. Bureau of Mines and U.S. Steel to "push the limit of research to see if anthracite could be combined with bituminous coal in the smelting process to obtain a much better fuel potential in the production of steel" (see Dan Flood, "New Use for Anthracite May be Found in Steel Industry," *Sunday Independent*, December 18, 1955). Similarly, Flood urged the U.S. Department of Agriculture to "institute an experimental program that will test coal and coal ashes as soil conditioners" (see "Flood Proposes Coal Ashes as Soil Conditioner," *Times Leader*, February 22, 1954; and letter of John A. Hipple, director of Mineral Industries Experiment Station, to Dan Flood, Penn State University, State College, Pa., April 22, 1955, KCL).

16. Flood quoted in Richard F. Bensel, *Sectionalism and American Political Development, 1880–1980* (Madison: University of Wisconsin Press, 1984), 220–21.

17. Rep. Price Preston quoted in ibid., 221.

18. Flood quoted in ibid., 221.

19. Ibid., 221.

20. *Congressional Record*, October 19, 1951; and "Flood Fights Coal Tax Boosts," *Sunday Independent*, February 12, 1950.

21. *Congressional Record*, July 2, 1955. Governor George Leader jumped on Flood's initiative by approving a $8.5 million grant to match the federal contribution to the mine drainage program. See "Leader Signs Bill for Money to Drain Mines," *Wilkes-Barre Record*, July 8, 1955.

22. "Eisenhower Signs Mine Flood Bill," *Sunday Independent*, July 17, 1955; and "Federal Aid to Halt Mine Subsidence," *Times Leader*, February 18, 1960.

23. Letter, Edgar J. Gealy, director of the Munitions Board, to Dan Flood, March 9, 1950, Washington, D.C., KCL; and letter, R.C. Miller, director of Office of International Trade, Department of Commerce, to Dan Flood, January 15, 1951, Washington, D.C., KCL. "Participating countries" were those allies who belonged to the North Atlantic Treaty Organization, which included Austria, Belgium, Denmark, France, West Germany, Greece, Iceland, Italy, Norway, Portugal, Sweden, and the United Kingdom.

24. Letter, Miller to Flood, January 15, 1951.

25. Letter, Dan Flood to Willard L. Thorp, State Department, September 14, 1951, Washington, D.C., KCL.

26. Letter, John K. McFall, State Department, to Dan Flood, October 5, 1951, Washington, D.C., KCL.

27. John L. Lewis quoted in United Mine Workers of America, "Shipping Pool to Boost U.S. Coal Exports Proposed by UMWA," *United Mine Workers Journal*, January 1, 1952, 10. Herbert H. Shaver, vice president of the Hudson Coal Company, made a similar proposal in 1955. According to Shaver's plan, the U.S. government would pay between six and seven dollars per ton to cover shipping costs to defray the current twenty-five-dollar-per-ton cost European consumers paid. See *Congressional Record*, July 20, 1955; and Joseph X. Flannery, "Coal Official Proposes Plan to Expand Anthracite's Overseas Market," *Scrantonian*, July 17, 1955.

28. "Deceit Charged in Coal Aid Plan," *New York Times*, October 1, 1955.

29. "Flood Asks Curb on Oil Imports to Help Miners," *Philadelphia Inquirer*, February 8, 1955.

30. "Congressman Flood Blasts St. Lawrence Seaway," *Anthracite Tri-District News*, July 8, 1949; "Flood Criticizes Truman Urgency on Waterway," *Sunday Independent*, February 4, 1951; and "Flood Exposes Fantastic Seaway Project as Injurious to Defense and Industry," *United Mine Workers Journal*, February 10, 1951.

31. Dublin and Licht, *Face of Decline*, 99–100.

32. Interview of Melvin R. Laird, Fort Myers, Fla., February 5, 2007; and "Congressman Flood Gets U.S. Officials to Change to Coal," *Sunday Independent*, June 20, 1954.

33. Interview with Rep. Daniel J. Flood by Richard F. Fenno, Jr., Washington, D.C., May 29, 1959, Center for Legislative Archives, National Archives and Records Administration, Washington, D.C.

34. Robert Higgs, "Hard Coals Make Bad Law: Congressional Parochialism Versus National Defense," *Cato Journal* 3 (Spring–Summer 1988): 4. All the congressmen represented districts in Pennsylvania's hard coal region: Flood's Eleventh district was Luzerne County; Walter's Fifteenth district included Carbon County; Scranton's Tenth district included Lackawanna County; and Fenton's Twelfth district included Northumberland and Schuylkill counties.

35. Interview of Rep. William W. Scranton, Scranton, Pa., October 24, 2005.

36. "Impact of the Army Tonnage," *Anthracite Institute Bulletin* 6 (October 19, 1961): 1.

37. Higgs, "Hard Coals Make Bad Law," 5.

38. "Impact of the Army Tonnage," 2; "Coal Operators Will Bid Today in German Fuel," *Wilkes-Barre Record*, July 13, 1961; "Anthracite Bidding Gets U.S. Approval," *Times Leader*, July 17, 1961; "Anthracite Wins Right to Bid on Army Coal," *Wilkes-Barre Record*, July 18, 1961; and "440,000 Tons of Coke Or Hard Coal Will Be Purchased by Army," *Wilkes-Barre Record*, October 4, 1961.

39. "Impact of the Army Tonnage," 2.

40. Higgs, "Hard Coals Make Bad Law," 6.

41. Interview of James Tedesco, Old Forge, Pa., June 7, 2005.

42. Flood quoted in Crile, "Best Congressman," 63.

43. Laird interview.

44. Flood quoted in Crile, "Best Congressman, 63.

45. Higgs, "Hard Coals Make Bad Law," 7.

46. Ibid.

47. Interview of Joseph M. McDade, Fairfax, Va., October 10, 2005.

48. Crile, "Best Congressman," 65.

49. "Hole Reported in River Bottom; 12 Still Missing; 3,000 Men Idled," *Wilkes-Barre Record*, January 24, 1959; and "Rescue Hope Fading for 12 Missing Men," *Times Leader*, January 24, 1959.

50. Interview of William Hastie, Pittston, Pa., March 20, 2007.

51. The most comprehensive account of the Knox Mine disaster is Robert P. Wolensky, Kenneth C. Wolensky, and Nicole H. Wolensky, *The Knox Mine Disaster: The Final Years of the Northern*

Anthracite Industry and the Effort to Rebuild a Regional Economy (Harrisburg: Pennsylvania Historical and Museum Commission, 1999).

52. Hastie interview.

53. Wolensky et al., *Knox Mine Disaster*, 28–30.

54. Ibid., 105–6.

55. Ibid., 70–78; and Dublin and Licht, *Face of Decline*, 111.

56. Wolensky et al., *Knox Mine Disaster*, 83–110; and Dublin and Licht, *Face of Decline*, 111–12.

57. Stephen Fox, *Blood and Power: Organized Crime in the Twentieth Century* (New York: William Morrow, 1989), 66–67; and Carl Sifakis, *The Mafia Encyclopedia* (New York: Checkmark, 2005), 31.

58. Letter, Santo Volpe to Cologero Volpe, Pittston, Pa., November 8, 1949, LCHS.

59. See "400 at Montedora Society Dinner for Dr. Volpe," *Times Leader*, March 20, 1950.

60. U.S. Department of Justice, "Memorandum: Daniel J. Flood, U.S. Congressman; Pagnotti Enterprises; Racketeer Influences and Corrupt Organizations," October 24, 1978, Document No. 183-1626-12, Federal Bureau of Investigation/United States Department of Justice, Washington D.C. (hereafter cited as FBI). See also Commonwealth of Pennsylvania, Pennsylvania Crime Commission, *1984 Report* (St. David's: Commonwealth of Pennsylvania, 1984), 40–42; and J. R. Freeman, "Flood Once Helped Crime-Linked Friends," *Sunday Tribune-Review* (Greensburg, Pa.), April 23, 1978.

61. See Pennsylvania Department of Labor, *The Unemployment Problem in the Northeast Anthracite Area of Pennsylvania* (Harrisburg: Bureau of Employment Security, 1959), appendix 6.

62. Dublin and Licht, *Face of Decline*, 122. In March 1954 the Northeast Pennsylvania Development Commission wrote a letter to senators and congresspeople describing the severe economic plight of the region and its need for federal aid. See Charles Weissman et al., Northeast Pennsylvania Industrial Development Commission, to Senator Edward J. Martin et al., March 24, 1954, Committee of Twelve Papers, 1930–1954, Historical Collections and Labor Archives, Pennsylvania State University, University Park, Pa.

63. U.S. House of Representatives, "Area Redevelopment Act," sponsored by Rep. Daniel J. Flood, House Report No. 2099, July 1, 1958, KCL.

64. *Congressional Record*, January 4, 1957.

65. Flood quoted in press release, August 8, 1958, KCL.

66. Interview of Rep. Robert Michel, Washington, D.C., March 8, 2007.

67. "Old Problem, Similar Approach," *Washington Daily News*, December 6, 1960.

68. Flood quoted in press release, July 29, 1959, KCL.

69. Governor David L. Lawrence quoted in press release, July 29, 1959, KCL.

70. See president Dwight D. Eisenhower, "Area Redevelopment Act—Veto Message," Senate Document No. 95, May 13, 1960, KCL; and Dickson Preston, "Douglas Sees Distressed Area Bill Being Pushed," *Washington Daily News*, December 5, 1960.

71. Dan Flood, "Statement on President Eisenhower's Veto of Area Redevelopment Act," June 7, 1960, KCL.

72. Interview of Ed Mitchell, Wilkes-Barre, Pa., January 30, 2007.

73. Wright interview. Dan and Catherine Flood exaggerated the closeness of their relationship with John F. Kennedy (see Jerry O'Brien and Tony Pavloski, "Dan Flood Recalls JFK's 'Deadpan Humor,'" *Citizens' Voice*, November 21, 1993). Since the congressman's constituents were largely Catholic and enamored of the young president, the Floods often spoke of JFK as if he had been a close, personal friend. Flood even went as far as calling himself a part of Kennedy's "Irish Mafia," the president's circle of intimates who had been with him since his first campaign for Congress in 1946 (see Sandy Grady, "Flood They Can't Dam," 8). But there is no documentary evidence of the kind of intimacy suggested by the Floods, aside from a May 11, 1962, get-well letter from JFK to Flood, who was recovering from cancer surgery at Georgetown University Hospital (located in personal scrapbooks kept by Catherine). What's clear, however, is that Flood respected and admired JFK, whom he called his "favorite president" (see Flood quoted in Libby

Brennan, "Dan Flood, Friend to Presidents, Powerful Figure in U.S. Congress," *Sunday Independent*, February 7, 1971).

74. Arthur M. Schlesinger, Jr., *A Thousand Days: John F. Kennedy in the White House* (Boston: Houghton Mifflin, 1965), 118. Pearson made the ghostwriting accusation in an interview with Mike Wallace, which was broadcast on ABC on December 7, 1957. He identified Theodore Sorensen, JFK's legislative assistant, as the author. Washington attorney Clark Clifford was hired to defend the young senator and, after reviewing Kennedy's handwritten notes, determined that JFK had written the book. Pearson was forced to retract the charge. Sorensen recently admitted that *Profiles in Courage* was a "collaboration." While he "assisted in the assembly and preparation of research, the book's concept, selection of stories, and writing" were Kennedy's. See Ted Sorensen, *Counselor: A Life At the Edge of History* (New York: HarperCollins, 2008), 148–52.

75. Wright interview.

76. Ibid.

77. Loftus interview.

78. "Kennedy Will Tour Valley Enroute Here," *Times Leader*, October 27, 1960; "Kennedy Visit Draws Public Square Throng," *Times Leader*, October 28, 1960; and Michael Clark, "JFK's Visit in 1960 Likely Won't Be Topped," *Citizens' Voice*, November 2, 2004.

79. "Luzerne's 'Dynamic Dan' Unseats FDR as Vote King," *Philadelphia Bulletin*, November 13, 1960; and "Flood and Murray Win by Record Vote Margin," *Times Leader*, November 9, 1960. Flood's total of 112,000 votes topped the 105,000 polled in 1936 by Franklin D. Roosevelt. It was an impressive achievement considering that in the six elections between 1942 and 1952, Flood won three times and was defeated three times. He won by 2,537 votes in 1954, 9,572 in 1956, and 23,818 in 1958. Flood was the first local candidate to go over the 100,000 mark.

80. Preston, "Douglas Sees Distressed Area Bill Being Pushed"; "Bolstering the Economy," *Washington Post*, December 6, 1960; and "Flood Presents Distressed Areas Bill," *Wilkes-Barre Record*, January 4, 1961.

81. *Congressional Record*, March 28, 1961; HR 186, "Area Redevelopment Act," April 26, 1961, 87th Cong., 1st sess.; and "Depressed Areas Aid Bill Passed by House," *Times Leader*, April 26, 1961.

82. Flood quoted in "Depressed Areas Aid Bill Passed by House."

83. "Depressed Area Aid Bill Signed by JFK," *Scranton (Pa.) Tribune*, May 2, 1961; Dublin and Licht, *Face of Decline*, 123; and Schlesinger, *A Thousand Days*, 577–78, 918.

84. "Depressed Area Aid Bill Signed by JFK."

85. President John F. Kennedy, "Statement by the President Following a Meeting with the Conference of Appalachian Governors, May 8, 1961," *The Public Papers of John F. Kennedy, January 20 to December 31, 1961* (Washington, D.C.: Government Printing Office, 1962), 365.

86. Dublin and Licht, *Face of Decline*, 123.

87. Letter of Rep. Dan Flood to W. J. McNeil, assistant secretary and comptroller for the Department of Defense, Washington, D.C., March 4, 1958, KCL.

88. Letter of W. J. McNeil, assistant secretary of defense, to Rep. Dan Flood, Washington, D.C., March 15, 1958, KCL.

89. *Congressional Record*, August 6, 1958.

90. Press release, April 4, 1958, KCL.

91. Miller and Sharpless, *Kingdom of Coal*, 326; and "30 Million to be Spent on Tobyhanna Depot," *Times Leader*, January 17, 1951.

92. "Local Site Proposed as Command Post," *Times Leader*, February 4, 1950; "Mine Factory Sites Offered," *Times Leader*, March 10, 1950; "Flood Warns Russia Has 300,000 Men Near Alaska," *Times Leader*, March 21, 1950; and Flood quoted in *Congressional Record*, March 19, 1950.

93. Flood testimony in U.S. Senate, *Area Redevelopment Act: Hearings Before a Subcommittee of the Committee on Banking and Currency*, 86th Cong., 1st sess., February 25, 27, 1959 (Washington, D.C.: Government Printing Office, 1959), 81.

94. The most comprehensive account of Min Matheson and the International Ladies' Garment Workers' Union is Kenneth C. Wolensky, Nicole H. Wolensky, and Robert P. Wolensky,

Fighting for the Union Label: The Women's Garment Industry and the ILGWU *in Pennsylvania* (University Park: Penn State University Press, 2002).

95. Min Matheson quoted in Wolensky et al., *Fighting for the Union Label*, 140.

96. Ibid., 142–45; and "Local Union Director and Congressman Are Witnesses at Capital," *Times Leader*, January 4, 1956.

97. Min Matheson quoted in Wolensky et al., *Fighting for the Union Label*, 138–39.

98. Rayburn and Flood quoted in "900 Attend Flood Dinner," *Wilkes-Barre Record*, June 8, 1959; and "Rayburn Lauds Flood," *Times Leader*, June 8, 1959.

99. "Dorris Not Fired Says VA Hospital," *Times Leader*, January 26, 1954; "Dorris Retains Chairmanship, but Loses 2 VA Posts," *Wilkes-Barre Record*, January 26, 1954; and "Minute Men Reiterate Opposition to Dorris," *Times Leader*, October 15, 1956. In 1954 Bernard O'Hara, acting manager of the Veterans Administration hospital in Wilkes-Barre, warned Dorris to resign as Democratic county chair because of a political conflict of interest or he would be dismissed from the staff. Dorris refused to relinquish the position and was fired from the VA.

100. See "Politics," *Sunday Independent*, May 13, 1956; and "Brown Quits as Counsel for Democratic Party," *Sunday Independent*, September 4, 1955. Brown, Flood's law partner, continued to serve as his campaign manager.

101. John "Dada" Kashatus quoted in "Kashatus Asks Leader to Put Dorris in Place," *Sunday Independent*, May 13, 1956.

102. John "Dada" Kashatus quoted in "Minute Men Reiterate Opposition to Dorris," *Times Leader*, October 15, 1956.

103. "Martin Murray Wins Senate Seat," *Times Leader*, November 7, 1956.

104. "Dorris Okayed for Another Term," *Pittston (Pa.) Sunday Dispatch*, June 17, 1964; and interviews of Clark, April 2, 2005, and Loftus.

105. Lou Rauscher, "Dan's Flooded with Requests," *Sunday Independent*, November 11, 1962.

106. See Richard F. Fenno, Jr. *Home Style: Members in Their Districts* (New York: Harper and Row, 1978), 136–40. Fenno uses the term "home style" to refer to the "explanation of power" that a congressperson uses to legitimize his actions on Capitol Hill in the eyes of the voters back home in his district. Fenno explains that the representative "legitimizes" his activities at the federal level by pursuing activities for the welfare of those he serves. In doing so, the congressperson hopes to achieve three goals: reelection, power on Capitol Hill, and good public policy.

CHAPTER 5

1. See John Lewis Gaddis, *The Cold War: A New History* (New York: Penguin Press, 2005), 9–34. Gaddis's book is the most comprehensive treatment to date on the cold war.

2. Flood quoted in *Congressional Record*, March 29, 1955.

3. "Flood Details Position on National Security," *Luzerne County (Pa.) Voters Guide*, May 17, 1950.

4. "Congressman Returns Home from Europe," *Times Leader*, December 22, 1949.

5. Pope Pius quoted in "Flood Visits Pope with Other Congressmen," *Times Leader*, November 28, 1949.

6. Flood quoted in "Congressmen Have Audience with Holy Father," *Catholic Weekly*, June 29, 1950.

7. Pope Pius quoted in ibid.

8. See "Daniel J. Flood," *Current Biography, 1978*, 132.

9. See telegram of Daniel J. Flood to president of the United States, Washington, D.C., December 31, 1956, KCL; *Congressional Record*, January 23, 1957; and letter of Assistant Secretary of State Robert C. Hill to Daniel J. Flood, Washington, D.C., January 24, 1957, KCL.

10. See *Congressional Record*, January 11, February 11, April 26, 1945; February 17, 1946; September 21, 1949; February 27, 1950; February 14, April 18, 1955; and January 17, 1956. The

editor of the *Polish American Journal* stated that Flood inserted editorials from his publication six times in 1949 alone. See "Rep. Flood Inserts Journal Editorial in Congressional Record," *Polish American Journal*, October 1, 1949.

11. See "Lithuanians' Plight Stressed by Flood," *Times Leader*, February 12, 1945; "Flood Says Russia Letting Him Down on Good Will Front," *Lansford Evening Record*, April 28, 1945; and "Lithuanian Underground Asks U.S. to Back Organized Guerrilla Warfare on Soviets," *Rome Daily American*, February 28, 1950.

12. Flood quoted in "Lithuanians Hear Flood," *New York Times*, February 18, 1946.

13. Laird interview.

14. Gaddis, *Cold War*, 21; and U.S. House of Representatives, *The Katyn Forest Massacre: Final Report of the Select Committee to Conduct an Investigation*, 82d Cong., 2d sess., 1952, H. Doc. 2505, 1.

15. U.S. House of Representatives, *Katyn Massacre Report*, 2, 8.

16. National Committee of Americans of Polish Descent, *Death at Katyn* (New York: National Committee of Americans of Polish Descent, 1945), 17–18.

17. "Russians Blame Nazis for Katyn Massacre," *New York Times*, January 27, 1944.

18. See National Committee of Americans of Polish Descent, *Death at Katyn*, 19; "Author William H. Chamberlain, Points to Russians in Death of Polish Soldiers in Katyn Forest," *Times Leader*, May 11, 1946; and "Katyn Massacre," *Polish American Journal*, October 13, 1951.

19. Flood quoted in "Katyn Massacre."

20. John Fisher, "U.S. Officials Facing Quiz on Katyn Massacre Gag," *Washington Times-Herald*, February 3, 1952.

21. U.S. House of Representatives, *Katyn Massacre Report*, 11–12, 37–38.

22. "House Report Charges Soviet with Massacre of Poles at Katyn," *Washington Evening Star*, July 2, 1952.

23. Sidney Weiland, "Khrushchev Attack Widely Known," *Washington Post*, March 18, 1956.

24. Rep. Daniel J. Flood, "Will the Soviet Union Confess to the Katyn Massacre?" (speech delivered at Convention of Polish American Congress, Philadelphia, Pa., June 1, 1956), 2–3.

25. Rep. Dan Flood to Secretary of State John Foster Dulles, Washington, D.C., May 2, 1956, KCL.

26. Rep. Dan Flood to Mr. Nikita S. Khrushchev, Washington, D.C., July 26, 1956, KCL.

27. Flood quoted in *Congressional Record*, May 6, 1957.

28. Clark interview, June 27, 2008.

29. The best accounts on McCarthyism are Richard H. Rovere, *Senator Joe McCarthy* (New York: Harper and Row, 1959); and Ted Morgan, *Reds: McCarthyism in Twentieth-Century America* (New York: Random House, 2003).

30. Laird interview.

31. See Flood quoted in *Congressional Record*, January 31, 1955.

32. Robert C. Albright, "House Passes Bill to Create Science Body," *Washington Post*, March 2, 1950.

33. "Flood Urges Congress to Outlaw Communists," *Washington Post*, March 7, 1949.

34. "Flood Warns of Taxes for Safety," *Hazleton Standard Sentinel*, October 17, 1952.

35. *Congressional Record*, May 29, 1957.

36. See David McCullough, *The Path Between the Seas: The Creation of the Panama Canal, 1870–1914* (New York: Simon and Schuster, 1977).

37. "American Enterprise Institute Report, No. 3," April 24, 1964, 88th Cong., 2d sess.

38. Paul B. Ryan, "Canal Diplomacy and Interests," *U.S. Naval Institute Proceedings* (January 1977): 45–46.

39. Letter, Daniel J. Flood to H. R. Parfitt, governor of the Panama Canal Zone, Washington, D.C., June 21, 1976, KCL.

40. See Bob Lawler, "Impressive Ceremonies Mark Gift of Trout Eggs to Panama," *Panama American*, January 9, 1950; "Congressmen a-Comin," *Panama American*, June 18, 1955; and "Flood Blasts Idea to Let Panama Flag into Zone," *Washington Evening Star*, January 12, 1960.

41. Earl Harding, *The Untold Story of Panama* (New York: Athens Press, 1959), 116–18.

42. "Rep. Flood Calls for Abolishment of Panama Corporation," *Panama Star and Herald*, June 18, 1955; and "PRR Ruckus Pops; Can Seybold Dam the Flood?" *Panama American*, June 18, 1955.

43. Flood quoted in "Rep. Flood Calls for Abolishment of Panama Corporation."

44. Rep. J. M. Murphy, "Introduction of Captain DuVal," June 28, 1978, KCL.

45. Interviews of Thomas A. Makowski, Wilkes-Barre, Pa., February 2, 2005; Sarah Sheerin, New Carrollton, Md., February 25, 2005; and Clark, April 2, 2005.

46. John Major, *Prize Possession: The United States and the Panama Canal, 1903–1979* (New York: Cambridge University Press, 1993), 332–33; and Harding, *Untold Story of Panama*, 119–20.

47. *Congressional Record*, May 29, 1957, and March 26, 1958. Among those "several well-positioned people in the United States" to whom Flood referred were: Senator Hubert Humphrey (D-Minn.); Senator Ralph E. Flanders (R-Vt.); former president Harry S. Truman; and Rep. James Roosevelt (D-N.Y.), son of Franklin D. Roosevelt. See Harding, *Untold Story of Panama*, 123–25.

48. Among the most complimentary letters are: Leigh Stevenson, Ft. Amador, Canal Zone, July 27, 1955; Louis Schmidt, Canal Zone, April 19, 1957; Norman J. Padelford, Boston, Mass., April 28, 1958; and Earl Harding, Washington, D.C., October 9, 1958, KCL.

49. Demaree Bess, "The Panama Danger Zone," *Saturday Evening Post*, May 9, 1959.

50. "Panama Solons Call Flood 'Public Enemy,'" *Plain Speaker* (Hazleton, Pa.), January 14, 1959; and "Flood Called Panama Foe," *Wilkes-Barre Record*, May 5, 1959.

51. Flood quoted in David Lawrence, "'America' Is a Dirty Word, Thanks to the Communists," *Patriot News*, March 5, 1959. See also John V. Horner, "Flood Blasts Idea to Let Panama Flag Into Zone," *Washington Evening Star*, January 12, 1960; and Elizabeth Ford, "Flood Urges Monroe Barrier; Sees Red in Panama," *Washington Post*, April 19, 1960.

52. "Congressman Flood at His Best During Debates on Defense Bills," *Army Times* (Washington, D.C.), May 13, 1962.

53. Mahon and Flood quoted in Robert K. Walsh, "Vital Decisions on Missiles Expected Soon from Military," *Washington Star*, November 21, 1957; and Robert C. Albright, "Vast Output of IRBMs Seen Soon," *Washington Post*, November 22, 1957.

54. Flood quoted in Drew Pearson, "Congressman Dan Flood Fights For More Air Force Funds," *Washington Post*, July 7, 1956.

55. Flood, "Rep. Flood Loses 10,000 Marines," *Washington Post*, May 12, 1962.

56. "Army Times Reports: Congressman Flood at His Best During Debate on Defense Bill," *Sunday Independent*, May 13, 1962.

57. Ford interview.

58. Flood quoted in *Congressional Record*, June 27, 1961.

59. "It's Spring on the Potomac—Dan Flood Is in Full Bloom," *Navy Times* (Washington, D.C.), April 8, 1962.

60. Ford interview; and Boldt, "Flood, the Flamboyant," 22.

61. In 1960 the Democrats held all of the most influential positions in Congress, from Speaker of the House (Sam Rayburn) to House majority leader (John McCormack of Massachusetts) to majority leader in the Senate (Hubert H. Humphrey of Minnesota), plus the chairs and a majority of seats on all the standing committees.

62. See Peter Wyden, *Bay of Pigs: The Untold Story* (New York: Simon and Schuster, 1979); and David Talbot, *Brothers: The Hidden History of the Kennedy Years* (New York: The Free Press, 2007), 48–52. Talbot argues that for weeks before the invasion Kennedy had "repeatedly made it clear to CIA director Allen Dulles and spymaster Richard Bissell that he would not commit the full military might of the United States to the Bay of Pigs operation." Kennedy believed that such "gunboat diplomacy" would destroy his effort to improve the United States's image in the hemisphere from a "bullying imperialist" to a "benevolent partner for reform in the new alliance for progress that characterized his Latin American policy." But Dulles and Bissell never believed that the president would stick to his plan. Convinced that in the heat of battle Kennedy would "cave

and send in U.S. warplanes and troops," the two CIA spymasters engaged in insubordinate behavior in planning the invasion. When Kennedy embarrassed them by refusing to save the operation, they were determined to remove him from office. See Talbot, *Brothers*, 44–48.

63. See J. F. terHorst, *Gerald Ford and the Future of the Presidency* (New York: Third Press, 1974), 76–77. Kennedy had actively opposed the reduction in defense spending since the mid-1950s when he was in the Senate. During a May 13, 1958, speech before the Wilkes-Barre Chamber of Commerce, Senator Kennedy insisted that Eisenhower's decision to cut defense spending not only resulted in a recession, but also brought into question the issue of whether "a democratic society can keep ahead of a single purposed Communist regime" (see Kennedy quoted in "Kennedy Addresses 1,000 Chamber of Commerce Diners," *Times Leader*, May 14, 1958).

64. Ford interview.

65. For a contemporary treatment of the Cuban missile crisis, see Robert F. Kennedy, *Thirteen Days: A Memoir of the Cuban Missile Crisis* (New York: Norton, 1969); for a more recent treatment of the missile crisis, see Ernest R. May and Philip D. Zelikow, eds., *The Kennedy Tapes: Inside the White House During the Cuban Missile Crisis* (Cambridge: Harvard University Press, 1997).

66. Glenn T. Seaborg, *Kennedy, Khrushchev, and the Test Ban* (Berkeley and Los Angeles: University of California Press, 1981).

67. See Talbot, *Brothers*; E. Howard Hunt, *American Spy: My Secret History in the CIA, Watergate, and Beyond* (Hoboken, N.J.: John Wiley and Sons, 2007); Lamar Waldron with Thom Hartman, *Ultimate Sacrifice: John and Robert Kennedy, the Plan for a Coup in Cuba, and the Murder of JFK* (New York: Carroll and Graf, 2005); Evan Thomas, *Robert Kennedy: His Life* (New York: Simon and Schuster, 2000); and Richard D. Mahoney, *Sons and Brothers: The Days of Jack and Bobby Kennedy* (New York: Arcade Publishing, 1999).

68. On plans to assassinate Castro, see: James Pierson, *Camelot and the Cultural Revolution: How the Assassination of John F. Kennedy Shattered American Liberalism* (New York: Encounter Books, 2007), 44; Robert Dalleck, *An Unfinished Life: John F. Kennedy, 1917–1963* (New York: Little, Brown, 2003), 439–40; Seymour Hersh, *The Dark Side of Camelot* (New York: Little, Brown, 1997), chaps. 13, 14; and Thomas C. Reeves, *A Question of Character: A Life of John F. Kennedy* (New York: Macmillan, 1991), chap. 12.

69. Waldron, *Ultimate Sacrifice*, 1–23. Since the mid-1970s there has been a growing body of literature suggesting that John F. Kennedy's assassination was the result of a conspiracy between organized crime and the Central Intelligence Agency. Waldron argues that Kennedy's refusal to give the Cuban nationalist freedom fighters the necessary support during the Bay of Pigs invasion led to the CIA to enlist Marcello, Trafficante, and Rosselli in a plot to assassinate the president in Dallas, using many of the same tactics in the CIA's secret plan to kill Castro. Their success was insured by the fact that the U.S. government could not disclose the real facts of the Kennedy assassination without admitting its own secret plans to kill Castro and risking nuclear retaliation. Accordingly, the Warren Commission, charged with investigating the Kennedy assassination, deflected any suggestion of a conspiracy by charging a lone gunman with the crime. Other conspiracy theorists also cite a connection between the CIA and organized crime. Some of the most persuasive accounts are: Robert S. Anson, *"They've Killed the President!" The Search for the Murderers of John F. Kennedy* (New York: Bantam, 1975); David S. Lifton, *Best Evidence: Disguise and Deception in the Assassination of John F. Kennedy* (New York: Macmillan, 1980); G. Robert Blakely and Richard N. Billings, *The Plot to Kill the President* (New York: Times Books, 1981); Jim Garrison, *On the Trial of the Assassins: My Investigation and Prosecution of the Murder of President Kennedy* (New York: Warner Books, 1988); John H. Davis, *Mafia Kingfish: Carlos Marcello and the Assassination of John F. Kennedy* (New York: McGraw-Hill, 1989); Mark Lane, *Plausible Denial: Was the CIA Involved in the Assassination of JFK?* (New York: Thunder's Mouth Press, 1991); and David R. Wrone, *The Zapruder Film: Reframing JFK's Assassination* (Lawrence: University Press of Kansas, 2003). Each and every one of these conspiracy theories have been disproved by prominent prosecuting attorney Vincent Bugliosi in his monumental work, *Reclaiming History: The Assassination of President John F. Kennedy* (New York: Norton, 2007), which reinforces the findings of the Warren Commission that Lee Harvey Oswald acted alone.

70. Commonwealth of Pennsylvania, *Pennsylvania Crime Commission, 1984 Report* (St. David's: Commonwealth of Pennsylvania, 1984), 40–42; "Crime Commission Report Says Bufalino's Family Is in Decline," *Citizens' Voice*, August 11, 1989; and Sifakis, *Mafia Encyclopedia*, 67.

71. Waldron, *Ultimate Sacrifice*, 349–52; and "Mafia Spies in Cuba," *Time*, June 9, 1975. Ironically, Bufalino later became the number one suspect in the disappearance of American trade unionist Jimmy Hoffa. See Charles Brandt, *"I Heard You Paint Houses": Frank "The Irishman" Sheeran and the Inside Story of the Mafia, the Teamsters, and the Last Ride of Jimmy Hoffa* (Hanover, N.H.: Steerforth Press, 2005), 2–4.

72. Commonwealth of Pennsylvania, *Pennsylvania's 1984 Crime Commission Report*, 42.

73. Ibid., 40; and Brandt, *"I Heard You Paint Houses,"* 64.

74. "Rep. Flood Helped Defense Firm," *Washington Star*, February 20, 1978; and Philip Jenkins, "The Actor as Politician: Daniel Flood," in Miller and Pencak, *Pennsylvania*, 347.

75. "Rep. Flood Helped Defense Firm."

76. Interview of Tom Medico, president, Medico Industries, Plains Township, Pa., March 26, 2007.

77. Ibid.

78. U.S. Department of Justice, "Memorandum: Daniel J. Flood, U.S. Congressman; Medico Industries, Inc; Racketeer Influenced and Corrupt Organizations—Bribery," June 30, 1978, FBI Document No. 183-1719-3; and FBI Document Nos. 183-1566-12 (April 15, 1978), FBI.

79. U.S. Department of Justice, "Memorandum to FBI Director from White Collar Crime Section: Daniel J. Flood, U.S. Congressman; Medico Industries, Inc.—Bribery," March 2, 1978, FBI Document No. 183-1709-1; see also FBI Document Nos. 183-1566-12 (April 15, 1978); 183-1709-4 (August 31, 1978); 183-1709-5 (May 9, 1979); 183-1709-6 (June 14, 1979); 183-1709-7 (September 10, 1979); and 183-1709-8 (September 17, 1979), all in FBI.

80. U.S. Department of Justice, "Memorandum to FBI Director from White Collar Crime Section: Daniel J. Flood, U.S. Congressman; Medico Industries, Inc.—Bribery," April 14, 1978, Document No. 183-1566-12, FBI.

CHAPTER 6

1. For biographical background on Lyndon Johnson, see Robert A. Caro, *The Years of Lyndon Johnson*, vol. 1, *The Path to Power* (New York: Knopf, 1982); Caro, *Years of Johnson*, vol. 2, *Means of Ascent* (New York: Knopf, 1990); and Doris Kearns, *Lyndon Johnson and the American Dream* (New York: Harper and Row, 1976).

2. According to Flood's staff members and congressional colleagues, the congressman never had any aspirations for the Senate or the executive branch. By the late 1960s, his desire to remain in the House might have been due to poor health. In 1962 Flood was hospitalized with esophageal cancer. Though cured, he lost a tremendous amount of weight and suffered recurring periods of fatigue. See interviews of Clark, April 2, 2005; Laird; McDade; Scranton; and Edward Mitchell, Wilkes-Barre, Pa., January 30, 2007.

3. Johnson quoted in Kearns, *Lyndon Johnson and the American Dream*, 210–11.

4. Remini, *House*, 400–403.

5. Lyndon Johnson, "State of the Union Address," January 8, 1964, *Public Papers of the Presidents of the United States, 1964* (Washington, D.C.: Government Printing Office, 1964), 281.

6. Kearns, *Lyndon Johnson and the American Dream*, 188–90; and Richard Bolling, *Power in the House*, 223–25.

7. See Adam C. Powell, chair of the House Committee on Education and Labor, "Remarks in the House of Representatives on H.R. 11377—Economic Opportunity Act of 1964," August 5, 1964, Flood Collection, KCL; Farmers Home Administration, *Facts and Fallacies About the Economic Opportunity Act of 1964* (Washington, D.C.: U.S. Department of Agriculture, 1964); Bolling, *Power in the House*, 225–26; and Harris Wofford, *Of Kennedys and Kings: Making Sense of the Sixties* (Pittsburgh: University of Pittsburgh Press, 1992), 294–96.

8. Kearns, *Lyndon Johnson and the American Dream*, 209, 235.

9. Eric Goldman, *The Tragedy of Lyndon Johnson* (New York: Knopf, 1969), 260.

10. Kearns, *Lyndon Johnson and the American Dream*, 216–25.

11. After the 1964 elections, Flood's seniority on the House Appropriations Committee increased as he moved from the fifteenth- to the thirteenth-ranking Democrat. See "Flood Gains in Seniority on Committee," *Times Leader*, November 9, 1964.

12. Flood's seniority on the HEW Appropriations Subcommittee increased rapidly. He was appointed to the subcommittee in 1964 and immediately became the fifth-ranking Democrat on it. Two years later, only Rep. John Fogerty of Rhode Island had greater seniority than Flood. When Fogerty died in January 1967, Flood became the new chair of HEW Appropriations with not even three years' experience on the subcommittee. See Clark interview, July 5, 2007.

13. Johnson quoted in "Johnson Says U.S. Wants Progress," *Wilkes-Barre Record*, October 15, 1964; see also "Johnson Greeted by 10,000," *Times Leader*, October 14, 1964.

14. Letter, Flood to E. V. Chadwick, Washington, D.C., June 24, 1964, Flood Collection, KCL.

15. Letter, Flood to Reverend A. Ward Campbell, Washington, D.C., June 25, 1964, Flood Collection, KCL.

16. Flood's letter, dated July 21, 1954, was sent to the following chamber of commerce presidents in the Eleventh district: Donald J. Allen, Pittston; Louis Feldman, Hazleton; John A. Mulhearn, Freeland; Joseph O'Karma, Nanticoke; Louis Schaeffer, Wilkes-Barre; and Frederick D. Schultz, Berwick, Flood Collection, KCL.

17. Letter, Albert N. Danoff, president of the Wilkes-Barre Welfare Planning Council, to Dan Flood, Wilkes-Barre, Pa., October 27, 1964, Flood Collection, KCL.

18. Flood's letter, dated November 16, 1964, was sent to the following mayors in the Eleventh district: Joseph Conahan, Hazleton; Robert A. Loftus, Pittston; Frank Slattery, Wilkes-Barre; and Vincent Znaniecki, Nanticoke, Flood Collection, KCL.

19. "County Prepares for Anti-poverty Projects," *Times Leader*, December 7, 1964.

20. Letter, Flood to Albert Danoff, president, Wilkes-Barre Welfare Planning Council, Washington, D.C., September 1965, Flood Collection, KCL.

21. Letter, Wesley E. Davies, superintendent of Luzerne County Schools, to Flood, Wilkes-Barre, Pa., September 10, 1965, Flood Collection, KCL.

22. Letter, Flood to Davies, Washington, D.C., September 13, 1965, Flood Collection, KCL.

23. Letter, Davies to Flood, Wilkes-Barre, Pa., September 15, 1965, Flood Collection, KCL.

24. See Theodore Berry, director, Community Action Programs, "Data for Financial Planning of Child Development Programs," Office of Economic Opportunity, Washington, D.C., Flood Collection, KCL. For fiscal year 1966, Allegheny County received $5,356,098 and Philadelphia, $8,122,296 for Child Development Programs under the Elementary and Secondary U.S. School Aid Bill. The average grant for all other Pennsylvania counties was $600,000.

25. "Poverty Hits War on Poverty," *Economic Opportunity Newsletter* 11 (October 1, 1965): 3, in Flood Collection, KCL.

26. "124 EOA-Created Jobs Paid $256,690 Total," *Times Leader*, June 20, 1966; and "Operation Medicare Alert Needs Volunteers Despite Federal Grant," *Wilkes-Barre Record*, February 3, 1966.

27. The Flood Collection at Wilkes-Barre's King's College contains several files of correspondence between Flood and Shriver, which begins on August 20, 1964, and ends on September 2, 1967, when inadequate funding for the War on Poverty began to take its toll on the program.

28. Letter, Flood to Sargent Shriver, Washington, D.C., October 3, 1965; and letter, Shriver to Flood, Washington, D.C., October 8, 1965, Flood Collection, KCL.

29. Letter, Flood to Shriver, Washington, D.C., March 10, 1967; and letter, Shriver to Flood, Washington, D.C., June 3, 1967, Flood Collection, KCL.

30. Letter, Shriver to Flood, Washington, D.C., February 9, 1967, Flood Collection, KCL.

31. Telegram, Eugene D. Hegarty, Flood's administrative assistant, to Joseph Murphy, editor, *Times Leader*, November 18, 1965, KCL; and Flood quoted in Crile, "Best Congressman," 64.

32. Wright interview.

33. "Daniel J. Flood," *Current Biography, 1978*, 133; and Crile, "Best Congressman," 64.

34. "Summary of Appalachian Regional Development Act Quick Start Projects—State of Pennsylvania, Calendar 1965," Appalachian Regional Commission, Washington, D.C., Flood

Collection, KCL. Most of the four million dollars allocated to Luzerne County went to put out a mine fire in the borough of Laurel Run, which began at the Red Ash Coal Company's operation more than forty years earlier. Efforts to extinguish the fire had failed because of an inadequate water supply. In 1948 the Alden Coal Company placed seals on the fire, but gas leaks forced the evacuation of many families in the borough. In the mid-1950s Flood secured $1.5 million to extinguish the fire by sponsoring the Mine Fire Control Act of 1954 and the Mine Water Control Act of 1955. But the fire continued to spread. By the 1960s, the underground fire had spread into neighboring Wilkes-Barre Township and threatened the City of Wilkes-Barre itself if not extinguished. See "Gov. Scranton Lends Hand in Mine Fire Battle," *Wilkes-Barre Record*, January 11, 1964; "Valley Gets Top Priority on Flushing Project," *Wilkes-Barre Record*, February 24, 1965; and "U.S. Bureau of Mines Doubtful Mines Can Be Flushed Successfully," *Sunday Independent*, June 20, 1965.

35. Clark interview, April 2, 2005.

36. "Stern Rep. Flood Drowns Out 'Tower of Babel,'" *Roll Call* (Washington, D.C.), October 20, 1965; and "House Gives Flood Ovation," *Patriot News*, July 4, 1965.

37. "Daniel J. Flood," *Current Biography, 1978*, 133. Under the Model Cities program, Wilkes-Barre received over $84 million in federal money to raze dilapidated properties on an area of 220 lots and build 200 low-income housing units as well as a new post office and an ACME service center. The balance of the $181 million grant was spent to redevelop similar plighted areas in Hazleton, Nanticoke, and Pittston. See "Wilkes-Barre Enters 1966 with 7 Projects Reshaping its Future," *Sunday Independent*, January 2, 1966; letter, Flood to Frank Walser, editor, *Hazleton (Pa.) Standard Speaker*, Washington, D.C., December 28, 1966; and letter, Flood to William G. Snyder, director of Nanticoke Redevelopment Authority, Washington, D.C., October 19, 1967, both in Flood Collection, KCL.

38. According to Allen Fisher, archivist at the Lyndon B. Johnson Presidential Library, there "is no definitive total federal expenditure figure on the Great Society," which was a "sprawling amalgam of programs running into billions of dollars" (see interview of Allen Fisher, Austin, Texas; September 11, 2009).

39. Wright interview.

40. Scranton interview.

41. "Dorris, Murray Failed Says Slattery," *Wilkes-Barre Record*, October 16, 1964.

42. "Martin Murray Wins Senate Seat," *Times Leader*, November 7, 1956.

43. Loftus interview.

44. Sheldon Spear, "Frank P. Slattery, Jr.: The Mayor Who Beat the Machine," *Citizens' Voice*, September 4, 2007.

45. Mayor Frank Slattery quoted in "Dorris, Murray Failed Says Slattery."

46. "Dr. Dorris Hears Boos at Airport Reception for President Johnson," *Sunday Independent*, October 18, 1964.

47. Interview of Bernard C. Brominski, Wilkes-Barre, Pa., March 13, 1996. Common Pleas judge Bernard Podcasy confirmed Brominski's assertion, stating that Dorris hoped to displace Flood as well as other long-entrenched politicians with candidates of eastern European extraction. Since the Poles, Lithuanians, and Slovaks in particular formed an influential voting bloc, Dorris believed that a candidate from one of those ethnic groups could unseat incumbents, who tended to be white Anglo-Saxon Protestants or Irish Catholics. See interview of Bernard J. Podcasy, Wilkes-Barre, Pa., December 7, 2007.

48. Clark interview, April 2, 2005.

49. Farrell interview; and Monsignor Andrew McGowan quoted in *Dan Flood: A Legend in His Own Time*, WBRE-TV, Scranton/Wilkes-Barre, Pa., May 30, 1994.

50. Flood's personal appointment calendars reflect his busy schedule. Most weekends he would return to the district on a Thursday evening and be in his Wilkes-Barre office on Friday and Saturday mornings. The late afternoons and evenings were spent attending a variety of functions, sometimes as many as eight to twelve affairs over the course of a three-day weekend. On Monday morning the congressman would return to Washington, either by car or private airplane. See appointment calendars, 1970–1978, Flood Collection, LCHS.

51. Interview of Monsignor Andrew McGowan, Laflin, Pa., January 15, 2004.

52. Ibid.

53. Flood quoted in Crile, "Best Congressman," 64; interview, James Lee, former editor, *Times Leader*, Wilkes-Barre, Pa., June 7, 2005; and "Daniel J. Flood," *Current Biography, 1978*, 132. In 1962 Flood secured another $8.5 million in federal funding to construct an interchange that would link routes 80 and 81, the major east-west and north-south interstates under construction at the time. See "County to Be 'Crossroads of the State,'" *Wilkes-Barre Record*, April 17, 1962.

54. Catherine Flood interview.

55. See interviews of Edward Mitchell; and Michael Cefalo, West Pittston, Pa., November 9, 2007; and Crile, "Best Congressman," 64.

56. Interviews of Mitchell; Clark; and Makowski, Nanticoke, Pa., October 11, 2005. See also "Flood Hails Construction of 7 New Post Offices in County—2 More on the Way," *Exeter (Pa.) Echo*, April 19, 1962; "Dedication of Shavertown Post Office Will Be On May 5," *Wilkes-Barre Record*, April 13, 1962; and "Ground Broken for $137,000 Post Office at Nanticoke," *Times Leader*, November 3, 1962.

57. See "Flood Explains How Candidates Are Picked for Service Academies," *Sunday Independent*, January 10, 1960. Flood's annual quotas for congressional appointments were: five for the United States Naval Academy; four for West Point; and one for the United States Air Force Academy. He also nominated several alternates. The United States Merchant Marine Academy did not have a quota, but Flood routinely nominated ten young men for admission from his district each year. A "qualified" candidate had to carry at least a 3.5 cumulative grade point average and be in top physical condition. Flood's office received between 150 and 200 applications each year in the decade of the 1960s. The congressman based his selections largely on the results of a written examination that was conducted at his district office in Wilkes-Barre. His final decision was also influenced by three character references, each written by a mutual acquaintance of the candidate and the congressman. Flood's nominations were given special consideration by the naval academy, on whose board he served. See "Flood Named to Naval Academy's Board," *Times Leader*, March 11, 1961.

58. See "Daniel J. Flood," *Current Biography, 1978*, 132; and Crile, "Best Congressman," 63.

59. To protect the privacy of those individuals who are still living, the case files of individual constituents are not accessible to researchers. Flood donated his collection of private and public papers to the King's College Library in 1964. After his resignation from Congress in 1980, the remainder of the collection was relocated from his Washington office there, with the exception of those records that had been confiscated by the Justice Department in 1977 and 1978 in preparation for the congressman's federal trial on bribery and perjury charges. Only those papers for the twenty-year period 1944 to 1964 have been indexed. See "Flood Papers Will Be Put in King's Library," *Times Leader*, November 1, 1964.

60. Flood was often referred to as "one of us" in local newspaper editorials and letters to the editor throughout his congressional district. The first time such a broad reference was made was in the newspaper endorsements of Flood's reelection bid in the 1964 campaign. See "Rep. Flood More Valuable Than Ever in Congress," *Times Leader*, October 31, 1964; "Flood for Congress," *Wilkes-Barre Record*, November 2, 1964; and "Dan Flood—A Man of the People," *Hazleton Standard Speaker*, November 3, 1964.

61. "500 Attend Dinner in Tribute to Flood," *Times Leader*, October 20, 1964.

62. Crile, "Best Congressman," 66; and Paul Golias, "Flood, Winner 15 Times, Knows How Losers Feel."

63. Interview of Paul Golias, Wilkes-Barre, Pa., May 3, 2005.

64. Lee interview.

65. Ibid.

66. Mitchell interview.

67. See "Press Release Files," Flood Collection, KCL.

68. See "Model Cities Head 'Happy with Report,'" *Times Leader*, September 27, 1971; "Model Cities Agency May Lose Director," *Times Leader*, October 14, 1971; and "Miscavage Named Model Cities Head," *Times Leader*, March 21, 1972.

69. Golias interview.

70. Paul Golias, "HUD Audit Shows Misuse of Model Cities Funds," *Times Leader*, March 30, 1971.

71. Schutter successfully responded to the various allegations against the Wilkes-Barre Model Cities Agency in a series of articles that ran in the *Times Leader* in August 1971. See "Model Cities Sees No Violation of Federal Policy in Local Buying," *Times Leader*, August 21, 1971; "Model Cities Disputes Charge Project Work Hasn't Kept Pace," *Times Leader*, August 23, 1971; "Model Cities Agency Moves to Strengthen Fiscal Monitoring," *Times Leader*, August 23, 1971; "Model Cities Agency Answers Attack on Costs of TV Series," *Times Leader*, August 26, 1971; and "Model Cities Head 'Happy with Report.'" Schutter resigned his position as the local HUD director on March 3, 1972, to run as a Republican candidate for Flood's congressional seat. But the bad publicity severely damaged his chances to capture the Republican nomination. Schutter lost to Dr. Donald Ayers in the primary election. Ayers was soundly defeated by Flood in the general election, 124,336 to 57,809. See Golias, "Flood, Winner 15 Times, Knows How Losers Feel."

72. Cosgrove interview.

73. Flood quoted in Binkley, "Flood Was Everyman's Champion," 42.

74. James Free quoted in "Flood Is 'Good Copy,'" *Sunday Independent*, February 9, 1958.

75. Flood quoted in "Reporter Untwists Knotty Secret from Dan Flood on That Mustache," *Sunday Independent*, May 2, 1965.

76. Cosgrove interview. Flood's image as a stage actor who took to the House floor in a cape and top hat to deliver his speeches has been grossly exaggerated according to Michael Clark, a former aide: "Dan never appeared on the House floor in a cape and top hat. Caucus rules prevent the wearing of any hat on the floor of the House of Representatives. Nor did he ever dress in formal wear or a cape in that forum. He had too much respect for Congress to do that. He simply revered the House floor" (see Clark interview, Washington, D.C., May 26, 2005).

77. See Jack Anderson with James Boyd, *Confessions of a Muckraker: The Inside Story of Life in Washington During the Truman, Eisenhower, Kennedy, and Johnson Years* (New York: Random House, 1979).

78. See Drew Pearson, "Congressman Flood Angry over Lag in Satellite Missile Program," *Washington Post*, November 27, 1957; and Pearson, "Top Brass Face Angry Solons," *Washington Post*, November 27, 1957.

79. Drew Pearson, "FBI Probing Flood's Office for Leaks," *Washington Post*, March 18, 1957.

80. Jack Anderson, "Flood and Medico," *Washington Post*, April 1, 1970.

81. Jack Anderson, "Flood's Fiscal Principles," *Washington Post*, November 9, 1970.

82. Ford interview.

83. Ibid., 66; and Francis X. Clines, "Flood Is Offstage at Closing of 36-Year Congress Run," *New York Times*, February 1, 1980.

84. "A Jaunty Dan Flood Walks from Hospital," *Times Leader*, May 25, 1962; "Daniel J. Flood," *Current Biography, 1978*, 133; and interview of William C. Kashatus, MD, Wayne, Pa., January 15, 2006.

85. See "Flood Unhappy with Plan for New District," *Sunday Independent*, February 20, 1966. The average congressional district population was 419,000 in the mid-1960s. Prior to 1966, Flood's Eleventh district, which comprised just Luzerne County, was under the national average with a population of 346,972. But with the addition of Carbon (pop. 52,889) and Monroe (pop. 39,567) counties, the Eleventh district's total population was 438,428.

86. Catherine Flood interview.

87. Clark interview, July 5, 2007.

88. Letter, Flood to Dr. H. Beecher Charmbury, secretary of mines, Washington, D.C., February 3, 1965; and letter, Flood to Rep. John E. Fogerty, chair, HEW Appropriations Subcommittee, Washington, D.C., February 2, 1965, Flood Collection, KCL.

89. Clark interview, July 5, 2007.

90. Crile, "Best Congressman," 60.

91. Flood quoted in Grady, "Flood They Can't Dam," 7.

92. See Flood, "Remarks for the Class of '94," Washington, D.C., February 4, 1975, 2, Flood Collection, KCL; see also "Labor-HEW Budget Estimates" in U.S. Congress, *Appropriations Budget*

Estimates, 88th Cong., 2d sess. (Washington, D.C.: Government Printing Office, 1964), 149; *Appropriations Budget Estimates,* 89th Cong., 1st sess. (1965), 165; *Appropriations Budget Estimates,* 89th Cong., 2d sess. (1966), 166; *Appropriations Budget Estimates,* 90th Cong., 1st sess. (1968), 166; *Appropriations Budget Estimates,* 90th Cong., 2d sess. (1969), 175; *Appropriations Budget Estimates,* 91st Cong., 1st sess. (1970), 288; *Appropriations Budget Estimates,* 91st Cong., 2d sess. (1971), 219; *Appropriations Budget Estimates,* 92d Cong., 1st sess. (1972), 236; *Appropriations Budget Estimates,* 92d Cong., 2d sess. (1973), 235; *Appropriations Budget Estimates,* 93d Cong., 1st sess. (1974), 170; and *Appropriations Budget Estimates,* 93d Cong., 2d sess. (1975), 192. The HEW Appropriations Subcommittee was not responsible for funding such Department of HEW programs as the Food and Drug Administration, Indian Health, and Indian Education, which were assigned to other subcommittees.

93. Flood, "Remarks for the Class of '94," 5–7.

94. See James MacGregor Burns, *Leadership* (New York: Harper and Row, 1978), 357–62. Burns offers an excellent explanation of legislative leadership as practiced in the American political system.

95. Ford, Laird, McDade, Michel, Rooney, Scranton, and Wright interviews.

96. See Alan Derickson, *Black Lung: Anatomy of a Public Health Disaster* (Ithaca: Cornell University Press, 1998), 147–65; and Dublin and Licht, *Face of Decline,* 105.

97. Dublin and Licht, *Face of Decline,* 106.

98. See Dan Flood, "Statement Before the U.S. Senate Labor Subcommittee on Coal Mine Safety," March 20, 1969, Flood Collection, KCL. In 1969 Flood's congressional district had 260 underground mines and 150 strip mines, accounting for a total workforce of approximately 10,000 workers.

99. Ibid.

100. HR 13950, "Federal Coal Mine Health and Safety Act of 1969," 91st Cong., 1st sess., No. 91-563, October 13, 1969.

101. Clark interview, April 2, 2005.

102. Flood quoted in Crile, "Best Congressman," 66.

103. Flood quoted in *Congressional Record,* October 27, 1969. Flood's impressive delivery of the speech and his simulation of an afflicted coal miner was confirmed in the interviews of McDade, Michel, Rooney, and Wright.

104. Flood quoted in Crile, "Best Congressman," 66.

105. McDade interview.

106. O'Neill and Casey quoted in Crile, "Best Congressman," 66.

107. Interview of Rep. Fred Rooney, Washington, D.C., February 1, 2007.

108. President Richard M. Nixon, "Statement on Signing the Federal Coal Mine Health and Safety Act of 1969," December 30, 1969, in John T. Woolley and Gerhard Peters, American Presidency Project (online), Santa Barbara: University of California, http://americanpresidency.org/.

109. Telegram, office of Congressman Flood to editor, *Sunday Independent,* Washington, D.C., December 20, 1969, Flood Collection, KCL.

110. See "Coal Mine Safety Act Becomes law," *Washington Post,* December 30, 1969; and Justin McCarthy, "Nixon Signs Health, Safety Law," *United Mine Workers Journal,* January 1, 1970.

111. Flood quoted in "Flood: Mine Bill World's Best," *Scranton Times,* January 2, 1970.

112. See Department of Health, Education, and Welfare, *First Annual Report to Congress on the Administration of Part B of Title IV of the Federal Coal Mine Health and Safety Act of 1969* (Washington, D.C.: Department of HEW, June 1971), 18–19, Flood Collection, KCL.

113. Clark interview, April 2, 2005.

114. PL 91-173, "Federal Coal Mine Health and Safety Act of 1969," 91st Cong., S 2917, December 30, 1969, 51–56.

115. Ibid., 21–22.

116. Ms. Maria Lispi, president, "Petition of the Anthracosilicosis League of Pennsylvania to Rep. Daniel J. Flood," Wilkes-Barre, Pa., March 1, 1971, Flood Collection, KCL; and "Unit Wants 10 Years in Mines as Asthma Proof," *Wilkes-Barre Record,* February 10, 1971.

117. Letter, Flood to Ms. Maria Lispi, Washington, D.C., March 12, 1971, Flood Collection, KCL.

118. See David P. Rall, MD, *Coal Workers' Pneumoconiosis: State of Knowledge and Research Needs* (Research Triangle Park, N.C.: National Institute of Environmental Health Sciences, April 12, 1971), 5–7, Flood Collection, KCL.

119. See PL 92-303, "The Black Lung Benefits Act of 1972," 92d Cong., 1st sess., May 19, 1972. The House bill (HR 9212) passed by a vote of 311 to 79 on November 10, 1971, and the Senate version of the bill (S 2675) passed by a vote of 73 to 0 on April 17, 1972.

120. Bill Barnes quoted in Crile, "Best Congressman," 66.

121. Dan Flood, "Address Before the Brookings Institute," Washington, D.C., April 11, 1972, 17–20.

122. Crile, "Best Congressman," 65. In a recent interview, Carlucci insisted that the "statewide adjustment was not true." "All decisions about which community action agencies were to be retained or closed were made on an individual basis," he said. "I told Dan Flood that if he wanted the Wilkes-Bare agency funded, he'd have to fund it himself. And he did. He arranged to fund that agency through an appropriations bill he presented in the House" (interview of Frank Carlucci, Washington, D.C., November 9, 2007).

123. Lashford quoted in Crile, "Best Congressman," 65.

124. See James T. Patterson, *America's Struggle Against Poverty in the Twentieth Century*, 4th ed. (Cambridge: Harvard University Press, 2000); Michael B. Katz, *The Undeserving Poor: From the War on Poverty to the War on Welfare* (New York: Pantheon, 1990); and Allen J. Matusow, *The Unraveling of America: A History of Liberalism in the 1960s* (1984; repr., New York: Harper, 1985).

125. Daniel J. Flood, "Memorial Tributes in the House of Representatives," *Memorial Services in the Congress of the United States and Tributes in Eulogy of Lyndon Baines Johnson* (Washington, D.C.: Government Printing Office, 1973), 64–65.

CHAPTER 7

1. Stanley Karnow, *Vietnam: A History* (New York: Viking Press, 1983), 170–78; and Douglas Kinnard, *The War Managers* (1977; repr., Annapolis, Md.: Naval Institute Press, 2007), 5. The works of Karnow and Kinnard are widely considered the best treatments on U.S. involvement in Vietnam. Karnow was a war correspondent for the *Washington Post*, and Kinnard a U.S. general who was chief of staff of the most important field command in Vietnam before his retirement in 1970. A more recent reinterpretation of the Vietnam War, Michael Lind's *Vietnam: The Necessary War* (New York: Simon and Schuster, 1999), argues that the military establishment was justified in going to war, considering the global context of the cold war. He also insists that the U.S. effort in Vietnam failed largely because the Department of Defense, the Joint Chiefs of Staff, and the Pentagon did not adapt to the demands of guerrilla warfare.

2. Karnow, *Vietnam*, 181–224; and H. R. McMaster, *Dereliction of Duty: Lyndon Johnson, Robert McNamara, the Joint Chiefs of Staff, and the Lies that Led to Vietnam* (New York: Harper-Collins, 1997), 33–37.

3. Stephen E. Ambrose, *Eisenhower: Soldier and President* (New York: Simon and Schuster, 1990), 332, 556; and Emmet John Hughes, *The Ordeal of Power: A Political Memoir of the Eisenhower Years* (New York: Atheneum, 1981), 208, 251.

4. Karnow, *Vietnam*, 20.

5. William J. Rust, *Kennedy in Vietnam: American Vietnam Policy, 1960–1963* (New York: Charles Scribner's Sons, 1985), 42–43; Talbot, *Brothers*, 35–36; Karnow, *Vietnam*, 249–50; and McMaster, *Dereliction of Duty*, 9–11. General Maxwell Taylor first articulated the military doctrine of flexible response in his book *The Uncertain Trumpet*, a scathing critique of Eisenhower's defense policy in which he called for "the unqualified renunciation" of the doctrine of massive retaliation. See Taylor, *The Uncertain Trumpet* (New York: Harper, 1959), 137, 146, 153. Similarly, secretary of defense Robert McNamara, even after his resignation in 1968, insisted that "massive

retaliation" was "useless as a guarantee of our national security" and "must continue to give way to both the theory and the practice of flexible response" (see Robert S. McNamara, *The Essence of Security: Reflections in Office* [New York: Harper and Row, 1968], x, 68–86).

6. Wofford, *Of Kennedys and Kings*, 68.

7. Several scholars have identified the U.S. military establishment's misperception of Vietnam and how the war should have been fought, including: Henry Brandon, *Anatomy of Error* (Boston: Gambit, 1969); Sir Robert Thompson, *No Exit from Vietnam* (New York: David McKay, 1970); Colonel Donald Bletz, *The Role of the Military in U.S. Foreign Policy* (New York: Praeger, 1972), 278–81; Bernard Brodie, *War and Politics* (New York: Macmillan, 1973), chap. 5; and McMaster, *Dereliction of Duty*, 4–8. The following statement by chair of the Joint Chiefs of Staff Earle G. Wheeler is often cited for supporting the military's limited view: "It is fashionable in some quarters to say that the problems in Southeast Asia are primarily political and economic rather than military. I do not agree. The essence of the problem in Vietnam is military" (see Brandon, *Anatomy of Error*, 23).

8. See David Halberstam, *The Best and the Brightest* (1972; repr., Greenwich, Conn.: Fawcett Crest, 1973), 274–78; Kinnard, *War Managers*, 7–8; and McMaster, *Dereliction of Duty*, 18–19, 105–6.

9. Halberstam, *Best and Brightest*, 366.

10. Ibid., 345–50; Karnow, *Vietnam*, 277–81; Rust, *Kennedy in Vietnam*, 94–112; and McMaster, *Dereliction of Duty*, 38–41.

11. See Peter D. Scott, *Deep Politics and the Death of JFK* (Berkeley and Los Angeles: University of California Press, 1996); John M. Newman, *JFK and Vietnam* (New York: Warner, 1992); David Kaiser, *American Tragedy: Kennedy, Johnson, and the Origins of the Vietnam War* (Cambridge: Harvard University Press, 2000); Gareth Porter, *Perils of Dominance: Imbalance of Power and the Road to War in Vietnam* (Berkeley and Los Angeles: University of California Press, 2005); and Talbot, *Brothers*. Kennedy's defense secretary Robert McNamara also believes that JFK, had he lived, "would have pulled us out of Vietnam," believing that the "South Vietnamese were incapable of defending themselves, and that Saigon's grave political weakness made it unwise to try to offset the limitations of South Vietnamese forces by sending U.S. combat troops on a large scale" (see Robert S. McNamara, *In Retrospect: The Tragedy and Lessons of Vietnam* [New York: Random House, 1995], 96).

12. Halberstam, *Best and Brightest*, 424–26.

13. McNamara, *In Retrospect*, 106–8, 118. When I contacted McNamara for an interview, he politely declined, stating his advanced age and poor memory. Telephone conversation with Robert S. McNamara, Washington, D.C., March 22, 2007.

14. Flood quoted in "Flood Details Position."

15. Flood quoted in *Congressional Record*, May 5, 1955.

16. Flood quoted in Sandy Grady, "Flood They Can't Dam," 8.

17. Clark interview, July 5, 2007.

18. Wright interview.

19. Karnow, *Vietnam*, 43–44.

20. Ibid., 328–29.

21. Ibid., 636–37; Thomas A. Bailey, *A Diplomatic History of the American People*, 10th ed. (Englewood Cliffs, N.J.: Prentice Hall, 1980), 926; and John Lewis Gaddis, *Cold War*, 109–12.

22. Flood quoted in *Congressional Record*, June 27, 1961.

23. Flood quoted in Ed Koterba, "Generals Do Live Dangerously . . . Especially when Rep. Dan Flood Is in Form," *Pittsburgh Post-Gazette*, March 9, 1961.

24. Karnow, *Vietnam*, 320–26.

25. House Appropriations Defense Subcommittee, "Discussion of Vietnam," *Hearings on Department of Defense Appropriations for 1965*, 88th Cong., 2d sess. (February 16, 1964), 106–8, microfiche, Van Pelt Library, University of Pennsylvania, Philadelphia, Pa.; and Robert Allen, "U.S. Considers Taking Over Command of South Vietnamese Combat Forces," *Macon (Ga.) Telegraph*, February 29, 1964.

26. House Appropriations Defense Subcommittee, "Discussion of Vietnam," *Hearings on Department of Defense Appropriations for 1965*, 88th Cong., 2d sess. (April 13, 1964), 3–7; "Flood Sees Command by U.S. Way to Win in South Vietnam," *Wilkes-Barre Record*, April 15, 1964; and "Flood Prods General over Vietnam Course," *Times Leader*, April 14, 1964.

27. McMaster, *Dereliction of Duty*, 104–5, 108–10.

28. Karnow, *Vietnam*, 366–85, chap. 12; and Remini, *House*, 411.

29. House Appropriations Defense Subcommittee, "Southeast Asia Budget Figures," *Hearings on Department of Defense Appropriations for 1966*, 89th Cong., 1st sess. (March 24, 1965), 411–13. Budget request figures were not provided in the original records of the hearings to avoid potential dissent from Congress, watchdog groups, or the American public.

30. McMaster, *Dereliction of Duty*, 312–13, 316–17.

31. Ibid., 20–21; and Laird interview.

32. Remini, *House*, 411.

33. Rooney interview.

34. House Appropriations Defense Subcommittee, "Ordnance," *Hearings on Department of Defense Appropriations for 1966*, 89th Cong., 1st sess. (February 16, 1965), 111–12.

35. House Appropriations Defense Subcommittee, "Navy Ordnance," *Hearings on Department of Defense Supplemental Appropriation for 1966*, 89th Cong., 1st sess. (March 2, 1965), 140.

36. House Appropriations Defense Subcommittee, "Marine Corps Procurement," *Hearings on Department of Defense Supplemental Appropriation for 1966*, 89th Cong., 1st sess. (March 24, 1965), 348.

37. House Appropriations Defense Subcommittee, "Discussion of Vietnam," *Hearings on Department of Defense Appropriation for 1968*, 90th Cong., 1st sess. (March 8, 1967), 415–16.

38. "Flood Says McNamara Outflanked Congress," *Wilkes-Barre Record*, January 7, 1966.

39. House Appropriations Defense Subcommittee, "Discussion of Vietnam," *Hearings on Department of Defense Appropriation for 1968*, 90th Cong., 1st sess. (March 8, 1967), 416–24.

40. Laird interview.

41. McMaster, *Dereliction of Duty*, 412–13.

42. Karnow, *Vietnam*, 511–12; and Kearns, *Lyndon Johnson and the American Dream*, 320–21. In the mid-1990s McNamara wrote that he "still [didn't] know whether [he] quit or was fired" from the Department of Defense. He insisted that he was "not ill" at the time, or "under medical care for stress," but rather "at loggerheads with the President of the United States." He told Johnson "point-blank, that we could not achieve our objective in Vietnam through any reasonable military means, and we therefore should seek a lesser political objective through negotiations." Johnson wasn't "ready to accept that," nor would McNamara "change [his] judgment." Thus McNamara's departure came about as the result of a stalemate. See McNamara, *In Retrospect*, 311–14.

43. House Appropriations Defense Subcommittee, "Cost of Vietnam War," *Hearings on Department of Defense Appropriation for 1969*, 90th Cong., 2d sess. (February 15, 1968), 90–93.

44. House Appropriations Defense Subcommittee, "Commendation of Secretary McNamara," *Hearings on Department of Defense Appropriation for 1969*, 90th Cong., 2d sess. (February 14, 1968), 321.

45. Flood quoted in *Dan Flood: A Retrospective* (see chap. 1, n. 72).

46. Karnow, *Vietnam*, 592–600; Richard M. Nixon, *The Memoirs of Richard M. Nixon* (London: Arrow Books, 1979), 392–97; Henry Kissinger, *White House Years* (Boston: Little, Brown, 1979), 226–38; and Robert Dalleck, *Nixon and Kissinger: Partners in Power* (New York: HarperCollins, 2007), 125–28, 143–44.

47. Karnow, *Vietnam*, 609–12, 623–34; Nixon, *Memoirs*, 445–59, 467–68, 508–15; Kissinger, *White House Years*, 239–71; and Dalleck, *Nixon and Kissinger*, 194–202, 257–64.

48. Daniel J. Flood, "Personal Correspondence: Vietnam Folder, 1967–1969," Flood Collection, KCL. For specific quotation, see Flood to Anna Timlin, Washington, D.C., March 5, 1968; and Flood to John Selecky, April 23, 1968.

49. See Ralph Nader, *Congress Project* (1972), Flood Collection, KCL.

50. "Daniel J. Flood," *Current Biography, 1978*, 133; "Kanarr Firm Gets Contract," *Times Leader*, September 4, 1969; and "Rep. Flood Helped Defense Firm," *Washington Star*, February 20, 1978.

51. Medico interview.

52. "Rep. Flood Helped Defense Firm."

53. Flood quoted in ibid.

54. "Daniel J. Flood," *Current Biography, 1978*, 132; and Crile, "Best Congressman," 63.

55. See McDade interview.

56. Ibid.; interview of James Dyer, clerk and staff director of House Appropriations Committee, Washington, D.C., May 26, 2005; and Clark interview, Washington, D.C., April 20, 2008.

57. Clark interview, April 20, 2008.

58. Karnow, *Vietnam*, 628–70; Nixon, *Memoirs*, 585–86, 704–50, 889; Kissinger, *White House Years*, 433–57, 1301–50, 1471–73; Dalleck, *Nixon and Kissinger*, 466–74, 483–85, 619–20; and Remini, *House*, 420, 431.

59. Flood quoted in Grady, "Flood They Can't Dam," 8.

60. Flood quoted in *Dan Flood: A Retrospective*.

CHAPTER 8

1. Michael Clark quoted in *Dan Flood: A Legend in His Own Time*.

2. "Daniel J. Flood," *Current Biography, 1978*, 133–34.

3. Clark interview, April 2, 2005.

4. See Barry A. Bukatman, MD, to Axel Kleiboemer, Bethesda, Md., October 26, 1979; James L. Foy, MD, "Pretrial Psychiatric Evaluation of Daniel J. Flood," Department of Psychiatry, Georgetown University Hospital, Washington, D.C., October 19, 1979; and Alex Kleiboemer to Marvin Small, MD, Washington, D.C., February 23, 1978, all in Flood Court Files in possession of Robert Kulick, Bear Creek, Pa. (hereafter cited as Flood Court Files). Prior to his 1979 trial, several physicians reviewed Flood's medical history. These evaluations were made available to the prosecution and Axel Kleiboemer, Flood's defense attorney. The records remained in Kleiboemer's Washington office until 1984, when they were sent to Robert Kulick, a Flood assistant. Kulick loaned the court records to the author for use in this book.

5. See Axel Kleiboemer, "Debriefing of Helen Tomascik," May 22, 1978, Flood Court Files; and Sheerin and Makowski interviews.

6. Kleiboemer, "Debriefing of Helen Tomascik"; and FBI interviews of Helen Tomascik, Washington, D.C., May 17, 1978 and November 9, 1978, Flood Court Records.

7. Clark, Makowski, and Sheerin interviews.

8. Clark interview; and FBI interview of Richard Altman, Washington, D.C., May 15, 1978, Flood Court Files.

9. Sheerin interview.

10. Makowski interview, October 11, 2005.

11. "Cresco Recommended Elko for Hegarty's Job as Dapper Dan's Chief Aide in Washington," *Sunday Independent*, March 18, 1978.

12. United States v. Daniel J. Flood, "Testimony of Stephen B. Elko," U.S. District Court, Washington, D.C., January 16, 1979, 2–4; and United States v. Daniel J. Flood, "Testimony of Stephen B. Elko," U.S. District Court, Washington, D.C., January 17, 1979, 175–76, both in Flood Court Files.

13. "Elko Testimony," January 16, 1979, 5. Another anonymous source on Flood's staff claimed that John Cresko, a close friend of the congressman's, "pushed Elko to succeed Hegarty" (see "Cresco Recommended Elko").

14. Clark interview, April 20, 2008; and FBI interview of Helen Tomascik, Washington, D.C., May 12, 1978, FBI Document No. 58-9839. Clark suspects that Elko threatened to expose both Flood's personal battle with alcoholism and the heavy doses of medication he was taking for various physical ailments. Tomascik suggested that Elko, who "talked out of both sides of his mouth," left her with the impression that "something was dirty" in his relationship with Flood.

15. "Elko Testimony," January 16, 1979, 5; and January 17, 1979, 183; and FBI interview of Tomascik, November 9, 1978.

16. "Cresco Recommended Elko."

17. "Elko Testimony," January 16, 1979, 7.

18. Blair Bolles, *How To Get Rich in Washington: Rich Man's Division of the Welfare State* (New York: Norton, 1952), 14–15, 23.

19. See Theodore J. Lowi, *The End of Liberalism* (New York: Norton, 1979). Lowi argues that New Deal liberals were parceling out federal power to a variety of special interests rather than exercising it effectively themselves. They operated on the misconception that out of the clash of special interest groups emerges the common interest. That misguided policy continued through the 1970s. Thus, while direct federal control was asserted in theory, it became more and more attenuated in practice.

20. Robert N. Winter-Berger, *The Washington Pay-Off: An Insider's View of Corruption in Government* (Secaucus, N.J.: Lyle Stuart, 1972), 15–16. The Legislative Reorganization Act of 1946 tried to regulate the activities of lobbyists by requiring them to report to the secretary of the Senate and the clerk of the House of Representatives their contacts with members of Congress, their expenses, and the political contributions they make to the campaign funds of congresspeople. But the lobbyist could easily circumvent the law by making campaign contributions with his client's money, which doesn't have to be reported.

21. Ibid., 17.

22. U.S. Department of Justice, "Daniel J. Flood, U.S. Congressman; Northeastern Training Institute—Bribery," August 11, 1978, FBI Document No. 183-1924-1; see also FBI Document Nos. 183-1924-2 (December 7, 1978); 183-1924-3 (April 11, 1979); and 183-1925-2 (April 28, 1978).

23. U.S. Department of Justice, "Memorandum from J. E. Henehan to Mr. Moore; Daniel J. Flood, U.S. Congressman; Airlie Foundation—Racketeer Influenced and Corrupt Organizations," October 19, 1978, FBI Document No. 58-9839-140. See also Rodney Smith, "Airlie Founder Indicted, Charged With Bribing Two Congressmen," *Washington Star*, July 13, 1979; and Karlyn Barker, "Airlie Director Is Charged with Bribery, Tax Evasion," *Washington Post*, July 13, 1979.

24. See Paul D'Ambrosio, "The Airlie Center—A Contemporary Think-Tank," *Hatchet* (George Washington University newspaper), September 29, 1980; and Stephen J. Lynton, "Airlie's Tranquility Shaken by Charges Against Director," *Washington Post*, October 9, 1979.

25. D'Ambrosio, "The Airlie Center."

26. "Elko Testimony," January 16, 1979, 13–14.

27. Ibid., 17.

28. Ibid., 18–20.

29. Stephen J. Lynton, "'Mustache,' 'Priest' Bribed By Head, Witness Testifies," *Washington Post*, October 4, 1979; and "Elko Testimony," January 16, 1979, 22–39.

30. Lynton, "'Mustache,' 'Priest,'"; and "Elko Testimony," January 16, 1979, 46–52.

31. See "Campaign Finance Law Change Sought," *Times Leader*, February 16, 1978.

32. Elko Testimony," January 16, 1979, 20, 36, 40, 47–48. In 1981 Head was convicted of conspiring to bribe Passman and Flood to obtain lucrative contracts for the Airlie Foundation. Judge Oren R. Lewis of Federal District Court sentenced him to four and a half years in prison. See Eric Pace, "Dr. Murdock Head Dies at 70; Was Jailed in Bribery Scandal," *New York Times*, July 31, 1994.

33. Sheerin interview.

34. Mitchell interview.

35. Kleiboemer, "Debriefing of Leona Yurishin," June 16, 1978, Flood Court Files.

36. Interview of Dr. Francis Michelini, Mechanicsburg, Pa., February 13, 2008.

37. Boldt, "Flood, the Flamboyant," 22.

38. See Donald Riegle with Trevor Armbrister, *O Congress!* (New York: Doubleday, 1972), 92–94.

39. Mitchell interview.

40. Makowski interview, October 11, 2005.

41. Michelini interview.

42. United States v. Daniel J. Flood, "Testimony of William Fred Peters," U.S. District Court, Washington, D.C., January 23, 1979, 8–9, Flood Court Files.

43. Ibid., 9.

44. Ibid., 14; and United States v. Daniel J. Flood, "Testimony of Deryl E. Fleming," U.S. District Court, Washington, D.C., January 19, 1979, 15–16, Flood Court Files.

45. "Fleming Testimony," 3–5.

46. Ibid., 13–14; "Peters Testimony," 12–13; and letter, "Congressman Daniel J. Flood" [i.e., Stephen Elko] to Sidney P. Marland, Jr., commissioner of education, Washington D.C., August 1, 1972. Copy of letter attached to U.S. Department of Justice, "Memorandum to FBI Director from Los Angeles FBI Bureau: Daniel J. Flood, U.S. Congressman; West Coast Trade Schools; Bribery; Perjury," June 23, 1977, FBI Document No. 58-9839-10.

47. "Fleming Testimony," 15, 26; and "Peters Testimony," 14.

48. "Elko Testimony," January 16, 1979, 75–78; and "Elko Testimony," January 18, 1979, 390–91.

49. Letter, "Flood" [i.e., Elko] to Marland, August 1, 1972.

50. "Elko Testimony," January 16, 1979, 80.

51. Ibid., 83, 87–88; and "Elko Testimony," January 18, 1979, 415–16.

52. "Fleming Testimony," 28–29; and "Peters Testimony," 22–24, 80–84.

53. "Elko Testimony," January 16, 1979, 89; "Fleming Testimony," 33; and "Peters Testimony," 26–27.

54. "Elko Testimony," January 16, 1979, 89–91.

55. See U.S. Department of Justice, "Memorandum: Daniel J. Flood, U.S. Congressman; Bribery; Interstate Transportation in Aid of Racketeering; Perjury," May 18, 1977, FBI Document No. 58-9839-2; "Peters Testimony," 31–34, 102–4; and "Fleming Testimony," 39–41.

56. "Elko Testimony," January 16, 1979, 92; and Letter, "Flood" [i.e., Elko] to Marland, August 1, 1972.

CHAPTER 9

1. Wolensky, *Better Than Ever*, 6–9.

2. Flood quoted in Marita Lowman, "Leading the Way Back," *Times Leader*, June 23, 1992, special report: "Agnes Revisited," 47.

3. Atkins Watkin, *The Wyoming Valley Flood of 1936* (Wilkes-Barre, Pa.: Collins Press, 1936), 1–7.

4. Dawn Shurmaitis, "Could It Happen Again?" *Times Leader*, June 23, 1992, special report: "Agnes Revisited," 91.

5. Ibid.; "Kennedy, Lawrence Will Be Asked for Help to Repair Dikes," *Times Leader*, February 14, 1961; "Story Behind the Story on Rover Flood Threat," *Sunday Independent*, February 19, 1961; "U.S. Emergency Funds to Be Used to Restore Wyoming Valley Dikes," *Times Leader*, January 25, 1964; and "Levee-Raising Pact Soon to Be Negotiated," *Wilkes-Barre Record*, February 5, 1964.

6. "Thousands Flee To Higher Ground As Raging River Breaches Dike; Crest To Top 40 Feet," *Times Leader*, June 23, 1972.

7. Wolensky, *Better Than Ever*, 4–5.

8. Michael Clark, "Agnes Stories: It Was One Flood Against Another," *Citizens' Voice*, June 23, 2002, C32; Clark interview, July 5, 2007; and Wolensky, *Better Than Ever*, 6.

9. Clark interview, July 5, 2007.

10. Laird interview.

11. Dyer interview.

12. Clark, "Agnes Stories," C32; and United States v. Daniel J. Flood, "Elko Testimony," January 16, 1979, 95.

13. Clark, "Agnes Stories," C32; "20,000 Flee Flood in Wilkes-Barre," *Scranton Tribune*, June 24, 1972; "Rep. Flood Takes Charge at Disaster Command Site, *Scranton Times*, June 25, 1972; and Lowman, "Leading the Way Back," 47.

14. Lowman, "Leading the Way Back," 47.

15. Crile, "Best Congressman," 62; Gene Coleman, "Evacuation Efforts Continue," *Scranton Times*, June 25, 1972; and Grady, "Flood They Can't Dam," 7.

16. Lieutenant Howard Glad quoted in Crile, "Best Congressman," 62.

17. "Medical Centers Alert To Aid Victims of Flood," *Scranton Times:* June 25, 1972.

18. McKeown interview.

19. Clark, "Agnes Stories," C33; and Crile, "Best Congressman," 62.

20. Clark, "Agnes Stories," C33.

21. Crile, "Best Congressman," 63.

22. Grady, "Flood They Can't Dam," 8.

23. Letter, Edward R. Janjigan, MD, to attorney Louis Feldmann, Kingston, Pa., November 12, 1979, Flood Court Files.

24. Clark, "Agnes Stories," C33.

25. Interview of Pennsylvania state senator Raphael Musto, Harrisburg, Pa., January 30, 2008.

26. Interview of James Kozemchak, Wilkes-Barre, Pa., September 13, 2005.

27. Wright, Rooney, Michel, and McDade interviews.

28. Crile, "Best Congressman," 63; and Wolensky, *Better Than Ever*, 9.

29. Crile, "Best Congressman," 63.

30. Laird interview.

31. Interview of Harold Rosenn, Wilkes-Barre, Pa., May 28, 2005.

32. Wolensky, *Better Than Ever*, 17–19.

33. Ibid., 19.

34. Judge Max Rosenn quoted in Marita Lowman, "Leading the Way Back," 41; and Wolensky, *Better Than Ever*, 21.

35. Senator Hugh Scott quoted in Marita Lowman, "Leading the Way Back," 41; and Wolensky, *Better Than Ever*, 24.

36. Wolensky, *Better Than Ever*, 25.

37. See "Model City Extension to All of Wilkes-Barre Proposed by Scott," *Times Leader*, July 8, 1972. Prior to the Agnes disaster, only Wilkes-Barre's Heights and Iron Triangle sections were included in the Model Cities program.

38. Ibid.

39. Wolensky, *Better Than Ever*, 25–26.

40. Ibid., 26–27, 34.

41. Frank Carlucci quoted in ibid., 28.

42. David Boldt, "Flood, the Flamboyant," 21.

43. Wolensky, *Better Than Ever*, 36–40; and Claire Schecter, "Money Changed Everything," *Times Leader*, June 23, 1992, special report: "Agnes Revisited," 64.

44. Carlucci interview.

45. Michelini interview.

46. Rosenn interview, May 28, 2005.

47. Wolensky, *Better Than Ever*, 40–42.

48. Carlucci interview.

49. Ibid.

50. Dawn Shurmaitis, "One Way To Rebuild: Move the Downtown," *Times Leader*, June 23, 1992, special report: "Agnes Revisited," 90.

51. Carlucci interview.

52. Ibid.

53. Letter, Janjigan to Feldmann, November 12, 1979.

54. Carlucci interview.

55. FBI Interview of Fred Peters, Los Angeles, Calif., April 19, 1978, Flood Court Files.

56. "Peters Testimony," January 23, 1979, 47–48, 115–16; and U.S. Department of Justice, "Memorandum to FBI Director from FBI Los Angeles Bureau: Daniel J. Flood, U.S. Congressman; Sterling-Homex; Bribery," May 13, 1978, FBI Document No. 58-9839-1.

57. "Peters Testimony," 39–40, 112–13.

58. Ibid., 52, 118–21.

59. See "Elko Testimony," January 16, 1979, 101–4; and letter, "Congressman Daniel J. Flood" [i.e., Stephen Elko] to Sidney P. Marland, Jr., commissioner of Education, Washington D.C., August 1, 1972. Copy of letter attached to U.S. Department of Justice, "Memorandum to FBI Director from Los Angeles FBI Bureau: Daniel J. Flood, U.S. Congressman; West Coast Trade Schools; Bribery; Perjury," June 23, 1977, FBI Document No. 58-9839-10.

60. Sidney Marland quoted in letter, "Congressman Daniel J. Flood" [i.e., Stephen Elko] to Sidney P. Marland, Jr., commissioner of education, Washington D.C., August 19, 1972. Copy of letter attached to U.S. Department of Justice, "Memorandum to FBI Director from Los Angeles FBI Bureau: Daniel J. Flood, U.S. Congressman; West Coast Trade Schools; Bribery; Perjury," June 23, 1977, FBI Document No. 58-9839-10.

61. Ibid.

62. "Elko Testimony," January 16, 1979, 106–8; and "Fleming Testimony," 43–46.

63. "Fleming Testimony," 53–55; and "Lobbyist Claims $1,000 Given to Flood in Hotel," *Times Leader*, February 16, 1978.

64. United States v. Stephen B. Elko, "Testimony of Daniel J. Flood," U.S. District Court, Los Angeles, Calif., October 11, 1977, 7; U.S. Department of Justice, "Memorandum to Director of FBI: Daniel J. Flood, Perjury," Washington, D.C., November 16, 1978, FBI Document No. 58-9839-155; and "Lobbyist Claims $1,000 Given to Flood in Hotel."

65. "Peters Testimony," 58. Peters was later placed on trial in federal court in Los Angeles and convicted of conspiracy, bribery, and fraud. Though he was sentenced to five years in prison, the trade school executive agreed to provide the FBI with information on Elko, Fleming, and Flood in return for immunity from further prosecution; his sentence was reduced to two years. See "Peters Testimony," 61–62, 138.

66. Flood quoted in *Dan Flood: A Retrospective.*

CHAPTER 10

1. See letter, Daniel J. Flood to H. R. Parfitt, governor of the Panama Canal Zone, Washington, D.C., June 21, 1976, KCL. Flood tells Parfitt that he "received [his] first inspiration on the problems of the Panama Canal from former President Theodore Roosevelt during his occasional visits to [his] grandfather's winter home."

2. Flood quoted in "Whose Canal Is It?" *60 Minutes Broadcast*, CBS-TV, July 7, 1974.

3. "Panama Solons Call Flood 'Public Enemy'"; and "Flood Called Panama Foe."

4. See U.S. Department of State, "Hay-Bunau-Varilla Treaty," November 18, 1903, National Archives, Washington, D.C. The best history of the Panama Canal is McCullough's *Path Between the Seas*. Other histories include: Charles Francis Adams, *The Panama Canal Zone* (Boston: Massachusetts Historical Society, 1911); Philippe Bunau-Varilla, *Panama: The Creation, Destruction, and Resurrection* (New York: Robert M. McBride, 1920); Ian Cameron, *The Impossible Dream: The Building of the Panama Canal* (New York: William Morrow, 1972); Captain Miles P. DuVal, Jr., *Cadiz to Cathay: The Story of the Long Struggle for A Waterway Across the American Isthmus* (London: Oxford University Press, 1940); Charles H. Forbes-Lindsay, *Panama: The Isthmus and the Canal* (Philadelphia: J. C. Winston, 1906); Harding, *Untold Story of Panama*; Walter LaFeber, *The Panama Canal: The Crisis in Historical Perspective* (New York: Oxford University Press, 1989); and Major, *Prize Possession.*

5. Edmund Morris, *Theodore Rex* (New York: Random House, 2001), 183–93; and Bailey, *Diplomatic History*, 500, 505–6.

6. Bailey, *Diplomatic History*, 443–44, 500–503.

7. Ibid., 489–97; Morris, *Theodore Rex*, 270–306; and McCullough, *Path Between Seas*, 351–57, 379–86.

8. The military significance of the Panama Canal became clear during World War II and the Korean conflict when the U.S. Navy was able to move vessels through the canal in half the

time it would have taken to sail around the tip of South America en route to the Atlantic or Pacific Ocean. See "American Enterprise Institute Report, No. 3."

9. Ryan, "Canal Diplomacy and Interests," 45–46.

10. Harding, *Untold Story of Panama*, 116–18.

11. "Rep. Flood Calls for Abolishment of Panama Corporation"; and "PRR Ruckus Pops."

12. Miles P. DuVal, Jr., "Biographical Record," KCL; and Murphy, "Introduction of Captain DuVal."

13. Interviews of Makowski, February 2, 2005; Sheerin; Michael Clark, April 2, 2005; and Mitchell.

14. Among the most complimentary letters are: Leigh Stevenson, Ft. Amador, Canal Zone, July 27, 1955; Louis Schmidt, Canal Zone, April 19, 1957; Norman J. Padelford, Boston, Mass., April 28, 1958; and Earl Harding, Washington, D.C., October 9, 1958, all in KCL.

15. Bess, "Panama Danger Zone."

16. "Panama Solons Call Flood 'Public Enemy'"; and "Flood Called Panama Foe."

17. Flood quoted in Lawrence, "'America' Is a Dirty Word"; see also Horner, "Flood Blasts Idea"; and Ford, "Flood Urges Monroe Barrier."

18. Bailey, *Diplomatic History*, 861.

19. Flood quoted in "Flood Says Commies Seek Control of Canal," *Times Leader*, January 13, 1960; and "Canal Zone Decree Urged," *Wilkes-Barre Record*, January 14, 1960.

20. See Major, *Prize Possession*, 333; and *Congressional Record*, February 9, 1960. On February 9, 1960, the House of Representatives passed the Gross Amendment, prohibiting the use of any appropriated funds, under the Department of Commerce Appropriations bill, "for the purpose of displaying the flag of Panama in the Canal Zone." It was a moot point since the Senate did not pass the measure.

21. Flood quoted in Major, *Prize Possession*, 332.

22. *Congressional Record*, May 5, 1964.

23. Ibid.

24. John McKelway, "The Rambler," *Washington Evening Star*, April 18, 1963.

25. Letter, anonymous to congressman Daniel J. Flood, Canal Zone, February 24 1964, Panama Canal Correspondence, 1960–1964, KCL.

26. "Students Hoist 'Old Glory' on Balboa High School Staff," *Panama American*, January 7, 1964.

27. See "Panama Ends Ties to U.S. Over Riot," *New York Times*, January 10, 1964.

28. Ibid.; and William J. Jorden, *Panama Odyssey* (Austin: University of Texas Press, 1984), 76.

29. Jorden, *Panama Odyssey*, 87.

30. Flood quoted in *Congressional Record*, March 9, 1964.

31. Flood quoted in letter to Edwin D. Canham, *Christian Science Monitor* editor, Washington D.C., March 31, 1964; see also letter, Flood to *Washington Post* editor, Washington D.C., March 23, 1964, both in Panama Canal Correspondence, 1960–1964, KCL.

32. Gallup release, February 12, 1964, Panama Canal Correspondence, 1960–1964, KCL.

33. See Rowland Evans and Robert Novak, "Inside Report: A Plan for Panama," *Washington Post*, January 15, 1964. Evans and Novak wrote nearly a dozen columns on the issue of Panama during the period January 1964 to December 1967.

34. See White House press release, December 18, 1964, Panama Canal Correspondence, 1960–1964, KCL.

35. Flood quoted in *Congressional Record*, April 1, 1965; and "Flood Claims Johnson Hides Canal Issues," *Wilkes-Barre Record*, April 2, 1965.

36. Bailey, *Diplomatic History*, 895; and "Panama Finds Defense Terms of New Treaty Extremely Offensive," *Chicago Tribune*, July 7, 1967.

37. Flood quoted in "A Forward Looking Treaty," *Boston Globe*, June 28, 1967.

38. Letter, Flood to Senator Strom Thurmond, Washington, D.C., May 1, 1967, Panama Canal Correspondence, 1967, KCL. Thurmond agreed to Flood's request. See letter, Thurmond to Flood, Washington, D.C., May 20, 1967, Panama Canal Correspondence, 1967, KCL.

39. Letter, Flood to House colleagues, Washington D.C., July 19, 1967, Panama Canal Correspondence, 1967, KCL. By November 1967 Flood had secured resolutions from 150 members of the House of Representatives.

40. Bailey, *Diplomatic History*, 895; and Murray B. Woldman, *The United States and the Panama Canal: A New Beginning?* (Washington, D.C.: Members of Congress for Peace Through Law, 1977), 3.

41. Clark interview, June 27, 2008.

42. Ryan, "Canal Diplomacy and U.S. Interests," 44.

43. Flood quoted in "U.S. Agrees to Surrender Sovereignty of Panama Canal," *Washington Post*, January 10, 1974; and "Press Release: January 10, 1974," Flood Papers, KCL.

44. Flood quoted in "Whose Canal Is It?" *60 Minutes*.

45. See "Panama Correspondence, 1974–1976," Flood Collection, KCL. For the period July 1974 to June 1975, Flood received more than 280 letters supporting his position on Panama, mostly from American citizens in California, New York, Texas, and the Canal Zone.

46. Wendell Rawls, Jr., "Rep. Flood Had Secret Ties to Haiti While Pushing U.S. Aid to Duvalier," *New York Times*, February 5, 1978; and "Flood An Agent for Haiti?" *Philadelphia Bulletin*, February 5, 1978.

47. U.S. Department of Justice, "Daniel J. Flood, U.S. Congressman; Racketeer; Influenced and Corrupt Organizations," February 21, 1978, FBI Document No. 183-1566-12; see also Letter, Nick F. Stames to John M. Dowd, Washington, D.C., June 15, 1978, FBI Investigation of Daniel J. Flood/U.S. Department of Justice, FBI Document No. 183-1566-13.

48. Rawls, "Flood Had Secret Ties to Haiti."

49. Ibid. Among the members of Congress who received Flood's letters were: Rep. Thomas E. Morgan (D-Pa.), chair of the House Committee on Foreign Affairs; Rep. Otto Passman (D-La.); Senator Daniel K. Inouye (D-Hawaii); and Senator William Fulbright (D-Ark.).

50. Ibid.

51. U.S. Department of Justice, "Daniel J. Flood, U.S. Congressman; Racketeer; Influenced and Corrupt Organizations"; see also FBI Document Nos: 183-1566-34 (August 31, 1979); 183-1626-3 (March 22, 1978); 183-1626-4 (February 7, 1978); and 183-1566-12 (April 15, 1978).

52. FBI Document Nos 183-1566-34 (August 31, 1979); and 183-1626-3; see also "Haiti Questions Inundate Flood," *New York Herald Journal*, February 6, 1978.

53. "Flood Attacks Kissinger Giveaway of Panama Canal," *Sunday Independent*, December 8, 1974; and Clark interview, July 5, 2007.

54. Clark interview, July 5, 2007.

55. Ibid.

56. See Rep. Matthew Rinaldo (R-N.J.) quoted in Robert S. Allen, Field Newspaper Service press release (Chicago), April 19, 1975, "Panama Canal Papers," Flood Collection, KCL. Similar sentiments were voiced by Rep. William Dickinson (R-Ala.), a senior member of the powerful House Armed Services Committee; Rep. Leonor Sullivan (D-Mo.), chair of the Merchant Marine Committee; Senator John McClellan (D-Ark.), chair of the Senate Appropriations Committee; Strom Thurmond (R-S.C.), the senior Republican on the Senate Armed Services Committee; and Senator Jesse Helms (R-N.C.). See Allen, Field Newspaper Syndicate, January 30, 1975, March 8, 1975. By April 1975 there were thirty-seven senators publicly on record against the U.S. surrender of the canal, three more than the thirty-four constitutionally required to reject a new treaty. See Allen, Field News Service, April 19, 1975.

57. Flood quoted in Allen, press release, May 6, 1975, KCL.

58. Jordan, *Panama Odyssey*, 285.

59. Rep. Daniel J. Flood, "Projected Surrender of U.S. Canal Zone: A Call for A National Crusade," *Vital Speeches of the Day*, August 1, 1975, 635–38.

60. Ryan, "Canal Diplomacy and U.S. Interests," 53.

61. Ford interview.

62. Ronald Reagan quoted in Gerald R. Ford, *A Time To Heal* (New York: Harper and Row, 1979), 374.

63. President Gerald Ford quoted in Ryan, "Canal Diplomacy and U.S. Interests," 44.

64. Ibid.

65. Robert D. Schulzinger, "The Decline of Détente," in *Gerald R. Ford and the Politics of Post-Watergate America*, ed. Bernard J. Firestone and Alexej Ugrinsky (Westport, Conn.: Greenwood Press, 1993), 2:410; and Douglas Brinkley, *Gerald R. Ford* (New York: Henry R. Holt, 2007), 112.

66. Schulzinger, "The Decline of Détente," 411; and Brinkley, *Ford*, 129.

67. See Allen, press releases, March 18, April 22, May 20, June 12, July 29, October 28, 1976. Kissinger enjoyed significant support on the Senate Foreign Relations Committee for a new treaty. The list of supporters included such influential senators as: George McGovern (D-S.D.); Gale McGee (D-Wyo.); Hubert Humphrey (D-Minn.); Dick Clark (D-Iowa); Frank Church (D-Idaho); Clifford Case (R-N.Y.); Jacob Javits (R-N.Y.); and Charles Percy (R-Ill.).

68. For campaign promise, see Jimmy Carter quoted in Ryan, "Canal Diplomacy and U.S. Interests," 53; and Jimmy Carter, *Keeping Faith: Memoirs of a President* (1982; repr., New York: Bantam Books, 1983), 154–55. For fear of growing Communist influence in Latin America, see Jimmy Carter, "Address to Organization of American States Council Outlining U.S. Policy Toward Latin America," *New York Times*, April 15, 1977.

69. Carter, *Keeping Faith*, 155; and Bailey, *Diplomatic History*, 963.

70. Letter, Dan Flood to president Jimmy Carter, Washington, D.C., January 27, 1977, "Panama Canal Papers," Flood Collection, KCL.

71. Carter, *Keeping Faith*, 158.

72. Ibid., 159–62; Major, *Prize Possession*, 341–57; and Jorden, *Panama Odyssey*, 413.

73. United States Supreme Court, "Complaint, Jesse A. Helms, James A. McClure, Strom Thurmond, Orrin G. Hatch and Daniel J. Flood, Plaintiffs v. Cyrus R. Vance and James E. Carter, Jr., Defendants," No. 75, October 13, 1977, "Panama Canal Papers," Flood Collection, KCL.

74. Ibid., 2–3. Flood's suit was reinforced by fifty-one other House members who, on October 3, 1977, filed a similar action in the District Court for the District of Columbia.

75. See interview of Rep. Daniel J. Flood by Richard F. Fenno, Jr., Washington, D.C., May 29, 1959, Center for Legislative Archives, National Archives and Records Administration, Washington, D.C.

76. U.S. House of Representatives, "Concurrent Resolution 430," December 1, 1977, 95th Cong., 1st sess., "Panama Canal Papers," Flood Collection, KCL.

77. Carter, *Keeping Faith*, 160–67.

78. Lou Rauscher, "Is White House Out to 'Get' Dan Flood?" *Sunday Independent*, November 6, 1977.

79. Edward Walsh, "Carter Takes Case For Canal Treaties to the U.S. Public," *Washington Post*, February 2, 1978; and Peter G. Bourne, *Jimmy Carter: A Comprehensive Biography from Plains to Postpresidency* (New York: Scribner, 1997), 393.

80. Bailey, *Diplomatic History*, 964.

81. Carter, *Keeping Faith*, 160.

82. Ibid., 181–82; and Barbara Sinclair, *Majority Leadership in the U.S. House* (Baltimore: Johns Hopkins University Press, 1983), 215–19.

83. Carter, *Keeping Faith*, 183; and Sinclair, *Majority Leadership*, 223–24.

84. Wright interview.

85. McDade interview.

86. Twenty senators who voted in favor of ratifying the first treaty in 1978 were up for reelection later that year. Of that number, six did not run, seven were defeated, and another seven managed to win reelection. Two years later, in 1980, when another third of the senators were up for reelection, eleven others who supported the treaties were defeated. See Carter, *Keeping Faith*, 184. Journalist Adam Clymer contends that Carter's success in Panama had a much larger impact on American political culture by giving Ronald Reagan a slogan that kept his 1976 candidacy alive and positioned him to win in 1980, helping elect conservative senators who made a Republican majority, and fueling the overall growth of conservatism. See Clymer, *Drawing the Line at the Big Red Ditch: The Panama Canal Treaties and the Rise of the Right* (Lawrence: University of Kansas Press, 2008).

87. See Remini, *House*, 453–54; Bourne, *Jimmy Carter*, 394; and Jerel A. Rosati, *The Carter Administration's Quest for Global Community* (Charleston: University of South Carolina Press, 1987).

88. To determine if there was any connection between the Justice Department's investigation and the Carter administration, whose efforts on the Panama Canal treaties had been frustrated repeatedly by Flood, I made several attempts to contact former president Jimmy Carter for an interview. After six month's time, Mr. Carter's press secretary finally informed me that the former president's "many international activities make it impossible to add any further commitments to his schedule" (see letter, Deanna L. Congileo to William Kashatus, Atlanta, Ga., May 8, 2007).

CHAPTER 11

1. See Arthur M. Schlesinger, Jr., *The Imperial Presidency* (Boston: Houghton Mifflin, 1973). Flood was not an enthusiastic supporter of president Richard Nixon. Still, he was careful not to criticize Nixon in public, probably in deference to the high regard he held for the presidency itself. Just three months before Nixon resigned from office in disgrace, Flood said that he would "support him when he acts for the best interests of the country" and would "fight him" when he "feels that he impinges on what is not in the best interests of the country" (see Flood quoted in "Flood Has Not Formed Opinion on Watergate," *Times Leader*, May 13, 1974).

2. Remini, *House*, 442–43; and Shelley Ross, *Fall From Grace: Sex, Scandal, and Corruption in American Politics from 1702 to the Present* (New York: Ballantine Books, 1988), 237–39.

3. Remini, *House*, 447–48; Ross, *Fall From Grace*, 235, 241; and David E. Rosenbaum, "Latest Scandal Shocks and Depresses Congressmen," *New York Times*, February 5, 1980.

4. Remini, *House*, 448; and Ross, *Fall From Grace*, 236–37. Hanna pleaded guilty to one count of conspiracy to defraud the government and served one year of a thirty-month sentence.

5. David R. Obey, *Raising Hell for Justice: The Washington Battles of a Heartland Progressive* (Madison: University of Wisconsin Press, 2007), 135–36.

6. Jack Anderson, "Flood and Medico," *Washington Post*, April 1, 1970. According to Anderson, Medico Industries "obtained at least 11.4 million in Army contracts alone, almost all from the ammunition agency in Joliet, Illinois," between 1967 and 1970.

7. Jack Anderson, "Flood's Fiscal Principles," *Washington Post*, November 9, 1970. Another of Anderson's columns charged Flood with forcing Capitol Hill garage attendants to babysit his pet terrier, Cocoa, during working hours and "at taxpayer's expense."

8. Anderson, "Flood and Medico."

9. See U.S. Senate, "Investigation of Improper Activities in the Labor or Management Field," Hearings Before the Select Committee on Improper Activities in the Labor or Management Field, 85th Cong., 2d sess., pursuant to Senate Resolution 74 and 221, 85th Cong., Part 32, June 30, July 1, 2, and 3, 1958, Washington D.C., 1958.

10. See U.S. Senate, "Organized Crime and Illicit Traffic in Narcotics, Hearings Before the Permanent Subcommittee on Investigations of the Committee on Government Operations," 88th Cong., 1st sess., pursuant to Senate Resolution 278, 88th Cong., Part 3, October 29, 1963; July 28, 29, and 30, 1964; Part 4, July 30, 1964; and Part 5, August 4 and 5, 1964, Washington D.C. For more information on McClellan's investigation of organized crime, see: Senator John L. McClellan, *Crime Without Punishment* (New York: Duell, Storn and Pearce, 1962); and manuscript, "Organized Crime Investigation, 1963–64," Papers of Senator John L. McClellan. Special Collections. Riley-Hickingbotham Library, Ouachita Baptist University, Arkadelphia, Ark.

11. See U.S. Department of Justice, "Memorandum: Daniel J. Flood, U.S. Congressman; Medico Industries, Inc.; Racketeer Influenced and Corrupt Organizations." See also FBI Document Nos. 183-1709-1, 183-1709-4, 183-1709-5; and "Rep. Flood Helped Defense Firm," *Washington Star*, February 20, 1978.

12. "The Mafia in Luzerne County—Who Are They?" *Wyoming Valley (Pa.) Observer*, October 30–November 12, 1969. The exposé identifies Dominick Alaimo, Russell J. Bufalino, William Medico, James Osticco, and Santo Volpe as members of Luzerne County's underworld.

13. "Flood's Voting Record Mixed on Campaign Financing," *Times Leader*, October 28, 1978.

14. See U.S. Department of Justice, "Memorandum: Daniel J. Flood, U.S. Congressman; Campaign Financing and Election Fraud," June 8, 1978, FBI Document No. 58-9839-125; and U.S. Department of Justice, "Memorandum: Daniel J. Flood, U.S. Congressman; Campaign Financing and Election Fraud," August 21, 1978, FBI Document No. 183-1905-1.

15. "Elko Testimony," January 17, 1979, 120–40; and U.S. Department of Justice, "Memorandum: Daniel J. Flood; Gateway Housing Corporation, Hazleton, PA," March 30, 1978, FBI Document No. 183-1626.

16. "Elko Testimony," January 17, 1979, 141–61; United States v. Leib Pinter, "Government's Sentencing Memorandum," U.S. District Court, New York, N.Y., June 21, 1978, 7–8; Arnold H. Lubasch, "Rabbi Who Said He Bribed Flood Gets Two Years and $17,000 Fine," *New York Times*, June 23, 1978; and "Elko Says Flood Expected $50,000 From Law Firm for Pushing Grant for Hahnemann," *Times Leader*, March 9, 1978.

17. "Flood Aiding Medical Unit Complex Vital to Health Care of Region," *Wilkes-Barre Record*, September 24, 1971; and "Flood Backs MD School; Wilkes Is Joined By Hahnemann in 6-Year Plan," *Beacon* (Wilkes College newspaper), September 30, 1971.

18. "Wilkes Plans Revolutionary Program to Produce Medical Doctors in Six Years," *Wyoming Valley Observer*, September 16–25, 1971. The Wilkes-Hahnemann program lasted for eleven years and produced more than three hundred primary care physicians, many of whom returned to the Wyoming Valley to practice. See "At Wilkes, Hahnemann Out, Temple's In," *Sunday Independent*, July 25, 1982. After a six-year hiatus, Hahnemann and Wilkes resumed the partnership with a new emphasis on producing specialists. The partnership continues today, but it is an eight-year program with students spending four years at Wilkes and four at Hahnemann. See interview of Dr. Ralph Rozelle, Wilkes-Barre, Pa., February 20, 2008.

19. Michelini interview.

20. Rozelle interview.

21. "Closed-Circuit TV to Tie Wilkes with Hahnemann," *Times Leader*, September 7, 1976.

22. Rozelle interview.

23. Clark interview, April 14, 2008.

24. Naomi Rogers, *An Alternative Path: The Making and Remaking of Hahnemann Medical College and Hospital of Philadelphia* (New Brunswick, N.J.: Rutgers University Press, 1998), 240–42.

25. Ibid., 242–43.

26. See William Kelly, "Catherwood Foundation, Cuban Aid Relief, and the Philadelphia CIA Operation," *Education Forum*, October 7, 2007, http://www.educationforum.ipbhost.com/. In Philadelphia, the Catherwood Foundation established the Cuban Aid Relief (CAR) "to provide assistance to Cuban exiles with no connection with the deposed Batista regime, and to make as wide use as possible for the professional men, artists and businessmen who fled the Castro forces." According to Kelly, in 1961 the directors of the CAR were "Cummins Catherwood, former U.S. Ambassador to Cuba Arthur Gardner, E. Wharton Shober of ATEK Corporation, and Enrique Menocal, a Cuban national." At the time, Shober was director of the ATEK Corporation, which sold printing machinery and provided financial services to anti-Communist publishers in Latin and Central America. For his work with ATEK, Shober in 1963 received the President's "E" Award from assistant secretary of commerce Franklin D. Roosevelt, Jr., for excellence in export, though, according to Kelly, "it more likely was for espionage." When Shober left ATEK he became president of Hahnemann Hospital in Philadelphia, replacing Dr. Charles Cameron, a cancer specialist, who had received a four-hundred-thousand-dollar research grant from U.S. Army Intelligence. Kelly writes that prior to Hahnemann, "every single business venture Shober was involved in failed, yet he simultaneously amassed a fortune and decided to turn his attention to philanthropy," and that he "actually took the job at Hahnemann without pay."

27. Rogers, *An Alternative Path*, 242.

28. Michelini interview; and Karl Abraham, "Hahnemann to Honor General Somoza Despite Student, Faculty Protests," *Philadelphia Bulletin*, June 7, 1972.

29. Rogers, *An Alternative Path*, 246.

30. See Martin Tolchin, "Two Pennsylvania Politicians: One Behind the Scenes and the Other at Center Stage: Joshua Eilberg," *New York Times*, January 31, 1978.

31. Rogers, *An Alternative Path*, 247–48.

32. William C. Kashatus, MD, interview, February 7, 2005.

33. See Anthony Marro, "Evidence on Eilberg Is Reportedly Given to a 2d U.S. Inquiry," *New York Times*, January 19, 1978; and Rogers, *An Alternative Path*, 267.

34. See "United States v. John P. Dixon," United States Court of Appeals, Third Circuit. No. 80-2289, April 23, 1981, 464A; "Dapper Dan's Toughest Scene"; and Rogers, *An Alternative Path*, 267. The Community Services Administration was a successor to the Johnson administration's Office of Economy Opportunity.

35. Rozelle interview.

36. William C. Kashatus, MD, interview, March 3, 2005.

37. "United States v. John P. Dixon," 471A. Flood's relationship with the Dixon brothers dated to the late 1960s, when companies operated by them obtained a total of fourteen million dollars in federal assistance to put out mine fires in the congressman's district. See Nicholas M. Horrock, "Contractors' Names Cited in Flood Case," *New York Times*, February 19, 1978.

38. Ibid., 813A.

39. Ibid., 814A.

40. Ibid., 813A–818A.

41. Ibid., 846A–847A.

42. Ibid., 877A.

43. Ibid., 594A.

44. Ibid., 590A–592A; see also Ellen Karasik, "How Shober Lost Out at Hahnemann," *Philadelphia Inquirer*, June 27, 1977.

45. Michel interview.

46. Rooney interview.

47. Aaron Epstein and Ray Holton, "Flood and the Ethics Panel: Life in a Glass House," *Philadelphia Inquirer*, February 15, 1978.

48. Phil Gailey and Edward T. Pound, "Ethics Panel Ignored Data About Flood," *Washington Star*, February 16, 1978.

49. Steve Elko quoted in ibid.; Elko made a similar statement to the FBI after his indictment by a federal grand jury in Los Angeles on charges of conspiring to obtain bribes to gain accreditation for the West Coast Trade School. See Elko quoted in "An Aide Aids: Congressman Flood Is Indicted," *Time*, September 18, 1978.

50. "Former Flood Aide Admits Burning Records," *Syracuse (N.Y.) Herald-Journal*, January 18, 1979.

51. U.S. Department of Justice, "Memorandum: Daniel J. Flood, U.S. Congressman; Bribery, Perjury, Conspiracy," September 1, 1978, FBI Document No. 58-9839-139.

52. U.S. Department of Justice, "Memorandum: Stephen Elko; Patricia Brislin; Bribery, Perjury, Conspiracy," June 9, 1977, FBI Document No. 58-9839-01.

53. "Elko Says Philip Medico Arranged $10,000 Consulting Job for Him," *Times Leader*, March 10, 1978; "Elko Paid $1,000 Monthly While Adviser to Chamber," *Wilkes-Barre Record*, March 10, 1978; and John Anderson, "Medico Records Are Subpoenaed," *Times Leader*, March 22, 1978.

54. U.S. Department of Justice, "Memorandum: Daniel J. Flood, U.S. Congressman; Bribery, Perjury, Conspiracy."

55. See Robert Fowler, "Marston Accused of Politics," *Philadelphia Inquirer*, February 13, 1978; and Senator Richard S. Schweiker, "The Marston Affair Calls for a Probe," *Philadelphia Inquirer*, February 13, 1978. Marston's reputation as one of the most effective prosecutors of political corruption in Pennsylvania came from his success at obtaining the convictions of several county and state politicians.

56. Nicholas M. Horrocks, "Former Aide Charges Rep. Flood Sold His Influence for $100,000," *New York Times*, January 28, 1978; "'Leak' to Eilberg Links Elko, Marston," *Chicago Tribune*, February 2, 1978; and Marro, "Evidence on Eilberg Given to 2d U.S. Inquiry."

57. "Aide to Flood Points Finger," *New York Herald Journal*, January 27, 1978; and George Larner, Jr., "Elko Is Subpoenaed for Testimony at a Closed Hearing," *Washington Post*, March 9, 1978. The sentencing took place on January 9, 1978. On March 12, 1978, Elko and Brislin were married in Las Vegas, Nevada. Five days later they began serving their prison sentences. See "Former Aide to Flood Is Married," *New York Times*, March 13, 1978.

58. Stephen Elko, "Affidavit Given to David R. Hinden, Assistant U.S. Attorney," U.S. District Court, Los Angeles, December 6, 1977, Flood Court Files; see also: "Dapper Dan's Toughest Scene"; Horrock, "Former Aide Charges Flood"; "Aide to Flood Points Finger"; and Marro, "Evidence on Eilberg Given to 2d U.S. Inquiry."

59. Wendell Rawls, Jr., "Republicans Call on Ethics Panel for Inquiry on Flood and Eilberg," *New York Times*, February 10, 1978; "House Probe Asked of Eilberg, Flood," *Philadelphia Bulletin*, February 17, 1978; Marc Schogal, "Trouble Is a New Star in Flood's Power Play," *Boston Globe*, February 19, 1978; "FBI, Others Probe Firing of Marston," *Scranton Times*, February 4, 1978; and Marro, "Evidence on Eilberg Given to 2d U.S. Inquiry."

60. President Carter, when asked about the federal investigation of Eilberg and Flood at a January 12, 1978, press conference, stated that he was "not familiar with it" and denied that there was any pressure to remove Marston. But a week later, Carter admitted in a letter to the Justice Department that Eilberg's name had surfaced as the subject of an investigation and that he had knowledge of it. During the last week of January, Carter administration officials stated that U.S. attorney Griffin Bell had told the president of his decision to remove Marston *before* Eilberg's November 4, 1977 request. See Marro, "Evidence on Eilberg is Given to 2d U.S. Inquiry."

61. See Rawls, "Republicans Call on Ethics Panel"; and "House Probe Asked of Eilberg and Flood." The request from the Republican leaders to the House Ethics Committee was made in a letter to chair John Flynt (D-Ga.) from congressmen John Rodes of Arizona, House minority leader; John Anderson of Illinois, the Republican Conference chair; Samuel L. Devine of Ohio, the Republican Conference vice chair; and Bill Frenzel, the Research Committee chair.

62. Aaron Epstein and Ray Holton, "Flood and the Ethics Panel: Life in a Glass House," *Philadelphia Inquirer*, February 15, 1978.

63. Edward T. Pound and Ron Sarro, "After Long Delay, Probe of Flood, Eilberg Gears Up," *Washington Star*, May 26, 1978.

64. Ibid.; and Joseph Nocera, "No Flood Probe: House Panel Won't Investigate Possible Wrongdoing by Lawmaker," *Allentown (Pa.) Morning Call*, February 16, 1978.

65. Pound and Sarro, "After Long Delay, Probe of Flood, Eilberg Gears Up." The lack of activity on a House Ethics investigation of Flood and Eilberg prompted a second letter from House GOP leaders on May 24, 1978. In addition, public interest groups like Common Cause were pressing for a House investigation of Flood and Eilberg. David Cohen, president of the watchdog group, insisted, "There is enough public evidence to warrant a Congressional investigation of the two lawmakers, regardless of a Justice Department probe" (see Cohen quoted in "Law Change Help Sought," *Times Leader*, February 16, 1978).

66. Pound and Sarro, "After Long Delay, Probe of Flood, Eilberg Gears Up"; and "Aide to Rep. Flood Starts Prison Sentence," *New York Times*, March 19, 1978.

67. "Ethics Committee Appoints Counsel for Flood Case," *Washington Post*, June 3, 1978.

68. The Racketeer Influenced and Corrupt Organizations Act (commonly referred to as RICO Act or RICO) is a U.S. federal law that provides for extended penalties for criminal acts performed as part of an ongoing criminal organization. RICO was enacted by section 901(a) of the Organized Crime Control Act of 1970 (Pub.L. 91-452, 84 Stat. 922, enacted October 15, 1970). RICO is codified as Chapter 96 of Title 18 of the United States Code, 18 U.S.C. § 1961–1968. It was intended to make it easier to prosecute organized crime figures, but has been applied in several other cases as well.

69. See U.S. Department of Justice, "Memorandum: Daniel J. Flood; Bribery, Conspiracy and Obstruction of Justice," March 28, 1978, FBI Document No. 183-HQ-1566; and Nicholas M. Horrock, "Flood Investigation Is Widened," *New York Times*, February 26, 1978.

70. U.S. Justice Department, "Memorandum: Daniel J. Flood Investigation," February 28, 1978, FBI Document No. 58-9839-83.

71. See U.S. District Court for the Central District of California, "Daniel J. Flood, Defendant; Indictment for Perjury," 18 U.S.C. 1623, March 1978, Flood Court Files; and "Perjury Laid to Rep. Flood," *Washington Post*, September 6, 1978.

72. Flood quoted in "Congressman Flood Is Indicted," *Time*, September 18, 1978; "Rep. Flood Arraigned in Perjury Case," *New York Times*, September 12, 1978; and "Congressman Flood Denies All Charges," *Syracuse Herald-Journal*, September 6, 1978.

73. U.S. District Court for the District of Columbia, "Daniel J. Flood; Indictment for Bribery, Conspiracy, Aiding and Abetting," 18 U.S.C. 371, 201, 2, April 1978, Flood Court Files; and "Flood Indicted on Charges of Conspiracy, Bribery," *Syracuse (N.Y.) Post-Standard*, October 13, 1978.

74. Flood, "Statement by Congressman Daniel J. Flood," October 12, 1978, Flood Court Files.

75. U.S. Department of Justice, "Memorandum: Daniel J. Flood Investigation," October 19, 1978, FBI Document No. 183-1626-12. For information regarding Flood's legal counsel, see: letter, Axel Kleiboemer to Frank Sherman, assistant U.S. attorney, Washington, D.C., February 14, 1978; and letter, Daniel J. Flood to Whom It May Concern, Washington, D.C., June 23, 1978, both in Flood Court Files.

76. "Flood Wins 16th term," *Times Leader*, November 8, 1978.

CHAPTER 12

1. Letter, Axel Kleiboemer to Marvin Small, MD, Washington, D.C., February 23, 1978, Flood Court Files.

2. Phone conversation, Tip O'Neill and Dan Flood, quoted in John A. Farrell, *Tip O'Neill and the Democratic Century* (Boston: Little, Brown, 2001), 10.

3. Kleiboemer/Small letter.

4. Ibid.

5. Ibid.

6. Commonwealth of Pennsylvania, Luzerne County, "Affidavit of Edward W. Jones, II, Vice President and Trust Officer of United Penn Bank," September 17, 1979, Flood Court Files.

7. "List of Assets: Daniel J. and Catherine S. Flood," attachment to ibid.

8. Luzerne County, "Affidavit of Edward W. Jones."

9. Ibid. Flood's attorney, Axel Kleiboemer, charged fifty dollars per hour for his services plus traveling and office expenses. See invoice, Axel Kleiboemer to Daniel J. Flood, "For Professional Services Relating to Investigation," July 6, 1978, Flood Court Files.

10. Advertisement, Friends of Dan Flood, "The Hour Has Come to Help Dan Flood," *Citizens' Voice*, December 4, 1978; and "Party for Flood Is 'Nightmare,'" *Syracuse Herald-Journal*, December 8, 1978.

11. "The Home Folks Stand by Dan," *Time*, March 27, 1978.

12. James F. Clarity, "Rep. Flood's District Remains Loyal Despite Federal Inquiry," *New York Times*, February 12, 1978; and Clarity, "Hometown Lions Hail Flood as the 'Citizen of the Year,'" *New York Times*, March 17, 1978.

13. Roy Morgan quoted in Clarity, "Flood's District Remains Loyal."

14. Ibid.; and Gar Kearney, "Garnering the Facts," *Scranton (Pa.) Sunday Times*, February 12, 1978.

15. Mariclare Wysocki-Hahn quoted in *Daniel J. Flood: Closest Thing to God*, WVIA-TV, Scranton/Wilkes-Barre, Pa., October 20, 2005.

16. "Flood Attends Jury Selection," *Syracuse Post-Standard*, January 15, 1979. Of the twelve jurors selected for the Flood trial, eleven were African Americans and one was white, and eight were male and four female.

17. Wendell Rawls, Jr., "Ex-aide Testifies He Delivered Money to Rep. Flood as Payoffs."

18. "Elko Testimony," January 16, 1979, 10–54.

19. "Elko Testimony," January 18, 1979, 326–29; and Rawls, "Flood Aide Says He Was Told to 'Get All You Can.'"

20. "Elko Testimony," January 18, 1979, 336–80; and "Flood Accuser Quizzed," *Syracuse Herald-Journal*, January 18, 1979.

21. Rawls, "Banker Says He Told Rep. Flood in 1972 of Top Aide's Solicitation."

22. "Elko Testimony" January 18, 1979, 312–15, 478–79; and "Former Flood Aide Admits Burning Records."

23. Wendell Rawls, Jr., "Assault on Credibility of Witness Backfires in Flood Bribe Trial," *New York Times*, January 22, 1979; and "Lobbyist Says Flood Pocketed $1,000 payoff," *Syracuse Herald-Journal*, January 20, 1979.

24. "Fleming Testimony," January 19, 1979, 53–55.

25. "Peters Testimony," January 23, 1979, 46–48.

26. Wendel Rawls, Jr., "Mistrial Declared for Rep. Flood as Jury Deadlocks on 11 Counts," *New York Times*, February 4, 1979. Fleming was the most suspect of the government's witnesses. At the time of Flood's trial, the lobbyist was under investigation by John Dowd for connections to organized crime. Fleming shared an office with Martin Martino, a Washington lawyer whose clients included Thomas and Joseph Gambino, sons of Mafia leader Carlos Gambino. Fleming was also good friends with Edward Lubrano, described by federal authorities as "an extortionist for the Gambino family" (see Susan Fraker and David C. Martin, "A Tangled Scandal," *Newsweek*, February 27, 1978, 24).

27. United States v. Daniel J. Flood, "Testimony of Michael Clark," U.S. District Court, Washington, D.C., January 25, 1979, 94–96. Flood Court Files.

28. United States v. Daniel J. Flood, "Testimony of John Jenkins," U.S. District Court, Washington, D.C., January 25, 1979, 17–19, Flood Court Files.

29. United States v. Daniel J. Flood, "Testimony of Thomas Visgilio," U.S. District Court, Washington, D.C., January 25, 1979, 32–33; United States v. Daniel J. Flood, "Testimony of Joseph W. Balz," U.S. District Court, Washington, D.C., January 25, 1979, 25–28; and United States v. Daniel J. Flood, "Testimony of Robert L. Rosholt," U.S. District Court, Washington, D.C., January 25, 1979, 36–40, all in Flood Court Files.

30. Cheryl M. Fields, "Flood Relinquished Key Congressional Post," *Chronicle of Higher Education*, February 5, 1979. Rep. William Natcher, a conservative Democrat from Kentucky, replaced Flood as HEW Appropriations chair. Although Flood resigned the subcommittee chair, he indicated that he expected to continue to serve on the full Appropriations Committee.

31. Wendell Rawls, Jr., "Story Holdout Gave to Flood Juror Similar to One a Witness Reported," *New York Times*, February 8, 1979; Gregory Gordan, "Flood Wins Mistrial," *Syracuse Herald-Journal*, February 4, 1979; and "The Twelfth Man Hangs a Jury," *Time*, February 19, 1979. Because a Justice Department investigation of juror William Cash failed to discover any evidence of tampering, the mistrial held.

32. Flood quoted in Rawls, "Mistrial Declared for Rep. Flood."

33. See Mary E. Reidy, PhD, clinical psychologist, "Psychological Report of Daniel J. Flood," September 27, 1979, Georgetown University Hospital, Flood Court Files; James L. Foy, MD, professor of psychiatry, "Confidential Pretrial Psychiatric Evaluation of Daniel J. Flood," October 19, 1979, Georgetown University Hospital, Flood Court Files; letter, Barry A. Bukatman, MD, to Axel Kleiboemer, Bethesda, Md., October 26, 1979, Flood Court Files; U.S. Justice Department, "Memorandum: Daniel J. Flood; RICO," December 7, 1979, FBI Document No. 58-9839-175; and "Doctor Says Flood 'Depressed, Senile,'" *Times Leader*, September 29, 1979. Flood was hospitalized for eight of the ten months between February and December 1979.

34. U.S. House of Representatives, "Statement of Alleged Violations of Daniel J. Flood," June 7, 1979, Committee on Standards of Official Conduct, Flood Court Files.

35. John Anderson, "Resignation tied to Flood 'deal,'" *Times Leader*, February 27, 1979.

36. Wendell Rawls, Jr., "Rep. Flood Resigns from Congress," *New York Times*, November 8, 1979.

37. Letter, Rep. Charles E. Bennett to Honorable Thomas P. O'Neill, Jr., Speaker of the House of Representatives, Washington, D.C., November 8, 1979, Flood Court Files.

38. Letter, Rep. Thomas P. O'Neill, Jr., to Rep. Charles E. Bennett, Washington, D.C., November 10, 1979, Flood Court Files.

39. Tip O'Neill quoted in Farrell, *Tip O'Neill and the Democratic Century*, 502–3.

40. "Flood, at Hearing, Unable to Identify the Day," *Philadelphia Inquirer*, January 16, 1980; and "After Hospital Stay, Flood Takes Stand," *Syracuse Herald-Journal*, January 16, 1980.

41. "Doctor: 'Flood's Not Faking,'" *Citizens' Voice*, January 18, 1980.

42. See Marjorie Hunter, "Former Rep. Flood Enters Guilty Plea," *New York Times*, February 27, 1980. Rabbi Pinter pleaded guilty in 1978 to a charge of bribing Flood and was sentenced to two years in prison. Dr. Murdock Head was convicted in federal court on October 12, 1979, of conspiracy to bribe Flood and former congressman Otto Passman and was sentenced to three years in prison.

43. Ibid.

44. Ibid.; and U.S. Justice Department, "Memorandum: Daniel J. Flood; Bribery; Perjury; Conspiracy," October 24, 1980, FBI Document No. 58-9839; and Mark Grossman, *Political Corruption in America: An Encyclopedia of Scandals, Power, and Greed* (Santa Barbara, Calif.: ABC-CLIO, 2003), 134.

45. On March 10, 1979, Flood was found not guilty of any wrongdoing in the Hahnemann scandal. Joshua Eilberg, on the other hand, pleaded guilty to receiving a portion of fees from Hahnemann after representing the hospital's interest before the government. He received five years in prison. Shober was indicted for paying a ten-thousand-dollar bribe to Stephen Elko for help in obtaining a federal grant for Hahnemann, but was found not guilty. He relocated to Saudi Arabia, where he found employment as a hospital administrator. See Rogers, *An Alternative Path*, 268. On March 13, 1979, Joel M. Friedman, head of the Philadelphia strike force investigating Flood's connections to organized crime, stated that he would "decline prosecution" of the former congressman after "reviewing various government contracts to Medico Industries and interviewing numerous military personnel involved in the awarding of those contracts" (see U.S. Justice Department, "Memorandum: Daniel J. Flood; Medico Industries," March 15, 1980, FBI Document No. 183-1709-11). Finally, the investigation into Flood's involvement with Haitian officials for private gain was dropped by the Justice Department on March 16, 1979, after prosecutors determined that they did "not have the necessary evidence to prove any type of conspiracy or payoffs" (see U.S. Department of Justice, "Memorandum: Daniel J. Flood; Racketeer Influenced and Corrupt Organizations," August 31, 1979, FBI Document No. 183-1566-34).

46. Francis X. Clines, "Flood Is Offstage at Closing of 36-Year Congress Run," *New York Times*, February 1, 1980.

47. Rooney interview.

48. Scranton interview.

49. Wright interview. The House Ethics Committee's report in early 1989 implied that Rep. Jim Wright had used bulk purchases of his vanity book, *Reflections of a Public Man*, to earn speaking fees in excess of the allowed maximum, and that his wife, Betty, was given a job and perks to avoid the limit on gifts. Faced with an increasing loss of effectiveness, he resigned as Speaker on May 31, 1989, effective upon the selection of a successor. On June 6 the Democratic caucus brought his speakership to an end by selecting his replacement, Tom Foley, and on June 30 he resigned from Congress. The charges against Wright were part of the increasing partisan infighting that plagued the Congress in the late 1980s and 1990s. Rep. Newt Gingrich filed the original charges in 1988, and their effect propelled Gingrich's to the role of minority whip and, seven years later, to the Speaker's chair itself.

50. Clark interview, June 27, 2008.

51. Makowski interview, October 11, 2007.

52. Rosenn interview, May 13, 2005.

53. Flood quoted in *Dan Flood: A Retrospective*.

54. "Flood's Aide Describes Feelings of Dan's Staff," *Sunday Independent*, November 11, 1979; and "Ray Musto, Man of the Year in 1980 Politics," *Pittston Sunday Dispatch:* January 4, 1981.

55. Interestingly, James Musto cosponsored Pennsylvania's Occupational Disease Act of 1965, which set the precedent for Flood's 1969 Coal Mine Health and Safety Act. See Musto interview.

56. Jean Hronich, "Jim Nelligan—Congressman," *Citizens' Voice*, November 25, 1980.

57. "Harrison Defeats Nelligan," *Times Leader*, November 10, 1982. Harrison was defeated in the 1984 election by Paul Kanjorski, but the Eleventh district's congressional seat has remained Democrat ever since.

58. *Dan Flood: A Retrospective.*

59. Marjorie Hunter, "Two Pennsylvania Politicians: Dan Flood," *New York Times*, January 31, 1978.

60. McGowan interview.

61. "In Wilkes-Barre, They Still Love Dan Flood," *Philadelphia Inquirer*, May 14, 1989.

62. Musto interview.

63. Breslin interview, September 3, 2005. Catherine Flood's devotion to Dan continued well after he died in 1994. According to Breslin, she "kept the house like a shrine to his congressional career, with all of the photographs and other mementos he once had in his Washington office. She even refused to take his bed down and left his pajamas folded at the end of it. Whenever she left the house, she'd turn to the portrait of Dan on the wall and say good-bye to him. Even when we'd take her out in her wheel chair near the end of her life, she'd do that. Dan had been dead for more than a decade by that time. She was just madly in love with him."

64. Interview of Joseph DeVizia, Larksville, Pa., September 13, 2005.

65. "Dan Flood Dies at Age 90; He Was Legend in His Own Time," *Citizens' Voice*, May 29, 1994.

66. "Hundreds Bid Final Farewell to Flood," *Times Leader*, May 31, 1994.

67. Dawn Shurmaitis, "Applause Caps Flood Funeral," *Times Leader*, June 1, 1994; and Kelly P. Kissel, "A Politician of the People Is Eulogized," *Philadelphia Inquirer*, June 1, 1994. Catherine Flood would survive her husband by more than a decade. She died on Sunday, August 14, 2005, and is buried alongside Dan Flood at St. Mary's Cemetery, Hanover Township, Wilkes-Barre. See "Obituary, Catherine Flood," *Times Leader*, August 16, 2005.

BIBLIOGRAPHY

*   *   *   *   *

PRIMARY SOURCES

Interviews

Breslin, William A., Wilkes-Barre, Pa., September 3, 2005; and December 30, 2006.
Brominski, Bernard C., Wilkes-Barre, Pa., March 13, 1996.
Brown, J. Lawrence, Forty Fort, Pa., January 22, 2008.
Carlucci, Frank, Washington D.C., November 9, 2007.
Cefalo, Michael, West Pittston, Pa., November 9, 2007.
Clark, Michael, Washington, D.C., April 2, 2005; July 5, 2007; April 20, 2008; and June 27, 2008.
Cosgrove, John, Washington, D.C., May 26, 2005.
DeVizia, Joseph, Larksville, Pa., September 13, 2005.
Dyer, James, Washington, D.C., May 26, 2005.
Farrell, Joseph, Mountaintop, Pa., December 5, 2007.
Flood, Catherine, Wilkes-Barre, Pa., August 12, 2003.
Ford, Gerald R., Rancho Mirage, Calif., October 28, 2003.
Ganley, Laura Kane, Annapolis, Md., January 30, 2007.
Golias, Paul, Wilkes-Barre, Pa., May 3, 2005.
Hastie, William, West Pittston, Pa., March 20, 2007.
Janosov, Robert A., Nanticoke, Pa., November 19, 1991.
Kashatus, John, Sr., Glen Lyon, Pa., July 10, 1984.
Kashatus, William C., Wayne, Pa., February 7, 2005; and March 3, 2005.
Kozemchak, James, Wilkes-Barre, Pa., September 13, 2005.
Laird, Melvin R., Fort Myers, Fla., February 5, 2007.
Lee, James, Wilkes-Barre, Pa., June 7, 2005.
Loftus, Robert, Pittston, Pa., February 14, 2005.
Makowski, Thomas, Wilkes-Barre, Pa., February 2, 2005; and October 11, 2005.
McDade, Joseph, Fairfax, Va., October 10, 2005.
McGowen, Andrew, Laflin, Pa., January 15, 2004.
McKeown, John C., Wilkes-Barre, Pa., May 11, 2005.
Medico, Tom, Wilkes-Barre, Pa., March 26, 2007.
Michel, Robert, Washington, D.C., March 8, 2007.
Michelini, Francis J., Mechanicsburg, Pa., February 13, 2008.
Mitchell, Edward, Wilkes-Barre, Pa., January 30, 2007.
Musto, Raphael, Harrisburg, Pa., January 30, 2008.
Podcasy, Bernard J., Wilkes-Barre, Pa., December 7, 2007.
Rooney, Fred, Washington, D.C., February 1, 2007.
Rosenn, Harold, Wilkes-Barre, Pa., May 13, 2005.
Rozelle, Ralph, Wilkes-Barre, Pa., February 20, 2008.
Scranton, William W., Scranton, Pa., October 24, 2005.
Sheerin, Sarah, New Carrollton, Md., February 25, 2005.
Tedesco, James, Old Forge, Pa., June 7, 2005.
Wright, Jim, Fort Worth, Tex., January 9, 2007.

Manuscripts

Commonwealth of Pennsylvania. Crime Commission Reports, 1980, 1984. Harrisburg, Pa.

Commonwealth of Pennsylvania. Reports of the Department of the Mines. Harrisburg, Pa.

Daniel J. Flood Papers. King's College Library, Wilkes-Barre, Pa.

U.S. Bureau of the Census. United States Census Records. National Archives, Washington, D.C.

U.S. Congress. *Congressional Record*, 1944–1980. Van Pelt Library, University of Pennsylvania, Philadelphia, Pa.

U.S. Customs Service. Passenger Lists of Vessels Arriving at New York, 1820–1897. National Archives, Washington, D.C.

U.S. Department of Justice. Congressman Daniel J. Flood Declassified Documents. FBI Freedom of Information Act Unit, Office of Public and Congressional Affairs, Federal Bureau of Investigation, Washington, D.C.

U.S. District Court (Washington, D.C.). United States v. Daniel J. Flood, 1979. Manuscripts of trial proceedings, depositions, testimonies, and evidence in possession of Robert Kulick, Bear Creek, Pa.

U.S. House of Representatives. Report of Hearings on Department of Defense Appropriations, 1960–1980. Microfiche, Van Pelt Library, University of Pennsylvania, Philadelphia, Pa.

Newspapers

Allentown (Pa.) Morning Call
Anthracite Tri-District News (Hazleton, Pa.)
Boston Globe
Chicago Tribune
Chronicle of Higher Education
Citizens' Voice (Wilkes-Barre, Pa.)
Hazleton (Pa.) Standard Sentinel
The Journal (Wilkes-Barre High School, Wilkes-Barre, Pa.)
New York Daily News
New York Herald Journal
New York Times
Panama American
Patriot News (Harrisburg, Pa.)
Philadelphia Bulletin
Philadelphia Inquirer
Pittston (Pa.) Dispatch
Roll Call (Washington, D.C.)
Saturday Evening Post
Scranton (Pa.) Times
Sunday Independent (Wilkes-Barre, Pa.)
Syracuse (N.Y.) Herald-Journal
Times Leader (Wilkes-Barre, Pa.)
United Mine Workers Journal
Washington Post

Washington Star
Washington Times-Herald
Wilkes-Barre (Pa.) Record
Wyoming Valley (Pa.) Observer

SECONDARY SOURCES

Ambrose, Stephen E. *Eisenhower: Soldier and President.* 1983. Repr., New York: Simon and Schuster, 1990.
Anderson, Jack. *Confessions of a Muckraker: The Inside Story of Life in Washington During the Truman, Eisenhower, Kennedy and Johnson Years.* With James Boyd. New York: Random House, 1979.
———. "Flood and Medico." *Washington Post*, April 1, 1970.
Bailey, Thomas A. *A Diplomatic History of the American People.* Englewood Cliffs, N.J.: Prentice Hall, 1980.
Barendse, Michael. *Social Expectations and Perception: The Case of the Slavic Anthracite Workers.* University Park: Penn State University Press, 1981.
Beers, Paul B. *Pennsylvania Politics Today and Yesterday: The Tolerable Accommodation.* University Park: Penn State University Press, 1980.
Bensel, Richard F. *Sectionalism and American Political Development, 1880–1980.* Madison: University of Wisconsin Press, 1984.
Boldt, David. "Flood, the Flamboyant." *Philadelphia Inquirer Magazine*, July 7, 1974, 20–25.
Boller, Paul F. *Congressional Anecdotes.* New York: Oxford University Press, 1991.
Bolles, Blair. *How To Get Rich in Washington: Rich Man's Division of the Welfare State.* New York: Norton, 1952.
Bolling, Richard. *Power in the House: A History of the Leadership of the House of Representatives.* New York: Dutton, 1968.
Bourne, Peter G. *Jimmy Carter: A Comprehensive Biography from Plains to Postpresidency.* New York: Scribner, 1997.
Brandt, Charles. *"I Heard You Paint Houses": Frank "The Irishman" Sheeran and the Inside Story of the Mafia, the Teamsters, and the Last Ride of Jimmy Hoffa.* Hanover, N.H.: Steerforth Press, 2005.
Brinkley, Douglas. *Gerald R. Ford.* New York: Henry R. Holt, 2007.
Capeci, Jerry. *Gang Land: Fifteen Years of Covering the Mafia.* New York: Alpha Books, 2003.
Caro, Robert A. *The Years of Lyndon Johnson.* Vol. 1, *The Path to Power.* New York: Knopf, 1982.
———. *The Years of Johnson.* Vol. 2, *Means of Ascent.* New York: Knopf, 1990.
Carter, Jimmy. *Keeping Faith: Memoirs of a President.* 1982. Repr., New York: Bantam Books, 1983.
Clymer, Adam. *Drawing the Line at the Big Red Ditch: The Panama Canal Treaties and the Rise of the Right.* Lawrence: University of Kansas Press, 2008.
Congressional Quarterly. *Guide to U.S. Elections.* Washington, D.C.: Congressional Quarterly, 1985.
Crile, George. "The Best Congressman." *Harper's Magazine*, January 1975, 60–66.
Dalleck, Robert. *Nixon and Kissinger: Partners in Power.* New York: HarperCollins, 2007.

————. *An Unfinished Life: John F. Kennedy, 1917–1963*. New York: Little, Brown, 2003.

Derickson, Alan. *Black Lung: Anatomy of a Public Health Disaster*. Ithaca: Cornell University Press, 1998.

Donovan, Robert J. *Conflict and Crisis: The Presidency of Harry S. Truman, 1945–1948*. New York: Norton, 1977.

Dublin, Thomas, and Walter Licht. *The Face of Decline: The Pennsylvania Anthracite Region in the Twentieth Century*. Ithaca: Cornell University Press, 2005.

DuVal, Captain Miles P., Jr. *Cadiz to Cathay: The Story of the Long Struggle for A Waterway Across the American Isthmus*. London: Oxford University Press, 1940.

Farrell, John A. *Tip O'Neill and the Democratic Century*. Boston: Little, Brown, 2001.

Fass, Paula S. *The Damned and the Beautiful: American Youth in the 1920s*. New York: Oxford University Press, 1977.

Fenno, Richard F. *Home Style: Members in Their Districts*. New York: Harper and Row, 1978.

Firestone, Bernard J., and Alexej Ugrinsky, eds. *Gerald R. Ford and the Politics of Post-Watergate America*. 2 vols. Westport, Conn.: Greenwood Press, 1993.

Fox, Stephen. *Blood and Power: Organized Crime in the Twentieth Century*. New York: William Morrow, 1989.

Frankfurt, Harry G. *On Bullshit*. Princeton: Princeton University Press, 2005.

Gaddis, John L. *The Cold War: A New History*. New York: Penguin, 2005.

Goldman, Eric. *The Tragedy of Lyndon Johnson*. New York: Knopf, 1969.

Golway, Terry. *The Irish in America*. New York: Hyperion Press, 1997.

Grady, Sandy. "The Flood They Can't Dam." *Philadelphia Bulletin Magazine*, August 31, 1975, 6–8.

Grant, Philip. "Northeastern Pennsylvania Congressmen and the New Deal, 1933–1940." Unpublished paper presented at the Northeastern Pennsylvania History Conference, Nanticoke, Pa., October 11, 1991.

Greene, Victor. *For God and Country: The Rise of Polish and Lithuanian Ethnic Consciousness in America, 1860–1910*. Madison: Historical Society of Wisconsin, 1975.

————. *The Slavic Community on Strike: Immigrant Labor in Pennsylvania Anthracite*. South Bend: Notre Dame University Press, 1968.

Grossman, Mark. *Political Corruption in America: An Encyclopedia of Scandals, Power, and Greed*. Santa Barbara, Calif.: ABC-CLIO, 2003.

Halberstam, David. *The Best and the Brightest*. 1972. Repr., Greenwich, Conn.: Fawcett Crest, 1973.

Hamby, Alonzo L. *Beyond the New Deal: Harry S. Truman and American Liberalism*. New York: Columbia University Press, 1973.

Handlin, Oscar. *The Uprooted: The Epic Story of the Great Migrations That Made the American People*. New York: Grosset and Dunlap, 1951.

Harding, Earl *The Untold Story of Panama*. New York: Athens Press, 1959.

Hersh, Seymour. *The Dark Side of Camelot*. New York: Little, Brown, 1997.

Higgs, Robert. "Hard Coals Make Bad Law: Congressional Parochialism Versus National Defense." *Cato Journal* 3 (Spring–Summer 1988): 4–16.

Hunt, E. Howard. *American Spy: My Secret History in the CIA, Watergate, and Beyond*. Hoboken, N.J.: John Wiley and Sons, 2007.

Kaiser, David. *American Tragedy: Kennedy, Johnson, and the Origins of the Vietnam War*. Cambridge: Harvard University Press, 2000.

Karnow, Stanley. *Vietnam: A History*. New York: Viking Press, 1983.

Kashatus, William C. "'Dapper Dan' Flood: Pennsylvania's Legendary Congressman." *Pennsylvania Heritage* 21 (Summer 1995): 4–11.

Katz, Michael B. *The Undeserving Poor: From the War on Poverty to the War on Welfare.* New York: Pantheon, 1990.

Kearns, Doris. *Lyndon Johnson and the American Dream.* New York: Harper and Row, 1976.

Kennedy, Robert F. *Thirteen Days: A Memoir of the Cuban Missile Crisis.* New York: Norton, 1969.

Kenny, Kevin. *Making Sense of the Molly Maguires.* New York: Oxford University Press, 1988.

Kinnard, Douglas. *The War Managers.* 1977. Repr., Annapolis, Md.: Naval Institute Press, 2007.

Kissinger, Henry. *White House Years.* Boston: Little, Brown, 1979.

LaFeber, Walter. *The Panama Canal: The Crisis in Historical Perspective.* New York: Oxford University Press, 1989.

Lowi, Theodore J. *The End of Liberalism.* New York: Norton, 1979.

MacGregor Burns, James. *Leadership.* New York: Harper and Row, 1978.

Mahoney, Richard D. *Sons and Brothers: The Days of Jack and Bobby Kennedy.* New York: Arcade Publishing, 1999.

Major, John. *Prize Possession: The United States and the Panama Canal, 1903–1979.* New York: Cambridge University Press, 1993.

Martis, Kenneth C. *The Historical Atlas of the United States Congressional Districts, 1789–1983.* New York: Macmillan, 1982.

Matkosky, Greg, and Thomas M. Curra. *Stories From the Mines.* Scranton: Lackawanna Heritage Valley and University of Scranton Press, 2002.

Matusow, Allen J. *The Unraveling of America: A History of Liberalism in the 1960s.* 1984. Repr., New York: Harper, 1985.

May, Ernest R., and Philip D. Zelikow, eds. *The Kennedy Tapes: Inside the White House During the Cuban Missile Crisis.* Cambridge: Harvard University Press, 1997.

McClellan, John L. *Crime Without Punishment.* New York: Duell, Storn and Pearce, 1962.

McCullough, David. *The Path Between the Seas: The Creation of the Panama Canal, 1870–1914.* New York: Simon and Schuster, 1977.

McMaster, H. R. *Dereliction of Duty: Lyndon Johnson, Robert McNamara, the Joint Chiefs of Staff, and the Lies That Led to Vietnam.* New York: HarperCollins, 1997.

McNamara, Robert S. *Essence of Security: Reflections in Office.* New York: Harper and Row, 1968.

———. *In Retrospect: The Tragedy and Lessons of Vietnam.* New York: Random House, 1995.

Miller, Donald L., and Richard E. Sharpless. *The Kingdom of Coal: Work, Enterprise, and Ethnic Communities in the Mine Fields.* Philadelphia: University of Pennsylvania Press, 1985.

Miller, Randall M., and William Pencak, eds. *Pennsylvania: A History of the Commonwealth.* University Park: Penn State University Press and the Pennsylvania Historical and Museum Commission, 2002.

Mittrick, Robert. "John S. Fine: The Rise and Fall of a Political Boss." Unpublished paper delivered at Northeast Pennsylvania History Conference, Nanticoke, Pa., October 13, 1995.

Mooney, Tom. "Dan Flood: The Man for All Seasons." *Times Leader*, April 27, 1991, special report, 100–108.

Moritz, Charles, ed. "Daniel John Flood." In *Current Biography Yearbook, 1978*, 131–34. New York: H. W. Wilson, 1979.

Morris, Edmund. *Theodore Rex*. New York: Random House, 2001.

Morrow, Lance. *The Best Year of Their Lives: Kennedy, Johnson, and Nixon in 1948*. New York: Basic Books, 2005.

Nixon, Richard M. *The Memoirs of Richard M. Nixon*. London: Arrow Books, 1979.

Obey, David R. *Raising Hell for Justice. The Washington Battles of a Heartland Progressive*. Madison: University of Wisconsin Press, 2007.

Patterson, James T. *America's Struggle Against Poverty in the Twentieth Century*. Cambridge: Harvard University Press, 2000.

Phelan, Craig. *Divided Loyalties: The Public and Private Life of Labor Leader John Mitchell*. Albany: State University of New York Press, 1994.

Pierson, James. *Camelot and the Cultural Revolution: How the Assassination of John F. Kennedy Shattered American Liberalism*. New York: Encounter Books, 2007.

Remini, Robert V. *The House: The History of the House of Representatives*. Washington, D.C.: Smithsonian Books, 2007.

Rogers, Naomi. *An Alternative Path: The Making and Remaking of Hahnemann Medical College and Hospital of Philadelphia*. New Brunswick: Rutgers University Press, 1998.

Rosati, Jerel A. *The Carter Administration's Quest for Global Community*. Charleston: University of South Carolina, 1987.

Ross, Shelley. *Fall From Grace: Sex, Scandal, and Corruption in American Politics from 1702 to the Present*. New York: Ballantine Books, 1988.

Rust, William J. *Kennedy in Vietnam: American Vietnam Policy, 1960–1963*. New York: Scribner's Sons, 1985.

Ryan, Paul B. "Canal Diplomacy and Interests." *U.S. Naval Institute Proceedings* 1 (January 1977): 40–52.

Schlesinger, Arthur M., Jr. *The Imperial Presidency*. Boston: Houghton Mifflin, 1973.
———. *A Thousand Days: John F. Kennedy in the White House*. Boston: Houghton Mifflin, 1965.

Seaborg, Glenn T. *Kennedy, Khrushchev, and the Test Ban*. Berkeley and Los Angeles: University of California, 1981.

Sifakis, Carl. *The Mafia Encyclopedia*. New York: Checkmark, 2005.

Sinclair, Barbara. *Majority Leadership in the U.S. House*. Baltimore: Johns Hopkins University Press, 1983.

Spear, Sheldon. *Chapters in Wyoming Valley History*. Shavertown, Pa.: Jemags, 1989.
———. *Daniel J. Flood: The Congressional Career of an Economic Savior and Cold War Nationalist*. Bethlehem: Lehigh University Press, 2008.

Talbot, David. *Brothers: The Hidden History of the Kennedy Years*. New York: The Free Press, 2007.

terHorst, J. F. *Gerald Ford and the Future of the Presidency*. New York: Third Press, 1974.

Thomas, Evan. *Robert Kennedy: His Life*. New York: Simon and Schuster, 2000.

Van Atta, Dale. *With Honor: Melvin Laird in War, Peace, and Politics*. Madison: University of Wisconsin Press, 2008.

Waldron, Lamar. *Ultimate Sacrifice: John and Robert Kennedy, the Plan for a Coup in Cuba, and the Murder of JFK*. With Thom Hartman. New York: Carroll and Graf, 2005.

Winter-Berger, Robert N. *The Washington Pay-Off: An Insider's View of Corruption in Government*. Secaucus, N.J.: Lyle Stuart, 1972.

Wofford, Harris. *Of Kennedys and Kings: Making Sense of the Sixties*. Pittsburgh: University of Pittsburgh Press, 1992.

Wolensky, Kenneth C., Nicole H. Wolensky, and Robert P. Wolensky. *Fighting for the Union Label: The Women's Garment Industry and the ILGWU in Pennsylvania*. University Park: Penn State University Press, 2002.

Wolensky, Robert P. *Better Than Ever! The Flood Recovery Task Force and the 1972 Agnes Disaster*. Stevens Point: University of Wisconsin–Stevens Point Foundation Press, 1993.

Wolensky, Robert P., Kenneth Wolensky, and Nicole Wolensky. *The Knox Mine Disaster: The Final Years of the Northern Anthracite Industry and the Effort to Rebuild a Regional Economy*. Harrisburg: Pennsylvania Historical and Museum Commission, 1999.

Wyden, Peter. *Bay of Pigs: The Untold Story*. New York: Simon and Schuster, 1979.

Zubrov, Alfred T. *Speakers of the U.S. House of Representatives, 1789–2002*. New York: Novinka Books, 2002.

INDEX